A HISTORY OF THE CHRISTIAN PRESENCE IN THE HOLY LAND

Saul P. Colbi

UNIVERSITY
PRESS OF
AMERICA

Lanham • New York • London

Copyright © **1988** by

University Press of America,® Inc.

4720 Boston Way
Lanham, MD 20706

3 Henrietta Street
London WC2E 8LU England

Library of Congress Cataloging-in-Publication Data

Colbi, S. P. (Saul P.)
A history of the Christian presence in the Holy Land / by Saul P. Colbi.
p. cm.
Bibliography: p.
Includes index.
1. Christianity—Palestine. 2. Christian sects—Palestine.
3. Palestine—Church history. I. Title.
BR1110.C65   1988
275.694—dc 19   88–14829 CIP
ISBN 0–8191–7036–4 (alk. paper)

To my wife, Leah

Acknowledgments

I am grateful to Ms. Shira Twersky Cassel and to Custom Graphics and Publishing Ltd., Jerusalem, who skilfully did the typesetting and layout of the book.

I am greatly indebted to Shalom Ben-Zakkai, editor of the periodical *Christian News from Israel,* whose familiarity and long experience with Christian affairs in the Holy Land and language skills were of inestimable help to me in the editing of my manuscript.

CONTENTS

LIST OF MAPS

PREFACE

The present volume is an expanded, updated edition of my book, *Christianity in the Holy Land, Past and Present*, published in 1969.

Since then, not a few political events have left their imprint on the general situation in the Holy Land. Yet, during the past few years, the development of the local Churches has continued at a steady pace in many areas—religious personnel, educational and charitable institutions and building activity. There has also been a marked trend towards giving indigenous clergy a greater say in Church matters.

Ecumenism, too, has made encouraging progress, and the attitude of the major Churches towards Judaism has shown improvement.

Given these many developments and the abiding interest of world Christendom in events in the Holy Land, it seemed to me worthwhile to publish a revised edition of the former book. In the revision, I have drawn on the experience and knowledge acquired in four decades of contacts with Church dignitaries, as well as on personal involvement in the many and complex problems of the Christian Churches in the Holy Land.

While it is difficult to follow an entirely independent and objective line when dealing with contemporary events, my book attempts to take a non-partisan view of the often conflicting concerns of the several denominations. I do not attempt to provide answers to contemporary political issues. Rather, since tradition is of such paramount importance in the Holy Land, my purpose is to elucidate the past and so clarify current problems.

The book is divided into two main sections. The first describes the Christian Churches from their origin to the present day, recording events under the successive regimes in the Holy Land. The history of each of the most important Churches during the past 150 years is discussed in a separate sub-chapter. The second section of the book, *People, Holy Places, Institutions, Interreligious Relations,* seeks to give an account of religious life in the Holy Land today.

Much of the data recorded in the book was collected during conversations with local Church representatives, and from the many publications of the local Churches.

PART ONE

The Christian Churches In The Holy Land From Their Origin Up To The Present Day

Chapter One

THE FIRST CENTURIES

When the Christian Era dawned, the population of the Holy Land was far from constituting a homogeneous entity. It might be looked upon rather as a mosaic of peoples belonging to a number of national and religious groups. The Hebrew element was predominant in the provinces of Galilee and Judaea; in the central part the Samaritans were populous; the Phoenicians inhabited the northern coastal strip, and the Nabataean Arabs dwelt in the southern region on the edge of the desert. Considerable Hellenistic colonies had also been established throughout, particularly along the maritime plain, and there was also the Roman factor represented by the civil servants of the empire and the legions stationed in "Palestine."

Thus, the constituents of the population were entirely diverse in composition, yet there is no doubt that, as the New Testament affirms, the Christian faith was spread by a Galilean Jew and was addressed to Jews at the start. Extensive evidence of this may be cited from the Books of the Gospels, where it is often said that great throngs gathered to hear the message preached by Jesus. The same sources concede that the teachings of Jesus, although they attracted wide interest at first, did not afterwards win massive popular support amongst the Jews to whom the Christian message was primarily directed. This apparent apathy led Jesus, and the disciples who followed in the footsteps of the Master, to bring it to the Gentile dwellers of the Holy Land, to the Greeks, the Romans and the Samaritans not least. But it is true that the new faith found by far its largest following beyond the borders of the Holy Land, and it was no accident that within those borders the Church could organize and develop more swiftly in the districts where Jews constituted a minority. Thus, from the second century, organized congregations came into being in such towns as Caesarea and

3

Ptolemais,[1] both of a palpably Roman or Greek character. There were Christian nuclei in other places, but usually where the chief element was Hellenistic. The notable exception was Jerusalem: its overwhelmingly Jewish citizenry did not, after all, prevent the emergence of the first Christian community.

The beginnings of that community, later known as the "Mother Church", with its centre on Mount Zion, are recorded in the Acts of the Apostles. According to that and other sources, the spiritual head was James the Less, who was put to death in the year 62 of the Christian Era and is remembered as the first Bishop of Jerusalem.[2] When considering the earliest references to the organization of the Church, one should bear in mind that a clear tendency exists to attribute to the infant Church elements which were developed much later.

The first centuries witnessed a steady rise in the number of adherents, and the Church acquired a firm foundation in the Holy Land. But the cradle of Christianity never became so powerful a stronghold or so compulsive a fashioner of the faith as to threaten the hegemony of the Churches of Rome, Alexandria and Constantinople. Those three Patriarchates always surpassed Jerusalem as dominant Sees of ecclesiastical hierarchies and headquarters of famous theological academies.

In the Holy Land, then, the Church recruited its followers mainly from among the Gentile population. Yet small groups of Hebrew-Christians also formed. What is curious is that Gentile Christians should have so greatly outnumbered them. After all, the Gospel was delivered to the Jews to begin with. It is even stranger as one considers that, in the inaugural days of the Church, on the occasion of the Council which was held in Jerusalem in the year 49 or 50 of the Christian Era, the Apostles— so runs the narrative in the New Testament[3]—debated hotly

---

1) Name given to Acre when conquered in 281 BCE by Ptolemy II Philadelphos, ruler of Egypt. The name Ptolemais is still employed in the onomasticon of the Greek Catholic Church and in the Greek Orthodox Church (metropolitan See). In the Roman Catholic Church "Ptolemais in Phoenicia" is a titular See.

2) The Armenian Orthodox Church marks a traditional site of the martyrdom of St. James the Less in St. James' cathedral, seat of the Armenian Patriarch of Jerusalem.

3) Acts, Chapter 15.

4

among themselves whether Gentiles could be admitted to the new
faith. The eventual answer was "yes", but it was in due course
made plain that Gentiles, on conversion, were not bound by any
means to observance of the precepts of Judaism.

Although their number was exiguous, the Hebrew-Christians
split further into several sects.[4] The most important was that of the
so-called Nazarenes, who adhered to Christian beliefs, whilst
continuing to practise many of the ways and behests of Judaism.
Another sect, that of the Ebionites (a Hebrew word for the poor), accepted only the Gospel of Matthew and while they venerated Jesus
as the Messiah, disavowed the doctrine of his divine nature and
rejected the Pauline doctrine. A derivative group, the Elkesites,
followed an ecclectic doctrine with marked gnostic influence. So
for a spell, varying "nuances" of Hebrew-Christianity made each
its brief appearance, their exponents differentiated by the measure, large or little, of Christian and Jewish customs and commands that they obeyed.

The Jews were soon repelled by the demeanor of the Hebrew-
Christians, who, continuing though they did to belong formally to
the Jewish community, held and practised beliefs which, for Jews,
were heretical. Quasi-believers straying from the true path, the so-
called "Minim" or "kinds" were, therefore, discriminated
against by the Jews and their heresy was denounced in a special
prayer.

After the year 70 of the Christian Era, Jewish dislike for the
Hebrew-Christians in the Holy Land was sharpened by the latter's
attitude of unconcern towards the national calamity which culminated in the destruction of the Temple. When the Holy City was
beleaguered, its Hebrew-Christians took no part in the defense, but
stayed in Pella (Transjordan), the site to which they had de-
camped in the troubled period prior to the siege of the Holy City.[5]

---

4) Reference to those sects is first found in *Adversus Haereses* by Irenaeus of
Lions. There are further references in Epiphanios' work *Panarion*. Mention of
Hebrew-Christian sects is also made in the writings of Origen, Eusebius Pam-
phili and St. Jerome.

5) The flight of the Jerusalem Church to Pella, reported by Eusebius in his *Ecclesiastical History* and by Epiphanios in *Panarion*, is considered by some
modern historians to be a legend; e.g., S.G.F. Brandon, *The Fall of Jerusalem
and the Christian Church*, (1951), and *Jesus and the Zealots* (1967). For a defense

Some of the recreant Hebrew-Christians are said to have returned from Pella and to have settled again in Jerusalem after the Roman conquest. Christian sources tell that they were led by Simon, cousin of Jesus, who is remembered as the second Bishop of Jerusalem.

In the second century, Hebrew-Christians may still be discerned as a distinct entity. For example, there is the embargo proclaimed by the Romans, after Bar-Kochba's rising in 135, on Jewish residence in Jerusalem; the Hebrew-Christians were specifically included in it. The historian Eusebius, Bishop of Caesarea and a contemporary of the Emperor Constantine, testifies that only Gentile Christians were allowed to be domiciled in Aelia Capitolina, the city built to usurp the ruins of Jewish Jerusalem. Further evidence that Hebrew-Christians might not live there is furnished by the circumstance that, whilst thirteen among the first fifteen Bishops of Jerusalem bore evidently Jewish names,[6] those who filled the office after the rising of 135 no longer did. The series of the bishops issued from the Gentility starts from that date with Marc, originally from Caesarea.

Hebrew-Christians, however, preserved an identity of their own in the Holy Land, long after the fraternity in the Diaspora had been totally submerged. The dissociation of the Hebrew-Christians from the Gentile Christians in the Holy Land was due not to the influence of the Jewish surroundings alone, but to expedience as well. Until the fourth century, Hebrew-Christians found it opportune to mingle with the Jews and take on their outward appearance, for Christianity was banned and Judaism, being a national religion, was tolerated by emperors.[7] Rome did not demur to the Christian cult as such, but required Christians to offer sacrifices to Roman gods; failure to conform to this edict was proof of godlessness and punished harshly. Archaeological evidence shows the persistence of a Hebrew- Christian presence in the Holy Land up until the fifth century. By the end of the century, every link with Judaism had been snapped and no vestige of Hebrew-

---

of the tradition, see the article by Ray Pritz, "On Brandon's Rejection of the Pella Tradition," in *Immanuel* 13, Fall 1981.

6) See list of Bishops of Jerusalem, Appendix C. According to Eusebius (*Ecclesiastical History III, 19*), from 111 to 134, the bishops lived in Pella.

7) See Jean Daniélou in: *Ebrei e Cristiani*, p. 66.

Christianity could survive because of the violent opposition mustered by the Church Fathers: in their eyes adherence to Jewish customs posed a threat to the true Christian faith.

A semantic factor of decisive influence in changing the character of the spiritual atmosphere was the name Aelia Capitolina[8] foisted upon Jerusalem, a name that evoked no religious or pietistic memories. Jerusalem shed most of its ancient glory, and it is not surprising that Caesarea, capital of the Roman province of Syria Palaestina and the headquarters of its governor, also became the province's hierarchical focus.

The history of Christianity in the Holy Land during the first centuries is still somewhat obscure. It seems that the Christian inhabitants were but a minority, and religious controversy frequently disunited them. An eminent figure in the second century was the apologist, Justin of Flavia Neapolis (the present-day Nablus), author of a "dialogue" in which he sought to prove the truth of Christianity to a Jew named Trypho. In the third century, Origen, the renowned theologian from Alexandria, visited the Holy Land on several occasions. He lived in Caesarea for some time and attracted a multitude of scholars to the town, imparting a major impulse to religious study in the Holy Land. But his school came to an early end in the middle of the century when, like in the rest of the Roman empire, Palestine was the cockpit of savage religious tyranny.

The Holy Land had its contemporary share of Christian martyrs, resolute men, who declined to make obeisance to a heathenism that demanded sacrifices to Roman gods. Persecution was most outrageous in the reigns of the Emperors Diocletian[9] and Galerius. Eusebius[10] has left us a grimly exact chronicle of the bloody events.

---

8) Aelia after the Emperor Hadrian, whose full name was Publius Aelius Hadrianus; Capitolina, after the deities appointed to be patrons of the new city, the Capitolina triad: Jupiter, Juno and Minerva.

9) Edict against the Christians, February 303.

10) Eusebius Pamphili (260–340), Bishop of Caesarea, is the author of an Ecclesiastical History which constitutes a primary source for the history of the Church up to 324.

Chapter Two

THE BYZANTINE PERIOD (324–636)

FROM CONSTANTINE TO THEODOSIUS

There was a spectacular change in the fortunes of Palestinian Christianity upon the enthronement of the Emperor Constantine. His term marks the beginning of the Byzantine period in the Holy Land.

Constantine, son of Emperor Constantius Cloros and of his first wife Helena, was born about 280 in Naissa (modern Nish in southern Yugoslavia). On becoming ruler of Rome in 313 he issued an edict in Nicomedia in conjunction with Lucinius, who ruled over the Eastern provinces of the empire. The writ, erroneously called the Edict of Milan, granted full tolerance to all the religions in vogue in the empire. It was published in Caesarea in 324 and was in force locally thereafter. In 325, Constantine saw to the removal of Lucinius and became sole ruler of the empire. It is not easy to discern what induced Constantine to favor the Christians. The opinions of the historians are divided: some maintain that it was calculated politics, others find it an honest inclination towards Christianity. The first view has this to support it, that the Christians had by now so multiplied that it was imprudent to wage a war of uncertain outcome against them. On the other hand, paganism must still have been fairly common among the empire's ruling classes, and this may explain why the emperor did not discard the rank of Pontifex Maximus, the highest dignity in the priesthood of heathen Rome. Even Constantine's formal conversion to Christianity seems to have been undergone only in "articulo mortis." In spite of that, his attitude was so important, even decisive, for the propagation of Christianity that he almost becomes a mythical figure, and it is difficult to distinguish which facts of his life-story are authentic and which are the embellishment of legend. The biography by Eusebius betrays a manifest leaning to extol Constantine's personality and scarcely makes for the drawing of objective and documented conclusions.

But what is both of paramount importance and historically in-controvertible is his foundation of a new metropolis on the shores of the Bosphoros, on the ancient site of the colony Byzantium which was settled by Greeks from Megara. The new, eponymous city, Constantinople, soon became the political and administrative heart of the empire. Subsequently, as capital of the Eastern empire and hierarchical center of Eastern Christianity, it exerted a por-tentous influence upon the destiny of the Holy Land.

Constantine's open interventions in affairs of religion are remarkable. It is enough to mention his part in the convocation of the Council of Nicaea in 325 and, personally, in the theological disputations during the assembly: his prominence in the christo-logical argument was such that the Greek theologians conferred upon him the title "Isapostolos", peer of Apostles.

The interest shown by him in the Holy Land may be gauged from his bidding to Makarios, Bishop of Jerusalem after the Council, to discover the sites of Calvary and the Holy Sepulchre. Apparently, no trace of either site was then extant: the version of Eusebius and St. Jerome is that a temple to Venus had blotted both out after the founding of Aelia Capitolina. Following that act of desecration the early Christians suffered a period of such torment that the Holy Places were perforce left untended and exact loca-tions obscured. But Bishop Makarios claimed successful identifi-cation of them and reported to the emperor on his researches and findings.[1] Constantine at once bade that a circular church arise on the site of the empty Sepulchre (the Anastasis, i.e., resurrec-tion), and that a great and splendid basilica, the Martyrion,[2] be constructed close by. Between the two churches, an edifice was built to mark the site where Calvary (the skull) had been found. The architectonic whole was the work of two famed architects of Constantinople, Zenobius and Eustathe. But the architectonics of those shrines differed remarkably from that of the later Crusader building which, with some changes, still stands. Soon after this, tradition has it, Constantine's mother Helena was a pilgrim in the

1) Among these, tradition includes the discovery of the "true Cross." The Church commemorates the event with the Feast of the Invention of the Cross, on May 3.

2) Remains of the Martyrion were recently uncovered below the Greek Ortho-dox Katholicon in the Basilica of the Holy Sepulchre.

Holy Land; it would seem that she had become a Christian before her son. She did very much in the Holy Land for a grateful Church, which in due time rewarded her with sainthood. To her, among many ascriptions, is credited the Basilica of the Nativity in Bethlehem, built above the grotto venerated by Christians as the site where Jesus was born. Like Calvary, the place of the Nativity, according to St. Jerome, had also been defiled by dedication to the heathen cult of Adonis.[3] The Basilica of Bethlehem is the one church in the Holy Land to be conserved to this day in its original form,[4] albeit only in part, substantial repairs and enlargement having been carried out on the initiative of Emperor Justinian in the sixth century. Another church of St. Helena's presumptive making was destroyed: the Church of Eleona on the Mount of Olives (in Greek, *elaion* means olive grove).[5] The building of the church in honor of St. Abraham in Hebron is attributed to the prompting of another member of the imperial family, Eutropia, Constantine's mother-in-law.[6] During the same period, several churches were built in Galilee, allegedly owing to the endeavors of a wealthy Hebrew-Christian called Count Joseph, who was a tax-collector for the Byzantine authorities. Churches in Nazareth, Capernaum and Sepphoris are attributed to the munificence of the Count.

These and other churches of the era of Constantine, raised to signalize and safeguard the shrines of Christendom, are described in the famous itinerary of the anonymous "Pilgrim of Bordeaux", who visited the Holy Land in 333, and in the account given of her travels by the Spanish Abbess Etheria or Egeria, who was in the Holy Land at the end of the fourth century.[7]

3) In classical mythology, a youth of remarkable beauty, the favorite of Venus.

4) During the Persian invasion (614–629), the church was spared on account of its mosaics depicting the "Wise Men" (the Magi) in Persian attire.

5) The ruins of the Church of Eleona are shown on the crest of the Mount of Olives, within the area of the "Pater Noster" Convent of the Carmelite Cloistered Sisters. In 1986, the remains of the Church of Eleona were restored with the financial aid of the "Oevre d'Orient."

6) It was built on the spot where, according to tradition, Abraham's terebinth stood. A Russian Orthodox church was erected nearby on a plot bought in 1868 by Archimandrite Antonin Kapustin.

7) See Palestine Pilgrims' Text Society (London). The Latin text of Etheria's itinerary was discovered in 1884 by Bishop Gamurini in a library of the town of Arezzo (Italy).

In that age, the Byzantine rite was generally followed and the liturgy was recited in Greek as a rule, but some sectors, especially in the countryside, may have used Syriac.

After a certain period of expansion in the fourth century, Christianity was set back briefly during the short reign of Julian (361–363), who sought to reinstate the old pagan pantheon. During his rule, churches were desecrated in Sebaste, Emmaus and Mayuma near Gaza.

A radical swing came with the accession of Theodosius the Great (379–395), who once and for all asserted the State recognition and primacy of the Christian faith above all others within the empire. He was the first Roman emperor to dispense with the pagan title of Pontifex Maximus. He convened the Second Ecumenical Council in Constantinople in 381, which was also attended by bishops of Palestine. By degrees Christianity became the religion of the bulk of the population of the Holy Land. At that time, Palestine was divided into three parts: Palaestina Prima, including Judaea and Samaria; Palaestina Secunda, including Galilee and the Decapolis; and Palaestina Tertia, or Arabia Petrea. These administrative districts were matched by corresponding ecclesiastical divisions, headed by Metropolitans, with seats respectively in Caesarea, Scythopolis[8] and Petra.[9]

RELIGIOUS MANIFESTATIONS

Strangely enough, this development in the birthplace of Christianity was the outcome not of activity by local elements, but rather of proselytizing by monks from neighboring lands where the faith had implanted itself with much greater strength and permanence. They did not content themselves with the conquest of the infidel; they are believed to have torn down heathen sanctuar-

---

8) Scythopolis was the name of the city in classical times. The ancient biblical city was called Beit Sheán.

9) In recent times, the Greek Orthodox Patriarch of Jerusalem, Benedictos I, conferred the historical titles of Metropolitan of Caesarea and of Petra on two leading members of the Fraternity of the Holy Sepulchre. Patriarch Diodoros I, Benedictos' successor to the patriarchal See, conferred the title of the Metropolitan of Scythopolis on another member of the Fraternity.

ies and shattered idolatrous statuary with their own impassioned hands. In the south-west, Egyptian monks were in the van of this missionary zealousness. Hilarion, born near Gaza but sent out as a youth to Egypt, where he became a disciple of St. Anthony, was by far the most outstanding, and St. Jerome holds that the origin of Palestinian monachism must be attributed to him. He had tenanted a hovel in the wilderness near Mayuma, the port of Gaza, in about 330, and his fame as scholar and worker of miracles was such that throngs of followers and admirers were attracted to this site. He never visited Jerusalem, on account of his belief that "God does not dwell in a particular place." The monastery he founded was the first established in the Holy Land. A contemporary of St. Hilarion was St. Chariton, who founded the Monastery of Fara.[10]

In the north-west of the country, it was the monks from Antioch who campaigned with greatest vigor. Monasteries sprang up everywhere. Foremost amongst them were the "lauras" or colonies of anchorites[11] who, each occupying a separate cell, were subject to the control of a single Abbot. The first laura, deep in Judaea, near the Dead Sea, was founded in 428 by Euthymius, a monk of Armenian origin. His success in healing the son of a sheik named Aspebet prompted the whole nomad tribe to convert and to settle near the cave where he dwelt. The proselytes were so numerous that a new diocese had to be established and Aspebet became their bishop. Another monastery, the "Great Laura",[12] was founded a few years later by St. Sabas in the steep valley of the Kidron, several miles west of Jericho;[13] its monks became famous for their fiery debates for and against the theories of Origen, the great theologian of Alexandria. Several of them, perfervid followers of Origen's ideas, seceded from the "Great Laura" and founded the "New

10) The ruins of the monastery are the property of the Russian Orthodox Church which has its center outside of Russia.
11) Laura means in Greek: narrow valley, lane.
12) So called because it numbered about 150 monks, many of Armenian origin. (See Life of St. Sabas by Kyrillos)
13) A Greek Orthodox monastery, named Mar Saba, commemorates its founder to this day. The fortress-like building comprises seven chapels, some of them very ancient and ornate, for example those in honor of St. Sabas, St. John Damaskinos and St. Nicholas. In October 1965, the remains of St. Sabas were brought back from Italy to be reinterred in the monastery, the original place of rest.

Laura" near Tekoa, south of Bethlehem. The monks of the "New Laura" were later evicted by Eustochios, Patriarch of Jerusalem, for the heterodox views they professed. Sabas, who died in 532 in his ninety-third year, was entrusted during his life-time with two missions to Constantinople: one in 511 to the Emperor Anastasios in support of the Orthodox faith as set out in Chalcedon; the second after the Samaritan uprising.

The tradition of St. Basil, too, had its followers; his rule was observed by several monasteries in the vicinity of Jerusalem. St. Basil the Great, one of the Cappadocian Fathers had succeeded Eusebius in 370 as Bishop of Caesarea. Rufinus of Aquileia (a town in northern Italy) also settled in Jerusalem. After his arrival in 379 he founded a monastery on the Mount of Olives, the members of which were active as manuscript copyists. Rufinus himself did valuable service as translator of theological works from Greek into Latin.

A most illustrious monk who lived in the Holy Land at the end of the fourth and the beginning of the fifth century was St. Jerome. He dwelt in Bethlehem and was assiduously active as editor and exegete. An ancient tradition has it that an underground room in the town, situated near the grotto of the Nativity, is where St. Jerome lived for many years whilst preparing his famous Latin translation of the Bible, the Vulgate, from Hebrew and Greek originals.

Among the other monks of fame who settled in the Holy Land in the middle of the fifth century was St. Theodosios, who tenanted a grotto in the desert of Judaea, some six miles east of Bethlehem, and was joined by hundreds of monks of various nationalities, Greeks and Georgians, Armenians and Syrians. He founded a large monastery with a hospital, hospices and workshops for the monks. On the ruins of this vast compound rose, in later times, the present Greek Orthodox Church and Monastery of St. Theodosios. One of his eminent followers was St. Theognios, known as "the Light of the Desert", who founded a monastery of his own. One of those who established monasteries in the Holy Land was St. Epiphanios, author of the *Panarion*. He was born in 315 in Palestine and served as superior of one of the monasteries he had founded.

The monastic map of Byzantine Palestine shows a prodigious

14

development: in the desert of Judaea alone, there is evidence of more than a hundred monasteries.[14]

So it was that the concluding years of the fourth century and the starting years of the fifth ushered in an epoch of unsurpassed Christian growth in the Holy Land. With the thriving economy and the relatively stable political situation, the population of the Holy Land expanded dramatically. According to recent estimates by leading historians, archaeologists and demographers, there were some 2,800,000 souls at that time, more than half Christians.[15]

Pilgrims poured in from West and East. In a letter to Marcella, who led in Rome a monastically oriented circle of Roman widows and virgins, St. Jerome mentions the Ethiopians and Armenians, the Egyptians and the Persians, the Syrians and the Indians. Inducements were offered to those coming to settle in the neighborhood of the Holy Places. The large influx of newcomers from Western Europe did much to enhance the weal of the local brethren. Several rich noblewomen of the Roman patriciate now wished to end their days in an environment of sanctity, and Jerusalem and Bethlehem were irresistible magnets for them.

Among the aristocratic ladies who, drawn by the renown of St. Jerome, made their homes in Bethlehem, were St. Paula and her daughter Julia—also known by the Greek name of Eustochium—foundresses of two convents in the vicinity of the Basilica of the Nativity in Bethlehem, and of a hospice for pilgrims. Their benefactions to the Church were equalled and even surpassed by Melania Junior,[16] another lady of noble descent who, at about the same time, adopted an ascetic form of life and founded a convent for women in Jerusalem on the Mount of Olives in the neighborhood of the monastery for men established by Rufinus. She also gave

14) In 1965, archaeologist Asher Ovadiah published a list of the remains of Byzantine churches and monasteries discovered in the Holy Land. It comprises 175 names of such ruins, situated on 127 sites. Since 1965, the remnants of tens of other Byzantine churches have come to light in the Holy Land.

15) See Bachi R, *The Population of Israel*, p. 360.

16) Her grandmother, whose name was also Melania, widow of the Senator Valerius Maximus, had settled in Jerusalem in 374. She is linked with the foundation of a convent on the Mount of Olives. Tradition has credited each of these holy women with the same act.

much monetary aid to the hospices and hermitages of the neighborhood. According to some sources, the monastery of Rufinus was among the foundations which benefitted from Melania's largesse. To another wealthy lady, Poemenia, is credited the building of the Rotunda of the Ascension on the Mount of Olives and of its annex, around the year 378.

By far the most outstanding benefactress to the Holy Land was the Empress Eudocia, estranged wife of Theodosius II. She visited the Holy Land as a pilgrim in 438 and returned in 443 to live there for seventeen years until her death in 460. Eudocia could be said to merit the title Queen of the Holy Land. The churches built through her endeavors in Jerusalem and its vicinity included: St. Sophia of the Praetorium, St. George in Nikephoria (in the Hinnom Valley), the trefoil-shaped Church of St. John near the Basilica of the Holy Sepulchre, St. Stephen's near the Damascus Gate[17], St. Peter near the palace of Caiaphas, the Siloam Church at the pool and St. Peter near the Laura of Euthymius. Eudocia also expanded the circuit of Jerusalem's walls to include Mount Zion, the Ofel and the Siloam spring.

She was buried in St. Stephen's Church, the construction of which she had sponsored.

Eudoxia, daughter-in-law of Eudocia and wife of Emperor Arkadios, took also a special interest in the fortunes of the Holy Land. She supported Porphyrios, Bishop of Gaza, who had foretold the birth of her son. Gaza, until the fourth century a stronghold of paganism, became a flourishing Christian center. Porphyrios, with the backing of the empress, brought about the destruction *manu militari* of the town's eight pagan temples. Among them was the famous sanctuary of Marnas, built in honor of the Cretan Zeus. It was replaced by a magnificent basilica, named after the Empress Eudoxia, who gave generous sums for its construction.[18]

No less important for the progress of Palestine, now that it was considered to be the center of Christianity, was the bounty that poured in from many other parts of the world. Every holy site

17) The Ecole Biblique of the Dominican Fathers now occupies the site.
18) Over the remains of the Eudoxian basilica, the Crusaders built a great church, dedicated to St. John. It was later converted into a mosque by the Moslems who named it Giameh-el-Kibir. The Greek Orthodox parish church in Gaza is dedicated to St. Porphyrios.

which the Gospels recorded could thus be immortalized in masonry; the Churches of St. Peter in Gallicantu (Cockcrow) and the Tomb of the Virgin Mary, the Church of Gethsemane, the Hagia Sion and a church in Bethany near the Tomb of Lazarus, all of them in or around Jerusalem, are some of the finest examples.

Magnificent churches also rose elsewhere in Byzantine Palestine: the churches in honor of St. Cornelius and of St. Procopius in Caesarea, those dedicated to St. Basil and to St. Thomas in Scythopolis, others in Eleutheropolis (Beit Jibrin) and throughout Galilee. Two beautiful basilicas, one dedicated to St. Sergius, the other to St. Stephanos, were erected in Gaza through the endeavors of Bishop Markianos.

In this context it should be noted that Gaza reached in the sixth century the peak of its cultural and artistic development. Its academy of rhetoric earned a distinguished reputation, its most renowned representative being the philosopher Procopios. Other outstanding scholars of Byzantine Gaza were the historian Zosimos, the rhetorician Chorikios and the celebrated savant John of Gaza.

The cult of relics became unprecedently popular and, not unnaturally, could be turned to some commercial advantage; if by modern standards that can be criticized, it was nevertheless of considerable financial benefit to religious institutions and helped to subsidize general welfare. There was traffic in objects alleged to be bound up somehow with the lives of the Hebrew Patriarchs and Prophets, with the saints and martyrs of the faith, and with the earthly days of Jesus and the Virgin Mary, and particularly the bones and robes of holy men and women, and exhibits of martyrology. Sometimes the authenticity of the bones of a Saint was based only on the revelation in a dream. No wonder that the worship of relics and the merchandizing of them had to be controlled by Government ordinances. Many relics were sent overseas to add saintliness to chapels and churches existing or planned; often if a relic was kept in the Holy Land, a memorial chapel or church was built where it had first come to light.

The presence of many Greek inscriptions gives ample evidence of the predominantly Greek character of this early Church, but other national Churches, notably the Armenian, were represented.[19]

The tempo and extent of ecclesiastical construction are demonstrated by recent finds of mosaic pavements and numerous vestiges of old churches all over Israel, from Northern Galilee to the farthest Negev. Ruins of about two hundred churches of the Byzantine period were discovered in Cis-Jordan. They are distributed in one hundred and thirty-seven localities, the largest concentration being in the Judaean Hills, followed by the Negev, Samaria, the Wilderness of Judaea and, finally, Galilee. Assuming that a multiplicity of churches is an indication of the density of the Christian population, one may conclude that Christians lived, for the most part, in the southern part of Palestine. Another sign of the wide diffusion of Christianity at this period is the great number of bishoprics then extant. No fewer than forty-seven bishops are recorded in a decision taken by a local council in 530, during the incumbency of Patriarch Peter. Even taking in account the relatively modest size of a Palestinian diocese of that time, it is clear from their sheer number in the sixth century that Christianity had a large following in the Byzantine period.

General conditions prevailing in the three hundred years of Byzantine sovereignty were, we may conclude, very gratifying for Christendom, but the Holy Land was caught up to some degree in the feuds which shook and split Eastern Christianity in the fourth and fifth centuries. The polemics were stimulated by a peculiar mentality that possessed the enlightened of the time and was fed by the subtlety of Greek philosophy. But there were not only theological and metaphysical motivations. Political divergences also had their say and, more than anything else, resistance in the main centers of Eastern culture to the intellectual suzerainty of Constantinople. That political interests should trespass upon the arena of theological disputation was an unavoidable result of the tight relationship between Church and State during the Byzantine period; it meant that religious beliefs were usually enforced by law.

19) Ruins of Armenian mosaics of the Byzantine period were found in Jerusalem on the Mount of Olives and outside the Damascus Gate. They belonged to Armenian churches and monasteries of the sixth century.

Coming to a climax in the fourth century, this wordy warfare, its concomitant almost from infancy, imperiled the unity of a rising Church. A novel topic of christological controversy was the view advanced by Arius, a learned priest of Alexandria, that Christ was not of the same "substance" as God the Father, but had been created by Him. Arius was violently impugned by the bishop in whose jurisdiction he ministered, and was obliged to quit Alexandria, finding asylum in Caesarea with Eusebius, who was evidently not antagonistic to his idea. The quarrel around the Arian conception grew in bitterness and in dimension, so that it was found necessary to convoke an ecumenical, or world-wide council to find a way out. Arianism endured a while in defiance of its condemnation by the majority of bishops at the Council of Nicaea, since it enjoyed the support of certain emperors, for example, Constantine's. Because of these imperial links St. Cyril (350–386), a non-Arian bishop of Jerusalem, was exiled from the See.[20] In the fifth century, however, Arianism faded out of existence in the Near East.[21] On the other hand, two theological controversies launched successively in the fifth century produced lasting schisms, and their impact on Eastern Christianity was felt acutely. One is named after Nestorius, Patriarch of Constantinople, who accented the human nature of Christ. Nestorius was condemned by the Council of Ephesus (431) and deposed from his See. He lived for some time in a monastery near Antioch, but later was exiled to Upper Egypt, where he died in 451. The headquarters of the Nestorian Church was established in Ctesiphon, capital of Persia (present-day Iran). The choice of location was prompted by the strained relations that existed between Persia and the Byzantine empire.

Followers of the Nestorian Church are to be found among the Christians of the Near East and in Southern India; in the Holy

20) He is the author of 24 catechetical lectures delivered to candidates for baptism. St. Cyril was declared a doctor of the Church in 1883. On October 21, 1986, 1600 years after his death, a special celebration was held in Jerusalem at the initiative of the Greek Orthodox Patriarch.

21) Arianism also had followers among the German tribes which invaded the Western Roman Empire. Their adherence continued until the seventh century.

Land there are a few families only.[22] In the ninth century, the Catholicos of the Nestorian Church was the first spiritual shepherd of a Christian flock to be recognized by Islamic authority.

The future of Christianity in the Middle East was even more potently swayed by the Monophysitic altercation, in the main fought in Egypt. For the Monophysites there was in the person of the Incarnate Christ only a single (Greek: monos) nature (phusis), an unconfounded blend of divine and human, whereas the Orthodox doctrine spoke of a double nature, divine and human. For the overthrow of Monophysitism, an ecumenical council met in Chalcedon (451), and the protagonists of duality triumphed. The rift was as much political as theological, an end product of the traditional hostility of the provinces of Egypt and Syria to Byzantium. The followers of the Chalcedonian Orthodox Church in the Middle East were called Melkites, followers of the "melek" (or emperor) of Constantinople. In Syria and in the Holy Land Monophysites became very numerous in the course of the sixth century, thanks to the apostolate of Jacob Baradai (c.500–578)[23], after whom the Syrian adherents came to be known as "Jacobites."

Apart from its decision on christological issues, the Council of Chalcedon adopted a resolution directly affecting the hierarchy of the Holy Land. The Bishop of Jerusalem, until then a suffragan of the Metropolitan of Caesarea, who was dependent in his turn on the Patriarch of Antioch, was raised to the rank of Patriarch of Jerusalem. Maximos, Bishop of Jerusalem (334–348) had already claimed that in view of the religious importance of Jerusalem, the episcopal See of the Holy City should be given pre-eminence over the metropolitan See of Caesarea. His contention was borne out during the incumbency of Bishop Juvenal.

Juvenal, formerly Bishop and thenceforth Patriarch of Jerusalem, had at first partly espoused the Monophysite conception, but at Chalcedon he bowed to the opinion of the Orthodox ma-

22) Today there is in Jerusalem a patriarchal vicar of the Chaldean Church, representing those former adherents of the Nestorian Church who sought union with Rome in 1552.

There are also in the Holy Land and in Transjordan former Chaldeans who joined the Roman Catholic Church, but preserved the family name Kaldany, an unmistakable indication of their ancient ethnic origin.

23) Baradäus, meaning "ragged" in Aramaic, was the name given to Jacob, who used to move around disguised as a beggar.

jority in rejecting Monophysitism, and his elevation to the hierarchy was the reward. On his return to the Holy Land, Juvenal encountered vehement antagonism from clergy and population, for most of them had turned Monophysites. Things had come to such a pass that, while he was absent in Chalcedon, a rival ecclesiastic had been enthroned as Bishop of Jerusalem, and it took the bloody intervention of Byzantine soldiery to win his patriarchal privileges back for Juvenal.[24]

The rift between the Monophysites and the Orthodox Church with its center in Constantinople seriously upset the internal politics of the empire. The attitude towards heresy depended, on the whole, on the more or less tolerant views of the current ruler. Emperors anxious to obliterate Monophysitism alternated with emperors inclined to compromise; fanatical emperors persecuted Christian stragglers from the Orthodox path and bore heavily on the members of the non-Christian creeds.

THE SAMARITAN REBELLIONS

Repression in the fifth and sixth centuries provoked the Samaritans, who were still numerous then, into mutiny. Their spasms of insurrection involved Christians in the Holy Land painfully, for Samaritan activism also pointed against them. The first revolt during the reign of Zenon started on the Feast of the Pentecost, in the year 484. The insurgents slew most of the Christians assembled in the cathedral of Neapolis (Nablus of today), and then, led by their king, marched to Caesarea, to be joined by the then populous Samaritan colony of the town. They burned the church of St. Procopios and killed Bishop Timotheos with many other Christians. But the rising was sternly repressed, and a church, named for the Virgin Mary, was built exemplarily on Mount Gerizim, sacred hill of the sect, and the Samaritan synagogue near Nablus, claimed to be an edifice of Jacob himself, was converted into a monastery.

In a second revolt, during the reign of the Emperor Anastasios

---

24) Patriarch Juvenal is credited with building a church dedicated to the Virgin Mary in Gethsemane, the traditional site of Mary's tomb.

(491–518), the Samaritans destroyed the church on Mount Gerizim, but were driven out again by Procopios, the Byzantine governor of Palestine.

There was a third and most dangerous outbreak under Justinian (529) in violent Samaritan reaction to laws which treated the sectaries as heretics. The Samaritans in their fury wrecked churches and convents, butchered bishops and priests, and for a while were masters of several towns in the Holy Land, including Caesarea and Beisan. The church of St. John in Ein Karem was razed to the ground by them, and the basilica of Bethlehem gravely damaged. As soon as the revolt was put down, Justinian, famed for his piety, gave orders to restore the harmed churches at once and to build new ones, among them the very beautiful "new" church in Jerusalem, in honor of the Theotokos, the Virgin Mary.[25]

END OF BYZANTINE RULE

At the beginning of the seventh century, Christian domination in the Holy Land came to its end; it had opened in 324 with the publication of the edict of Constantine in Caesarea and had abided for three hundred years. The domestic friction between Christians and the Samaritan unrest, do not invalidate an assessment of the situation in the Holy Land in that interval as having been, all in all, calm and stable, compared to what characterized imperial provinces vulnerable to barbarian irruption. Besides, the mere attribute of religious centrality brought a degree of prosperity which the Holy Land was long to lack.

Persia now supplanted Byzantium. Persia and Rome had been implacable foes for generations. At the onset of the seventh century, the rivalry was keener than ever: the Persians succeeded, if

---

25) The remains of the "Nea", the new church built in the year 540 in honor of the "Theotokos" were discovered during the restoration work in the Jewish Quarter of Jerusalem's Old City. Part of the original structure has been cleared of debris and is preserved *in situ*. Theotokos is the Greek word for "Mother of God." During the christological debates of the first centuries, use of the appellative Theotokos was strongly opposed by the theologians who averred the human nature of Christ. (See: Nestorians)

only for a short while, in overrunning Syria, Egypt and the Holy Land, and advanced as far as the gates of Constantinople. Before many years had gone by, however, Byzantium mustered enough vigour to threaten Persia's domains and speedily bring its military triumphs to naught. But all this bloodletting only served to enfeeble both contestants to the advantage of a third party, the Moslem Arabs, who now loomed upon the horizon.

The short-lived victory of Persia had reflected a Byzantium riven by inner conflict and the religious intransigence of the emperors. The policy of discrimination against the Monophysites, who held on stoutly in Syria and Egypt, inspired those dissidents with a deep hatred of the Orthodox and a vindictiveness that egged them on to side openly with the Persians. Again and again we find a similar phenomenon during the Crusader epoch, when congregants of the local Churches, hounded by the Latins, in their resentment made common cause with the Moslems.

In 614, the Persian monarch, Cosroes II, surnamed Parvez (the victorious), took Jerusalem after a siege of twenty days: for three days that followed, most of its Christian inhabitants were done to death, churches were burned down, among them the Church of the Holy Sepulchre, the Hagia Sion on Mount Zion, the "Nea", dedicated to the Theotokos and the Church of the Ascension on the Mount of Olives. Before the Holy City fell, the churches outside the walls had been reduced to ruins. Thousands of ablebodied Christians were sent to Persia as serfs; Zacharias, Patriarch of Jerusalem, was among the captives. The "true Cross" was taken to Ctesiphon, capital of Persia, as loot of war, with countless things, beyond all price, pillaged from the churches of the Holy Land. It was an irreparable loss of infinite anguish.

In the end, the Persian rule lasted no more than fifteen years, but that was long enough for the brief, and ostensibly repentant, conquerors to grant Christians license to return to Jerusalem and to start the rebuilding of devastated churches. This very likely was a political move, aimed at achieving reconciliation with the Christian inhabitants in the newly occupied provinces.

Modestos, a monk from the monastery of St. Theodosios was exceptionally to the fore in collecting the funds needed for the restoration of the churches and, doubtless in recognition of his merits, he was elevated to the Patriarchal See of Jerusalem when Zacharias died.

The Byzantine Emperor Heraklios, who assumed the crown in 610 and succeeded in reorganizing State and army, took the field in 622 against the Persians and routed their troops. In the turbulence that followed, Chosroes was deposed and killed by his son Kavadh II (628). When Kavadh himself died a few months later, the ensuing anarchy made it easier for Byzantine Heraklios to reconquer lost territory. In March 629, he entered Jerusalem, and with exceeding but justifiable pomp led a procession to the restored Church of the Holy Sepulchre; there he replaced what was left of the "true Cross."[26] The Persians had returned it, being eager to make peace with their enemies without and to free themselves to reinstate order within.

Byzantine re-entry was not fated to be prolonged either. The fiery sword of Islam soon swept Egypt, Syria and the Holy Land in a lightning conquest, rendered all the simpler by Byzantium's frailty after its protracted sanguinary combat with Persia. Moreover, the Monophysites in the Eastern provinces, at daggers drawn with Orthodox authority, had little compunction about backing Byzantium's assailants. In 634, the Arabs, led by Amr Ibn al-As, to whom Caliph Abu-Bakr had entrusted the command, were at Gaza and in the neighborhood of that city they easily defeated the Byzantine commander Sergius, whose army numbered only five thousand men. The garrison of Gaza duly capitulated. A Greek officer named Kallinikos, and sixty soldiers from the citadel guard were taken to Jerusalem. Given the choice between conversion to Islam or death, they opted for the latter. To this day they are venerated by the Church as the sixty martyrs of Gaza. Advancing northward from that town and devastating the territory that they crossed, the Arab forces reached Caesarea. An attempt by Theodoros, brother of the Emperor Heraklios, to stop their advance failed dismally and, with the routing of his large army in July 634, practically the whole of the open country was in the hands of the invaders; the inhabitants had to take refuge in the walled towns. The crucial battle was fought in 636 close to the river

26) The Feast of the Exaltation of the Cross is celebrated on September 14 to commemorate the event.

Yarmuk, a tributary of the Jordan, and the day went to Abou Obeida, entrusted by the Caliph Omar Ibn al-Khattab with the supreme command of the Arab forces. Jerusalem was invested within a twelvemonth. The Patriarch Sophronios hoped against hope that a Byzantine army would come to the salvation of the Holy City, and he inspired a long and gallant resistance. At last, in spring, 638, the terrible ordeal which the citizens had undergone a quarter of a century before at Persian hands still fresh in his memory, Sophronios decided to surrender. To Moslems, no less Jerusalem was sacred, and Caliph Omar came in person to negotiate the capitulation and take the city over. In 640, after a bitter siege of seven months, Caesarea, ultimate stronghold of the Byzantines, also capitulated.

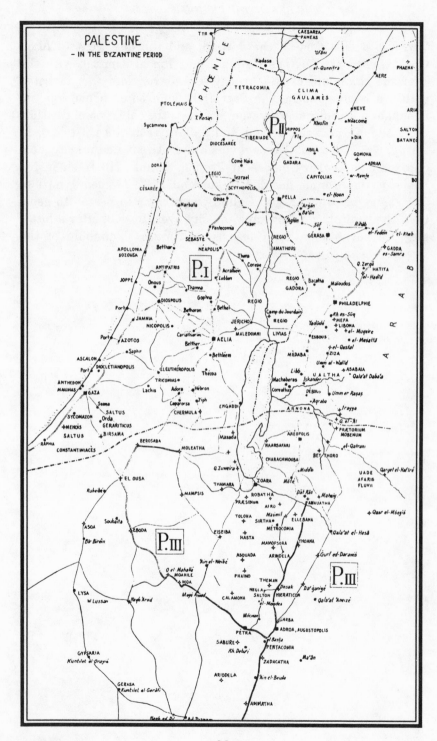

PALESTINE
– IN THE BYZANTINE PERIOD

Chapter Three

THE ARAB CONQUEST (636–1099)

The conquest of Jerusalem by the Moslem Arabs had momentous repercussions in the world at large; beyond question, it was a landmark in the history of the Holy Land. Understandably, the reports of the replacement of Byzantine by Moslem rule captured the imagination of the early historians, who were not slow to add a plethora of fictitious detail and embellishment. Greek sources are insistent on portraying the atmosphere of dignity which surrounded the first meeting between the Caliph Omar and the Patriarch Sophronios on the Mount of Olives. The climax of the meeting, we are told, was the delivery of a warrant of protection to the Patriarch by the conqueror, whereafter the two made a pilgrimage to the Holy Sepulchre; but the Caliph would not worship within the church and prostrated himself outside it. Omar's own explanation for his restraint was that, had he prayed within, his followers might have turned the Holy Sepulchre into a Moslem shrine and so robbed Christianity of its major Holy Place.[1] Thence, the sources continue, the thoughtful Caliph moved on with the Patriarch to the ruins of the Temple, a site with religious significance for Moslems, because of its connection with the life of Mohammed.

This tale of friendliness on Omar's part towards the vanquished Patriarch is, however, gainsaid by evidence that Sophronios died in the very year—638—of the surrender of Jerusalem and his successor, Anastasios, in 702. We do not know when Anastasios became Patriarch, but we may conclude that there was a lengthy hiatus in the patriarchal succession, pointing to a troubled period and radical changes. Nor can it be doubted that, as wars are wont to do, the Arab conquest dealt the Holy Land immense wastage of life and property.

The warrant of protection, said to have been given by the Caliph Omar to Patriarch Sophronios, plays an important role in

---

1) To commemorate the incident, the Omariya mosque was later built near the Holy Sepulchre.

the succeeding events in the Holy Land. This "ahtname," or edict, is regarded by the Greeks as their "Magna Carta of Rights." But its authenticity is challenged by not a few reputable scholars, who argue, *inter alia,* that only later copies of it are in existence. Indeed, it seems strange that a victorious Caliph should grant a worsted Patriarch conditions as indulgent as those dictated over a thousand years afterwards by the European Powers to the masters of a decadent Ottoman empire, but the tendency is not uncommon to project to earlier times a subsequent legal conjuncture. The "ahtname" certainly figured decisively in the conflict for the Holy Places, when a document supposedly promulgated by the first Caliph could not be ignored by any of the Ottoman Sultans who bore the title after Omar. But one must ask whether a deed issued by a Moslem Caliph binds non-Moslem overlords with equal validity. Or, conversely, does a Christian Church possess no more authentic an original title to its rights in the Holy Places than a deed given by a Moslem Caliph?

On the other hand, doubts regarding the authenticity of the "ahtname" should not sway us to assume that the Greek element in the Church of the Holy Land disappeared, a thesis propounded with obvious tendentiousness by Latin sources. The burden of that thesis is that Jerusalem's fall led to a mass exodus of Byzantine clergy and Greek citizens, and that, with the thin alien stratum withdrawn, the Christian population—so it is claimed—was left essentially Arab and Syrian.

Against this is the evidence of the unbroken presence of the Orthodox Church in the Holy Land and in the Holy Places, notwithstanding the crisis following the Moslem conquest. Nor is it material whether the membership of the Orthodox Church was made up to a larger or lesser degree of Arab-speaking Orthodox, for in this context it has to be remembered that the influx of Greek colonists into the Near East, behind the all-conquering phalanxes of Alexander the Great, had a powerful cultural and ethnic impact on the peoples of the area. Nor can it be denied that, in the centuries after the Moslem conquest, the Byzantine emperors never failed to evince deep concern for the fate of the Holy Places, and on many occasions underwrote their restoration generously.

Admittedly, the Moslem conquest affected Christian life in the

Holy Land adversely. That is not, however, to say that it wiped that life out by any means.

As soon as fighting ended, it seems that the Moslems treated the subdued population humanely, and for a time the Christian majority in the Holy Land were undisturbed in their professions. But all the non-Moslem inhabitants without exception were regarded as "second-class citizens" and constrained to behave in such a way as not to offend Moslem susceptibility. They must not attempt to proselytize among Moslems, nor could their men marry Moslem women. They were looked down upon as "dhimmis," as protégés, and had to pay a personal toll, a "djiziah." The Christians, although humiliated in many ways, were allowed to pursue an independent communality, to keep their places of worship, observe their own laws and customs: this considerable measure of autonomy in religion and in matters of personal status is called the *millet* system to this day.

The first of the three dynasties which ruled in succession in the Holy Land was the Omayyad dynasty (660–750). Its founder, Muawiya, who had been appointed governor of Syria by Omar ibn al-Khattab, was proclaimed caliph in Jerusalem in 660. Succession was promised to his son Yazid.

At the time of the first Omayyads the situation of the Christians was tolerable. Christian pilgrimage to the Holy Land, at all events to start with, was not interrupted by the Moslems; Arculf, a Frankish Bishop, who was on a visit in 670, described conditions as satisfactory. As the Omayyads consolidated their power they became less tolerant.

During the reign of Omayyad Caliph Abd-al-Malikh (685–705)[2] and his successor, Christians were once more victimized and in this duress many began to seek respite in conversion to Islam. Not a few, and mainly those of Greek extraction, chose to emigrate; their houses were occupied by incoming Moslems.

The advent of the Abbasids made things even worse, for the members of that dynasty were more rigid in their religious de-

2) He is credited with the construction of the celebrated Moslem shrine "The Dome of the Rock" in Jerusalem. It was built in order to enhance Jerusalem as a center of Moslem pilgrimage, and thereby diminish the religious and political influence of Mecca and Medina.

mands. In 756, Abu Djafar al-Mansour[3] forbade the building of new churches and any display of the cross; if there was already one upon a church, it had to be taken down. Not only that but, by an ordinance in most general terms, all Christians were obliged to brand their garments with a distinctive sign.

In 765, Pipin the Short, King of the Franks, dispatched a mission to Caliph al-Mansour, and the caliph in turn sent envoys to France. Chronicles of the time do not relate the results of this exchange.

The Caliph Harun al-Rashid (786–809)[4], for all his "humanism" and for all his friendship with Charlemagne, the great Frankish king, brought little relief. In his reign, too, many churches in the Holy Land were put to the torch and many Christians were killed because of the wars that he waged.

Charlemagne, lauded by the Western world as the champion of Christianity, was understandably concerned with the Holy Places and bargained amicably with Harun al-Rashid on matters pertaining to them. In 797, some thirty years after the mission sent by his father Pipin to al-Mansour, a delegation representing Charlemagne left France for Baghdad, the Abbasid capital, with Jerusalem a staging post along the way. The mission to the caliph consisted of two Palatine counts, Lanfred and Siegmund, and a Jew Isaac, who acted as guide and translator. In response, a delegation from Baghdad reached France in 801 with gifts for the king of the Franks. In 802, Charles again sent envoys to Baghdad, and the reciprocal gesture came four years later. During the same period, contacts were also established with Patriarch George of Jerusalem. Charles sent gifts for the Christians of the Holy Land, and in turn received from the Patriarch religious artifacts delivered by two Jerusalem monks, one from the Greek Orthodox Monastery of Mar Saba, the other from a Latin Monastery on the Mount of Olives.

There is a tradition that the caliph's envoys, despatched in 801 to Charlemagne in Aix-la-Chapelle, bore as a gift to the king the keys of the Church of the Holy Sepulchre and the banner of Jerusalem. Upon this alleged presentation of the keys of the Holy

---

3) al-Mansour means "the divinely aided."
4) al-Rashid means "the upright."

Sepulchre was subsequently based the Frankish assertion of a right of "protectorate" over the Holy Places, the entire Holy Land and its Christian inhabitants. Whatever the fact or legend concerning the caliph's gifts, history records that Charlemagne succeeded in securing better terms for the Christians of the Holy Land. Under his patronage a Benedictine monastery was founded near the Basilica of the Holy Sepulchre. In the same vicinity was built the Church of Sancta Maria Latina, later called "Maior."[5] Within its precincts were a library and a hospice for pilgrims from Western Europe.

In the eighth century, with the rising number of pilgrims to the Holy Land, such further lodgings were needed.

In 825 the Benedictine Monastery on the Mount of Olives was transferred to Haceldama (Field of the Blood), near Jerusalem. At the end of the tenth century the Benedictine monks founded a hospital for pilgrims in Jerusalem, naming it after St. John Eleemon of Egypt.

The amity between Harun al-Rashid and Charlemagne may at first seem curious, in the antithesis of Harun's harassment of his Christian subjects and Charles' renown in history and folklore for his remorseless warring against the Moors in Spain. Yet the two monarchs found a mutual enemy in the emperor of Byzantium and that made them allies, at least in diplomacy. Charles had taken the title of "Roman Emperor of the West"; this damned him as a usurper in the eyes of the Byzantine, who claimed to be the only inheritor of that title in East and West alike. The emperor of Byzantium besides, had never abdicated his provinces in the East, long and firmly occupied by Moslem invasion, and this pretension was a constant danger for the Caliph of Baghdad.

On the death of Harun al-Rashid, feuding between his two sons over the succession made the Christians' plight more wretched yet; it was then that the famous monasteries of St. Theodosios, St. Sabas and St. Chariton were so ill-used.

Of all the Abbasid rulers, Jafar al-Mutawakhil (847–861) was the most cruel and tyrannical. He intensified the degrading and cramping prohibitions imposed on the Christians: they were for-

5) So called in order to distinguish it from the later Church of Sancta Maria Latina "Minor."

bidden to ride on horseback or carry a sword, liturgy in public was circumscribed, tapers were not to be kindled or church bells rung. Christians had to affix wooden images of pigs or monkeys to their houses and wear yellow-colored outer garments. When riding on mules or asses, they had to use wooden saddles marked with pomegranate-like balls on the cantle. The effect of these measures was a steady exodus of Christians into Byzantine territory, which the Moslems did nothing to prevent. Moslem animosity was especially virulent against Christians of pure Arab stock who resisted forcible conversion; they, too, had to seek asylum beyond Moslem domain.

Special status among the Christian minorities was, however, granted to the Nestorians, possibly because of their enmity of Orthodox Byzantium. Thus the head of their community was the first Christian leader to obtain recognition from Moslem rulers.[6]

Abbasid domination in the Holy Land came to an end, for all practical purposes, in the second half of the ninth century: the local military commanders, who were able generals of Turkish origin, contrived to make themselves altogether independent of their Arab sovereigns. The most successful of them was Ahmed-ibn-Tulun, who became ruler of Egypt and conquered Palestine in 877. After his death in 884, under his sons and successors twenty years of misrule followed. In the ensuing disorders, the churches of Ramla and Ascalon were destroyed and the Church of the Holy Sepulchre was badly damaged.

In 905, Egypt and Syria reverted for thirty years to the Abbasids, and Palestine was dominated by mercenary captains who ruled in their name. During the reign of Caliph Jafar al-Muktader (908–932)[7], a decree was issued which removed all Christian clerks from official positions, with the exception of tax collectors and doctors. The caliph also called for a more rigorous adherence to the 200-year-old regulations concerning garments—a move which suggests that the rules had not been strictly enforced.

After 960, the Emperor Nikephoros Phocas, a great soldier, campaigned against the Moslems, winning back some of the ter-

---

6) A Nestorian bishop was appointed in Jerusalem as early as 893. It was his duty to care for Nestorian pilgrims. After 1065, Nestorian bishops in Jerusalem ranked as metropolitans.

7) al-Muktader means "the powerful through God."

ritories lost by his predecessors: many Christians, inhabitants of former Byzantine provinces, were thereupon aroused and saw deliverance at hand. But in 966, as a kind of reprisal for the victories of Phocas, Patriarch John VII was murdered in Jerusalem by Moslem assassins and the Church of the Holy Sepulchre once more profaned. In 969, Patriarch Thomas II repaired the churches with a donation from a wealthy Christian official from Baghdad.

In the same year, the Holy Land was conquered by the Fatimids, an Islamic dynasty which had risen to power in Northern Africa and, in the mid-tenth century, disputed the claim of the Abbasids to be the only and exclusive heirs to the caliphate of Baghdad.

The turmoil raging in the second half of the tenth century, the internecine rivalries of the Arab satraps of the Middle East and the crisis in the caliphate gave the Byzantine Emperor John I Tzimisces his opportunity to try and wrest the Eastern provinces from what was now a slackening grasp. In 975, John could safely advance into the Holy Land: Tiberias, Nazareth and Acre yielded to his assaults, and the North of the Holy Land, down to Caesarea, was soon in his possession. The campaign may be regarded as a holy war, not very different from the Crusades which were yet to come, but John did not trust his strength enough to march on southwards towards Jerusalem, even though heralds were sent out to him from the city bearing its keys. The death of the emperor in January 976 was perhaps the main reason for the withdrawal of the Byzantine army.

So his was a short conquest of the Holy Land and only a partial one. It did, however, establish an important precedent that was invoked by the emperor of Byzantium at the time of the First Crusade, in laying claim to all the lands of the Middle East. The emperor could, in the circumstances, afford to shelve the rights that were four centuries old and rely upon comparatively fresh contacts and conquests.

The Fatimids resumed their rule of the Holy Land on John's withdrawal, and under Abu Manzur Nizar al-Aziz (975–996) the Christians enjoyed a spell of quietude, only to suffer a recrudescence of hardship under his successor Abu Ali al-Manzur al-

Hakim (996–1021).[8] Al-Hakim passed ordinances directed against the Christians; he banned pilgrimages, confiscated Church property, ordered crosses to be burned and small mosques to be built on the roofs of the churches. Hundreds of churches were pillaged and destroyed during his reign, among them the Church of the Holy Sepulchre itself, on the pretext that the annual miracle of the Holy Fire, celebrated in it on the Saturday before Easter, was an impious deception.[9] Despairing, many Christians left the Holy Land, again fleeing to Byzantine territory. Yet al-Hakim abandoned his anti-Christian policy at the end of his reign: thousands of recent apostates were allowed to return to the Christian fold, Church property was returned to its owners, and the Greek Orthodox Patriarch Nikephoros was permitted to renew worship in the ruins of the Holy Sepulchre.

After al-Hakim's death, the Emperors Romanos III Argyropoulos, Michael IV Paphlagon and Constantine X Monomachos, in patient and successive negotiations, extracted from the Caliphs al-Zahir (1021–1036) and al-Mustansir (1036–1094) their recognition of the special status of Byzantium as protector of the Christian Holy Places. The price of license to rebuild the church of the Holy Sepulchre was a huge indemnity to the Fatimids, not to speak of other "douceurs." To supervise the work of rebuilding, imperial officers were sent to Jerusalem.

In 1048, it appears, the work of reconstruction was finished, so that at the end of the century the Crusaders could find a new church, replacing the two sacred buildings, Anastasis and Cal-

8) Caliph al-Hakim, who was later proclaimed divine, is accepted by the Druze as an incarnation of godhead.

9) The ceremony of the Holy Fire is still celebrated by the Greek Orthodox as a focus of devotional fervor. It was abolished for Catholics by Pope Gregory IX in 1238. The order of the ceremony is described in *The Status Quo in the Holy Places*, by L.C.A. Cust. According to Cust, the origin of the ceremony is uncertain, but in essence it symbolizes the triumph of the Christian faith, and is renewed year after year in commemoration of the first victory after Calvary. A legend regarding its origin relates that when the lamps in the Church of the Holy Sepulchre were short of oil, Patriarch Narkissos went to the brook of Siloam for water and filled the vessels therewith; fire came down from heaven and ignited the water so that it burned like oil and the illumination lasted throughout the Easter service. Tradition has it that every Easter Saturday since then fire has appeared from heaven at the Sepulchre.

vary, which once had marked the sites of the Resurrection and the Crucifixion.

At that stage, to avoid communal friction, the Christians of Jerusalem were bidden to give up their assigned quarter there, and be segregated from the Moslem citizens. This migration may have drawn the faithful of the several Eastern Churches more closely together and simplified access by Christians, other than the Orthodox, to the rebuilt church.

In the middle of the eleventh century, the lot of the Christians was not unsatisfactory. A strong Byzantine empire obliged the Caliphs to be lenient towards their Christian subjects; more apostates of al-Hakim's days were permitted to return to Christianity, and pilgrimages from the West multipled. In 1063, merchants from Amalfi in Italy, a sea-port with manifold commercial links with the Near East, were authorized by the Fatimid rulers of Egypt to establish a hospice and a chapel over the ruins of the Church of Sancta Maria Latina and over the hospice built under the patronage of Charlemagne. The hospice founded by the Amalfitans was named after Johanan the Pious (Patriarch of Alexandria in the seventh century.) During the Crusader period the hospice and adjacent buildings were converted into a hospital, which, being located in proximity to the Church of St. John, was called St. John's Hospital. This institution attained importance during the Crusades, owing to its connection with the order of the knights which took the name of the institution as its own, the Hospitallers of St. John.

But the short breathing space came to a sudden end in 1071, when, under the leadership of Sultan Alp Arslan, the Seljuk Turks crushed the Byzantine army at Manzikert, in Armenia. The last third of the eleventh century was an unusually agitated period for the Holy Land, in the successive grasp of suzerain after suzerain. It started with Aziz ibn Abay, one of Alp Arslan's generals, albeit acting independently to further his own ambitions; ravaging far and wide, he seized Jerusalem, but, unlike so much else of the Holy Land, left it unharmed. In 1076, the city had reverted to the control of the Fatimids, but Aziz expelled them again after a not too arduous siege. Then Aziz was assassinated, and the Holy Land was governed by another Seljuk prince, Tutush, one of Alp Arslan's sons, or, to be exact, by his lieutenant Ortok, resident in Jerusalem. Ortok was succeeded by his sons Soqman and Ilghazi, who had to withstand beleaguerment by the Fatimids of Egypt, by now recovered from the shock of the Turkish onslaught. In 1098, the city was once more, if not for long, in the hands of the Fatimids who, at that juncture, made common cause with the advancing Crusaders. But the Crusaders very quickly crushed their ephemeral authority.

Chapter Four

THE CRUSADER KINGDOM (1099-1291)

The Crusader kingdom in the Holy Land had a life of about two hundred years, from 1099 to 1187, and again, after a brief interregnum, from 1189 to 1291.

The promptings and motives of armed Christian penetration into the Holy Land, the influences that marshalled the men who took part in the First Crusade, are complex and manifold, material and self-seeking as well as spiritual and pious. There is no questioning the profound and earnest religious feelings characteristic of mediaeval society or the directive concept of honor to which the feudal chivalry in particular was wedded. But there was also the natural appetite for adventure and for lucrative conquest, the demands of economic expansion, the urgency of easing the pressure of over-population, in many regions of Europe.

But in the final analysis, it is plain that the precipitant of the First Crusade was the very real alarm which was aroused in Christendom by the precarious state of things in the Holy Land after the incursion of the Seljuk Turks. Moving violently westward, the Seljuks had occupied the Land, massacring its inhabitants right and left, profaning the Holy Places and rendering devout approach to them hazardous, if not altogether impossible. The remnant of the Christian population sent forth pitiful calls for help; the tales told by pilgrims who escaped the Turkish executioners of the atrocious crimes perpetrated in the Holy Land, left an indescribably inflammatory impression on Western Europe.

According to Latin sources, which as so often Greek sources contradict, the appeal from the Holy Land was reinforced by a no less pressing solicitation of military aid on the part of the Byzantine empire itself. It had been disastrously humbled in 1071 at Manzikert by Alp Arslan, and a major part of Byzantine territory in Asia Minor passed into Seljuk ownership in consequence. It was this that meant so much for Christians in the West: landward access to the Holy Land was virtually cut off.

37

Pope Urban II, of French origin, was among the most fervid instigators of the First Crusade. His exhortation went out from Clermont, in France, and impressively numerous and powerful contingents of French barons in every Crusade are vouched for historically. Conspicuous in the first and following French contingents were the Normans of South Italy, and English knights of Norman origin and Gallic culture should be counted with them. This made considerably for the French character of Crusader rule in the Holy Land, for the dominant texture of its governing class, and, markedly, for the identifiably French cultural norms and nomenclatures of the kingdom of Jerusalem.

It is outside our province here to discuss the adventures of the Crusaders as they traversed the Balkans and Asia Minor, or their military successes in Syria and Lebanon which led them to the establishment of the principality of Antioch and the counties of Edessa and Tripoli. It was from Lebanon, at the beginning of 1099, that they entered the Holy Land, and moving down the coastal highway took a number of towns along this route. Jaffa was bypassed at that stage, but Ramla, abandoned by its inhabitants, was easy prize. Entering adjacent Lydda, the Crusaders found only the smouldering ruins of the famous Church of St. George, burnt down by infuriated Moslems. And from there, brushing aside resistance, on to Jerusalem the Golden, destination of their long dream. The city had no more than twenty-five thousand inhabitants, for its Christians had been driven out by the Moslem defenders as the Crusaders approached; their dependability, in such circumstances, was not unnaturally suspect. The defense of the city was in the hands of the Fatimid governor, Iftikhar ad-Dawla. For only forty days Jerusalem held out: a frightful slaughter of all Moslems and Jews taken in it was the final act. The only Moslems spared were the governor and his bodyguard: he offered to deliver to Raymond of Toulouse the Tower of David which was in his hands, together with a large sum of money, in return for the lives of his bodyguard and himself; the terms were accepted and Iftikhar and his men could depart for Ascalon and join its Moslem garrison.

Now, most of the Holy Land was held by the Crusaders. How were they to defend their conquest, how set up an enduring and orderly administration? At the beginning, it looked as though the character of the new "State" would be predominantly religious; papal encouragement had contributed largely to its founding and the influence of the local clergy was strongly felt. Eventually the laity got the upper hand, and a baronial majority chose Godfrey of Bouillon, Duke of Lorraine,[1] as their overlord, whereupon he modestly demurred to accepting any title more honorific than "Defender of the Holy Sepulchre."[2] Simultaneously, influential barons chose the Norman Arnoulf of Malcorne to be Latin Patriarch of Jerusalem. The patriarchal dignity had until that time been exercised by the Greek Patriarch Simon who, the Greek account says, had to flee to Cyprus,[3] but the Latin version has it that Simon died about the time when the Crusaders entered the city. Proof of one or the other version would touch directly upon the validity of Arnoulf's appointment. Arnoulf's ecclesiastical politics were aimed at "latinizing" his See. To that end, he installed twenty Latin canons in the Holy Sepulchre to conduct daily services, and banished the clergy of the Orthodox and the other Eastern rites, who had officiated till then. With all the other Christians, that clergy had been forced by the Moslems to quit Jerusalem as the Crusader threat approached, and on the morrow of the Latin victory they made their way eagerly back, hoping to be reinstated in their priestly places in the Holy Sepulchre.

Patriarch Arnoulf's successor was Diambert, Archbishop of Pisa, who arrived in the Holy Land commanding a fleet recruited by the maritime republic of Pisa. As Godfrey needed Diambert's fleet, he was not in a position to resist his demands. Irregularities were discovered in Arnoulf's election and Diambert was elected in his place at the patriarchal See. What Diambert intended to create was not a theocratic constitution, but a principality for him-

---

1) Bouillon is a town in Belgium (province of Luxembourg). It was inherited by Godfrey from his uncle, Godfrey the Hunchback, but in 1096 the duke pledged the town to the Bishop of Liège in order to raise funds for his crusade. For centuries the Bishops of Liège bore the title "Duke of Bouillon."

2) According to some modern historians, the choice of title might have been determined by political and financial considerations, since the designation "Advocatus Sancti Sepulchri" carried with it well-defined rights to authority over Church lands.

3) According to Greek sources, the Greek Patriarch proceeded to Constantinople, and Greek Orthodox Patriarchs of Jerusalem continued to reside there for the following eighty-eight years.

self. He succeeded in obtaining from Godfrey important territorial concessions, but his position was weakened when, after Easter in the year 1100, the Pisan fleet sailed for home. Diambert behaved even more harshly than his predecessor towards the native Christians: not content with dismissing the Eastern clergy from the Holy Sepulchre, he cast them out of all of the monasteries and religious establishments in Jerusalem.

Jerusalem now theirs, it was left for the Crusaders to conquer the regions still controlled by the Egyptian Fatimids. Godfrey clashed with their troops in August of 1099 and near Ascalon overcame them in a victory which, in effect, closed the First Crusade. But the town itself was not taken and the Fatimid ruled it for fifty more years; in this forward and strategic enclave, they constituted an everpresent danger.

The occupation of the Holy Land was gradually accomplished thereafter. Jaffa was abandoned by its Moslem citizenry and its port became a vital base for supplying Jerusalem from overseas when, in June 1100, a Venetian fleet landed there. Bethlehem had fallen, earlier than Jerusalem, to Tancred, a scion of the Norman nobility which reigned in southern Italy; it was not a hard battle, for there was a fairly large, pro-Crusader, Christian element in the town. Tancred, an exceptionally gifted and valiant baron, expanded the area of his bold authority, occupying Beisan and Nazareth; he next carved out an autonomous principality for himself in Galilee, with Tiberias as capital.

The Crusader conquest of the Holy Land, over and above the great expanses previously overrun in Asia Minor, Syria and Lebanon, was not on the whole especially difficult. And yet, in the concluding phases of the campaign, the invading army in all probability numbered less than twenty thousand men. Success may be explained in part by disorganization and disunity in the Moslem ranks, in part by the numerous Christian congregations in the Middle East. Within the bounds of the Kingdom of Jerusalem proper, the Greek Orthodox, most of them Arabic-speaking, and the Syrian Jacobites were still present in considerable number; further north in Lebanon, Maronites were heavily concentrated; Christians of the Eastern Churches tipped the scales in such towns as Tyre and Acre. Indeed, in Jerusalem, besides the Greek Orthodox, one found adherents of almost every Eastern

Church—Ethiopians, Copts and Armenians, Jacobites, Nestorians and Georgians.

As the Moslems had degraded "infidels" to an inferior citizenship, it was to be expected that the Christians of the Holy Land would respond favorably to the Crusaders. But as we shall see, the tactless and overweening attitude of the Latins towards the Eastern Christians, manifested particularly in religious affairs, was to engender bitter dislike to a degree that Eastern Christians would eventually prefer Moslem to Latin sovereignty: towns and districts *en bloc*, where the indignant "Easterners" were many, were to go as far as to welcome the re-entry of Islam.

Godfrey of Bouillon died in 1100 and was succeeded by his brother Baldwin, who took the royal title "King of Jerusalem." Baldwin I (1100–1118) was a valiant warrior and a gifted ruler, deeply respected for his energy, his foresight and the justice of his rule. He had inherited from Godfrey a tenuous realm, its jurisdiction circumscribed to Jerusalem and its environs, Jaffa, Nablus and St. Abraham (Hebron); Baldwin saw to improving their fortifications. Galilee under Tancred enjoyed virtual independence, as did several minor fiefs inside the realm's narrow borders. Anxious to win the support of the native Christians, Baldwin insisted on righting the wrongs done to them, and especially to the clergy. Greek canons had access again to the Holy Sepulchre, to officiate according to the Orthodox rite; Orthodox monasteries could carry out their works without hindrance; lands were given to the Abbot of St. Sabas, the principal Orthodox hierarch; and easements were granted to the other Eastern Churches.

Under Baldwin, Crusader occupation was extended to the coastal towns which, so as not to hold up the march on Jerusalem, had been side-tracked during the first rapid sweep; they mattered a great deal for communications from Europe by sea, to guarantee or anyhow simplify the provisioning of the garrisons and the landing of reinforcements from Europe. One after the other, the harbors were subdued: Haifa, in 1100, Arsouf and Caesarea in 1101[4], Acre in 1104, and Beyrouth and Sidon in 1110. As the sequel

---

4) During the pillage that followed the capture of Caesarea, Genoese soldiers discovered a bowl which the Crusaders believed to be the Holy Grail. Taken to Genoa, it is still preserved in the Cathedral of San Lorenzo and it became known as "Sacro Catino."

shows, the mass of the Frankish population was to be centered in those places.

All this mastery of the littoral was made possible and swift by partnership of the fleets of the great trading interests of Venice and Genoa, of Amalfi and Pisa, of Marseilles, Montpellier and Barcelona. The maritime republics were the most powerful in the Mediterranean and the Crusaders, with no naval strength of their own, now turned to them for help. The ships of the republics were indispensable for the transport of troops, for procuring foodstuffs and materials of war and, above all else, for military sorties against Moslem armadas or for completely blockading such strongholds as had to be stormed from the sea as well as landward.

The shrewd and businesslike Italians, eager to expand their seaborne traffic and acquire new naval bases, neglected no opportunity to extract due requital for whatever they did. Very often, the indemnity took the form of commercial rights and privileges. It might even be as exorbitant as the cession of a special quarter in the conquered town: a typical example of this high fee is provided by Acre, main port of the Holy Land, where Venice, Genoa and Pisa were each assigned an autonomous zone.

With the coast under control, military operations were mainly directed against the southern part of the Holy Land, where the Fatimids were still more or less in power and had made several attempts to reconquer their lost possessions. The army of the Egyptian Fatimids reached the environs of Hebron and Jerusalem and their fleet threatened Jaffa and even Sidon and Beyrouth. Baldwin struck back manfully and advanced to the extreme south. To strengthen his conquests he built the great castle of Le Crac du Moab (Pierre du désert) south of the Dead Sea, and the castle of Montréal (Shobak in Arabic) where he had control over the road to Elath at the tip of the Red Sea.

By the time of his death, in April 1118, he had expanded his kingdom into a compact State, taking in the whole of Palestine from Beyrouth in the north to Beersheba in the south, with the Jordan as its eastern frontier and outposts in the far south-east to command the approaches to Arabia. The only enclaves out of his grasp were Ascalon and Tyre. Tyre was entirely cut off from its hinterland with the construction of the two fortresses of Toron and Scanderion. Only in 1124 did it fall to the Crusaders.

Baldwin I was succeeded by his cousin, Baldwin II, called Baldwin of Bourcq (1118–1131). This second King of Jerusalem gave the Crusader realm its grandest power and amplest prosperity. Not only did he consolidate his royal imbalance, but he succeeded in gaining recognition as the unquestioned overlord of the Crusader principalities established in the Near East. Like his predecessor, he too had to war against Egyptian Fatimids and in 1124, with the help of the Venetians he conquered Tyre, last Fatimid stronghold in the north. He embarked upon a series of campaigns in the north-east of the kingdom aimed at the city-states of Aleppo and Homs, Hama and Damascus. In one such campaign he was taken prisoner, to be ransomed only after a captivity of two years; during his absence, the barons chose Eustace Guarnier, lord of Sidon and Caesarea, to act as Bailli (i.e., regent). He was released in summer 1124 in return for pledges he did not keep.

By now, the original numbers of the First Crusade, small enough to begin with, had dwindled in the continuous depletion of combat. It is true that newcomers from Europe kept arriving in a now firmly-held Holy Land, and swelled the Frankish population, but even during the period of the greatest influx, that population, it would appear, never exceeded the figure of a hundred and twenty thousand: this census may have yielded a maximum of twenty thousand able-bodied combatants, even allowing for the quite high percentage of young men who joined the Crusades and settled in the Holy Land.

Considerations of self-defense impelled the Franks, from the outset, to cling together in towns; the Moslem element, and to a less degree the native Christians, tended to favor the rural areas.

The Crusaders were nothing like sufficiently numerous or entrenched to populate a territory which comprised both the Holy Land and the southern Lebanon.

Even less could a garrison constantly preoccupied with territorial watch and ward effectively perform unaided the multifarious tasks demanded by the crafts and professions which are indispensable for any society that seeks to be self-supporting and organized. So the jobs were done in part by indigenous Christians, the so-called Syrian element, and the Moslems were left in the

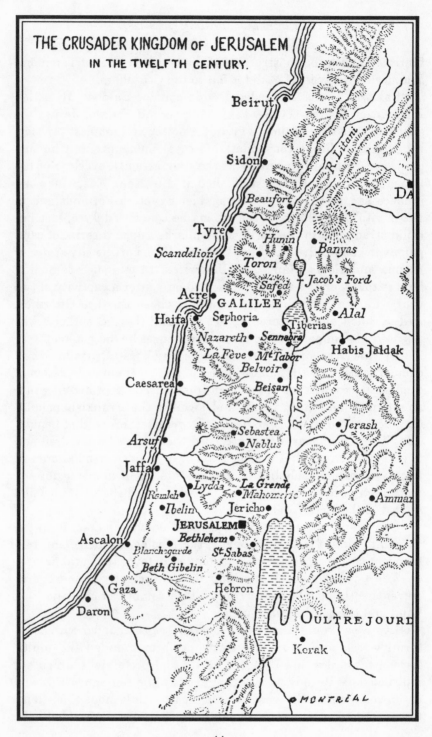

THE CRUSADER KINGDOM OF JERUSALEM
IN THE TWELFTH CENTURY.

Beirut

Sidon

Beaufort

DA

Tyre

Scandelion

Hunin

Banyas

Toron

Jacob's Ford

Safed

Acre

GALILEE

Alal

Haifa

Sephoria

Tiberias

Nazareth

Sennabra

La Fève

Mt Tabor

Habis Jaldak

Belvoir

Caesarea

Beisan

R. Jordan

Jerash

Sebastea

Arsuf

Nablus

Jaffa

Lydda

La Grende

Ramleh

Mahomerie

Amman

Ibelin

Jericho

JERUSALEM

Bethlehem

Ascalon

St Sabas

Blanchgarde

Beth Gibelin

Gaza

Hebron

Daron

OULTREJOURD

Korak

MONTRÉAL

44

main to till the soil and assure a supply of farm produce; it was for such prosaic and utilitarian motives that the Moslem farmers were spared after the first victory-intoxicated outbursts of violence.

For offensive and defensive warfare without respite, a standing army was wanted, ready and equipped for any crisis. The nucleus of this army were the knights, at most two or three thousand in all, for the cost of each knight's upkeep was heavy; the infantry was formed of groups of retainers, six foot-soldiers to every knight. At first, the knights, mounted and in massive armour, were vastly superior to the lightly-cuirassed Moslem cavalry, but in the end the mobile tactics of the Saracens and their surprise forays wiped out that early advantage.

The large outlay of knightly maintenance, and all the complexities of that continuing and rising responsibility, led in the natural course of things to the emergence of the military Orders.

The first among them was the Order of Knighthood of the Holy Sepulchre, created by Godfrey, or more probably, by his successor, Baldwin. It comprised a corps of knights entrusted with custodianship of the Holy Sepulchre, and an ecclesiastical branch, namely the Canons of the Holy Sepulchre.[5] The most noteworthy of the military Orders were those established during the reign of Baldwin II. They were the Order of the Hospitallers dedicated to St. John[6], with headquarters in the vicinity of the Church of the

5) After the fall of Jerusalem in 1187, Knights and Canons left for Acre, and in 1291, when Acre was lost to the Crusaders, they settled in various European countries, where national branches of the Knighthood were established. The Canons were surpressed in 1489 by Pope Innocent VIII, whilst the Knights continued to subsist; the privilege of knighting worthy or distinguished pilgrims was granted first to the Franciscan Guardian of the Holy Sepulchre of the Holy Land, later to the Custos. When the Latin Patriarchate was reinstalled in Jerusalem in 1847, the Holy See entrusted the Latin Patriarch with the administration of the Order.

6) The Order of the Hospitallers of St. John had its headquarters in the precincts of a hostel founded in 1063 by Amalfi merchants, near the Benedictine Monastery and the Church of Sancta Maria Latina, which was built at the end of the eighth century. The church was later called Sancta Maria Maior to distinguish it from the nearby Church of Sancta Maria (Minor) erected by the Knights between 1130 and 1140. The hostel founded by the Amalfitans had been enlarged after the Crusader conquest of Jerusalem, so that it could serve as a hospital. In 1113, a Bull issued by Pope Paschal II granted special privileges to Fra Gerardo, superior of the fraternity which administered the hospital. Gerardo's successor,

Holy Sepulchre, and the order of the Templars[7], operating from a wing of the royal palace next to the mosque of el-Aqsa, in the Solomonic Temple area (whence the name); the French knights were prominent in both. The Order of the Teutonic Knights, its chief center in Acre, had a German membership, and was established at the beginning of the second kingdom of Jerusalem, along the lines of the Order of the Hospitallers. The knights of the Orders were also ordained monks and had taken the prescribed vows; it was within their mission to help the sick and offer hospitality and shelter to the pilgrims. But, first and foremost, the Orders may be regarded as a sort of regular militia, always alerted and under arms. The fortresses which were built and garrisoned at strategic points along the border, and at crucial highway junctions, guaranteed the security of the Holy Land; the count of fighters in each sometimes ran into the hundreds. In time of danger, the fortresses provided a refuge for the population round about, and for the peasantry in particular, who depended utterly upon their proximity and protection.

The Orders were subsidized munificently by European monarchs and nobles and rapidly amassed exceeding strength and riches; they waxed exceptionally independent, not hesitating to flout the authority of Jerusalem's king and Patriarch. Their claim was that they owed sole and direct responsibility to the Pope.

The Frankish knighthood, installed with such seeming finality in the Holy Land by the First Crusade, grafted on to itself the feudal system of Europe, but local conditions and incessant warfare lent a special character to the system and gave its evolution a new bias. At the summit of the feudal pyramid was a king, who had already suffered a "clipping of wings" early in the days

---

Raymond de Puy, transformed the function of the hospital's fraternity, combining the medical duties with military ones in the knightly tradition. When Jerusalem was conquered by Saladin in 1187, the Knights of St. John founded a hospital in Acre. In 1291, after the defeat of the Crusaders, they retired to Cyprus and Rhodes and afterwards to Malta. At present, the center of the Sovereign Order of St. John of Jerusalem is in Rome. In 1886, the Knights of Malta acquired land in the locality of Tantur, on the road leading from Jerusalem to Bethlehem. This land, part of a larger tract given by Baldwin II to the Knights of St. John, was chosen for the construction in 1972 of the Ecumenical Institute for Theological Research.

7) The Order was founded in 1119 or 1120 by Hugues de Payns. Recognition was accorded to the Order a decade later at the Council of Troyes.

of the Crusader monarchy, and ultimately became a mere figurehead. On the other hand, the High Court made up of the principal barons had great prestige, exercising the widest political and judicial prerogatives: it was competent to choose the king, and to determine the royal right of succession. Beneath this supreme judicature were established secondary courts, which maintained considerable civil and religious jurisdiction, and there existed even lower tribunals with authority to try criminal, commercial and maritime suits. The canon of laws and customs applicable during the Crusader period, known as "The Assizes of Jerusalem", is an excellent compendium of the feudal system of the time.

In summary review of the pervading political and administrative situation, one is struck by the emergence of so many institutions and organizations which arrogated so large an autonomy to themselves: the monarchy first of all, and the administration that served it, notably the commander of the army and his deputy. Then there were the baronies, the military Orders, the autarchic colonies of the trading republics and, last but far from negligible, the towns in which the citizens set up and, with no interference from above, managed a local self-government resembling that which was contemporaneous in many a European city.

Diversity of nationalities matched this heterogeneity of "independences": all manner of unlike Europeans and Jews, local Christian sects and the Moslems. Schism, indiscipline and dis-coordination among the Christians produced a state of things which weakened the kingdom's capacity to resist. The danger mounted after Zangi, Lord of Mosul, had succeeded in unifying the dissident Moslem factions, and with most of the faithful of Syria and Iraq rallying to his standard, could threaten the Crusaders alarmingly.

Baldwin's successor, named during his lifetime, was his son-in-law, Fulk of Anjou. Melisande, the king's eldest daughter, was formally recognized by a council as heiress of the Kingdom. Ambassadors were sent to France to negotiate her betrothal to Fulk, count of Anjou, with the promise that upon their marriage he would become heir to the throne, ruling jointly with Melisande.

It was at the time of Fulk of Anjou (1131–1143), that Zangi took Edessa and a large slice of the Crusader principality of that name. The tidings reverberated throughout Europe. This was a rebuff

47

that Christendom could not stomach, and the Second Crusade, led by the Emperor Conrad II and Louis VII of France, was the swift rejoinder. But the new venture was ill-fated and left no mark upon the destiny of the Holy Land. Even before setting foot on the sacred soil, the royal columns suffered more than one reverse: in their passage through Asia Minor, they lost heavily in clashes with the Seljuks. Arriving at length in Syria with sadly decimated forces, the kings made no effort to retake Edessa, and instead attacked Damascus, then an independent emirate. The attack failed dismally and Conrad II made haste to return home in 1148, followed by Louis VII the next year. In 1154, Nur- ed-Din[8], son of Zangi, triumphed where the Second Crusade had given up; he annexed Damascus to domains which already embraced Iraq and most of Syria. When Fulk of Anjou died, his widow Queen Melisande assumed the government of the kingdom with her thirteen-year-old son Baldwin as co-regent. When he was twenty-two, Baldwin ousted his mother, who had to satisfy herself with Nablus and its environs, which she had brought Fulk as her dowry.

It was during the joint rule of Melisande and Baldwin that Nur-ed-Din had seized Damascus.

Baldwin III (1143–1162) was thus to find a too powerful neighbor on his northern flank, and for the time being, the Crusaders were obliged to suspend military operations in Syria and divert their troops southwards, where they achieved a remarkable success. By building a fortress over the ruins of the town of Gaza, Baldwin's men succeeded in blocking the route between the Fatimid south and Ascalon, and thus completed the encirclement of the town. A year later, in 1153, Ascalon surrendered and with it fell the last Fatimid stronghold. Amalric, the king's brother and Count of Jaffa, was duly made Count of Ascalon. This development was to draw his attention south to the irresistible wealth and resources of Egypt.

It was during Baldwin's reign that Berthold of Limoge (France) brought together the solitary hermits living on Mount

---

8) Nur-ed-Din means, in Arabic, "Light of the Faith."

Carmel, and built for them a small monastery and chapel. Berthold later became prior general of the Carmelite Order.

When Baldwin III died childless in 1163[9], he was succeeded by his younger brother Amalric (1163–1174). The latter was quick to profit from Fatimid decay and, by successful expansionist campaigning, reduced Egypt to vassalage for a spell. The Egyptians were not less quick to turn for help to Nur-ed-Din, and he despatched Shirkuh, a Kurdish-born general of intelligence and ability, to be his viceroy or vizier in Egypt. Shirkuh's nephew, Salah-ed-Din, or Saladin,[10] as he is better known in the West, followed him in that rank. In 1174, Nur-ed-Din died and Saladin became the real ruler of Egypt in his own right. Not content with that distinction, he aspired to lay hands on Syria and Iraq as well and, great soldier that he was, he realized his ambition. The Crusader kingdom now saw itself almost wholly encompassed by a formidable enemy; only the sea-border was open.

In view of the dangerous situation, Amalric became more dependant on Byzantium. He visited Constantinople in 1171 and enjoyed a friendly reception by Emperor Manuel Comnenos I. The nature of the agreement reached during their encounter is unclear, but the result was seen in Greek initiatives in the Holy Land. Manuel Comnenos had the Church of the Holy Sepulchre repaired, and ordered new mosaics for the Church of the Nativity in Bethlehem. On his order, the monasteries of Mar Elias and of St. John near the Jordan River were reconstructed. In 1173, an Orthodox Archbishop suddenly appears in Gaza and a community of Orthodox monks at the Church of the Holy Sepulchre.

At Amalric's untimely death in 1174, the Crusader Kingdom included the entire Holy Land, both banks of the Jordan, northward as far as Beyrouth, southward to Elath on the Red Sea. The great dominion crumbled only too quickly under the hammer-blows of Saladin as he bore down upon it from all sides. No help could now be sought from Manuel Comnenos, who had been com-

9) In 1158 he had married the Byzantine princess, Theodora, a niece of Emperor Manuel Comnenos I. Their union was a mark of reconciliation between the Crusader and the Byzantine powers.

10) His full name was al-Malik al-Nazir Salah-ed-Din Yusuf. Salah-ed-Din is Arabic for "Honor of the Faith." He was born in Tikrit (Iraq) to a Kurdish family which had emigrated from Armenia.

pletely routed by the Anatolian Seljuks at Myriocephalum in Phrygia.

Once Saladin was firmly in the saddle of an independent sovereignty, the Crusaders began to feel how fearsome a neighbor he could be. His first foray was against the south of the kingdom, where a chain of fortresses, among them the reputedly inpregnable Le Crac and Montréal, fell into his hands. While his victory was a tribute to outstanding generalship, the domestic misfortunes of the kingdom under Baldwin IV (1174–1185) Amalric's son, also worked in Saladin's favor. Baldwin was not only a stripling at his coronation, he was a leper too. He was not lacking in valor or wisdom for all that, but he could not stave off the ultimate dissolution of the realm. It is true that he won a brilliant victory at Montgisard near Ramleh in 1177, but he could not prevent Saladin from capturing, in 1179, the newly-built castle of Chastellet on the Jordan near Jacob's Ford, north of the Lake of Galilee. The loss of this stronghold represented a serious threat to Galilee.

At Baldwin's death in 1185, he was succeeded by his nephew, an eight-year-old child who reigned nominally as Baldwin V until his premature death in the summer of 1186. Undoubtedly, the downfall of the kingdom was hastened by the intrigues and irresponsibility of Sybil and Isabel, sisters of Baldwin IV. Sybil, bride of Guy de Lusignan, plotted the accession of her handsome but foolish husband after her brother's untimely death; it was a most unlucky choice and its consequences for the kingdom were to be disastrous.

In 1185, a truce was declared between Saladin and the Crusaders; it was violated, however, when Raynald of Chatillon, lord of Kerak (Crac du Moab), ambushed a Moslem caravan travelling from Damascus to Egypt. This gave Saladin the "casus belli" he needed to start the campaign.

Now the battleground was Galilee. For a time, the outcome was uncertain, and the Crusaders won resounding victories here and there, but the last and fatal battle went badly for them and that was the finale. On July 3, 1187, at the Horns of Hittin, between Nazareth and Tiberias, legendary burial place of Jethro, father-in-law of Moses, they were irrevocably undone. Of an army of fifteen thousand fighting men, only a thousand escaped death or slavery. Guy de Lusignan was taken prisoner and sent with his senior knights to Damascus. The fragment of the "true Cross", which the Crusaders carried into the fray, was lost to the Saracens. The knights in cumbersome armor were at a disadvantage in manoeuvering upon uneven ground; the Moslem horsemen, not so hampered, could swing and shift with devastating speed. The enemy's light archers were also favored by a longer bowshot. But the severest handicaps for the Crusaders were a blazing sirocco and unquenchable thirst.

After this virtual annihilation of their main strength, the castles and keeps of the Crusaders were practically unmanned and defenseless, and succumbed in rapid sequence to the ubiquitous onslaughts of Saladin.

In the month of August, Acre, Jaffa and Beyrouth collapsed and Ascalon held out only a little longer. On September 30, Saladin laid siege to Jerusalem, its population greatly swollen by fugitives from the villages around. In a month it was all over. The Eastern Christians were suffered to stay on in the vanquished city and Latins were ejected, a discrimination that is again highly suggestive of the incompatibility of the two persuasions and their variant attitudes towards the advent of the Moslems. It would be disingenuous not to contrast the humane behavior of the Saracen conqueror with the bloodthirsty rioting of the Crusaders in Jerusalem a century earlier, for then the Moslem and Jewish citizens were massacred to a man. If Saladin drove out the Latin citizens now, he spared their lives, though he showed less reverence for the churches of Jerusalem and converted most of them into mosques; the cross over the Dome of the Rock was taken down and all signs of Christian worship in the mosque were obliterated, as well as in the mosque of el-Aqsa. But the Greek and the Syrian Orthodox were undisturbed in their residence in Jerusalem, even if they had to pay a ransom and afterwards a poll-tax. Saladin exempted the poor from these levies and the affluent Christians of the Oriental communities did not fare badly either, as they bought up much of the property abandoned by the departing Latins.

When the news of Saladin's triumph reached Constantinople, the Emperor Isaak Angelos sent a delegation to congratulate him and petition for the return of Christian Holy Places to the Orthodox Church. It is reported that after some delay, the Sultan re-established the Greek Orthodox in the privileges which had been theirs before the Crusader conquest. Moslem leaders, it may be noted, had counselled that the Church of the Holy Sepulchre be destroyed, but Saladin did not heed their advice, sensing that the Christians would continue to venerate the site, even if the edifice no longer stood. In fact, the church was shut for just three days, and the Christians were then free to enter again, though on payment of a fee, which was exacted thereafter for many centuries and only abolished in 1831 by Ibrahim Pasha. But the Moslem janitor, posted on Saladin's order to guard the portal, is still in evidence today.[11]

Except for Tyre, the Kingdom of Jerusalem was wholly under Moslem hegemony now. Nevertheless, a few places beyond its borders, on the coast of Lebanon and Syria were still held by the Crusaders, and from these rallying points, heartened by the arrival of reinforcements, they once more took the offensive. The Third Crusade, a passionate and impressive response to the appeal to make Jerusalem Christian again, was led by the Emperor Frederick Barbarossa, by Philip Augustus, King of France, and by Richard Coeur-de-Lion, King of England. Barbarossa was not destined to enter the Holy Land: he was drowned in the fording of the Saleph River in Cilicia (Asia Minor), and his army broke up. The battered remnants of the once big army, led by Barbarossa's son Frederick of Swabia, reached Acre in October, 1190. There they met the German Crusaders who had chosen the sea route. Frederick died in January 1191 and the German soldiers, who found themselves leaderless, were rallied under the banner of Frederick's cousin, Leopold V, Duke of Austria. In all, however, the Germans played an insignificant part in the Third Crusade.[12]

11) According to another version, it was the Sultan As-Salib-Ayoub who, in 1246, entrusted the keys of the Holy Sepulchre to one Arab family and charged another with the opening and closing of the Basilica door. There is no contradiction between the two versions, since between 1229 and 1244 the Basilica had been in Christian hands, following the treaty signed between Frederick II and the Sultan Al-Kamil. The descendents of the two families, the Judeh family and the Insaibe, are to this day serving in the same capacity.

12) Of great importance for the future was the founding near Acre of a German hospital community by some citizen of Luebeck and Bremen in 1190. In spring 1198, the hospital—not to be associated with an earlier institution at Jerusalem— was transformed into a purely national Order of ecclesiastical knights, and began to describe itself as the Hospital of St. Marie of the German House of

Meanwhile, Guy de Lusignan, whom Saladin had freed on his swearing an oath to go back across the seas and never take up arms against the Moslems, embarked upon a siege of Acre; he justified himself by the contention that "an oath given to an 'infidel' is not binding." Philip Augustus and Richard, each in the vanguard of a large force, joined him. The terms of surrender of the fortress stipulated, *inter alia*, that the Saracen prisoners would be set free against ransom and by exchange with Christian prisoners. Richard, however, cold-bloodedly decreed the massacre of the twenty-seven hundred survivors of the garrison, on the pretext that the Saracens had not adhered to the conditions of the bargain.

The re-taken city was quickly restored and its churches reconsecrated. Acre was now to be the most important Crusader bastion for the next hundred years.

After its conquest, Philip Augustus, who had suffered from almost uninterrupted illness and was convinced that he had accomplished his full Christian duty as a Crusader, left for Europe. Richard led the Crusader army out of the city and moved south along the coastal highway, so that his flank would be protected by the sea and the fleet could support him.

There was more than one clash between the Crusaders and Saladin's troops, but the main engagement was fought near Arsouf (September 1191), and there the Crusaders had the upper hand.

Richard might then have proceeded to Jerusalem, but he thought it prudent to make certain of Jaffa first. The delay was fatal, because it enabled Saladin to strengthen the defenses of the Holy City. Whilst the Christian army enjoyed a respite in Jaffa, Saladin methodically demolished Ascalon, fearful that Richard could take it and turn it into a stronghold which would sever communication with Egypt. Richard, however, did occupy Ascalon and rebuilt and refortified it. Fighting between the Crusaders and the Saracens went on during the first half of 1192 until, on September 2 of that year, a treaty was signed, giving the coastal towns as far south as Jaffa to the Christians, and allowing the pilgrims to visit the Holy Places freely; Moslems and Christians would be allowed to pass through each other's territory; Ascalon

---

Jerusalem. The Order of Teutonic Knights, as it was called, was confirmed by Popes Celestine III and Innocent III.

must be razed to the ground. Saladin gave sanction besides to a handful of Latin priests to officiate in the Church of the Holy Sepulchre, as well as in Bethlehem and Nazareth. This concession to the Latins aroused Greek suspicions. It will be recalled that a delegation was sent to Jerusalem at the instance of the Emperor Isaak Angelos, asking Saladin that the Orthodox be given back entire control of the churches which had been theirs in the days of the Fatimids. Saladin would not grant the petition, as he was unwilling that any one denomination should be in charge of all the Holy Places: he preferred to arrogate to himself the authority of arbiter between the several denominations, as in after days the Ottoman Sultans did.

When the treaty had been concluded, Richard left the Holy Land, where he had campaigned for sixteen months. His departure marked the end of the Third Crusade. Thanks to the gallantry of those that took part in it, the Kingdom of Jerusalem had been resuscitated. It was, however, a kingdom now of modest dimensions, stretching from Tyre to Jaffa, and in spite of its name it did not embody the Holy City within its borders.

When Queen Sybil died of disease in autumn 1192, Guy of Lusignan, who had won the crown of Jerusalem as Sybil's husband, was dropped as King of Jerusalem and compensated with the crown of Cyprus. Heiress to the Kingdom of Jerusalem was now Isabella, the younger daughter of King Amalric I. Her second husband, Conrad, Marquis of Montferrat, a gifted leader, was recognized as king, but shortly after his appointment was murdered by two Assassins, sent by the "Old Man of the Mountains", the Sheik Rashid-ed-Din Sina (April 1192). Isabella's next husband, Henry of Champagne, Count of Troyes, was never crowned king. He died in September 1197 and early the following year, Isabella—ever mindful of the dynasty—was remarried, this time to Amalric I, King of Cyprus, younger brother of Guy of Lusignan. As King of Jerusalem, he was crowned Amalric II.

Saladin died in 1193. His successors were not the heirs of his military and political genius, but all the same, the Crusaders could make little further headway against them because of internal divisions in their own midst and the lack of an efficient and stable leadership. Too, it often happened that the rulers of the Kingdom of Jerusalem were victims of violence or malady and left the throne to minors; the need to appoint regents provoked quarrels among the factions seeking influence in the disposition of the crown.

A treaty which merely recognized the *status quo* of Crusader sovereignty in Crusader-occupied territory, and from which Jerusalem was barred, could not be looked upon by Christendom as to its full liking.

A Moslem-held Jerusalem rankled insufferably in the minds and emotions of Christian Europe, whose sorely troubled conscience inspired a fourth Crusade. This was, however, a Crusade "by indirection", for it never touched the Holy Land and contented itself with a vain assault upon Constantinople. Not only did the diversionary purpose misfire, the rift between Western and Eastern Christians became, if possible, even wider and deeper as a result. Collaboration between Byzantium and the Kingdom of Jerusalem was almost totally ruled out thenceforth, and the inevitable weakening of the Byzantine empire, made it child's play in the long run for the Ottoman Turks to conquer its capital and burst in upon Europe.

The failure of the Fourth Crusade to enter the Holy Land was not without its measure of compensation, for the Kingdom of Jerusalem enjoyed an interval of ten years of comparative tranquility, under a truce negotiated in 1198 between Amalric II of Lusignan and the Sultan al-Adil Saif-ad-Din, brother of Saladin.

In 1217, Crusader reinforcements arrived from Hungary, led by King Andrew II, and from Austria under Duke Leopold VI. A small contingent came also from France, but still the re-conquest of Jerusalem was not attempted. There was only minor campaigning in Galilee and Beisan and at Mount Tabor, if we overlook the fortification of Caesarea and the building of a citadel at Athlit. After a space, however, the Crusaders turned on Egypt again, realizing that the Holy Land could not be governed securely unless the enemy were smashed in what was, after all, his chief base. John of Brienne, the current King of Jerusalem, took Damietta. The discreet Sultan al-Kamil, feeling himself in jeopardy, chose to parley with him and offered to cede Jerusalem and all the western bank of the Jordan in return for Crusader evacuation of Egypt. John and the Frankish barons were willing to accept the exchange, but not so the papal delegate Cardinal Pelagius, who had accompanied the army of invasion, or the spokesmen of the military Orders and of the mercantile republics. They demanded the territory on the eastern bank as well, but for the Sultan to go that far would be to disrupt free communications between Syria and Egypt.

As all this bargaining went on, the initial strategic advantage of the Crusaders evaporated and they came off second best in a battle at the site where Mansourah would later be located, supply problems became aggravated and a profitless withdrawal was the upshot. In September 1221, al-Kamil entered Damietta in triumph. The Holy City was as irrecoverable as ever.

One episode in the Egyptian campaign had a bearing on the future of the Holy Land, to the extent that it was to revolve round Franciscan custody of the Holy Places: Francis of Assisi was in Damietta and is said to have had an audience with the Sultan al-Kamil, arguing the truth of the Christian doctrine with superb courage and fiery faith. The sultan was unyielding, and Francis left for Acre, where he spent some six months before returning to Italy in 1220. A number of friars remained behind. They were compelled to leave with the collapse of the Crusader Kingdom, but after a short interval they returned to establish themselves in Jerusalem.

At the beginning of the thirteenth century, the Crusader Kingdom fastened great hopes on the prospect of intervention by Frederick II of Hohenstaufen, Emperor of Germany and King of Sicily, who under papal pressures had solemnly pledged himself to organize a new Crusade, but had put it off from year to year. Living in Sicily most of the time, fairly near the Holy Land, he was well placed to intervene. Nevertheless he dallied, although many German Crusaders were less laggard. The Teutonic Order of German knights grew in influence, and the German element began to leaven the long supremacy of the Franks.

German prestige was further enhanced when Frederick won the right of succession to the crown of Jerusalem by marriage in 1225 to Yolande, daughter of John of Brienne. Frederick was a gifted diplomat with a working knowledge of Arabic, acquired from his Arab subjects in Sicily and the Arab scholars among his counsellors at the court in Palermo. So he fitted out no military expedition, but applied his talents in negotiations with the Egyptian sultan for the peaceful handing back of Jerusalem. However, his tactics drew down upon him the wrath of the Pope: Jerusalem must be re-conquered by derring-do against the infidels. Frederick was excommunicated and left no choice but to launch his tardy venture, and proceeding by way of Cyprus, his army landed in Acre in September 1228. Even now, he avoided open belligerency and, on February 18, 1229, he signed a peace treaty in Jaffa with the Sultan al-Kamil, which granted him Jerusalem, Bethlehem, a corridor running through Lydda to the sea at Jaffa, and Nazareth, as well as the Galilee, without a blow struck. The fly in the ointment was that Jerusalem had to be unfortified and the mosques of Omar and el-Aqsa were left in the hands of the Moslems.

Frederick, now the son-in-law of John of Brienne, had himself crowned King of Jerusalem in the Church of the Holy Sepulchre, although after the death of his wife Yolande in 1228, he ranked only as regent of the kingdom on behalf of Conrad, his infant son by Yolande and legal heir to the throne. In this insistence on coronation, cut off as he still was by the Pope from communion with the Church, he was opposed by the clergy, the Order of the Templars, by the Hospitallers and the Frankish chivalry; only his soldiers and the Teutonic knights sided with him.[13]

Urgent affairs soon required his return to Germany. The imperial marshal Richard Filangieri, whom he appointed regent in the Holy Land was repudiated by most of the local population, led by the powerful Ybelin family, and there was open hostility, degenerating into a period of continuous disorder. The kingdom grew weaker. Each body and organization pursued its own wayward policy and royal power dwindled almost to zero.

In 1239, Thibault of Champagne, King of Navarre, heading a distinguished company of French noblemen, arrived in the Holy Land and set out on an expedition from Acre to the Egyptian frontier, only to be beaten there by an Egyptian column under the Mamluk Rukn ad-Din, but he did secure territorial concessions from Ismail, Lord of Damascus, as reward for loyal services

---

13) Among those who joined Frederick on his Crusade was Philip d'Aubigny, a signatory to the "Magna Carta." He died in Jerusalem in 1236 and was buried near the main portal of the Church of the Holy Sepulchre. His burial place was recently discovered when an old stone platform, used by the Moslem doorkeeper, was removed.

against the rulers of Transjordan and Egypt, Ismail's adversaries. This gave the Crusader kingdom Beaufort and Safed, Tiberias and Galilee. But there was a rapid switch of allegiances. The Crusaders, their number augmented, and their confidence swollen by an army under Richard of Cornwall, Brother of King Henry III of England, abandoned the Lord of Damascus and joined with Egypt; the payment for that *volte face* was the territory which included Ascalon and Beit Gubrin.

In 1240–1241, therefore, the kingdom took in an area larger than at any other phase of the second period: the coastal strip from Beyrouth to, but not including, Gaza, all of Galilee and a major slice of Judaea, less Hebron. Richard of Cornwall left the Holy Land in 1241: he had behaved with wisdom and made himself generally acceptable as brief viceroy.

As we saw, after the death of Yolande, who had been the "vector" of the original rights of the crown, the party antagonistic to Frederick was in ascendant: her infant son, Conrad, became the rightful heir, and Frederick counted only as regent. According to the custom and law, in 1243, having attained the age of fifteen, Conrad had to come in person to Jerusalem for enthronement. He did not appear, and his opponents seized the chance to declare him as abdicant. It was a puzzling quandary: no crowned king, and a constitution that provided for no substitute ruler. All the easier for the barons, for the townships and the military Orders to cultivate individual aims and interests.

In the same year, see-sawing again, the Crusaders swerved from the line followed by Frederick and made a pact with Damascus, Hamath and Kerak that gave back the mosques of Omar and el-Aqsa to Christendom. When war broke out in the spring of 1244 between Ayub, Sultan of Egypt, and Ismail of Damascus, the Crusaders intervened actively on Ismail's behalf. The riposte of Ayub was to ask for help from the Khwarzimian (Chorasmian) Turks, who had broken away from the Mongols. Nothing loth, the Khwarzimian Turks invaded the Holy Land and laid it ruthlessly waste, capturing Jerusalem and destroying the churches, not sparing the Holy Sepulchre, defiling the tombs of the kings of Jerusalem. A few aged Latin priests, who had not left

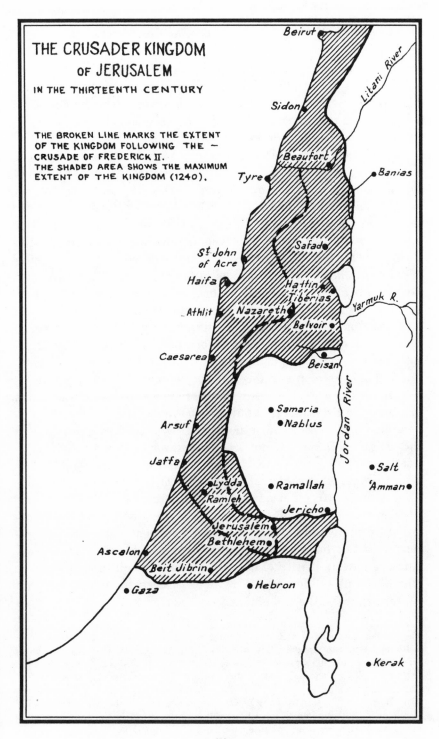

THE CRUSADER KINGDOM
OF JERUSALEM
IN THE THIRTEENTH CENTURY

THE BROKEN LINE MARKS THE EXTENT
OF THE KINGDOM FOLLOWING THE —
CRUSADE OF FREDERICK II.
THE SHADED AREA SHOWS THE MAXIMUM
EXTENT OF THE KINGDOM (1240).

Beirut

Litani River

Sidon

Beaufort

Banias

Tyre

St John
of Acre

Safad

Haifa

Hattin
Tiberias

Yarmuk R.

Athlit

Nazareth

Belvoir

Caesarea

Beisan

Jordan River

Samaria
Nablus

Arsuf

Jaffa

Salt

Lydda
Ramleh

Ramallah

'Amman

Jericho

Jerusalem
Bethlehem

Ascalon

Beit Jibrin

Hebron

Gaza

Kerak

Jerusalem and were celebrating Mass in the Holy Sepulchre, were slain on the spot, and the same fate befell the priests of the Oriental denominations. Some thousands of Christians who had at first been allowed to depart in safety from Jerusalem, were ambushed on their way to Jaffa, and most of them killed.

In October 1244, a pitched battle was fought at La Forbie, near Gaza, between the Crusaders and an Egyptian army commanded by the young Mamluk Emir, Rukn ad-Din Baibars[14], reinforced by the Khwarzimian Turks. The Crusaders were shockingly defeated with a loss, it is said, of two thousand knights and four times as many foot-soldiers; it was as crushing as the rout of the Horns of Hittin. Baibars had little trouble then in taking Jerusalem, and the city was to be in Moslem control thereafter for seven unbroken centuries. Hebron, Beit Gubrin and all of Samaria were also spoils, and roving bands of Khwarzimian Turks did havoc in Galilee. The Sultan of Egypt had, however, to overcome Ismail of Damascus before be could venture to finish with the Crusader kingdom, and this meant a short respite for it. But by 1247, Ascalon and Tiberias, too, were in thrall to Egypt.

The pattern of European retaliation was repeated. Again a Crusade, led this time by Louis IX of France, a gallant and pious sovereign who was to earn sainthood. He attacked from Cyprus and regained Damietta, but was ignominiously put to flight soon after and made captive. Freed for an astronomic ransom, he retired to Acre, whence actual governance of the kingdom was exercised by him with great advantage to "outre-mer."

The titular King of Jerusalem was still Frederick's son, Conrad of Germany, and Henry I of Cyprus was entrusted with the regency, as the next adult recognized heir.[15] A very curious conjuncture indeed. Until 1254, Louis applied himself to fortifying the coastal towns—Sidon and Acre itself, Caesarea and Haifa—but left for France at the end of that year.

---

14) Daher Rukn ad-Din Baibars Boundukdari was a native of Kipchak, a locality between the Caspian Sea and the Ural Mountains. He took the name Boundukdari from his first master, who bought him as a slave. A gifted soldier, he rose quickly in the echelons of the military and was regarded a second Saladin in the making.

15) Henry I of Lusignan, King of Cyprus, succeeded his mother Alice in 1246 as regent of the Kingdom of Jerusalem, claiming the title "Lord of the Kingdom of Jerusalem." Alice was the daughter of Henry of Champagne.

In that same year, Conrad of Germany died and the kingly title of Jerusalem passed to his two-year-old son Conradin, whose nominal prerogatives were scrupulously safeguarded in the laws of the kingdom.

In the middle of the thirteenth century, the kingdom had shrunk to a small coastal strip from Tyre to Jaffa, with some hinterland in the northern part, including Western Galilee, Nazareth and Safed, the strategic castle garrisoned by the Templar Knights, which controlled the Acre-Damascus road and Jacob's Ford, the crossing point on the River Jordan.

After the departure of Louis of France, there was an interlude of truce between the Crusaders and the neighboring Moslem states, but any advantage that the Crusaders might have gained from it was deplorably wasted by internal quarrels arising out of conflicting Venetian and Genoese claims to ownership of the Monastery of St. Sabas in Acre. Fighting broke out in the Christian possessions of "outre-mer", with the Templars and the Teutonic Order supporting the Venetians and the Hospitallers siding with the Genoese. Agreement was not reached until 1261, and then only thanks to intervention of a special delegate of the Pope and the endeavors of Geoffrey of Sargines, who had been appointed *bailli* (or governor) by Queen Plaisance of Cyprus, regent of the Kingdom of Jerusalem, an office to which she had acceded on the death of her husband, Henry, in 1257.

While all this was happening, the military Mamluk caste had seized power in Egypt, and Baibars, hero of the battle at La Forbie, became sultan in 1260. Simultaneously, a new enemy, the Mongols of Central Asia, assailed the northern front of the Crusaders: Mongol expansionism in the Middle East was backed by the Kingdom of Armenia and the Principality of Antioch. It is well to emphasize that the Nestorian form of Christianity was not alien to the Mongols, and had even won over members of the ruling dynasty.[16] the Mongol ruler sent delegations to the Pope and to the Christian courts and suggested making common cause against the Mamluks, so as to eject them from Syria and Palestine. Al-

16) The Mongol Dynasty, which reigned in the thirteenth century, was closely allied with the Christian Kingdom of Armenia and Georgia. It is uncertain if Holagu, the Mongol leader who led the Mongol armies in the conquest of Syria and Palestine, was a baptized Christian, but his wife certainly was.

liance with the Crusaders against the Moslems was logical and might have had incalculable consequences for Christianity, but the Crusaders missed a wonderful opportunity and kept strictly neutral in the tussle between Mongols and Mamluks. It is conceivable that the habitual prejudice against Eastern Christians played a part here and influenced the Crusaders against a Mongolian involvement, but certainly Crusader inertia helped Baibars to repel the Mongols led by Holagu at Ain Jalud (Goliath's Spring) near Ein Harod (September 1260), and the invaders withdrew from the Holy Land and Syria, turning their faces finally northward. The ill-advised Crusaders were now at the mercy of the Mamluks, and Baibars systematically reduced city after city of their kingdom. The churches of Nazareth, with the famous Basilica of the Annunciation, were wrecked[17]; the church and Benedictine monastery on Mount Tabor lay in ruins.

At the beginning of 1265, Caesarea fell, and next came the turn of Arsouf. Both were razed to the ground, lest they should again become "infidel" strongholds. By refinement of insult, the Christian defenders of the conquered fortresses were compelled to help dismantle them and were then led, with broken crosses round their necks and banners reversed, to grace the victors' triumphal entry into Cairo. Safed likewise was conquered and taken from the Templars (1266). Safed's capture gave Baibars control of Galilee. In 1268, Jaffa was taken after a siege of only twelve hours. The fine marble of the churches was utilized to decorate the mosques of Cairo. The Mamluks were ruthless in their conquest of "outre-mer." Every Christian who fell into their hands was slaughtered and very often this was the grim collective lot of the garrisons which capitulated under Mamluk promise that their lives would be spared.

Before quitting the field, Baibars rewarded the prominent emirs, some fifty in number, by gift of the fertile lands in Palestine which he had stripped from the Crusaders.[18] Nothing of con-

---

17) According to a pious tradition, the house of the Virgin, which was located near the site of the Annunciation, was miraculously transferred the night between the 9th and the 10th of May 1291 from Nazareth to Tersatto, near Fiume (now Rieka in Yugoslavia), and thence, on the 10th of December 1294, to Loreto, near Ancona.

18) The Mamluk settlers built themselves fortified residences; the remains of

sequence was left in Crusader hands except Acre, with a population of fifty thousand, very many of them stout fighters, but internal rivalry and especially a rift within the local colonies of the Italian trading republics undermined resistance. More domestic friction followed when, after the death in 1268 of the titular King of Jerusalem, Conradin of Hohenstaufen, the question of his succession had to be ventilated. Eventually, the choice fell on Charles of Anjou, King of Naples and Sicily, brother of Louis IX of France.[19] In 1277, Charles sent out Roger of Saint Séverin as Governor of Acre, with an armed force.

A few years previously, in May 1271, Prince Edward, the future Edward I of England, had arrived in Acre. He stayed in the Holy Land until September 1272, engaging the Moslems in battle on several occasions. At his request, Baibars granted the Crusaders a ten-year truce, during which time the Latins indulged in fratricide quarrels.

On Baibars' death in 1277, his successor, Qalaun, pursued his offensive methodically against the crumbling remnants of a kingdom now confined to Acre and a few coastal cities on the Lebanese coast. When, in 1282, a revolution broke out in Sicily (the notorious "Sicilian Vespers"), Charles withdrew part of his troops from Acre, and the troubles that he faced in his European dominions prevented him from paying effective heed to "outremer."

On Qalaun's sudden death, his son al-Ashraf Khalil renewed the siege of Acre, having mustered a large army and one hundred siege engines.

So, in 1291, Acre fell and the once splendid town crumbled into a heap of ruins.[20] Only a handful of the panic-stricken citizenry could make their way to safety by sea; the Latin Patriarch of Jerusalem, Nicholas of Hanape, was drowned, amid a multitude, in the attempt. Next, Haifa was occupied; the Mamluks burned the

---

some of them can be seen until today in several Arab villages.

19) Charles had purchased the claims to the crown of Mary of Antioch, grandchild of Isabella and Amalric II, through their daugher Melisande, wife of Bohemond of Antioch.

20) The fine doorway of St. Andrew's Church was transferred to Cairo to become part of the sepulchre of the victorious Sultan al-Ashraf Khalil. It remains in place to this day. At the beginning of the nineteenth century, the Franciscan Church of St. John was built over the ruins of St. Andrew's.

monasteries on Mount Carmel and slew the monks. Athlit and Tyre surrendered after a few of their inhabitants had escaped to Cyprus.

Appendix 'A' to Chapter Four

LIST OF CRUSADER KINGS AND THEIR RIGHT TO SUCCESSION

Godfrey (of Bouillon), Defender of the Holy Sepulchre	Sept.1099–1100
Baldwin I (of Boulogne), brother of Godfrey	1100–1118
Baldwin II (of Bourcq), cousin of the above kings	1118–1131
Melisande, heiress, daughter of Baldwin II	1131–1152
Fulk (of Anjou), consort of Melisande	1131–1143
Baldwin III, son of the above two	1143–1163
Amalric I, brother of Baldwin III	1163–1174
Baldwin IV, son of Amalric I	1174–1185
Baldwin V, nephew of Baldwin IV	1185–1186
Sybil, heiress, daughter of Amalric I, mother of Baldwin V	1186–1190
Guy (of Lusignan), consort of Sybil	1186–1192
Isabella (I), sister of Sybil	1192–1205
Conrad (of Monferrat), consort of Isabella	1192
Henry (of Champagne)—not king—consort of Isabella	1192–1197
Amalric II (of Lusignan), consort of Isabella	1198–1205
Mary, heiress, daughter of Isabella and Conrad	1205–1212
John (of Brienne), consort of Mary	1210–1225
Isabella (II) or Yolande, heiress, daughter of Mary and John	1212–1228
Frederick II, Emperor, consort of Isabella II	1225–1243

After Federick II, there were several pretenders to the crown of Jerusalem: the descendents of Frederick of the House of Hohenstaufen; the Kings of Cyprus of the House of Lusignan, as descendants of Amalric II and Henry of Champagne's daughter, Alice; the Angevins of Naples, descendents of Charles of Anjou, who had purchased the rights. Several Kings of Jerusalem were buried in the Church of the Holy Sepulchre, while the Church of the Tomb of Mary was the burial place for a number of Queens.

Appendix 'B' to Chapter Four

LATIN PATRIARCHS OF JERUSALEM AT THE TIME OF THE CRUSADER KINGDOM

Arnoulf of Rohes or Chocques—elected but not consecrated	1099
Daimbert of Pisa	1099–1101
Evremar of Chocques	1102–1108
Gibelin of Sabran, Archbishop of Arles	1108–1112
Arnoulf of Chocques	1112–1118
Gormond or Warmund of Picquigny	1119–1128
Stephen de la Ferté, Abbot of Chartres	1128–1130
William I, Prior of the Holy Sepulchre	1130–1145
Fulcher, Archbishop of Tyre	1145–1157
Amalric of Nesle	1157–1180
Heraclius	1180–1191
Aimery the Monk	1197–1202
Soffred, Cardinal of Saint Prassede	1203
Albert of Vercelli	1205–1214
Ralph of Merencourt	1215–1224
Gerald of Losanne	1225–1239
Robert of Nantes	1240–1254
James Pantaleon	1255–1261
William of Agen	1262–1270
Thomas Agni of Lentino	1272–1277
Elias of Perigueux	1279–1287/8
Nicholas of Hanapes	1288–1291

Appendix 'C' to Chapter Four

TITULAR KINGS OF JERUSALEM

The title "King of Jerusalem" was claimed by some of the leading European dynasties, among them the Royal Houses of Savoy, Habsburg and Bourbon. The House of Savoy used the appelation "King of Jerusalem and Cyprus" on the basis of a link with the House of Lusignan, which, after 1267, furnished the Kings of Cyprus, who continued to carry the nominal title of Jerusalem.

Charlotte, daughter of John, the last King of Cyprus, who died in 1458, had married Louis of Savoy. On her husband's death, she bequeathed her rights to Charles of Savoy, her husband's nephew.

The claims of the Habsburgs can be traced to three sources: to Frederick II of Hohenstaufen, since the Habsburgs inherited the crown of the sacred Roman-German Empire; to Charles of Anjou, King of Naples and of Jerusalem, since Charles VI of Habsburg was also King of Naples; and to Godfrey of Lorraine, since Francis, Duke of Lorraine, had married Maria Theresia of Habsburg, and their descendants bore the title Habsburg-Lorraine.

The claim of the House of Bourbon to the crown of Jerusalem is based on the fact that the Bourbons of Spain were the inheritors of the primogenital branch of the House of Habsburg. To reinforce their pretension to the exalted title, the sovereigns of this branch of the Habsburgs could also invoke their descent from the Kings of Aragon, who had acquired the title by lavishing largesse and attention upon the Holy Places.

Chapter Five

THE MAMLUK PERIOD (1291-1517)

In the mid-thirteenth century, the Mamluk Sultan Baibars and his successor, Qalaun, were already masters of the Holy Land. In 1291, with the capture of Acre, al-Ashraf Khalil, the next in line, extended Mamluk rule over the entire land.

The Mamluks were slaves—which is the meaning of the name—originally of Turkish or Circassian stock, or even "islamized" Christians. They were bought by the Ayyubid sultans to serve in the army. The military caste which they succeeded in establishing governed vast domains in Egypt and the Holy Land and in Syria for two hundred and fifty years; they produced many gifted commanders, some of whom rose to royal eminence.

Under the first dynasty, the Bahris[1], there were no fewer than twenty-five sultans in swift succession between the years 1250 and 1381, with many a reign ending in violent death. The Mamluks had a decisive influence on history, for it was their repulsing of the Mongols that helped secure a long-lived Islamic supremacy in the Middle East. The Mongols, nevertheless, after sacking Damascus, managed to infiltrate the Holy Land once more in 1303, doing much harm to the City of Jerusalem and killing many of its inhabitants. But this was their last incursion and the Holy Land thereafter remained an exclusively Mamluk preserve.

It was administered by the Mamluks in three districts, each under a governor: in Judaea, Samaria and Gilead, with headquarters in Damascus; on the coastal strip as far as Mount Carmel, with Gaza at its center; and in Galilee, with headquarters in Safed. Jerusalem came directly under Damascus at first, and in the second half of the fourteenth century it was made headquarters of an autonomous district. But, all in all, the Holy Land was only a peripheral and neglected province of the Mamluks; the chief cultural and commercial center was in Egypt. Through the

---

1) So called because they were drawn from the bodyguard of the Sultan Ayyub, which was quartered in barracks adjacent to a river near Cairo. ("Bahr" is Arabic for "river.")

port of Alexandria passed the precious trade in spices, to Alexandria came ships from Europe laden with all the stuffs that Egypt wanted. The ports of the Holy Land, so busy and prosperous in the Crusader period, had been smitten by war after war and were practically derelict. Special care was taken by the Mamluks to pull down the ramparts defending the ports, in order to prevent hostile fleets from establishing military bases along the littoral. The movement of pilgrims had dwindled to a trickle, for they were coerced into paying burdensome tolls as a condition of entry and had to bribe local officialdom for access to the Christian shrines. The life of the Christian residents became more and more difficult and dangerous, in subjection to the fanaticism of Moslem neighbors or the rapacity of local governors. Spreading bigotry was a constant threat to Christian shrines and places of worship. Many of the churches so numerously built in the time of the Crusader kingdom were destroyed, and if one was damaged or in decay it could not be put to rights without massive bribery.

The Bahri dynasty was succeeded by the Circassian, which ruled from 1381 to 1517. Under Sultan Saif ad-Din Barkouk (1382–1389), founder of the Circassian Mamluk dynasty, an order was given to destroy all the new buildings erected by the Christians in Jerusalem and Bethlehem. Again under Sultan Ashraf Bursbay (1422–1438), searches were conducted in all the monasteries of Jerusalem and Bethlehem and any new structures found were either demolished or their material was carried away to embellish a mosque. This was the fate of the Cathedral of Acre, whose ornaments were used to beautify a great mosque built in Cairo by Sultan Nazir ibn Qalaun.

Churches were often seized and turned into mosques under the "legal" plea of "right of conquest": the victorious Moslems claimed ownership of all religious buildings formerly in "heretical" hands. But such sequestration may be also explained by Moslem veneration for personages of the Bible and the New Testament; the Tomb of the Virgin Mary, the Sepulchre of Abraham, the Room of the Last Supper and the Grotto of Elijah are cases in point.

Persecution of Christians and seizure of their houses of prayer were, however, often in retaliation for the military actions of Christian States against Islam. Reprisals of that kind took place even before the Crusader epoch, when the Byzantine emperors had got the better of the Moslems, and the climax came when spearheads of the armies of Constantinople had marched triumphantly as far as Syria and the Holy Land. Thus, in 1305, during the reign of Sultan Nazir ibn Qalaun, Mamluk hostility against the Christians flared up because of the treacherous behavior of a delegation sent by James II of Aragon[2], and in spite of the protests of European Powers, the intolerant prescriptions of several centuries back were promulgated again.

An edict was enforced over the Mamluk dominions requiring Christians to wear a blue turban so that one might distinguish them at a glance, and their women had to wear a peculiar covering over their bosoms. They were not permitted to carry weapons nor to mount horses or mules. They could ride only donkeys, using packsaddles and seated with both feet on one side of the animal. They had to make way for Moslems, giving them the middle of the road. At assemblies, they had to rise before the believers and lower the pitch of their voice. Palm Sunday could not be observed with any public ceremonial. The use of church bells for worship was forbidden. Churches had instead to beat upon a wooden shield called "nakus", which produced a weak sound.[3] The least attempt to proselytize a Moslem was criminal; no Christian might possess Moslem slaves or captives, or any article that had fallen into Moslem hands as booty. A Christian resorting to a public bath had to have a belt tied around his neck. There was a ban on inscriptions in Arabic script on Christian rings. Needless to say, familiarity with a Moslem woman was punishable by death. Christians were forbidden to sell wine or to show wine in public. By Sultan Bursbay's order, Christian houses were searched for wine and any wine vessel found was emptied and smashed.

In 1327, an envoy from the Pope arrived to urge Sultan Nazir to treat his Christian subjects humanely, promising in return that

---

2) James II (1291–1327) had attempted earlier, in 1296, to establish a kind of protectorate over the eastern Christians in the Holy Land and likewise over the Holy Places. Again, in 1300, he sought to obtain possession of a part of Palestinian territory through alliance with the Mongols.

3) A "nakus" can be seen in the parvis of the Armenian Cathedral of St. James.

71

Mohammedan subjects living in Christendom would be given the greatest possible protection from harassment.

Notwithstanding the harsh and oppressive treatment of their own Christian subjects, as described above, in general the Mamluk rulers were eager to keep up friendly relations with Christian States and granted privileges to their consuls and merchants. There were, moreover, periods when the humiliating prescriptions were less strictly enforced. From time to time, however, they were re-emphasized by new edicts, as happened under Sultans Sikh (1417), Bursbay (1422), Djakmak (1452) and Khuskadam (1463). In 1365, when Peter I of Lusignan (1359–1396), King of Cyprus and Pretender to the crown of Jerusalem, jointly with the Venetians and the Knights of Rhodes, conquered Alexandria and, in 1367, ravaged the ports of the Holy Land, the Moslems promptly retorted by destroying churches and forbidding Christians entry into the Church of the Holy Sepulchre for five years. It was the intervention of the Emperor of Constantinople, John V Paleologue (1355–1391), which obtained the release of Patriarch Lazaros of Jerusalem and the reinstatement of the Greek clergy in the shrines from which they had been evicted. As usual, persuasion took the form of generous gifts. In 1423, during the reign of Alfonso V the Magnanimous, an attack launched by a Catalan fleet against the port of Alexandria provoked retaliatory action by the Mamluk rulers, and Catalan pilgrims were arrested in the Holy Land.

In 1429, in spite of the assaults by Catalan ships and the raids on Egyptian and Syrian ports, Sultan Bursbay sent Angel, the Franciscan Custos of the Holy Land, on a diplomatic mission to the Aragonese court. There he proposed that peace negotiations be held on the Island of Rhodes. Accordingly, Alfonso V dispatched to Rhodes ambassadors who were instructed, among other things, to ask the Sultan that his Christian subjects, the Franciscan monks and the pilgrims visiting the Holy Land, should be well treated.

Even in fairly normal times the Moslems still considered themselves the legal owners of Christian churches by right of conquest. In the circumstances, they looked upon and permitted reversion of a Christian shrine or a holy site to their Christian subjects as nothing more than a concession, or indulgence, revocable at will. Consequently, political reckoning or plain *bakshish* was the motivation of most of the easements allowed to Christian denominations in respect of their use of the Holy Places.

In 1330, Philip, King of France, sent an envoy to Nazir demanding that the Sultan hand over to the Christians the City of Jerusalem and part of the coast of Palestine. Predictably, the request was dismissed with contempt. Political reasons may have largely actuated the grant of rights to the Georgians, for their territory occupied a highly strategic area in the Caucasus and its inhabitants were doughty fighters. They owned the Monastery of the Cross in Jerusalem where, it is said, the tree had grown whence the true Cross was made.[4] The monastery had been occupied by the Moslems and turned into a mosque, but in 1305, following the intervention of the Byzantine Emperor Andronikos II Paleologue, it was returned by Sultan Nazir ibn Qalaun to its former owners. The Georgians also owned the Monastery of St. James, and the whole of the Calvary, and held the keys of the Church of the Holy Sepulchre. They were also in possession of a monastery dedicated to St. Theodoros at a place called Bir el-Qutt, near Bethlehem. This is confirmed by a dedicatory inscription in the Georgian language, discovered in 1951. In the fourteenth and fifteenth centuries, the Georgian community was most influential in the Holy Land; dwindling support from abroad led to a decline in its status in Palestine.[5]

The Ethiopians too, during the Mamluk era, possessed important rights in the Church of the Holy Sepulchre as well as in the

4) Inscriptions in the Georgian language can still be seen in the Monastery of the Cross. Scholars recently identified in the monastery a portrait of the great thirteenth-century Georgian poet, Shot'a Rust'avely, author of the epic poem, "The Man in the Panther's Skin." Rust'avely lived his last years in the Monastery of the Cross and is said to have been buried there. According to a Georgian tradition, Rust'avely was compelled to leave his native land because of a love affair with Queen Tamara of Georgia.

5) In the middle of the seventeenth century, the Georgian community lost its hold on Golgotha and retired to the Monastery of the Cross, its one remaining possession. Towards the end of the seventeenth century, the financial position of the Georgians became hopeless, and the monastery was entrusted to the Greek Orthodox Patriarchate to prevent its falling into the hands of the Turks or a non-Orthodox community. Patriarch Dositheos duly paid the debts and taxes owed by the Georgians and took possession of the monastery as well as a number of other Georgian properties.

Church of the Nativity in Bethlehem and in the Church of the Tomb of the Virgin Mary near Gethsemane. Here again, political reasons may have influenced the Mamluks, who were obviously interested in preserving Egypt's southern border from molestation by their Ethiopian neighbors.[6] Subsequently, all these ancient assets were to be lost by Georgians and Ethiopians and would be acquired, respectively, by the Greeks, the Armenians and the Latins.

The Nestorian and the Jacobite Churches, the Armenian and the Coptic Churches, which had enjoyed certain minor rights in the Holy Places under the Crusaders, held on tightly to them under the Mamluks and eventually managed to enlarge them.[7] Once more, "reasons of State" had a say; the Mamluks were concerned to solicit local Christian support. But the Greeks and the Latins had to fight to regain their forfeited standing in the Holy Places, and it was usually a question of—how much?

With the downfall of the Crusaders, the Greeks had attempted immediately to re-enter into possession of the Holy Places which had been theirs before the Latins dislodged them. Although it might have been possible to revive the Greek Orthodox Patriarchal See in Jerusalem, the Patriarch's position in those troubled times was far from secure. According to Greek sources, the year 1236 saw the accession of Patriarch Sophronios III, while 1298 is given as the final year of his successor Gregorios I. However, no mention is made of the duration of either incumbency. The Byzantine Emperors Andronikos III Palaeologue (1328–1341) and John VI Cantacuzenus (1347–1354) intervened time and again on behalf of the Greeks, making munificent gifts to the Mamluk sultans of Egypt, Nasreddin Muhammed (1309–1340) and Nasreddin Hassan ibn Nasser (1347–1351). They appear to have got their way in the end; the Greeks, according to their own sources, were rein-

6) In 1444, when Pope Eugene preached a new Crusade, the Christian shrines were in danger of destruction by the Mamluks. It was then that an Ethiopian king saved the shrines by threatening to pull down all the mosques in Ethiopia and to kill all the Moslems there if the Holy Places suffered damage or destruction.

7) The German pilgrim, Ludolf of Sudheim, who wrote an account of his visit to the Holy Land in 1348, reports that the Christian shrines were occupied by seven sects in all: the Latins, the Greeks, the Armenians, the Nubians, the Syrians, the Georgians and the Nestorians.

stated in their traditional authority in the Christian shrines of Jerusalem and Bethlehem. They did not, however, enjoy exclusivity in the shrines since right of worship had also been assigned to other groups, some of them Mamluk subjects—like the Greeks—and others from foreign lands, such as the Copts, Jacobites, Armenians, Ethiopians and Georgians.

The Latins, no less anxious to recover their footing in the Holy Places, soon undertook a similar campaign, which was waged mainly by the Franciscan Fathers of an Order founded at the beginning of the thirteenth century by Francis of Assisi. The Franciscans had established themselves in the Holy Land shortly after the visit of their founder, but were later to be expelled when the Crusaders lost Acre, their last foothold in Palestine.

In a short space of time, the Franciscans managed to consolidate their position and even to expand it remarkably. It may be that a superior education and discipline gave them an advantage over their indigenous rivals in matters of title deeds and archives. Finally, and most importantly, they enjoyed the support of Catholic polities with which the Mamluks entertained profitable commercial relations.

Thus, as early as 1327, the intervention of James of Aragon (1291–1327) secured for the Franciscans the Monastery and the Church of the Nativity in Bethlehem. They were obtained from the Sultan of Egypt, al-Malik al Nazir Muhammed ibn Qalaun (1310–1341). Six years later, in 1333, the sovereigns of Naples, King Robert of Anjou and his wife, Sancha of Mallorca, by dint of much effort and expenditure, received a rescript giving the Franciscans the right to live permanently in the Holy Sepulchre and to worship there.[8] Furthermore, at their behest, the Sultan ceded the Coenaculum on Mount Zion, and two years later the friars installed themselves on the storied hill. The Coenaculum held a deep religious significance for Christianity, being the traditional site of the Last Supper shared by Jesus with his disciples. It was also linked with other hallowed events in Christianity. In the first half of the fourteenth century, the Franciscans, besides being reinstalled in the Coenaculum, had repossessed the Church of the

---

8) In the twelfth century, at the time of the Crusader Kingdom, the Augustinian canons had worshipped in the church.

Holy Sepulchre and part of the Church of the Nativity and could claim undivided authority over the Tomb of the Virgin Mary.

The special interest shown by Robert of Anjou probably stemmed in part from the consideration that, as a grandchild of Charles of Anjou, he was a pretender to the Kingdom of Jerusalem. As for James of Aragon, besides being a nephew of Queen Sancha, he enjoyed friendly relations with the Sultan of Egypt and greatly favored the Franciscans.

On November 21, 1342, the two Bulls, "Gratias agimus" and "Nuper charissimae"[9] of Pope Clemens VI, vested the Franciscans, who had gained a stable footing in the Holy Land, with the guardianship of the Holy Places. The sphere within which they functioned in the Middle East in that vigilant capacity became known as the "Custody of the Holy Land", with a "Custos" or Custodian presiding.

During the fifteenth century, the friars also cared for the sick in Jerusalem and in Bethlehem and were assisted in their charitable work by several "Poor Sisters of Saint Claire." The Franciscans now felt secure enough to found hospices for pious visitors. It is recorded that a hospice or hospital existed in Ramla in 1437, on the road leading from the port of Jaffa to Jerusalem. Franciscans have lived in Ramla since 1396.

The serenity of the Franciscans was, admittedly, somewhat clouded and even shaken occasionally by the animus of Greek Orthodox fellow-Christians and by the bias of Moslems. But the King of Naples was an ever-present ally. The Dukes of Burgundy were likewise anxious to remain involved and their protection was extended following the visit to Jerusalem in 1432 of the Burgundian Knight Betrandon de la Braquière, who wrote an account of his pilgrimage. Influential merchants of Venice and Genoa also were always ready to help, just as the Sultans of Egypt had good commercial reasons, as a rule, for being friendly with Venice and Genoa.

Consular agencies of the two maritime republics operated in Jerusalem, at least between the years 1413 and 1467. The consuls met pilgrims on their arrival, exacted a tax for the protection

---

9) The Bull "Gratias agimus" was addressed to the superior general of the Franciscans, the Bull "Nuper charissimae" to the King of Naples.

granted, and entrusted them to the care of the Franciscan Fathers on Mount Zion. A Venetian consulate had been established in 1304 in Safed, center of the Mamluk Government in Galilee.

In spite of the support given to the Franciscans by the Catholic Powers, the situation of the Greeks remained fairly satisfactory. It was only when Patriarch Athanasios IV (1450–1460) sought and obtained from the Turkish conqueror of Constantinople, Mehmet II, a *firman* reconfirming the rights of Greeks, that the Mamluks reversed their policy and began to oppose the Orthodox.

During the fourteenth and fifteenth centuries, the Franciscans contrived more than once to carry out major repairs in the shrines of Jerusalem and Bethlehem with the ever forthcoming help of Christian kings and princes, who had to pay the Mamluks dearly for this privilege. In 1482, King Edward of England supplied the lead needed to repair the roof of the Church of the Nativity.

The Holy Places were not only a source of substantial income to the Sultans of Egypt, they were levers of political pressure as well. In 1487, when the Moors of Spain were hard pressed by King Ferdinand, the Mamluk Sultan Kaitbai sent him a delegation of monks of the Holy Sepulchre, with the threat that if Ferdinand did not spare Granada, the churches in the East would be laid waste and pilgrimages halted. When, at the end of the fifteenth century, the Portuguese and the Spaniards endangered Egyptian traffic in the Indian Seas, the Mamluk Sultan Qansu al-Ghuri forewarned the Pope, through the Franciscan Prior of Mount Zion, that should the Pontiff not check the two kings, Ferdinand of Spain and Emanuel I of Portugal, in their naval marauding, he would destroy all the Catholic Holy Places and treat the Christians as these two monarchs were treating the followers of Islam.

In the final analysis, Mamluk governance did immense harm to the Holy Land. The Christian minority, a chronic target for Moslem intolerance in matters of faith, was almost taxed out of existence; certainly, hunger was never far away. In addition, Christians and Moslems and Jews alike were decimated and depressed by the plague of the "Black Death" which raged in 1349, by war and by earthquake: it was a sad and shrunken population which greeted the close of that unhappy interval.

Chapter Six

THE OTTOMAN PERIOD (1517–1917)

GENERAL CONSIDERATIONS

It was inevitable that the predicament of the Byzantine Empire at the beginning of the fifteenth century should upset the Holy Land, and indeed the last emperors were so bitterly vexed by the Turks that they could not maintain their traditional policy of intervention in favor of its Christian inhabitants. Symptomatic of the resultant hardships was the bidding of the vindictive Djakmak, Sultan of Egypt (1438–1453), within a series of repressions, that every newly-built church in Jerusalem and Bethlehem should be pulled down.

Greek sources say that, after the conquest of Constantinople by Mohammed II in 1453, the Patriarch of Jerusalem, Athanasios IV, travelled secretly to that city to procure an imperial edict which would confirm the Caliph Omar's warrant of protection that had given the Greek Orthodox exceptional prerogatives in the Holy Places. The visit, its actuality scouted by Latin writers, shrewdly anticipated an imminent Turkish dominion of the Holy Land; it may well have flattered the Sultan and predisposed him to grant the petition of Athanasios. And, indeed, Turkish dominion was asserted in 1517, in the reign of Selim I, to endure exactly four hundred years, until the British occupation.

The history of Christianity in the Holy Land under the Ottomans is mainly a struggle for possession of the Holy Places; the Christian population was impoverished, its numbers were so exiguous, that all other aspects had little significance.

The Holy Land was now divided in four *sanjaks:* Jerusalem, Gaza, Nablus and Safed, dependent on the pasha or governor of the *vilayet* of Damascus. In the middle of the seventeenth century, Galilee was detached from Damascus and attached to the *pashalik* of Sidon. Jerusalem rose in importance only in the nineteenth century, when the problems connected with the Holy Places became a matter of international interest. It was then that the Governor (in Turkish, *sanjak bey*) of Jerusalem became directly subordinate to the Sublime Porte. Each *sanjak* or district was conceived as an organizational, military, economic and judicial entity. At the start, the new administrative reorganization brought about an improvement in the general conditions of the country, which had suffered so much under Mamluk rule. Soon enough, however, the method of decentralized administration proved catastrophic. The pashas, residing in carefree comfort in the provincial capitals, were utterly oblivious to the welfare of their districts; all that concerned them was to collect taxes and furnish a quota of troops for the Turkish army, and the most barbarous and ruinous devices were employed to either end. The greed and venality of the pashas and their staffs drained local resources and thinned the population: this was a total consequence, but non-Moslems felt it more sharply.

The situation was exacerbated by the fact that not a few feudal landowners and Beduin sheiks made themselves virtually independent of the local Pashas. A local chief would rise to particular eminence and manifest a tolerant attitude towards the religious minorities, in order to gain the support of the Christian Powers at odds with Constantinople. Such was the case of Emir Fakhr ad-Din (1583–1635)[1], a Druze who kept control of Galilee and Mount Carmel. With a few exceptions, local rulers made life wretched for the populace.

Under Ottoman rule, Christians and members of other religious minorities[2] continued to enjoy a certain degree of autonomy in matters of religion and personal status, as they had under pre-

---

1) Fakhr ad-Din acted equitably towards the religious minorities. Another example is that of the Beduin Sheik Dahir al-Umar (1690–1775). It was during Dahir al-Umar's rule that the Franciscans received permission to build their first small church dedicated to the Annunciation in Nazareth (1730). In Acre, too, the capital of Dahir al-Umar's domains, Christians were allowed to put up churches. Extant shrines in Acre that date from this time are the Greek Orthodox Church of St. George, the Maronite Church and the Latin of St. John. By far the most striking example of benign rule was that of Mehmet Ali and his son Ibrahim Pasha, in the nineteenth century.

2) This included the Jews. The Moslems regarded both Christians and Jews as "People of the Book" (*"Kittabis"* in Arabic), who were entitled to protection under Moslem rule, though never to full equality with the Moslems.

vious Moslem regimes. However, the new ruler created a legal framework, delimiting with more precision the position of the religious minorities. Communities legally recognized by the Ottoman regime were called *millets*.[3] They were obliged to pay a poll-tax.

The historical Patriarchates of Constantinople, Alexandria, Antioch and Jerusalem were now all within the bounds of Turkish hegemony; this made for a degree of centralization and put greater power in the hands of the Ecumenical Patriarch of Constantinople, so that he came to be regarded as head of the Roum–Orthodox *millet*. ("Roum" was the contemporary way of saying "Greek.") Under Ottoman rule, the title "Millet Bashi" was conferred on the Greek Orthodox Patriarch of Constantinople.

At first, the Moslems ignored any difference between the Churches and recognized only the Roum-Orthodox *millet*, but in the end they accepted the presence of a number of Christian "nations", namely the Armenian Orthodox, the Armenian Catholics and the Roman Catholics.

The Greeks rose to greatest distinction among the Christian subjects of the Ottoman empire, for they represented the educated class: those that were particularly illustrious at court or in office were known as "Phanariotes", Phanar being the name of a Greek quarter in Constantinople.

The Struggle for Possession of the Holy Places

This privileged status of the Greeks at the Ottoman court had a direct bearing upon the affairs of the Holy Places.

Greek and Latin writers alike ascribe growing Greek influence in the Holy Land to the energy of Patriarch Germanos (1534–1579), a Peloponnesian. Latin historians go further and claim that even the Greek Orthodox Brotherhood of the Holy Sepulchre only came into being during his Patriarchate; such a claim, decrying a monastic Order which had already been in control of the Holy

---

3) The word *millet* derives from the Arabic *"milla"* meaning "religion, rite." Members of the religious minorities in the Ottoman Empire were called *"rayas"*, the Arabic for "flock."

Places for several centuries, seems tendentious in the extreme. On the other hand, it would in truth appear that the exclusive Greek character of the Brotherhood can be traced to Germanos' activity. Before his time, Arab Christians also were to be found in the membership, even assuming patriarchal dignity itself. Greek sources claim that Patriarch Germanos obtained an audience with Sultan Suleiman the Magnificent in Constantinople and was given a *firman* which granted the Greek far-reaching rights in the Holy Places.

It goes without saying that the reorganization of the Brotherhood into an exclusively Greek body, and the superior authority which it exercised in matters of the Holy Places at the start of Turkish rule, evoked a sharp reaction from the Latins, and until the end of Turkish dominion, the annals of Christianity in the Holy Land are little more than a chronicle of quarrel after quarrel between Latins and Orthodox for possession of the Holy Places.

The Latins had not waited long after the fall of the Crusader Kingdom to renew contacts with the Holy Land. Repossession of the Holy Places was, we recall, the special assignment of the Franciscan Order, behind which stood the Republic of Venice and cities and principalities with mercantile interests in the Mediterranean. As the power and importance of these allies fell away, France became the protector of Latin interests: a united national State had just emerged, and France could point to an early tradition of defence of Roman Catholic holdings and ambitions in the Holy Land.[4] Thus, in 1535, its King, Francis I, negotiated with Sultan Suleiman the Magnificent a treaty that is generally known as "Capitulations", for it was set down in seventeen *capitula* or chapters. The aim of it was to put Europeans dwelling in the Ottoman Empire or on visit to it under the aegis and jurisdiction of the consuls of France: the primary purpose was commercial, but the religious consequences turned out to be far-reaching. The

---

4) The relations maintained between Harun al-Rashid and the Emperor Charlemagne were recalled in this connection, with the addition of not a few legendary embellishments. The reference to Charlemagne, intended to stress French links to the Holy Land, is not convincing, as Charles was of German stock, held sovereignty over Germany as well, and had his residence in Aachen. A more convincing commitment to the Holy Land is the predominant role played by France in the Crusader movement.

treaty proved a boon to European pilgrims as a whole and to the Franciscan Fathers, as guardians of the Holy Sepulchre, in particular, and although no specific mention of the Holy Places was made in the Capitulations, France felt entitled to intervene on behalf of the Order whenever Latin rights in the Holy Places were flouted.

While French advocacy on behalf of the Latins in their struggle for the possession of the Holy Places was preeminent, Spain's role was by no means inconsiderable. The policy pursued early in the fourteenth century by the sovereigns of Aragon was followed by the kings of Spain, when the country attained national unity. In 1498, the "Obra Pia" was established with the main purpose of providing financial help for the upkeep of the Christian shrines.[5]

In the second half of the sixteenth century and at the start of the seventeenth, the Franciscans frequently succeeded, with French help, in securing precedence for themselves in the Holy Places of Jerusalem and Bethlehem; they incurred a major loss, however, when in 1552 the Moslems ejected them from the Coenaculum. The building, deeply venerated by the Christians, was converted into the Mosque of Nebi Daoud, the name reflecting the traditional link of the site with King David. The Franciscans, thus dislodged from their chief center, took over the site where today stands the Church and Monastery of St. Savior, present headquarters of the Custody; it had been held by the Georgians before them. The achievements of the Franciscans perturbed the Greek Orthodox and their alarm knew no limits when, in 1555, the Custos Boniface De Stefanis from Ragusa won permission to restore the edicule of the Holy Sepulchre, which was in very bad shape, for restoration meant Latin possession of that site. The Latins likewise secured for themselves a privileged place in the Grotto of the Nativity in Bethlehem.

French diplomatic activity in support of Latin claims in the Holy Places culminated in 1604 in the prescription of new Capitulations within the Ottoman Empire. They were negotiated by Francis Savary, Count of Brèves, Minister to King Henry IV of

---

5) Churches and monasteries under Spanish patronage in the Holy Land still benefit today from the assistance of the Obra Pia. See "P. Juan R. De Legisma", in *"Huella de Espana en Tierra Santa,"* pp. 19-32.

France in Constantinople. These Capitulations for the first time make mention of the Holy Places: protection was guaranteed to pilgrims visiting them, as well as to the religious personnel in charge.[6]

The balance of rights in the Holy Places was, however, being continuously upset under the influence of international politics and, to an ever greater extent, of the corruption of Turkish officialdom. Already in 1605, only a year after the Capitulations, the Greek Patriarch Sofronios IV was able to obtain a *firman* from Sultan Ahmed I, giving the Greeks the northern part of the Calvary, the place of the Crucifixion, and this highly revered site is in Greek possession still.

As a result of local and external influences between 1630 and 1637, the right of pre-eminence in the sanctuaries alternated between the Greek Orthodox and the Roman Catholics no fewer than six times. While France was the main defender of Latin rights in the Holy Places, the powerful maritime Republic of Venice also assisted the Franciscans and made it possible for them to carry out repairs in the Christian shrines in 1615 and 1632.

In 1637, the tide turned decisively in favor of the Greeks. Patriarch Theophanes extracted from Sultan Murad IV a *firman* which ceded to the Greek Orthodox possession of the Basilica of the Nativity in Bethlehem and the gardens, the Holy Sepulchre, the Stone of Unction and the Calvary. The *firman* went so far as to require the Latins to seek the authorization of the Greek Orthodox Patriarch for performance of their religious services in the Holy Places.

From 1637 until 1689, therefore, the Greeks had the upper hand and all Latin attempts to regain their lost rights were to no avail. During the first part of the seventeenth century, the Greek Orthodox could rely on some support from the Protestant Powers, since Cyril Lucaris, Patriarch of Constantinople, was considered to in-

---

6) In 1612, the Netherlands concluded a treaty with Turkey in which an article referred to religion and stipulated that Dutch subjects should be entitled to visit Jerusalem, although they were Protestants. After the Reformation, the Franciscans were responsible to the Turkish authorities for all western pilgrims, who now comprised Lutherans, Calvinists and other Protestants. Up to the eighteenth century, the Franciscans cared for those pilgrims, exacting due payment for the hospitality extended.

cline towards Reformation. When, contrary to Protestant expectations, opposition to Lutheran and Calvinist propaganda came to prevail among the Greeks, the diplomatic representatives of the Protestant countries in Constantinople withdrew their support for the Greek cause.[7]

New Capitulations agreed upon in 1673 between France and Turkey, and negotiated by Charles Marie Francois Olier of Nointel, French ambassador in Constantinople, confirmed the former Capitulations. They incorporated several articles concerning the Holy Places, but this mark of French-Ottoman friendship did not change the disposition of rights in the Holy Places, and the primacy of the Greeks was in fact confirmed in a new *firman* of 1675.

The triumph of the Greek Orthodox was mainly due to the advocacy of the outstanding Patriarch of Jerusalem, Dositheos (1669-1707) and his nephew and successor, Chrysanthos, who were aided at the Sublime Porte by the Grand Dragoman, the Phanariot Alexander Mavrocordato.

In March 1672, during the tenure of Dositheos, an important synod was held in Jerusalem with the participation of seventy-one bishops and other clergy. From this synod there issued the last notable pronouncement of the Orthodox Church in matters of Faith. It was convened with the prime purpose of denouncing the calvinizing "Confession of Orthodox Faith",[8] attributed to Cyril Lucaris, Patriarch of Constantinople.

In the middle of the seventeenth century, the Greek Orthodox Brotherhood of the Holy Sepulchre underwent a period of reorganization and reinforcement. The standing that it had acquired was such that it could occupy Ethiopian religious property (1656)[9] and evict the Armenians from their Monastery of St. James (1658) for a time. The Armenians were also expelled from the Church of the Nativity in Bethlehem. Taken over by the Greeks, the church underwent extensive repairs and in 1672 was rededicated by the Greek Orthodox Patriarch Dositheos. At about

---

7) See: Nicephore Moschopoulos: *La Terre Sainte*, p. 177.
8) "Confession", in this context, refers to a statement of faith.
9) On the occupation of Ethiopian property, see the sub-chapter on the Ethiopian Church.

the same time, the Greeks also acquired the properties of their impoverished co-religionists, the Georgians.

In 1689, the pendulum swung back again to the side of the Latins, with the turn in international politics. The Ottoman Empire, which only a few years earlier had thrust forward to the ramparts of Vienna, was now hard–pressed by a military alliance of Austria, Poland and Venice. This was the judicious moment for France, premier State in Europe, to manifest its traditional friendship to the Sublime Porte and seek in recompense a restitution of rights lost by the Latins in 1637.

The outcome of this demonstration was a *firman* of April 23 1689, according the Latins a superior status in the Holy Places: in the Church of the Holy Sepulchre in Jerusalem, this meant the Holy Sepulchre itself, both domes, the Stone of the Unction, half the Calvary, the Seven Arches of the Virgin and the Chapel of the Holy Cross; in Bethlehem, it meant the Basilica of the Nativity, the grotto and the two gardens.

Patriarch Dositheos maintained good relations with Tzar Peter the Great, to whom he wrote several letters. Early in 1693 he sent his nephew Archimandrite Chrysanthos to Moscow to seek the Tzar's support in the struggle against the Latins. Chrysanthos returned laden with gifts from the Tzar, but since Russia was at odds with Turkey at that time, no assistance was forthcoming with regard to the Holy Places. Consequently, there was no provision in favor of the Greeks in the peace treaty that followed between Turkey and Russia.

The overall pre-eminence of the Latins in the seventeenth century had official recognition in new Capitulations negotiated in 1740 between France and Turkey. Turkey had suffered a sequence of frightful reverses at Austrian and then at Russian hands. The campaigns, ending successively in the Treaties of Carlowitz (1699), Passarowitz (1718) and Beograd (1739)[10], had discomfited and enfeebled Turkey; only the good offices of France could save it from dismemberment. And, indeed, during the negotiations which led to the Peace of Beograd, Marquis Louis

---

10) Carlowitz is now called Sremsky-Karlovci; Passarowitz is now called Pozarevac. Both localities lie within the borders of Yugoslavia.

Sauveur de Villeneuve, representative of Louis XV, was an energetic and successful mediator between Turkey and the allied Powers of Austria and Russia, and exceedingly helpful in securing reasonable terms for the Turks. France's reward was the liberal indulgences of 1740. The pact concluded between Mahmud I and Louis XV on May 29, 1740, in its eighty-five Capitulations reasserted the far-reaching rights in the Holy Places that had been granted in the *firman* of 1689, but with the important difference from the previous pacts of the kind that it bound not only the signatories, but their successors, too (art. 85 of the Capitulations of 1740). In clear terms, it expressed concern for the safety of the Franciscans and, consequently, each time that claims respecting the Holy Places were put forward by the French, as the chief protectors of Latin rights, the argument was that any change in those rights was a breach of an international treaty and so invalid without the consent of France, as the other party to it. For the Latins, then, the *firman* of 1740 is the "Magna Carta" of their prerogatives and demands and is invariably cited as the veritable foundation and basis in and upon the Holy Places.

Seventeen years later, in 1757, matters were again reversed, this time in favor of the Orthodox, who exploited a fracas in the Church of the Holy Sepulchre during Holy Week to gain a *firman* restoring the rights they had enjoyed until 1689[11] in the Holy Places from the Sultan Osman III. On the strength of this *firman*, the Greeks also occupied the Tomb of the Holy Virgin Mary in Gethsemane, dispossessing the Latins, whose rights to the shrines had been recognized only a few months before by the Grand Vizier Mehmed Reghev Pasha. It is relevant to remark that the sultans were naturally inclined to show more benevolence to Orthodox Christians, their subjects, than to Latin nationals of European States with which the Ottomans were often at loggerheads. Moreover, on the eve of the Seven Years' War, France was no longer in a position to assist the Ottoman Empire in its struggle with Russia

---

11) The *firman* of 1757 was obtained chiefly through the prompt intervention of Patriarch Parthenios (1737–1766), who, after the turmoil in the Holy Sepulchre, betook himself to Constantinople and succeeded in winning over the right supporters.

and thus lost reciprocal concessions that had favored the Franciscan claim to the Holy Places.

The *de facto* conditions of 1757 decisively favored the Orthodox and were to be the infrastructure of all *firmans* and treaties of the nineteenth and twentieth centuries.

Ecclesiastical and political jockeying to secure control of the Holy Places in Jerusalem and Bethlehem was the main preoccupation and pursuit of Latins and Greeks all through the Ottoman period, but it did not exclude continuous activity towards recovery of other sacred shrines.

In the first half of the seventeenth century, the monk Prosper bought an area on Mount Carmel from the local governor and in due course a new monastery was built there by the Carmelite Fathers. That Order had been expelled in 1291 by the Mamluks.

At about the same time, the Franciscans won the right to enter the Grotto of the Annunciation in Nazareth, although it was only in 1730 that the church was rebuilt on the site. It was Father Thomas of Navarre, the Custos of that time, who in 1620 got permission from the Druze Emir Fakhr ad-Din[12], ally of the Grand Duke of Toscana[13] and sworn enemy of Turkey, to occupy the ruins of the former Byzantine and Crusader church. At the beginning of the seventeenth century, Nazareth was inhabited by Moslems only. The Franciscans asked the Maronite Patriarch to send some Maronite families from Lebanon to settle in Nazareth. They were the first Christians to live there in modern times. An Orthodox family and an Orthodox priest also came from Transjordan.

In 1629, the Franciscans could regain a foothold in Acre, where they built a small church eight years later dedicated to St. John. After Fakhr ad-Din's death in 1635, conditions for Christians in Galilee worsened. In 1679, the Franciscans purchased the ruins of the Church of the Visitation in Ein Karem and restored it in part and, in 1690, rebuilt the Church of St. John in the village. The Franciscans were joined by Christians from

12) Fakhr ad-Din means "the Glory of the Faith."
13) The Emir resided in Italy from 1613 to 1618, mainly as guest of Cosimo II, Grand Duke of Toscana, on whose assistance he could depend in his struggle against the Turks.

Bethlehem and Beit Jala and developed a small Christian community in Ein Karem.

Dahir al-Umar, who ruled Galilee from 1720 to 1775, also favored Christian settlement in Nazareth and maintained good relations with the Franciscans with a view to gaining the support of France. In 1762, twenty Christian families left Bethlehem, then stricken by a severe famine, and settled in Nazareth. It was also during Dahir al-Umar's rule that the Franciscans bought the traditional site of Joseph's workshop (1754) and the building popularly believed to be the synagogue where Jesus had expounded the Bible (1741).

The Greeks were just as busy in construction, and churches and monasteries were founded in Cana (1566) and Nazareth (1767). In the face of Franciscan opposition, Dahir al-Umar gave permission to the Orthodox Bishop of Acre to construct the Church of St. Gabriel in Nazareth.

In 1799, the Holy Land suddenly found itself in contact with Europe again during the brief and partial occupation by an army of Napoleon Bonaparte. Advancing through Egypt, the French speedily took Gaza, Jaffa and Ramla, and besieged a strongly fortified Acre, but lack of artillery denied Napolean success there. To offset that disappointment, the French scored a notable victory at Affula in the Valley of Esdraelon and entered Nazareth and Safed. Napoleon as a rule lodged in monasteries, which were among the few places in the Holy Land that offered a modicum of comfort, and there is still a record of the chambers occupied by him in Jaffa (in the Armenian convent) and in Ramla and Nazareth (at the Franciscan). Jerusalem, for some strange reason, lay beyond the bounds of his expedition, and his swift short transit did not impinge upon the status of the Holy Places. When he was forced by political developments to return hastily to France, the Turks wreaked a vicarious vengeance on the Christians of the Holy Land. Ramla was brutally damaged; the Carmelite monastery on Mount Carmel was destroyed and its monks were massacred, together with two thousand wounded French soldiers who had been in their care. In 1876, a modest memorial was set up in front of the main entrance to "Stella Maris" Monastery in their memory.

On the night of October 11, 1808, a disastrous fire swept the

Church of the Holy Sepulchre. It had broken out in the quarters of the Armenian monks and taken hold of most of the church, causing the collapse of pillars that supported the dome over the edicule of the Holy Sepulchre, and eventually of the dome itself. The rapid spread of the conflagration is only too understandable in the light of the situation within the church. Besides the main chapel, the church houses stores for religious vestments, and rooms and cells which are the habitations of the monks who perform the religious services celebrated day and night. With so much inflammable material about, it is little wonder that the innumerable votive lamps and candles in this place of worship could cause such a fire which extended swiftly and furiously in all directions.

The "secular" distractions of a Europe in the throes of the Napoleonic wars provided the Greeks with an opportunity to wheedle authorization from Sultan Mahmud II to put the church to rights. Funds for reconstruction of the dome were provided by contributions raised during the Patriarchate of Polycarp by Greeks throughout the Ottoman Empire, as recorded in an inscription in the church. Authorization to reconstruct was given to the Greeks in the teeth of violent antagonism by Latins and Armenians, who feared that if the Greeks were vouchsafed a monopoly of reconstruction, their own rights in the Holy Sepulchre would be jeopardized. For law and custom of the time granted the restorer possession of any part of a building which he restored. Moreover, renewal of a roof transferred the entire building into the ownership of the party which renewed it. Nevertheless, the Latin States were successful in procuring a subsequent declaration from Turkey that the restoration of the Holy Sepulchre by the Greek Orthodox was without prejudice to rights and privileges claimed in it by other Christian denominations.

An uprising of the Janissaries hampered and complicated the work, but the dome was at last in place again in 1810. It had, however, been a hurried and unskilled performance and had to be reenacted within a few decades. This necessity was to give rise to technical problems, to say the least, and would be a source of grave political repercussions.

The Latins claim that during the first decade of the nineteenth century the Greeks made other radical changes in the basilica with the purpose of obliterating, as much as possible, any vestige of its Latin character. Latin sources claim, for example, that the tombs of the Latin kings were removed. This might have been done when the single stairway ascending to Calvary was replaced by two flights of steps. For their part, the Greeks took objection to the installation by the Franciscans of a large organ opposite the altar of Mary Magdalene.

At the turn of the nineteenth century, the Holy Land was inextricably enmeshed in the general turbulence of the Ottoman Empire. Revolutions and revolts were a matter of course, crisis followed crisis, foreign Powers interfered more and more blatantly. Russia was the chief menace and had indeed been such in the previous century as well. Russian involvement concerning the Holy Land dates back to the Treaty of Carlowitz, when Tzar Peter the Great tried formally to mediate between the Sultan and his Christian subjects. However, the only benefit reaped by Russia from that treaty was the agreement of 1700, whereby Russian subjects were to be allowed free access to the Holy Land and its Christian shrines. The threat to Ottoman rule became more pronounced after Russia sealed its victory in two major campaigns with the treaties of Küchük Kainardji (Bulgaria) on July 21, 1774, and of Jassy (Romania) on January 9, 1792. As a result of these two treaties, Russia began to take a direct interest in matters pertaining to the Holy Land. The treaty of Küchük Kainardji, between Catherine the Great of Russia and the Sultan guarantees exemption to pilgrims on their way to the Holy Places from any levy and, more important, the Sublime Porte engaged itself to protect the Christian religion and its churches, to abstain from any oppressive policy and to allow repairs to existing churches and the construction of new ones. The treaty does not specifically mention the possibility of active interference by Russia to protect the Christian subjects of the Ottoman Empire. An extensive right of that nature was, however, claimed by Russia during the first half of the nineteenth century, on the basis of the two pacts in question.

While Russia's influence grew apace, the "Hellenic" element, once so influential in the Sublime Porte, had forfeited its standing in the aftermath of the Greek War of Independence, 1821–1830. In Turkish eyes, that insurrection proved each Greek an adversary and a potential traitor. Even the Ecumenical Patriarch, Gregorios V of Istanbul, recognized head of the Orthodox *millet*, fell victim to this wind of change and was hanged in the first year of the rising from the gate of his residence.

In 1831, the Holy Land was occupied by Ibrahim Pasha in the name of his father, Mehmed Ali, who had achieved enormous power and set up a semi-independent regime in Egypt.[14] From that base, Mehmed Ali lost little time in attempting to assert himself over adjacent Turkish provinces, and in 1840 his troops had advanced beyond the northern frontier of Syria into the very heart of Turkey, and were threatening the survival of the empire itself. A European coalition hastened to the Sultan's rescue and Mehmed Ali was forced to withdraw and be content with the *pashalik* of Egypt.

The controversy round the Holy Places was inflamed in 1847 by the vanishing of the silver star which was believed to mark the exact birthplace of Jesus in the grotto of the Nativity. The main rights in the grotto proper were then enjoyed, as they are today, by the Greek Orthodox and the Armenians. On the other hand, the star with its engraved Latin inscription[15] could be interpreted as evidence of existing Latin rights. Consequently, the presence of the star in the grotto was disturbing to the Orthodox. The Latin owners, of course, imputed its disappearance to the Orthodox, who naturally brought countercharges. The disputants, with French and Russian support respectively, engaged in long and stormy exchanges before the Turkish Government: in 1855, that Government sensibly wound up the interminable argument by placing a new star in the grotto at its own expense.[16]

In the meantime, another problem involving the Holy Places cropped up. It had to do with the urgently needed repairs to the dome of the Holy Sepulchre, which had been restored hastily and unskillfully in 1808. The Greeks, backed by Russia and basing themselves on the *firman* of 1808, claimed to be the only ones authorized to do the work; the Catholic Powers vehemently objected.

---

14) Mehmed Ali was born in Kavalla (Macedonia) to a Turkish family and came to Egypt as an officer of the Albanian contingent dispatched by the Turks to fight Napoleon.

15) "Hic de Virgine Maria Jesus Christus natus est. 1717." The star bearing this inscription was installed by the Latins on the eve of the Treaty of Passarowitz.

16) The star was cast in Vienna and sent from there to Bethlehem.

The dispute concerning the right to replace the star in the grotto of the Nativity and the altercation about the right to repair the dome of the Holy Sepulchre gave France an excuse to exert pressure on the Sublime Porte and gain concessions for the Latins. The main diplomatic activity in that regard was carried out by General Aupick, the French Ambassador in Constantinople who, on May 28, 1850, presented successive Notes insisting on a return to the situation in the Holy Places agreed upon by the treaty of 1740. This insistence was endorsed by several European States, mainly Austria, Spain, Belgium, Sardinia and Naples, but all this unison of diplomacy was helpless against the open threats of Russia, opposing any change detrimental to the rights enjoyed by the Greek Orthodox Church.

A thoroughgoing enquiry into the question of the Holy Places was obviously overdue. On February 8, 1852, therefore, upon the advice of an imperial commission, Sultan Abdul Medjid despatched a *firman* to the Vizier Hafiz Ahmed Pasha, Governor of Jerusalem, authoritatively determining the rights of the several Churches; save for minor amendments, this confirmed the *de facto* situation that had been in existence ever since 1757. Among the amendments, there was a small innovation in favor of the Latins in the Tomb of the Virgin. They were permitted to worship in the shrine, as other denominations were, without prejudice to the pre-eminent position of the Greeks. But they never took advantage of this concession, for it might be interpreted as an implicit renunciation of their claim to exclusive possession of the Tomb.

Another amendment of the *firman* was the permission given to the Greek Orthodox to worship on Ascension Day according to the Julian calendar inside the sanctuary of the Ascension on the Mount of Olives. The Greeks, however, in their turn did not avail themselves of it and continued to worship outside the sanctuary. This was, and still is, the practice of the Latins and, respectively, the Greeks on their Ascension days.

The *firman* of 1852 did not satisfy the importunings of the parties, and all strove with might and main to overbear the Turkish Government and get it altered, each to its particular fancy. Russia was adamant in its claim for official recognition of its protectorate of all subjects of the Ottoman Empire who were of Orthodox

93

faith, and a status of privilege in respect of the Holy Places. To press its claims, a delegation headed by Prince Mentchikoff was sent by the Tzar to Constantinople. Turkey's reluctance to admit those claims, considered to be an encroachment on its rights as a sovereign State, led to the outbreak of the Crimean War (1853–1856). The Treaty of Paris (March 30, 1856), which was the upshot of the fighting, reaffirmed the provisions of the *firman* touching upon the Holy Places.

Though vanquished in Crimea, Russia held on to its prestige in the Holy Land, and the years that followed saw the re-establishment of a Russian ecclesiastical representation and the building of many Muscovite churches and hostels and a variety of religious institutions.

The Treaty of Paris left open the question of the dome of the Holy Sepulchre, which was once more in danger of collapsing, but on September 5, 1862, France, Russia and Turkey came to an agreement that the costs be borne in equal parts by the three.

The architects were enjoined to follow the principle that no decoration, emblem or inscription could adorn the dome that might establish a link with possessory rights of the Christian denominations in the Holy Sepulchre. The replacement of the dome was eventually carried out six years afterwards. Through his representative, Cardinal Antonelli, the Vatican's Secretary of State, Pope Pius IX officially proposed that he himself assume responsibility for the dome and the costs of its restoration. The offer was turned down by the Porte.

By 1877, Russia was warring with Turkey again, in ostensible concern for the welfare of all Ottoman nationals confessing Christianity. But the considerations of the rest of Europe, which called for preservation of the current balance of power, soon put an end to the hostilities: in 1878, the Congress of Berlin purported to adjust the issue that agitated the Western Powers and to re-examine the question of the Holy Places generally. In that regard, the Congress confirmed the *de facto* rulings of the *firman* of 1852, and in Article 62 of the Treaty of Berlin (July 13, 1878), for the first time the expression *status quo* is used, as it was to be so often employed thereafter, to describe the "factuality" in respect of the Holy Places.

One sequel of the Crimean War was certainly a betterment of

the legal status of the Christians throughout the Ottoman Empire. In theory, the Sublime Porte had promised important reforms (in Turkish: *tanzimat*), on November 3, 1839, in the *hatt-i-sherif* of Gulhané (the rescript of the Rose Chamber), but that pronouncement was stillborn. A *hatt-i-hümaioun* (imperial decree) of February 1856, after the Crimean War, was in requital of military help rendered by France, Britain and Sardinia; it granted some equality of rights of citizenship to non-Moslem subjects of the empire, but although its gist was reproduced in the Treaty of Paris in the same year, these reforms were hardly actualized.

In 1901, an intervention by France which was anxious to assure the creditor-claims of the French bankers, Lorando and Tubini, against Turkey, was resolved by the Treaty of Mytilene[17], confirming the privileges and customs exemptions enjoyed by French institutions and institutions under the protection of France; after revision and renewal in December 1913 (the Maurice Bompard-Said Halim agreement) the treaty entered into force in 1914, just before the outbreak of the First World War.[18]

17) Main town of the Isle of Lesbos in the Aegean Sea.
18) In 1905, the Italian Government concluded an agreement with the French Government, which enabled Italian patronage over Catholic institutions of unmistakable Italian character, therein replacing French protection in this regard.

Appendix to Chapter Six

EXCERPTS FROM INTERNATIONAL TREATIES

A) *Treaty of Carlowitz negotiated between the Emperor Leopold I and Mustafa Khan on January 26, 1699.*

Art. XIII. In behalf of religion and the practice of the Christian religion, according to the rite of the Roman Catholic Church, whatever privileges the preceding emperors of the Ottomans have favorably granted in their realms, either by earlier sacred treaties or by the imperial seal, either by edict or by special mandate, the Most Serene and Most Powerful Emperor of the Ottomans will also confirm completely to be observed in the future, so that the adherents of the aforementioned religion can restore and repair their churches and may carry on the customary rituals which have come down from earlier times. And let no one be permitted to establish any kind of vexation or monetary demand on the religious peoples of any order or condition, against the sacred treaties and against the divine laws, to hinder the practice of that religion, but rather let the adherents of it flourish and rejoice in the customary imperial sense of duty. Moreover, let it be permitted for the Most Serene and Most Powerful Emperor of the Romans (i.e., the Austrian Monarch) to set forth to the Sublime Porte the matters entrusted to him concerning the religion and the places of Christian pilgrimage in the Holy City of Jerusalem, and to bring his request to the Imperial (Ottoman) throne.

B) *Treaty of Passarowitz negotiated between the Emperor Charles VI of Habsburg and Sultan Ahmed Khan on July 21, 1718.*

Art. XI is identical to art. XIII of the Treaty of Carlowitz. There is, however, an addition regarding pilgrimages. While the former treaty refers solely to pilgrimates to the Holy City of Jerusalem, the Treaty of Carlowitz adds: "...and the other places where the aforementioned religious people have churches."

Art. XIII of the Treaty of Passarowitz extends to Austrian merchants trading in the Ottoman Empire the same treatment enjoyed by other Christian nations and provides for the appointment of Austrian consuls in Ottoman territories.

C) *The Treaty of Belgrade negotiated between the Emperor Charles VI of Habsburg and Sultan Mahmoud Khan on September 18, 1739.*

Art. IX. All the privileges granted to monks and to insure the freedom to practice the Christian religion according to the rites of the Roman Catholic Church by the predecessors of the Most Exalted Emperor of the Ottomans in his kingdoms, either by the previous holy Capitulations or other imperial decrees, or by special edicts and orders, both prior to the Treaty of Passarowitz and since, all the privileges and particularly those which were granted, at the request of the Most Sainted Holy Roman Emperor, to the monks of the Order of the Most Sainted Trinity regarding the ransoming of captives, his Most Serene Highness, Emperor of the Ottomans, shall confirm them that they may be respected in the future so that the aforementioned monks may freely repair and restore their churches, carry out their duties as was formerly their wont, and no one may disobey the above–mentioned Capitulations and laws by molesting and insulting or by exacting money from these monks or others or any order or status, but they may enjoy the Emperor's protection as usual. In addition, the Ambassador of the Most August and Powerful Roman Emperor to the Ottoman Porte may state what shall be entrusted to him in connection with the religion and the places that Christians visit in the Holy City of Jerusalem and other places where the above–mentioned monks have their churches and to make all the necessary requests in that connection.

D) *The Treaty of Küchük Kainardji of the 10/21 July 1774.*

Art. VII. The Sublime Porte promises a lasting protection of the Christian religion and churches of that religion. She permits the Minister of the Imperial Court of Russia to represent on every occasion the cause of the church constructed at Constantinople (which is mentioned in art. XIV), as well as the cause of those who serve the church, and she promises to give her attention to these observations as coming from respected persons and belonging to a neighboring and sincerely friendly Power. (A new Russian–Greek church on the outskirts of Galata.)

Art. VIII. All the subjects of the Russian Empire, clerical and secular, shall be permitted freely to visit the Holy City of Jerusalem and other places worthy of attention, and the pilgrims and travellers shall not be asked, whether in Jerusalem or in other places, to pay any *karatsch* (right of passage), tribute, assessment or any other tax. Moreover, they shall be provided with proper passport or *firmans* as are given to subjects of other Powers. No wrong or injury shall be done them as long as they are in the territory of the Ottoman Empire; on the contrary, they shall be protected according to the law in the most extensive and efficient manner.

E) *Treaty of Paris negotiated on March 30, 1856 between Great Britain, France, Sardinia, Turkey and Russia.*

Art. XXV. The final agreement with the suzerain Power shall be recorded in a Convention to be concluded at Paris between the High Contracting Parties, and a *hatt-i-sherif*, in conformity with the stipulations of the convention, shall constitute definitively the organization of those provinces, placed thence forward under the collective guaranties of all signing Powers.

F) *Treaty of Berlin negotiated on July 13, 1878 between Great Britain, Austria-Hungary, France, Germany, Italy, Russia and Turkey.*

Art. LXII. The Sublime Porte, having expressed to maintain the principle of religious liberty, and give it the widest scope, the Contracting Parties take note of this spontaneous declaration. In no part of the Ottoman Empire shall difference of religion be alleged against any person as a ground of exclusion or incapacity as regards the discharge of civil or political rights, admission to the public employments, functions and honors, or the exercise of the various professions and industries. All persons shall be admitted, without distinction of religion, to give evidence before the tribunals. The freedom and outward exercise of all forms of worship are assured to all, and no hindrance shall be offered either to the hierarchical organizations of the various communities or to their relations with their spiritual chiefs. Ecclesiastics, pilgrims, monks of all nationalities travelling in Turkey in Europe, or Turkey in Asia, shall enjoy the same rights, advantages and privileges. The right of official protection by the Diplomatic and Consular Agents of the Powers in Turkey is recognized both as regards the above-mentioned persons and their religious, charitable and other establishments in the Holy Places and elsewhere.

The rights possessed by France are expressly reserved and it is well understood that no alteration can be made in the *status quo* in the Holy Places.

Chapter Seven

DEVELOPMENT OF CHRISTIAN INSTITUTIONS DURING THE LAST CENTURY OF OTTOMAN RULE

GREEK AND RUSSIAN ORTHODOX

The Greek Orthodox Church

At the beginning of the nineteenth century, the Christian population of the Holy Land numbered between thirteen and sixteen thousand, four-fifths or more being Greek-Orthodox. From then on, the population rose steadily as the state of things improved generally, but the proportion of Orthodox became smaller, as more and more members of that denomination went over to the Catholic and Anglican Churches.

These defections had several causes, but were provoked in the main by discord between the "Hellenic" and the Arab clergy. Since the time of Ottoman intrusion into the Holy Land, the former had acquired a monopoly of senior ecclesiastical appointments and dominated the Brotherhood of the Holy Sepulchre, preventing local priests from attaining high Church office. Moreover, the Brotherhood considered its main duty to be the safeguarding of the rights of the Greek Orthodox Church in the Holy Places and the conduct of liturgy there, and were little concerned with the cultural needs of the Arab Orthodoxy.

Following this policy, the Greek Patriarch Polycarp (1808–1827), directed most of his efforts towards the restoration of the Church of the Holy Sepulchre, which had been damaged by fire in 1808.

It was during his term of office that Archimandrite Arsenios, a Russian subject and a member of the Brotherhood of the Holy Sepulchre was dispatched to Russia to secure financial aid. His mission opened a new era, as it brought about large-scale Russian enterprise in the Holy Land.

During that period, the Christian inhabitants of Jerusalem and Bethlehem revolted in protest against the crippling exactions of the Pasha of Damascus, but the uprising was harshly repressed.

101

The situation improved somewhat during the Patriarchate of Polycarp's successor, Athanasios V, whose term coincided with the rule of Ibrahim Pasha. Ibrahim, intent on winning the friendship of the Christian Powers, inaugurated a pro-Christian policy. He abolished the taxes formerly levied on pilgrims, as well as the fee that had been demanded of those wishing to enter the Church of the Holy Sepulchre since Saladin's time. In 1834, as a sign of goodwill, he attended the Greek Orthodox ceremony of the Holy Fire in the Church of the Holy Sepulchre. The financial position of the Brotherhood of the Holy Sepulchre at that time was disastrous, and only the voluntary contributions of the Greek people at home and abroad rescued the Patriarchate from bankruptcy.

After the death of Athanasios V, the Brotherhood elected Cyril II (1845–1872), who was the first Greek Patriarch to establish his residence in Jerusalem (1843). In previous centuries, the Patriarch of Jerusalem lived in the "Phanar" of Constantinople and visited Jerusalem only rarely.[1] This transfer of residence was probably due to the persuasion of the Russian Government. At that time, the Protestant Missions in the Holy Land were undergoing an expansion which precipitated greater activity among the Catholic institutions; this situation could hardly be overlooked by St. Petersburg. Russia had just initiated its own religious penetration into Palestine and not having its own official hierarchy in the Holy Land, needed the cooperation of the Greek Patriarchate. The Greeks, though resentful of the growing influence of the Russian Orthodox Church in Palestine, had recently benefited from Russia's political support in the settlement concerning the Holy Places (the *firman* of 1852) and had to acquiesce.

Major events of Cyril's Patriarchate included the establishment of a theological seminary in the Monastery of the Holy Cross in 1855 and, in the same year, the construction of the Church of St. Elias on Mount Tabor, on the foundations of former churches, as well as the reconstruction of the dome of the Holy Sepulchre in 1869. Cyril's Patriarchate also saw the erection in 1860 in Beit Jala of a large church dedicated to the "Theotokos." His Patriarchate came to a critical end in 1872. In that year, the Greek Patriarchs

---

1) Among the reasons why the Patriarch of Jerusalem desired to live in Constantinople was the advantage that he would derive from being near the main sources of income of the Patriarchate, namely the rich religious endowments in the principalities of Wallachia and Moldavia, which had to be controlled. From Constantinople, it was easier for the Patriarch to travel to Russia on his frequent money-collecting missions.

had assembled in Constantinople to deal with the problem of the Bulgarian Church, which had proclaimed its independence from the Ecumenical Patriarchate. Cyril, at the probable direction of the Russians, refused to associate himself with the decision of the Synod which condemned the Bulgarian Church and as a consequence was deposed by the Brotherhood of the Holy Sepulchre. In protest, the Russian Government seized the properties in Russia which had been endowed to the benefit of the Holy Sepulchre. With that example to inspire them, the Arab Orthodox of Jerusalem stood up in favor of the Patriarch and against the decision of the Brotherhood. The Sultan, however, put an end to the quarrel and ordered Cyril deported to Constantinople.

Relations between Greek and Arab Orthodox were strained almost to the breaking-point in the second half of the nineteenth century, with the Arab element displaying more fervent nationalism. In the seventies they demanded the right of franchise in patriarchal elections and a share in administering the property of the Church. The Patriarch and the Brotherhood passionately resisted this attempt to diminish the exclusively "Hellenic" character of both privileges. They upheld the conviction that the Patriarch, alone and wholly, represented the interests of Greek Orthodoxy in the Holy Places, and that the property of the Patriarchate consisted of gifts by pious "Hellenes" for the upkeep of "Hellenic" shrines, so that any outlay in favor of the local Orthodox was but gratuitous charity and implied no legal obligations.

On March 13, 1875, the Turkish Government issued a special statute[2] concerning the Greek Patriarchate of Jerusalem which upheld the claims of the local congregants in some measure. Not surprisingly, the Brotherhood rejected it and none of the articles favorable to the native population was ever enforced during the remainder of the Ottoman period.

Hierotheos, Patriarch from 1875 to 1882, made a number of concessions to the local congregants and tried to ease the strained relations with Russia. The recurrent financial straits of the Patriarchate made it imperative to reach a settlement with Russia concerning the confiscated property and this settlement was realized in 1881.

---

2) A translation of the 1875 statute from the Turkish original into English is annexed to the Report of the Commission appointed by the Government of Palestine to inquire into the affairs of the Greek Orthodox Patriarchate (See *The Bertram-Luke Report*, Oxford Press, 1921).

Nicodemus (1881–1891), Hierotheos' successor, had for many years been the representative of the Brotherhood of the Holy Sepulchre in Moscow and was, therefore, *persona grata* to the Russian Government. With the financial assistance of Russia, he was able to build several churches, among them the patriarchal residence "Viri Galilaei" on the Mount of Olives and the Church of the Virgin Mary nearby, as well as the churches of Rama and Mujedel in the Galilee. In 1887, he built a new church in the village of Cana to replace an older one dating from 1566. Among his works of special note were the reorganization of the theological seminary in the Monastery of the Holy Cross and the collection of many precious manuscripts from ancient Orthodox monasteries at a central library in the Monastery of St. Constantine and St. Helena in Jerusalem. The generous gifts which poured in from Tzarist Russia and from the Orthodox countries in the Balkan peninsula, induced the Patriarch to embark on even more ambitious projects, such as an extensive commercial center in the formerly uninhabited Muristan area in Jerusalem. In addition, the Patriarch built a new hotel near Jaffa Gate in Jerusalem and added a new wing to the edifice housing the headquarters of the Patriarchate. But his building activity was a drain on the finances of the Patriarchate and caused the halt of other vital activities.

Although cooperating with the Russians, Nicodemos always resisted Russian intervention in the internal affairs of the Patriarchate. Ultimately, however, he encountered such strong criticism from the members of the Brotherhood as a result of his pro-Russian policy that he was forced to resign.

He was succeeded in 1891 by Gerasimos, previously Greek Patriarch of Antioch. Gerasimos was instrumental in building several new churches, but was particularly concerned with the construction of new schools: he sought to neutralize the effects of the proliferation of Russian schools in the Holy Land. This policy was continued by his successor, Damianos, so that in the years before the outbreak of the First World War, the Patriarchate could pride itself on as many as eighty-three schools for boys and girls within the territory under its jurisdiction: notably two large institutions for boys—one in Jerusalem and the other in Jaffa.

During the Patriarchate of Damianos, the nationalistic consciousness of the Arab Orthodox element became stronger, encouraged by the successes of the Young Turks, and put forth more insistent claims to share in the administration of the Patriarchate in 1908. These circumstances forced Damianos to grant several concessions to the Arab community; in this he was opposed by the Synod, which decided to depose him.

In 1910, a Government Commission intervened to reconcile Patriarch and Synod, and Damianos remained in office. This Commission also set up a mixed council in which representatives of the Arab community would take part, but the council met only sporadically and lapsed at the outbreak of the First World War.

In 1917, as the British army advanced towards the borders of Palestine, the Turks exiled Damianos to Damascus.

In fine, it can be said that the Greek Patriarchate enjoyed fairer treatment at the hands of the Ottoman Government during the last century of Turkish rule than during the three preceding centuries. Moreover, the Greek Orthodox Church obtained a very satisfactory settlement of its rights in the Holy Places. On the other hand, it was endangered by the activities of the Russians who were anxious to supplant it in the Holy Places. Nevertheless, the Patriarchate could not forgo Russian cooperation as it needed financial help and political support against the encroachments of Catholics and Protestants.

An added development was the emergence in the nineteenth century of a national consciousness among the Arab-speaking Orthodox, which threatened the supremacy of the "Hellenic" element within the Patriarchate.

The Russian Orthodox Church

Russia had taken an active interest in the Holy Places and in the welfare of Russian pilgrims since the signing of the Treaty of Küchük Kainardji in 1774, but the establishment of a Russian Ecclesiastical Mission in Palestine materialized only in the 1840's. Until that time, Russian intervention in the affairs of the Holy Places had been designed to favor and aid the Greek Orthodox Church.

The first suggestion that there should be a permanent Russian presence in the Holy Land came from Archimandrite Arsenios, a Russian subject and a member of the Brotherhood of the Holy Sepulchre, who had been sent to Russia in 1816 by Patriarch Polycarp to raise funds for the Holy Places. In order to ingratiate himself with the Russian Holy Synod, Arsenios stressed the desirability of a regular representation of the Russian Church in Palestine. This was not taken up at the time, but came under consideration several years later, when Russia's Minister of Foreign Affairs, Count Karl Robert Nesselrode (1780–1856), began to feel concern at the growing influence of the Anglican and Protestant institutions in Palestine, which culminated in the appointment of an Anglican Bishop in Jerusalem. This situation could not be lightly overlooked by the Russian Government or the Holy Synod in Moscow, any more than it had been overlooked by the Catholics, who in 1847 had re-established the Latin Patriarchate in Jerusalem.

Now a straightforward and broader Russian interest in the Holy Land began to express itself. The setting up of the first Russian Ecclesiastical Mission was prepared by the preliminary enquiry carried out by an erudite Russian monk, Archimandrite Porphyrios Ouspensky, and the practical proposals in his report submitted to Tzar Nicholas I led to its establishment. Porphyrios was appointed Head of the Mission and upon his arrival in Jerusalem installed himself in the Monastery of the Archangel, which was placed at his disposal by the Greek Patriarch Cyril. It is significant that his arrival, on February 18, 1848, coincided with the installation of the Latin Patriarch Valerga on January 17 of that same year.

The outbreak of the Crimean War six years later created a difficult situation for the recently established Mission, and so, in 1857, following the hostilities, a second Mission was dispatched to the Holy Land. This time Russia could claim the credit for advancing Orthodox interests, as its political intervention had swayed the Sultan to issue the *firman* of 1852 which favored the Orthodox Church over the Catholics. In the hope of raising the prestige of the Mission, a Bishop was appointed to head it, and the choice fell on Monsignor Cyril Naoumov, Bishop of Melitopolis. The principal aims which Naoumov pursued during his incumbency were the rehabilitation and revival of the Arab Orthodox community and the acquisition of rights in the Holy Places at the expense of the Greeks. This policy alienated the Greek Patriarchate and as a consequence, Naoumov had to be replaced. His successor was not a Bishop but merely an Archimandrite. When the second Mission was installed, a special committee was appointed in St. Petersburg (Leningrad) to take charge of Palestinian affairs. The President of the Palestine Committee was the Grand Duke Constantine Nikolaievich, brother of Tzar Alexander II, who visited the Holy Land in 1859 and was instrumental in providing the Russians with an important foothold in Palestine.

Besides acquiring a historic spot near the Church of the Holy Sepulchre, the remarkable sums of money contributed by the Palestine Committee[3] made it possible to purchase ten acres near the Jaffa Gate[4] in Jerusalem and to build what is now known as the Russian Compound.[5] This comprised a hostel, a hospital, the magnificent five-domed Cathedral of the Holy Trinity[6], a residence for the Russian Consul and a house for the Mission with a private chapel. Smaller establishments went up in Nazareth, Jaffa, Haifa, Ramla and the hill-towns of Judea. In April 1864, with most of the buildings in Jerusalem completed, the usefulness of the Palestine Committee was at an end and the Tzar ordered its dissolution. In its place, he founded the Palestine Commission which was no more than a department of the Ministry of Foreign Affairs.

In 1865, Archimandrite Antonin Kapustin came out to head the Russian Mission. His interest in archaeology led him to work systematically for the acquisition of places of biblical purport for the Russian Church, among them the Oak of Mamre in Hebron[7] and important sites on the Mount of Olives. Moreover, he built homes for pilgrims who had decided to spend the rest of their days in the Holy Land. He was also involved in the affairs of the Greek Patriarchate, siding with the Russophile Patriarch Cyril, who was overthrown in 1872 by the Brotherhood of the Holy Sepulchre, and encouraging the anti-Greek tendencies of the Arab Orthodox community. Thus, Russia's ecclesiastical policy in the 1870's became more and more a function of its general diplomacy, and this sought to advance Russian political interests in the Middle East.

After the Turco-Russian War of 1877–1878 and the Treaty of St. Stefano, which European diplomats tried to reverse at the

---

3) The Imperial Treasury made a grant of 500,000 rubles and the people of Russia added 600,000.

4) It served formerly as a parade ground for the Turkish garrison (the so-called Maidan).

5) The Russians called the compound "New Jerusalem." The two sponsors of the project, the Grand Duke Sergei Alexandrovich and Nikolai Nikolaievich, gave their names to buildings in the compound: the Sergievsky, constructed in 1889, and another edifice built in 1903. The emblem carved on many façades in the compound incorporates the initial letters of Jesus Christ and a quotations from Isaiah 62:1, "For Zion's sake I will not hold my peace, and for Jerusalem's sake I will not rest."

6) It was consecrated in 1872 by Cyril, Greek Orthodox Patriarch of Jerusalem.

7) The Church of the Holy Trinity and Saints Abraham and Sarah was built in that place.

Congress of Berlin in 1878, a different approach was clearly called for in order to achieve religious and cultural objectives in the Holy Land.

To that end, the Orthodox Palestine Society was founded in 1882. Its first president was the brother of Tzar Alexander III, the Grand Duke Sergei, who had visited the Holy Land in 1881 and evinced a great interest. The purposes of the Society, according to the first article of the constitution, were exclusively scientific and charitable. It proposed to "collect, elaborate on and propagate in Russia news of the Holy Places in the East, to render assistance to the Orthodox pilgrims, to found schools, hospitals, hostels and, simultaneously, to render material aid to the native citizens, to churches, monasteries and clergy."

The Orthodox Palestine Society was recognized by the Tzar as a major organization occupied with Palestinian affairs in March 1889, and the Russian Ecclesiastical Mission and the Palestine Commission were relegated to a secondary role. The interests of the "Imperial" Russian Palestine Society embraced archaeological excavations carried out near the Holy Sepulchre at a site purchased from the Ethiopians. Russian scholars began to concern themselves with the past connections between the Church of Georgia, a territory which had now come into Russia's boundaries, and the Holy Land. Georgian influence in the Holy Land had been significant before its decline in the seventeenth century and now Georgian inscriptions in the Holy Sepulchre and in the Monastery of the Holy Cross became subjects of antiquarian research.

More important was the work of the Society in the care of pilgrims and in establishing educational and benevolent institutions for the local Orthodox community. The number of pilgrims to the Holy Land had increased steadily during the second half of the nineteenth century, and in 1913 fifteen thousand Russians made the pilgrimage. To answer this need, the Society added large new hostels to those already existing, not only in Jerusalem but also in Nazareth and Jericho, and in the 1880's schools were opened in Mujaidel, Rama, Kefar Yassif, Sejera, Nazareth and Beit Jala. At that time, the Society was maintaining twenty-three schools in Palestine, including 1,074 pupils and many more in the neighboring Arab countries.

Relations between the Society and the Greek Patriarchate were marred by constant rivalry, yet it was mutually essential that they work together. The Greeks were interested in Russian financial support, the Russians needed a maximum of collaboration from the Patriarchate, because the Sultan had not given them official permission to operate schools in Palestine and the Society was, to a certain degree, the client of the Greeks. At last, in 1902, that permission was vouchsafed.

The Russians gave financial aid to the Greeks to build a church in Mujaidel in 1884 and another in Rama in 1890. Many more churches, however, were built for their own use: the Church of the Ascension on the Mount of Olives in 1886, the Church of Alexander Nevsky near the Church of the Holy Sepulchre, and in 1886 the Church of Maria Magdalena on the Mount of Olives, in pure Muscovite style with its seven bulbous gilded domes. It was inaugurated by Grand Duke Sergei[8] who, on this same trip, laid the corner-stone of the Church of St. Peter and Paul in Abu Kabir on the outskirts of Jaffa. At the beginning of the twentieth century, the Church of St. Elias went up on Mount Carmel and a monastery was founded in Ain Farah, with the intention of setting up a monastic colony and renewing the tradition of the "lauras" of the first centuries of Christianity.

The Society also pursued an active medical program, maintaining a hospital in Jerusalem and dispensaries there and in Bethlehem, Beit Jala and Nazareth.

At the outbreak of the First World War, Russian influence in Palestine was at its peak. In Jerusalem alone, there were four churches, several hostels and schools[9] and a hospital. Places of worship and other educational and charitable institutions had been established all over the Holy Land. Moreover, the Russians had succeeded in awakening national feelings among the Arab laity, a ferment which was later to create many a problem for the Greek Patriarchate.

But once fighting began, pilgrimages from Russia ceased and the schools had to be closed down. They were never opened again.

---

8) The crypt in the same church was the last resting place of the Grand Duchess Elisabeth, wife of Grank Duke Sergei. She had been put to death during the Russian revolution in 1918, but her body was recovered by the White Russian army and brought to the Holy Land. In January 1982, following the decision of the Russian Church Outside Russia to canonize the Grand Duchess, a solemn ceremony was held at the Church of Mary Magdalena on the slopes of the Mount of Olives, with the participation of visiting dignitaries of the Orthodox Church Outside Russia.

9) The only school still run today by the Russian Orthodox Church is an Arab girls' school maintained in Bethany by the New York-based Orthodox Church Outside Russia. Its pupils are taught in Russian as well as in Arabic and English.

PROTESTANTS AND ANGLICANS

The Common Enterprise

Law and order were reasonably good during the term of Mehmed Ali. Clergymen and scholars interested in biblical and archaeological research were more free to follow this pursuit in the Holy Land, and their writings and findings stimulated interest in this subject among co-religionists.

Until the first decades of the nineteenth century, contacts of the Protestant Churches with the Holy Land had been irregular; now they became stronger and more continuous. The first Protestant missions were established in the Middle East notably by the American Board of Foreign Missions and, even more important for the Holy Land, by the Church of England through its London Society for Promoting Christianity among the Jews (LJS). Following exploratory sojourns to Jerusalem in 1820 and 1824, the Society and afterwards the Mission despatched its first medical missionary, Dr. George Colward Dalton, to launch the enterprise. The first ventures encountered obstacles and work of a permanent nature was made possible only in 1833 when Rev. John Nicolayson, a Dane from Schleswig, secured a vantage in the Holy City. Defying the Ottoman Law, he purchased the property inside Jaffa Gate and the building which is today known as Christ Church Hostel, and laid the foundation of Christ Church itself. The work of construction was stopped by the Ottoman authorities, as the "Porte", while it allowed existing churches to function, did not permit the building of new ones. When Nicolayson was establishing his Mission, German and Swiss missionaries began also to be conspicuous in evangelism.

A notable American missionary was Orson Hyde, one of the twelve Apostles of the Church of the Latter-Day Saints (Mormons), who was delegated by the head of the Church, Joseph Smith, to travel to the Holy Land. Standing on the Mount of Olives on October 24, 1841, he offered a dedication prayer for the Land of Israel, for the ingathering of the Jewish people and their constitution as a distinct nation and a government.

Anglicans and Protestants were badly handicapped from the outset, for unlike the "veteran" Christian Churches, they had no legal status in the Ottoman Empire: building activity on their part was plagued with obstruction, the new faith of their converts was not recognized and last, but by no means least, they did not have the benefit of backing by a powerful European State, which the Catholics and the Orthodox enjoyed.

In order to mitigate this state of affairs in the Holy Land, Frederick William IV of Prussia conceived the idea of setting up an Anglican bishopric to which a Protestant mission might be appended. More than one hurdle had to be overcome. There was, first of all, the substratum of a Church of England that stood solid on the episcopal office; the Church of Prussia was non-episcopal. In the second place, in sending a new Bishop to the Holy City, extreme circumspection was essential if the resentment of pre-existing Patriarchs and Bishops of Jerusalem was not to be aroused.

Frederick's proposal was put to Queen Victoria and to the Archbishop of Canterbury and an agreement was duly arrived at: the nominee for the new bishopric, if he were not already an Anglican, must be taken into that faith; nomination would be alternately by the British sovereign and the Prussian king; the Anglican Bishop must eschew any meddling in the affairs of the Eastern Churches, and his titles would consequently be "Bishop in Jerusalem", not "Bishop of Jerusalem", so that no infringement of the established rights of the hierarchy of other Churches could possibly be imagined.

The first incumbent was Dr. Michael Salomon Alexander (1841–1845), a convert from Judaism—his original name was Wolf—whom the British crown had named; his main task was to be conversion of local Jewry. For this purpose, he founded a training school in Jerusalem for missionaries, but it was shortlived. In September 1845, a few months before his death[10], a *firman* was secured, finally permitting the much-interrupted building of what was to be Christ Church. It was merely to be a chapel for the personnel of the British consulate, which had recently been opened in Jerusalem. The church was completed under Bishop Alexander's successor, and consecrated on January 21, 1849; it was the sole evangelical church in the entire East at that time.

On Prussian nomination, Samuel Gobat (1846–1879), a Swiss Protestant, succeeded Alexander and began proselytizing among the non-Protestant population. Direct work among the Moslems was virtually impossible and likely to endanger the status of the missions, but work among Christians was looked upon with indifference by the Ottoman Government. So Gobat turned to the

---

10) Bishop Alexander was buried in the Protestant cemetery on Mount Zion, as was the Rev. Nicolayson who died in 1824.

Eastern Christians. Mindful though he was of the engagement entered into when the bishopric was established not to interfere in the affairs of the Eastern Churches, he thought that opening schools and distributing Bibles among the Eastern Christians would not infringe it. He may well have been pursuing these educational activities in good faith, but the ultimate result was that not a few young people educated in Anglican schools abandoned the Eastern communities to join the Anglican Church. In this way, congregations sprang up in all the main Christian towns, mainly under Arab clergy, using an Arab translation of the Book of Common Prayer.

In 1852, the Ottoman Government issued a *firman* which recognized and legalized the conversion to Protestantism of Christians who were Ottoman subjects. It is not clear whether it yielded to pressure of Protestant Powers or was prompted by a further desire to stir up division and dissension among its Christian subjects. The legal recognition given to the Protestant community by the Turkish Government was not upheld during the British Mandate.

After 1849, Bishop Gobat enlisted the moral and monetary support of the Church Missionary Society to expand his work. The Society began to be active in 1851 and set up missions in towns and villages, built new churches, opened schools and clinics; the first schools were in Jerusalem, Bethlehem and Jaffa. The Crimean War provided Bishop Gobat and the Society with a wonderful opportunity to extend their educational enterprises, with the Russian Orthodox prevented from operating their own schools or supporting those of the Greek Orthodox. In 1853, Gobat opened a school on Mount Zion in Jerusalem, which was later enlarged and named after him. It was to remain open until 1948.

In the 1860's, Gobat opened schools in Bethlehem, Beit Jala, Ramla, Jaffa, Nablus, Rafidiah, Nisf al-Jabal, Zebabdeh, Burkin and Shfaram. Most were quite small, with from ten to fifteen pupils in each, and not infrequently were obliged soon to close down.

The greater part of these schools were afterwards entrusted to the Church Missionary Society, whilst those of Bethlehem and Beit Jala were taken over by the Berlin Missionary Association[11] . On its own initiative, the Church Missionary Association opened

---

11) In 1873, Beit Jala's thirty-five Lutheran families became an independent congregation with their own pastor.

several schools in and around Nazareth and by the end of the nineteenth century it was maintaining thirty-one schools with 1,762 pupils in the whole of Palestine.

Thanks to the extensive educational activity of the episcopate of Samuel Gobat, the Arab-Anglican congregation grew to more than a thousand faithful, largely Greek Orthodox and Catholic converts. Special churches had to be built for them: Christ's in Nazareth (1871), St. Paul's outside of the New Gate in Jerusalem (1874), St. Philip's in Nablus (1882) and St. Andrew's in Ramallah (1888).

When Bishop Gobat's term ended, his successor, designated by the Church of England, was Bishop Joseph Barclay. After barely a year and a half in office, in 1881, Bishop Barclay died and a hiatus of six years followed in the Anglican See.

The English branch of the Order of St. John in Jerusalem opened an ophthalmic hospital in temporary premises in 1883. Subsequently, the Sultan presented the Order with a suitable site outside the city walls overlooking the Hinnom Valley and a new building was erected there.

The Anglican Church

On November 3, 1886, the union between the Lutheran Church and the Church of England in affairs of the Anglican bishopric of Jerusalem had come to its early end and each denomination thereafter conducted an independent activity.

Bishop George Francis Popham Blyth (1887–1914) was the first Bishop of the purely Anglican establishment. A violent controversy between Blyth and the Church Missionary Society concerning proselytism among the Eastern Churches led to his seeking the independence of the Society's financial support, and accordingly he founded the Jerusalem and East Mission, controlled and directed by the Anglican Bishop exclusively.

The London Society for Promoting Christianity among the Jews continued to enjoy his full sympathy and was considerably strengthened by the building of a new home for the English Mission Hospital in Jerusalem in 1897,[12] which was destined to be enlarged several times. In Haifa, St. Luke's Church was conse-

12) The first hospital of the Church Mission to the Jews (CMJ) was located in the Old City (Watson House)

113

crated in 1899,with its own school and hospital. On October 18, 1898, the Collegiate Church of St. George the Martyr was consecrated in Jerusalem, a magnificent edifice that owed its construction to the efforts of Bishop Blyth.[13] The compound included the Bishop's residence, the house of the clergy, the choir-school (later to develop into St. George's Boys' School) and St. Mary's Girls' Home or Orphanage. In 1910, Edward's Tower was added to the main church. To emphasize the pan-Anglican character of St. George's, six Bishops of the Anglican world (Australia, Britain, Canada, South Africa, the United States of America and India) were invited to accept the honorary title of Episcopal Canon of the cathedral.

The Church Missionary Society started its work during the second half of the nineteenth century in Gaza, where it opened four schools, two for boys and two for girls, with a total enrollment of four hundred. A clinic opened in 1882, and in 1908 a hospital was established to serve the growing number of patients. Later, the work in the hospital was taken over by the Southern Baptist Convention.

Most important for the development of Palestine's Anglican congregation was the handing over of several of its institutions and responsibilities by the Church Missionary Society in 1906 to a body of Anglican-Arab Christians, governed by the "Palestine Native Church Council." Like the Church Missionary Society and the Church Mission to the Jews, the Arab-Anglican communities recognized the authority of the Bishop only in spiritual matters and were entirely independent in all their other concerns.

Bishop Blyth died in 1914, shortly after the outbreak of the First World War. His successor, Bishop Rennie MacInnes (1914–1931) was unable to enter his cathedral until the hostilities ceased.

The Lutheran Church

The Anglican-Lutheran joint venture lasted thirty-five years. The period coincides, in the main, with the term of Bishop Gobat, who seconded the work of German missionaries in their active foundation of cultural and welfare institutions.

A small Evangelical community was formed early in Bishop

---

13) The church is also known as St. George's Cathedral, but as the real cathedral of Jerusalem is the Church of the Holy Sepulchre, this name is avoided.

Gobat's tenure, composed of four Deaconesses of Kaiserswerth[14], four brothers of Chrischona[15] and some craftsmen. The Deaconesses of Kaiserswerth began their educational and charitable work early in 1851 in buildings situated in the Old City of Jerusalem in the vicinity of Christ Church. In 1868, the Society of the Deaconesses in Germany sponsored the construction of the Talitha Kumi Girls' School[16] in the new sector of the Holy City. The Deaconesses also began medical work in Jerusalem in 1851, in a small hospital with ten beds. In 1891, the Society in Germany saw to the construction of a new hospital in Jerusalem's new sector and, in addition, a hospital for children was built in 1873. Known as Marienschaft, it owed its inception to Dr. Sandreczky. The Deaconesses also founded welfare institutions in Bethlehem and Haifa. In 1858, a hospice sponsored by the Evangelical branch of the Knights of St. John was established in the Via Dolorosa. In 1860, the family of the German missionary, Johann Ludwig Schneller, embarked upon its work of orphan care and rehabilitation and in due course was responsible for the founding of the great "Syrian" orphanage in Jerusalem, with branches in Nazareth and in Bir Salem near Ramleh. In the lower section of Prophets' Street in Jerusalem an entire compound of Lutheran institutions was established, among them the residence of the "Propst" or Provost, head of German Lutheran institutions in the Holy Land. A landmark in the development of Lutheran missionary work in the Holy Land was the acquisition of the Muristan area in the vicinity of the Church of the Holy Sepulchre; it had been a gift of the Sultan to the Crown Prince of Prussia, later King Frederick IV, during his visit to Jerusalem after attending the inauguration of the Suez Canal. Muristan is a Persian word

14) The Deaconesses of Kaiserswerth are a Lutheran female congregation founded in Germany in 1836 by Theodor Fliedner. In 1852, Fliedner bought a small house for the deaconesses in Jerusalem, in the neighborhood of Christ Church.

15) The Pilgrim's Mission of Chrischona, founded by Christian Friedrich Spittler, had its center in Basel (Switzerland). One of the Mission's disciples sent to the Holy Land was Conrad Schick, who was to build some of the most impressive buildings in Jerusalem. (See article in *Zeitschrift des Deutschen Palestina Vereins*,1983, by Alex Carmel.)

16) The Talitha Kumi building was designed by the German architect Conrad Schick. During the Second World War, it came under the Custodian for German property. The building was demolished in 1980, but a small section was preserved and reconstructed near the original site as a historic landmark of nineteenth-century Jerusalem.

which means "lunatic asylum" and there had originally been such an institution on the site, but in Crusader times the Church of Sancta Maria Latina was located in the Muristan compound and nearby was the seat of the Knights of St. John. It was there that the Lutheran Church built the Muristan chapel in 1871 and this chapel served the German congregation until 1898 when the construction of the Church of the Redeemer was completed.

After 1873, the Lutheran Church established its own school, the children of the German-Lutheran congregation of Jerusalem having until that time attended the Anglican school. Several developments account for this change: the larger number of children of the local communities, the agreement of the newly established Templers' "colony" to join the undertaking, and the unification of Germany in 1871, which was undoubtedly a stimulus to the Jerusalem "colony" to give their children a German education. Initially, the Lutheran school was situated in a rented building in Jerusalem's Russian Compound. In 1910, a new building was erected in the vicinity of the Propstei.

The union between the Lutheran Church and the Church of England came to an end in 1886. There was more than one reason for this severance. When the association was embarked upon in 1840, the Lutheran Church was a newcomer to the Holy Land and was interested in benefiting from the support of the already established Anglican missionary institutions. This is the reason that the King of Prussia had agreed to the stipulations of the Anglican Church, among them the uneasy condition that the Lutheran ministers of the common enterprise should seek Anglican consecration. Half a century later, when the King of Prussia became Emperor of a united Germany, that arrangement was patently no longer compatible with German prestige.

The only remnant of the "union" of the two Churches is the Protestant cemetery on Mount Zion.

A Jerusalem Evangelical Associaton had been formed in Berlin in 1852 to help local members of that Church. In the same year, Jerusalem's first German pastor, Propst Friedrich Valentiner, was dispatched to Jerusalem to assist Bishop Gobat in his work. The Association was instrumental in furthering the development of German-sponsored institutions. An Arab community was founded in Beit Jala and a church was built there in 1886; a primary school for boys had been built in 1870, followed by the establishment of a girls' school in 1889. In addition, an Arab primary school was run by the Jerusalem Association in Hebron.

The community, founded by Samuel Mueller in Bethlehem in 1861, was able to consecrate its Christmas Church in 1893. The Association also established two primary schools—one for boys and one for girls—in Bethlehem where the Chrischona Brothers had been active since 1856.

The Jerusalem Evangelical Foundation was created by Emperor William II in 1888; it inherited funds left behind by the Lutheran Church in Jerusalem following the dissolution of its "partnership" with the Anglican Church. The Foundation built schools, a residence for the "Provost" of Jerusalem and a Church of the Redeemer, the latter opened in 1898 by William II.[17]

The Carmel Mission was active in Haifa and in the northern sector of the Holy Land. Its founders, Martin Bleich and Johannes Seitz, initially had ideological links with the "Temple Movement", but these were soon severed. In 1887, Martin Bleich opened a hospice on Mount Carmel in a building purchased from the Carmelite monks. The hospice was transferred to a larger building in 1904, and in that year Pastor Martin Schneider joined the Carmel Mission. Three Mission schools were inaugurated in Haifa: on Mount Carmel and in the western and eastern sectors of the town, respectively. School projects also were initiated in Acre and in the village of Bassa on the Lebanese border.

The Lutheran Church also opened further classrooms in the village of Beit Sahour near Bethlehem in 1901.

A large Lutheran complex came into being in Jaffa: the construction of the Immanuel Church, begun in 1901, was completed in 1904; three plots away, a large house was put up as a home for the pastor and a school for the children of German citizens of the area.

By general consent, in site and splendor, the Augusta Victoria Stiftung on Mount Scopus, including the Church of the Ascension, transcends all German establishments in the Holy Land; it was a strange quirk of history that made it the headquarters of Allenby's Egyptian Expeditionary Force in the First World War and, in succession, of the British Military Administration of Occupied Enemy Territory (South) and finally of the Mandatory Administration of Palestine and official residence of the High Commissioner during the early years of the Mandate.

---

17) After World War I, the Berlin Foundation, formerly connected with Emperor William II, came under the supervision of the Evangelical Church of Germany.

Other Protestant Churches

In 1866, one hundred and fifty-three followers of the *Church of the Messiah*, an American millenarian sect led by George Jones Adams, settled in the Holy Land to await the Second Advent of Jesus. The initiative proved disastrous and those who survived returned to America in 1868. The land they had bought near Jaffa, and the huts which they had occupied during their brief stay were later bought by the German Templers.

In the mid-nineteenth century, a pietistic movement began in Wuerttemberg in South Germany, seceding from the Lutheran Church. The movement called itself "Der Tempel" (The Temple) and its members called themselves *"The Templers"*, according to the reference in Ephesians 2:21.[18] The leaders of the movement, Christoff Hoffman and George David Hardegg, finding themselves persecuted, resolved to settle with their followers in the Holy Land and await the Second Coming of Jesus. In 1868, after unsuccessful attempts to put down permanent roots in the Holy Land, several families finally realized their aim. Industrious farmers and craftsmen, the Templers founded agricultural villages and built suburbs of their own in the principal cities which contributed much to the progress and modernization of the Holy Land.

The first settlement was Sarona near Jaffa, established on landed property purchased in 1871. The agricultural colony of Wilhelma, near Lydda, named after Emperor Wilhelm II, was founded in 1902. This was followed by Waldheim (1906) and Bethlehem (1907), both in Galilee. The inhabitants of the two latter settlements opted for reunion with the Lutheran Church from which the "Temple movement" had split in Wuerttemberg. In Jerusalem, Haifa and Jaffa, the neighborhoods founded by the Templers are still known as the "German colonies." Such a Jerusalem suburb, which was founded in 1873, carried the biblical name Rephaim. In 1914, the Templers in the Holy Land numbered approximately 2,200.

The Church of Scotland first began to interest itself in missionary work in the Holy Land in 1839. It was the outcome of a visit by a commission of inquiry to Palestine that year. As the Church of England had begun its proselytizing activities in Judea, the members of the Scottish commission suggested that the work of

---

18) There is no connection with the Order of the Templars of the time of the Kingdom of Jerusalem.

their Church be confined to the Galilee. Consequently, missionary work among the Jews was initiated in Safed in 1852 but had later to be given up because of the difficult conditions prevailing.

Eleven years later, in 1863, a Scotswoman by the name of Miss Jane Warner-Arnott established a small mission for girls in rented premises in Jaffa.[19] The mission was named Tabitha, and was taken from Acts 9:36 where it is written that Tabitha (or Dorcas) was a disciple who had lived in Jaffa and had performed good deeds for the poor. When she died, Peter brought her back to life. The mission was enlarged in 1875 when a boarding-school and later a day-school were established outside the city walls. When Miss Arnott died in 1911, she left the school to the Church of Scotland.[20]

Meanwhile, other institutions—a clinic and a hospital—were opening in Jaffa under the supervision of Miss Morgan, a Mildmay deaconess.

In 1885, Dr. David Watt Torrance embarked upon his pioneering medical work in Tiberias, in what, at that juncture, was virtually a medical vacuum. He began by renting a small house but eventually managed to collect the funds necessary for a hospital. This building, situated on the shores of the Sea of Galilee, was formally inaugurated on the first of January 1894. A maternity-ward was added in 1912.

Besides its medical work, the Church of Scotland also launched educational activities in Tiberias with the opening of a small school for girls in 1888, followed by a school for boys. Two small schools, one for boys and one for girls, were likewise opened in Safed. At about the same time, the Edinburgh Medical Missionary Society (EMMS) began work in Nazareth. The hillside on which the EMMS hospital was built in 1914 had been purchased by the Church Missionary Society despite the difficulty experienced by Christians wanting to purchase plots in the Holy Land. The edifice was used by the Turkish army during the First World War and extensive restoration was necessary before the dedication in 1924. In the 1960's, the hospital was enlarged and a school for nurses was added.

At the turn of the nineteenth century, medical work was begun in Hebron by the Mildmay deaconesses and in due course a hospital was built. This was taken over by the Church of Scotland,

19) The venture started with fourteen girls and enrolment soon rose to 50.
20) In the school year 1984–1985 there were 300 pupils at Tabitha School.

which in 1922 transferred it to the Church Missionary Society, a body connected with the Anglican Church. With the outbreak of the First World War, the educational and medical work of the Church of Scotland in Galilee was disrupted, since most of the missionary workers being enemy subjects were forced to leave the country.

The Christian and Missionary Alliance, an evangelistic and missionary movement founded in the United States, started its work in Jerusalem in 1889, and about twenty years later began missionary activity in Beersheba, which was then a townlet inhabited solely by Arabs. The Mission also maintained a center in Haifa, and was active in a number of villages and towns.

The American Friends (Quakers) opened a girls' school in 1869 in Ramallah and a boys' school thirty years later. Both schools are still operative.

The Seventh-Day Adventists established a clinic in Jaffa in 1900.

The Assemblies of God, a religious sect belonging to the Pentecostal group, started work among the Arabs in Jerusalem and bought a building in the city. Miss E. Brown, a missionary connected with the Assemblies, had come to the country in 1908.

The Moravian Church devoted itself to the healing of lepers, a vocation considered particulary worthy in the Holy Land. A leper house dedicated to St. Lazarus had existed in Jerusalem at the time of the Crusaders in Jerusalem, but by the middle of the nineteenth century it had disappeared and lepers were huddled together in hovels outside the city walls. Pilgrims visiting the city were shocked by these conditions.

In 1867, a home for lepers called "Jesushilfe" was set up in Jerusalem, under the supervision of the brethren of the "Herrenhut Community."[21] As numbers grew, responsibility was handed over to the Moravian Church, which in 1887 built a leper house on a plot of land in Katamon, just outside of Jerusalem. The construction was sponsored by the German Baroness Keffenbrink-Ascheranden; nursing care was entrusted to the "Deaconesses of Emmaus" from Niesky in Saxonia, Germany.

In 1881, Horatio Gates Spafford of Chicago and his wife Anne arrived in the Holy Land, seeking peace and solace in the wake of a series of numbing personal tragedies. They came to Jerusalem, accompanied by several other Americans, and founded the

---

21) The German branch of the Moravian Church is called "Herrenhuter Bürgergemeinde" (Herrenhut is a locality in Saxonia).

"American Colony", a name which probably echoed the precedent of the German "colony" there. Their aim was to render Christian service to the needy of Jerusalem and of all Palestine, without distinction of race or creed. Before long, constructive and successful commercial enterprise went, quite legitimately, with praiseworthy social voluntary works. In 1899, the group moved its premises from the Old City of Jerusalem to a former Pasha's palace outside the City walls, and this new location, together with several smaller adjoining buildings, was to become the American Colony Hotel which continued to serve as a base for charitable works. The efforts of Horatio and Anne Spafford were continued by their daughter, Bertha Spafford Vester, and her sons: counted among their undertakings were the American Colony Hotel and the Spafford Memorial Childrens' Hospital, founded in 1952 and supported by a committee in New York City, the American Colony Charities Association.

CATHOLICS

The Latin Church

After a gap of half a millennium and more, the Latin Patriarchate was re-installed in the Holy Land on July 23, 1847 by the apostolic letter, "Nulla celebrior", of Pope Pius IX, who was gravely troubled by the proselytising of Protestant Churches among the Christians of Palestine and by the appearance of a Protestant Bishop in Jerusalem. It should be noted that, whereas the installation of a Greek or Armenian Patriarch required a formal *bérat* of investiture from the Sultan, there was no such stipulation in the case of a Latin Patriarch. The Turkish authorities acquiesced in such appointments and the successive Governments of the Holy Land likewise tacitly accepted the Vatican nominees.[22]

The first resident Patriarch was Monsignor Joseph Valerga.[23] The Greek Orthodox Patriarch took instinctive exception, and not all Catholic circles were particularly enthusiastic. The Greek

---

22) It should be remembered, in this context of jurisdictional power, that the Latin Patriarch carries a purely honorary title of historical meaning, giving the incumbent precedence over Primates, Archbishops and Bishops. (See: article 438 of the new Canon Law and art. 271 of the Canon Law of the year 1917.)
23) From 1291 until 1847 there were only titular Patriarchs of Jerusalem.

Catholic Patriarch of Antioch, Maximos III Mazlum, who bore the titles of Patriarch both of Antioch and of Alexandria and Jerusalem, was none too happy about this development either. He claimed jurisdiction over all Catholics in the Middle East and felt no need for the appointment of an independent Latin Patriarchate to look after the devotional requirements of, to quote Latin sources themselves, no more than four thousand adherents. It certainly was not fortuitous that the Greek Catholic Patriarch built his own cathedral-church in Jerusalem in 1848 and a year later, held the first Greek Catholic Synod in the Holy City instead of in Ein Taraz (Lebanon) where he had his residence.

The view that the Latin Patriarch is a redundant duplication was upheld by the Greek Catholic Melkite Patriarch Maximos IV Sayegh, who passed away in 1967. His successor, Maximos V Hakim, has not relinquished this view.

The Franciscan Fathers, hitherto the guardians of Latin interests, were also put out by the appointment being that the Custos of the Holy Land, by virtue of exceptional prerogatives, wields an authority which in certain respects matches that of a Bishop, and a resurrected Latin Patriarchate was likely to entail friction and collisions of competence. Instruction had, therefore, to be given by the Holy See, in the decree "Licet" on September 9, 1851, to delimit the prerogatives of the Patriarch and the Custos. *Ad hoc* intervention by the Holy See, however, continued to be necessary to clarify the situation. Only on April 12, 1923, was a final settlement reached and a *modus vivendi* worked out, demarcating the respective jurisdictions. According to this agreement, the Franciscans cannot vindicate a sanctuary lost by them without the authorization of the Congregation of Propaganda Fide, nor initiate a major restoration in a Holy Place without the approval of the Patriarch.

One of the means employed to remove or to narrow this area of sensitivity was the appointment of a Franciscan monk to the Patriarchal See, in spite of the fact that only secular clergy are ordinarily employed there. This was the case of the third Patriarch, Monsignor Louis Piavi, formerly a Franciscan, and in latter years, by the appointment of Monsignor Alberto Gori who, besides being a Franciscan, was also a former Custos. Moreover, the former Apostolic Delegate of "Jerusalem and Palestine", Monsignor Augustin Sepinsky, was chosen in 1966 from the Franciscan Order and was a former Superior-General of this Order. Was this pure chance, or a new concession to the ancient rights of the Franciscan Friars in the Holy Land? Monsignor Valerga (1847–1872) was a man of boundless activity, educational and missionary. In 1853, he opened the first Latin mission station in the village of Beit Jala, now a townlet near Bethlehem, and entrusted the work to Dom Jean Maritaine. The Christians of Beit Jala were at that time solely of Greek Orthodox persuasion, although several had requested a Latin priest because of the higher standards of the Latin clergy and the benefits anticipated from the Latin educational and charitable institutions. Initially, the Latin Patriarch had to withstand the fierce opposition of the Orthodox clergy, who enjoyed the support of the Turkish authorities, but finally, after intervention by the French Consul of Jerusalem, Paul Emil Botta, and the French Ambassador in Constantinople, Valerga was issued a *firman* authorizing him to build a church and mission in Beit Jala. In the years that followed, he succeeded in opening mission stations in Gifneh (1855), Lydda (1856), Ramallah (1856), Birzeit (1859), Taibe (1859), Beit Sahour (1859), Rafidiyah (1856), Yafie (1866) and Nablus (1860), and in two villages in Trans-Jordan.

To set his diocese on a sound basis, Valerga had to create an indigenous clergy or at least one of locally educated priests. In 1853, he opened a seminary in Jerusalem which was later transferred to Beit Jala, where, in 1936, it moved into premises specially built for it. The seminary underwent expansion in the years 1956–1959, with the financial assistance of the Order of the Holy Sepulchre.

Patriarch Valerga prudently enlisted the cooperation of pioneer monks and nuns; to the Franciscans and the Carmelites were now added, in response to his call, the Sisters of St. Joseph of the Apparition (1848), the Sisters of Our Lady of Nazareth (1854), and the Sisters of Our Lady of Sion (1858). In the last year of his Patriarchate, Patriarch Valerga consecrated the Cathedral of the Latin Patriarchate, to fill a need due to the fact that the Church of the Holy Sepulchre, which is the Cathedral of the Latin Patriarch, is shared by several denominations and so, not always available for Latin ceremonies.

The second Patriarch was Monsignor Vincent Bracco (1872–1889), who had served as Auxiliary Bishop to Patriarch Valerga. He succeeded in doubling the number of missions run directly by the Patriarchate by means of establishments in Ain Arik (1882),

Zebabdeh (1883), Reneh (1878), Shfaram (1879), Gaza (1881) and Cana (1881) and several locations in Trans-Jordan. During the same period, other religious Orders and Congregations opened schools, orphanages and hospitals, clinics and hospices for pilgrims; among them the Brothers of the Christian Schools (1887), the Fathers of Sion (1884),[24] the White Fathers (1878), the Fathers of the Holy Heart of Bétharram (1879), the Dominicans (1884), the Assumptionists (1887), the Charitable Brothers of St. John of God (1879),[25] the Religious of Mary Reparatrix (1888), the Cloistered Carmelite Nuns (1873), the Poor Sisters of St. Claire (1884), the Daughters of Charity of St. Vincent of Paul (1886), and the Sisters of St. Charles Borromeus (1887). Monsignor Bracco was also instrumental in forming in 1880 a new, purely indigenous congregation, the Sisters of the Rosary. This congregation grew in numbers and good works in succeeding years and at present is in charge of the girls' schools of the Patriarchate. Among the religious Orders invited by Monsignor Bracco were the Dominican Fathers who, in 1884, established the Biblical and Archaeological School in their Monastery of St. Stephen in Jerusalem, a School which has acquired an international reputation.

The third Patriarch, Monsignor Louis Piavi (1889–1905), worked to consolidate the existing missions, building churches, presbyteries and schools. Among the churches was the Basilica of Emmaus, consecrated in 1902 by Cardinal Andreas Ferrari, Archbishop of Milan. But the foundation of new missions was precluded by the promulgation, in 1894, of the famous Encyclical "Orientalium ecclesiarum dignitas", which brought to a halt proselytizing by Roman Catholics among the followers of Eastern Churches and entrusted their conversion to the Uniate Churches.

---

24) A religious Order established by Alphonse Marie Ratisbonne, a converted Jew. He bought an extensive plot in Jerusalem, on which a large monastery was built and named after him. In 1935, a 99-year lease was concluded between Jewish contractors and the Fathers of Sion concerning landed property in the vicinity of the monastery. The land now forms part of the present-day Rehavia Quarter of Jerusalem and in the year 2034, the buildings erected on it may become the property of the Fathers of Sion.

25) The Brothers of St. John of God were invited by Count B. Caboga, Austrian consul general in the Holy Land, to join a newly established hospice at Tantur. In 1882, a group of Brothers went to Nazareth and built a hospital there. Inaugurated in 1884, it was initially an Austrian venture under the patronage of the Austrian Emperor. Since 1957, it has been run by Brothers from an Italian branch of the Order. The hospital, now modernized and enlarged, is named after the Holy Family.

In the time of Monsignor Piavi, a number of new communities began to be active in the Holy Land: the Trappists settled in Latrun (1890), the Discalced Carmelite Nuns in Haifa (1892), the German Lazarists (1890), the Salesians (1891), the Benedictine Nuns of Calvary (1896) and the French Benedictines (1899) all in Jerusalem; the Passionists in Bethany (1903); the French Lazarists (1904) and the Benedictines of Beuron (1906) in Jerusalem; and the Sisters of the Hortus Conclusus in Ortas near Bethlehem (1901).[26]

The fourth Patriarch was Monsignor Philip Camassei (1907–1919), who founded the Mission of Rameh (1912) and three others in Trans-Jordan. During his term, several more communities were installed in the Holy Land: the Tertiary Carmelites (1907) and the Carmelites of St. Joseph (1914) in Haifa; and the Sisters of Cottolengo (1914) and the Sisters of Ivrea (1919) in Jerusalem.

Of all the religious Orders and Congregations, the Franciscan Custody of the Holy Land was especially reputed for its prolific activity. The following religious edifices went up under its auspices in the second half of the nineteenth century and at the beginning of the twentieth: monasteries and hospices in Emmaus (1861), in Tiberias (1872), on Mount Tabor (1873), Cana (1878), Haifa (1891), Capernaum (1905), Bethphage (1906) and the Church of St. Saviour (1882–1885) in Jerusalem.

But when the Holy Land became a theatre of operations in the First World War, the consequences were disastrous for the religious communities, many of which were closed down and their buildings requisitioned by the Turkish army. The Patriarch himself was exiled on November 24, 1917, and did not return until November 3, 1918.

France did not fail in its role of defender of Catholic interests in the Holy Land even during the period of estrangement between Church and State on the national level. Besides its dismay at the development of the Protestant establishment, France was greatly perturbed by the steady expansion of Russian Orthodox institutions. It is no coincidence that, in the immediate proximity of the Russian compound, monumental edifices were built, such as Notre Dame de France and Saint Louis Hospital, nor that the initiative for such ventures came from a French Catholic, Count Amédé de Piellat. Other French-sponsored buildings that went up

---

26) In 1894, Bishop Mariano Soler of Montevideo bought a plot there and built a convent for the Sisters of St. Mary of the Hortus Conclusus.

during the last decades of Ottoman rule in the Holy Land were the Ratisbonne Monastery and the Dominican Ecole Biblique et Archéologique Française. The churches which are national French property include St. Anne's in Jerusalem and the Church of St. Saviour at Abu-Gosh, just west of the city. The latter became French property in 1873 through the endeavors of the Marquis de Vogüe, French Ambassador at the Porte.

France, with its traditional role as protector of Latin interests, was not alone in such matters. There were other nations that sought to reinforce a Catholic presence in the Holy Land.

Germany, for example, saw to promoting not only its Protestant establishments, but Catholic institutions as well. "Das Deutsche Verband fuer das Heilige Land" (The German Association for the Holy Land) was founded in 1855. To this day, the seat of the Association is in Cologne, and that city's Archbishop serves as the Association's President.

Among the monasteries, churches and institutions created and sponsored by the Association are the Dormition Church and Abbey on Mount Zion in Jerusalem.[27] They were built on a plot donated in 1898 by Sultan Abdul Hamid to the Emperor William II. Other institutions under the aegis of the Association are the Schmidt Girls' School in Jerusalem[28], the church and monastery at Tabgha at the shores of the Lake of Galilee and the Home for the Aged in Qubeibe.

The Association also owns a hospice and extensive landed property on the shore of the Lake of Galilee, near Tabgha. During the 1948 Israel War of Independence, the Benedictine Fathers, who held the hospice on behalf of the Association, were forced to evacuate the hospice and its environs for security reasons. When the border with Syria was relocated further east, following the Six-Day War in 1967, the Association could claim that security was no longer a factor and that the German Catholic property should be returned to its legal owners. Agreement on this was reached early in 1982.

27) Since 1951, the Dormition Abbey has come directly under the aegis of the Holy See.

28) During the Second World War, the building constructed in 1886 in West Jerusalem, and which first housed the Schmidt Girls' School was placed in the care of the Custodian of Enemy Property; it never returned to its German owners. A new school building was put up by the Association in East Jerusalem, opposite Damascus Gate. A pilgrim hospice, "Paulushaus", was also built nearby.

Uniate Catholics

The Greek Catholic Melkite Church. In the first half of the eighteenth century, one could discern a sizeable separatist movement in the Greek Orthodox Church in Syria and Lebanon, its aim being union with the Catholic Church. So Greek Catholic congregations, with their own priests were formed, and these independent Catholic congregations were headed since 1724 by their own Patriarch. This separatist movement was strongly resisted by the long-established Greek Orthodox Church, which, as the only officially recognized community, could count on Ottoman backing.

Until 1772, the Greek Catholics living in the vicinity of the Patriarchate of Jerusalem, mostly immigrants from Lebanon and Syria, were under the spiritual aegis of the Franciscans. In 1773, Pope Clemens XIV gave the Patriarch of Antioch Theodosios V jurisdiction over Greek Catholics in the Patriarchates of Jerusalem and Alexandria (Decree of the Congregation of Propaganda Fide, July13, 1773).

Acre and Nazareth, and the whole territory of Galilee, were then under the ecclesiastical jurisdiction of Tyre and Sidon in Lebanon. As the number of Greek Catholics in the area had risen considerably, an independent Greek Catholic bishopric was established, and the first incumbent was Bishop Makarios Oujami (1752–1763). As the young community succeeded in attracting more and more proselytes from the Orthodox Church, it had to withstand the fiercest reactions from Orthodox quarters. It was only in 1804 that Bishop Makarios Nahas could establish his residence in Acre. In 1838, finally, the Greek Catholic Patriarch of Antioch, Maximos III Mazlum, and his community were granted recognition by Sultan Mahmoud II. At about the same time, Pope Gregory XVI bestowed on Maximos the supplementary title of Alexandria and of Jerusalem, but *ad personam*, with no right of transmission to his successors. The title was later, however, extended *ad personam* to his successors.

Once Jerusalem came under his jurisdiction, Mazlum began to dream of building a patriarchal residence in the Holy City and transferring to it the Greek Catholic Seminary of Ain-Taraz (Lebanon). Buying a plot in Jerusalem near the Jaffa Gate, he built a church dedicated to the "Annunciation", and a residence (1848). The residence is still the seat of the Greek Catholic Patriarchal Vicar of Jerusalem. In 1849, Mazlum held a council of Greek Catholic Bishops in Jerusalem.

The Greek Catholics were still few in number in Jerusalem and in the rest of Judea, but much more numerous in Acre and in Galilee where the autonomous bishopric had been established. Among the twelve Bishops who subsequently ministered to the diocese of Acre, three own particular distinction, and were raised to the dignity of Patriarch of Antioch.

The nineteenth century saw the Greek Catholics grow steadily in numbers. Their proselytizing was even more successful after the promulgation in 1894 of the Encyclical "Orientalium ecclesiarum dignitas", in which, as we noted, Pope Leo XIII banned missionary work by the Latin Church among the followers of the Eastern Churches and assigned the task to the Uniate Churches. In 1846, the Greek Catholic Patriarch appointed a Patriarchal Vicar in Jerusalem, in charge of Judea and Samaria. In the second half of the nineteenth century, the Greek Catholic Church was able to establish small congregations in the area administered by the Vicariate and built churches in Bethlehem, Beit Sahour, Beit Jala, Ramallah, Taibe, Bir Zeit, Jaffa, Ramla and Lydda.

A very important event in the development of the community was the opening of a Greek Catholic Melkite seminary in Jerusalem to train its clergy. It was built in 1882, near the Church of St. Anne, and enlarged in 1896. The Church of St. Anne was a Crusader building on the traditional site of the birthplace of the Virgin Mary, erected during the reign of Baldwin I, and Sultan Salah ed-Din had converted it in 1192 into the Moslem religious school "Salahieh", but it was presented by Sultan Abdul Madjid to Napoleon III (1859), in recognition of the help extended by France to Turkey during the Crimean War. That the seminary could be opened in buildings erected near the church, was due to the joint endeavors of Cardinal Charles Martial Lavigérie and the Greek Catholic Patriarch Gregory II Youssef. The training of seminarists was put in charge of the learned White Fathers. In November 1914, after the outbreak of the First World War, the seminary was confiscated by the Turkish authorities and for three years, used as a Koranic school. After the interruption of World War I, St. Anne was again the seat of a Greek Catholic seminary, and many Archbishops and priests serving in the Middle East were trained there.[29]

---

29) Following the reunification of Jerusalem in 1967, the seminary was transferred to Larissa (Lebanon). At present, groups of White Fathers come to the restored premises of St. Anne Seminary for lectures and retreat sessions. St. Anne also houses the offices of the journal *Proche Orient Chrétien* and a center for

In 1884, the Greek Catholics, whom the *status quo* had barred from a share in the major Holy Places, acquired the sanctuary of the Veronica, the Sixth Station in the Via Dolorosa. The site underwent radical restoration. The Little Sisters of Jesus have their regional headquarters there.

In Nazareth, the Greek Catholics own a church built in 1741, called "Madrasad Al-Masihi." According to Christian tradition, it stands on the site of the synagogue where Jesus preached and expounded verses from the Book of Isaiah. In Nazareth, the Greek Catholic Church originated in 1741 as the result of a disagreement between two Orthodox priests. One of them, named Gabriel Handousi, adopted Catholicism and was followed by 220 friends and members of his family. Expelled from Nazareth, they moved to Safed and did not return until 1770. The parish church of the Greek Catholic community in Nazareth was built over a hundred years later, in 1887. In Tiberias, a church was put up in 1884.

The Maronite Church. Most of the Maronite community in the Holy Land was concentrated in Galilee, near the Lebanese border; immigration from the Lebanon gave rise to small communities in Acre, Nazareth and Haifa. A small community also developed in Jaffa where, in 1857, a Maronite Order bought land for the later construction of a church and a presbytery. A Maronite Patriarchal Vicariate was established in Jerusalem in 1895.

The Syrian Catholic Church. A Uniate Syrian Church had been formed of Syrian Orthodox at the end of the seventeenth century.

The Syrian Catholic Church, however, was only recognized as an independent community within the Ottoman Empire in 1845. At the end of that century, Monsignor Moussa Khouri Sarkis purchased a plot near the Damascus Gate where, in 1901, he built a chapel, the residence of the Patriarchal Vicar, and a hospice.

In 1903, Pope Leo XIII, anxious to foster the development of the Uniate Churches, recommended the establishment of a Syrian Catholic seminary in Jerusalem. This was initiated in a building on the Mount of Olives, and the instruction was entrusted to the French Benedictine Fathers. From 1930 to 1953 their seminary was for junior pupils only.

African clergy, not functioning at present.

The Armenian Catholic Church. The Armenian Catholic Church, whose origins can be traced to the year 1741, has had a representative in Jerusalem since 1855. For the first twelve years, the incumbent was an Armenian Catholic Bishop. Later, Jerusalem became the seat of a Vicar-General of the Armenian Catholic Patriarch of Cilicia, who resides in Lebanon. The first Vicar was Reverend Seropè Tavitian, who had to take up residence in the Latin Patriarchate until the year 1885, when a residence was established for him on a plot that had been purchased in 1856 with the financial assistance of a wealthy Armenian Catholic, Anton Bey Missirli. A tradition linked this site with a thirteenth-century church built over the ruins of a Byzantine shrine which had marked the site of the Third Station of the Via Dolorosa. In 1897, a chapel was built on this spot.

In 1877, the Armenian Catholic Vicar, Father Tavitian, was succeeded by Father Joachim Toumayan, who four years following this date discovered the mosaic floor which depicted a pair of sandals. It was concluded from this find that the site was none other than that of the Fourth Station of the Via Dolorosa, and a chapel was built there to enshrine this memory. The year 1905 saw the consecration of a church, encompassing the traditional sites of both stations.

The Chaldean Catholic Church. The origin of this community is in Iraq, where in the middle of the sixteenth century, a number of members of the Nestorian community sought to unite with the Catholic Church.

Since 1908, the Chaldeans in the Holy Land have had a Patriarchal Vicar representing the Patriarch of Babylon, who has his seat in Baghdad. The first nominee was Bishop Itzkhak Khudabakhsh, who lived in Latin monasteries and worshipped in Latin churches, having no place of his own.

MONOPHYSITES

The Armenian Orthodox Church

The presence of the Armenian Church in the Holy Land goes back to the very beginnings of the Christian era, as ruins of churches and mosaics from Byzantine times attest.[30]

In the first centuries, Armenian monks lived together with Greek monks in the famous "lauras."[31] Like the Greeks, the Armenians suffered from the Persian and later from the Arab invasion. At the time of the Arab conquest, there is mention of a Bishop Abraham (638–669), who stood up for the rights of the Armenians in the Holy Places. Armenian historians name twenty-one Armenian Bishops of Jerusalem, who held office during the Arab period and until the end of the Crusader Kingdom; the incumbents had to face the same difficulties as afflicted the other Orthodox communities. In certain respects, however, their situation was better under the Crusaders owing to the fact that the Armenian Kingdom of Cilicia maintained friendly relations with the Kingdom of Jerusalem. A number of Armenian kings travelled to Jerusalem and visited the Holy Places. It was the Armenian King Hethoun I of Cilicia, on his visit to the Holy Land in 1227, who ordered the erection of an interior door of timber in the Church of the Nativity in Bethlehem. Intermarriage with Crusader families was common.[32]

Patriarch Sarkis (Sergius), who was in office in 1311, played a significant role in preserving the independence of the Patriarchate when the Holy Land came under Mamluk rule. He is referred to, by non-Armenian historians, as the first Armenian Patriarch of Jerusalem.

At the beginning of the Ottoman period, the Armenian Patri-

---

30) The mosaics in the Russian monastery on the Mount of Olives are an eloquent example of the beauty of the Armenian establishments of the first centuries of the Christian era. The mosaics belonged to the Armenian St. Garabed Monastery of Banta which stood on the present site of the Russian Church of the Ascension. The mosaics were discovered in 1868 and 1893. Another outstanding example of Armenian mosaic is that of the Polyeucte Monastery near Damascus Gate in Jerusalem. It is one of the most ancient Armenian inscriptions, bespeaking the earliest instance of a memorial to the "Unknown Soldier": "For the salvation of those Armenians who fell and whose names are only known to God." This mosaic was discovered in 1894.

31) Euthymios, founder of the first Laura, was an Armenian of Melitene (now Malatya in Asia Minor). The Armenian historian Vartabed Anastasios, who visited the Holy Land in 634 before the Arab conquest, relates that he found seventy Armenian monasteries in and around Jerusalem. Although this might be a somewhat exaggerated account, it does at least give evidence of a remarkable Armenian presence in the Holy Land.

32) Arda, wife of Baldwin I, and Morphia, wife of Baldwin II, were of Armenian stock. Queen Melisanda's mother was an Armenian princess and the Queen's upbringing bore a strong Armenian imprint.

131

arch was recognized by Sultan Selim as head of the other Mono-physite Churches. The start of the seventeenth century found the Armenian Patriarchate in critical financial straits, but thanks to the efforts of Patriarch Krikor (Gregory) Baronder (1613–1645) and the generosity of the Armenian people the world over, not only were the monetary problems overcome, but important restorations could be carried out in the churches and the buildings of the Patri-archate. Indeed, almost half of the present residential quarters of the Armenian monastery were built during Krikor's term. In 1667, during the Patriarchate of Yeghiazar, a bishopric was estab-lished in Bethlehem. The following two centuries were vexed by a protracted dispute between the Armenians and the Greek Orthodox over the Monastery of St. James: not until 1813 was it settled in fa-vor of the Armenians, by an edict of Sultan Mahmoud II.

Gregory the Chainbearer (1717–1749) was a Patriarch of great distinction. In his time, the Patriarchate was again deeply in debt, as a result of bribes and heavy taxes exacted by the Turks. Gre-gory decided to wear an iron chain around his neck and to travel through Armenia, seeking contributions. He was most successful and besides settling the debts of the Patriarchate, was able to re-store the Armenian churches in Jerusalem, especially the Church of the Archangels (the House of Annas).

In 1813, the Armenians obtained from the Sultan an *Iradè* (written decree), giving them the right to hold daily religious ser-vices in the Church of the Tomb of the Virgin in Gethsemane, and to hold one of the keys of the Basilica of the Nativity in Bethlehem, which enabled them to conduct religious services every day in the Grotto of the Nativity. A *firman* of the year 1827 confirmed the Armenians in their possession of one-third of the Basilica of the Holy Sepulchre.

In the nineteenth century, there was a considerable expansion in the educational activities of the Patriarchate. In 1833, a print-ing press was founded which, since the year 1866, prints the monthly review "Sion." This press provides Armenian liturgical and ritual books to Armenian churches all over the world.

Through the efforts of Patriarch Zacharias, a theological sem-inary was founded in 1843, and in 1863, the Kayaniantz School—the first girls' school in Jerusalem—was established. By the close of the nineteenth century, the Armenians had purchased large plots outside the walls of the Old City of Jerusalem and the build-ings later constructed there still earn a considerable income for the Armenian Patriarchate.

Prior to 1863, the members of the Fraternity of St. James (which constitutes the Patriarchate) used to submit the name of the person elected by them as Patriarch directly to the Sultan in Constantinople. In 1862, the Armenian National Assembly promulgated a new constitution concerning election of the Patriarch, which was ratified by a *bérat* of the Sultan on March 14, 1863, in which the position of the Patriarch vis-à-vis the Ottoman authorities was determined. The election of Patriarch Yesayi Garabedian was confirmed in 1864 accordingly.

In March 1888, the constitution was amended to provide for two lists of candidates—one of seven, and the other of three taken from the list of seven—to be chosen by the General Assembly of the Fraternity of Jerusalem. These lists were sent to Constantinople, and the General Assembly there selected the Patriarch, to be confirmed by the Sultan.

In 1910, upon the death of Patriarch Haroutioun Vehabedian, the See of Jerusalem remained vacant under a *locum tenens* until the outbreak of the First World War. It was then that the Turkish authorities deported the Catholicos of Cilicia, Sahac (Isaac) from Cis (near Adana) to Syria, and subsequently brought him to Jerusalem and imposed him upon the congregation of St. James as the Catholicos of all the Armenians. In 1917, the Catholicos was taken by the Turks to Damascus, along with all the ecclesiastical heads of Jerusalem. This was only one—and a minor— example of the inhuman policy pursued against the Armenian minority, which claimed more than a million innocent victims.

After the war, Patriarch Sahag paid a short visit to Jerusalem, but when the armistice was signed between Great Britain and Turkey, he relinquished the title thrust upon him by the Turks and reverted to his former rank of Catholicos of Cilicia.

The Syrian Orthodox (Jacobite) Church

This is one of the oldest, if not the very oldest, of the Christian Churches in Jerusalem. The liturgical language of the Syrian community is still the ancient Syriac, closely akin to the Aramaic spoken by the Jews at the time of the Second Temple.

The first Bishop of the community is said to have been Mark, who was originally from Caesarea, and whose episcopate might have begun during the first half of the second century, following the founding of Aelia Capitolina.

133

According to Syrian Orthodox tradition, the Church and Monastery of St. Mark in Jerusalem were built over the ruins of the site of the Last Supper. The Syrian Orthodox likewise place important events linked by other Christian denominations with the Coenaculum on Mount Zion at this site. If there is no proof of a first-century church on the site of St. Mark's, evidence is forthcoming for the fifth or sixth century in an Aramaic inscription and in the ruins of Byzantine buildings within the area of the monastery.

Although Greek was the language of prayer of the upper classes during the first centuries in the Middle East, and of the Greek enclaves within the territory of Palestine, there is no doubt that Syriac was also used by the Church, being the speech of the majority of the population. When Abbess Aetheria made her pilgrimage to the Holy Land in 385, she noted that the native Syriac was also used at the ceremonies in the Holy Sepulchre. The presence in the Holy Sepulchre of clergy officiating in Syriac was especially emphasized by Latin quarters which were interested, by this means, to diminish the prestige of the Greek Orthodox Church, who were their most formidable rival in the battle for the Holy Places.

The Council of Chalcedon in 451 led to an open rift between the Greek Orthodox Church and several national Churches that had adopted the Monophysite creed; the Syrian Church was among the adherents of Monophysitism. In the sixth century, it underwent reorganization and development, thanks to the indefatigable activity of Jacob Baradai, who was under the protection of Empress Theodora, wife of Justinian I, and it was in recognition of his work that the Syrian Church was also called the Jacobite.

During the reign of Harun al-Rashid, all the newly built churches were destroyed. Charlemagne's intervention, though intended to assist Western Christians, was also beneficial to the Syrians.

From 793 until 1099 there were Syrian Orthodox Bishops in Jerusalem and in Tiberias. In the twelfth century, Syrian Orthodox Patriarch Michael of Antioch records a long list of Syrian Archbishops who served in Jerusalem, and thirteen Archbishops who served in Tiberias. Their names are recorded as Isaac, Severus, Gabriel, etc., and it is possible that they were born outside the Holy Land.[33] Syrians were allowed to worship in the Holy Places during the Crusader period, following the intercession of Patriarch Michael of Antioch who visited Jerusalem three times between 1166 and 1178. Syrians obtained similar privileges from Salah ed-Din in 1187, and Syrian Bishops are said to have been residing in Jerusalem since the mid-twelfth century.

Bishop Ignatios III is said to have been the first to take up residence in the Monastery of St. Mark, in the year 1471. In 1718, the Syrian Bishop of Jerusalem, Gregorios Shimon, restored the ancient monastery, and his successor, Bishop Abd el-Ahad Ben Panah, took heed for the library where ancient manuscripts and valuable icons are kept. Bishop Gregorios Georgios el-Halabi and Bishop Bishara, who both lived during the eighteenth century, also enlarged and beautified the church and the monastery.

The Syrian Church, although its membership is small, claims our attention both by virtue of its rich history, which extends back to the dawn of Christianity, and for its present-day share in the Holy Places.

The Syrians have the right to celebrate in the Holy Sepulchre in the Chapel of Nicodemos, and in the Church of the Tomb of the Virgin, they are permitted to celebrate once weekly on the Armenian altar of St. Bartholomew. They can also celebrate at the altar of the Circumcision in the Armenian Church of the Nativity in Bethlehem at Christmas, as well as at the altar of the Nativity in the Grotto. They also have a share in the Ascension Sanctuary on the Mount of Olives during the celebration of Ascension Day. Their position in the ceremonies at the Holy Places is, however, always subordinate to the Armenians. According to the technical expression utilized in the *status quo* regulations, they are "yamklak", or clients, of the Armenians.

It should be added that they own a monastery on the Jordan River at the traditional site of the baptism of Jesus, and a parish church in Bethlehem, dedicated to the Virgin Mary.

---

33) After this period, there is a hiatus in the records. From the fifteenth century onwards, many Syrian Archbishops are named in manuscripts preserved in the library of St. Mark's Monastery in Jerusalem. However, precise dates for tenure of the Archbishops of Jerusalem is known only for those who were in office during the past hundred years.

The Coptic Orthodox Church

The ties of the Church of Egypt with the Holy Land are very ancient. The Egyptian monks, and foremost among them Hilarion, born in Gaza but educated in Egypt where he became a disciple of St. Anthony, were among the first to proselytize among the heathen of Roman Palestine. After the Ecumenical Council of Chalcedon (451), the Church severed its links with Byzantium and became autonomous. Theological causes, mainly the monophysite conception of Christ, but also political controversies, brought about this schism. Islamic rule meant a serious setback in the development of Coptic Christianity in Egypt and, in parallel, of its establishments in the Holy Land. According to the historians Ibn el-Mukaffah and Abu el-Makarrem, a Coptic church in honor of St. Maria Magdalena was built in Jerusalem in the middle of the ninth century by an Egyptian magistrate named Makarios el-Nabrauwi.[34] A fourth Coptic church was built in 1092 during the hegemony of the Seljuk Turks by Mansur al-Tilbany, a Copt who was an aide to the Governor of Jerusalem. The Crusader conquest was an added blow to the Coptic establishments, as indeed it was to all the other Eastern Christian Churches. But when Salah ed-Din, marching north from Egypt, captured Jerusalem, the Copts could depend on his support, chiefly because many of them were serving in administrative capacities on his staff, and there are records that he exempted the Copts in the Holy Land from taxation. During the Mamluk period, the Copts, again backed by the rulers of Egypt, succeeded in gaining a more important position in the Holy Land: they were allowed a Bishop of their own, Basilios, who was subordinate only to the Coptic Patriarch of Alexandria. This was during the time of Patriarch Cyril III (1235–1242); until then, they had been under the authority of the Syrian Orthodox Patriarch of Antioch. Coptic sources maintain that prior to the appointment of a Bishop in Jerusalem, the Bishop of Damietta in Egypt held the title of Damietta and Jerusalem. According to the historian Abu-el-Makarrem, during the early years of the thirteenth century, there were three churches in Jerusalem which belonged to the Copts: the Chapel of the Virgin Mary in the Church of the Holy Sepulchre, the Church of Mary Magdalena, and the church built by Mansur at-Tilbani. Ever since the fourteenth century, Coptic monks had

---

34) The Church of Mary Magdalene is now in Greek Orthodox possession.

rooms to live in at the Holy Sepulchre. A pilgrim of 1497 relates that they had a small chapel behind the edicule, and they maintain it to this very day. The Copts have long enjoyed other rights in the Holy Sepulchre: lamps hanging inside the Tomb, in the Angel's Chapel and over the Stone of Unction; a share in the processions, incensing and other celebrations. In the fifteenth century, the Copts acquired rights to celebrate in the Church of the Tomb of Mary, in the Chapel of the Ascension and in the Church of the Nativity in Bethlehem. Their connection with the Monastery of Deir es-Sultan, adjoining the Holy Sepulchre, goes back to the thirteenth century, but it is difficult to establish the respective shares of the Copts and the Ethiopians there.

But in 1838, the Copts definitely had the upper hand in Deir as-Sultan and since that time they regard the Ethiopian monks living on its premises as their "guests." This was the situation during the regime of Mehmed Ali, ruler of Egypt. It was in his rule of the Holy Land that Bishop Abram established the Coptic khan near the Pool of Hezekiah. In the second half of the nineteenth century, Bishop Basilios II built St. Anthony's Cathedral and Monastery near the Holy Sepulchre. In the compound is the residence of the Archbishop, constructed in 1912, and the St. Anthony's Boys' School, as well as two churches—St. Helen, with the ancient cistern of Queen Helen, and the Virgin's Apparition. Before the gate is the Ninth Station of the Via Dolorosa, owned by the Copts. At the beginning of the eighteenth century, the Coptic Church established St. George's Convent and Church near the Jaffa Gate, and the convent includes the St. Dimiana's Coptic Girls' College. There are also Coptic monasteries and chapels in Bethlehem, Jericho and near to the Jordan River. The church in Jericho, dedicated to St. Anthony, was constructed in 1922 by Archbishop Timotheos and the monastery near the Jordan River was founded by Archbishop Jacobus (1946–1956).

Until the end of the nineteenth century, the Archdiocese of Jerusalem also encompassed Lower Egypt (the districts of Al-Sherkia, Damiat and Garbia). During the tenure of Archbishop Theophilos, who served until 1946, the district of Al-Sherkia was still under the spiritual jurisdiction of Jerusalem. At present, the Archdiocese comprises Israel, Jordan and Sinai.

The Ethiopian Orthodox Church

The Ethiopian is one of the oldest Christian Churches in the Holy Land. There were strong links between Ethiopia and Palestine even before the evangelization of the Ethiopians. An Ethiopian is also mentioned in the Acts of the Apostles (8:27–38) among those who accepted the teaching of Christ and was baptized. The presence of Ethiopian monks in the Holy Land, and visits of Ethiopian pilgrims to the Holy Places, are mentioned in records of pilgrims of the first centuries. As early as the end of the fourth century, St. Jerome mentions the presence of Ethiopian monks, and Ethiopians are referred to in documents and *firmans* of successive Governors of the Holy Land.

In 1172, during the period of the Crusader Kingdom of Jerusalem, the monk Theodoric found the Ethiopians possessing altars in the Holy Places. In contrast to other Monophysite Churches which had established bishoprics in the Holy Land, they maintained monasteries in the vicinity of the Holy Places. After the downfall of the Crusader Kingdom, they won more extensive rights in the Holy Places. The fourteenth-century Italian pilgrim, Giacomo da Verona, describes them celebrating in the Church of the Tomb of the Virgin, and there is evidence from that same century to indicate they owned the Chapel of St. Mary of Egypt. In the fifteenth century, they possessed the Chapel of the Derision in the ambulatory of the Holy Sepulchre. For a time, they also owned the Chapel of St. Helen in the Holy Sepulchre. Chronicles of travellers and pilgrims of the sixteenth and seventeenth century tell of important rights enjoyed by the Ethiopians in the Holy Places. According to Bernardino D'Amico, a Franciscan friar who lived in Jerusalem at the end of the sixteenth century, the Ethiopians were in possession of a chapel in the Church of the Holy Sepulchre, and owned the Monastery of Deir as-Sultan in the same complex. A chapel in the Church of the Tomb of the Virgin Mary was also Ethiopian property. In 1614, an Italian pilgrim, Barbone Morosini, mentions several chapels in the Church of the Holy Sepulchre, and an altar in the Church of the Nativity in Bethlehem as belonging to the Ethiopians. At the end of the seventeenth century, however, like other smaller Christian communities which could not afford to pay the exactions of the Turkish pashas, they lost most of their holdings in the Church of the Holy Sepulchre.

In 1656, the Greek Orthodox Patriarch Paissios obtained a *firman* from Sultan Mehmed IV authorizing him to take over the charitable foundations (*waqfs*) of the Ethiopians. By 1670, the Ethiopians seem to have disappeared from Jerusalem and no more is heard of them throughout the eighteenth century. At the beginning of the nineteenth century, the situation of the Ethiopian monks was appalling. They were concentrated on the roof of the Chapel of St. Helen, one of the chapels of the Holy Sepulchre, in a monastery known as Deir es-Sultan.

From earliest days and until the beginning of the nineteenth century, they had rights of consequence in that monastery. According to Ethiopian account, the Copts occupied the monastery when all the Ethiopian monks perished in 1838 in a plague. We recall that the Ethiopian Church was dependent upon the Coptic Patriarch in Egypt at that time, and an Egyptian, Mehmed Ali, was in power in the Holy Land.

The *firman* of 1852 established the *de facto* situation in the Holy Places and, consequently, in Deir es-Sultan as well, but the Ethiopians have never ceased to claim their right to live in the monastery and to worship in the Chapels of the Archangel Michael and of the Four Living Creatures.

According to Cust[35], the Ethiopians had the right *ab antiquo* to officiate in the Chapel of the Four Living Creatures, but never in the lower Chapel of St. Michael. Since 1882, it may well be that the Copts have prevented the Ethiopians from worshipping in the Chapel of the Four Living Creatures, in retaliation for Ethiopian opposition to their tearing down a wall surrounding the monastery.

In the years between 1882 and 1893, the Emperors Yohannes IV and Menelik II built a monastery called Dabre Gannet (Mount of Paradise) in West Jerusalem, and nearby a circular church dedicated to the Virgin Mary, under the title "Covenant of Mercy." At the end of the nineteenth century, Mamher Walde Sama'et, who was the head of the Ethiopian community in Jerusalem, bought a house in the neighborhood of the Via Dolorosa, which became the residence of the Ethiopian Archbishop. From 1907 until 1969, Ethiopian monks lived in individual wooden huts at the traditional site of Jesus' baptism beside the River Jordan. Formerly, the monks had held their prayers in a small timber church. A stone church and a monastery, Deir Ahbash, were later built on that spot.

---

35) *The Status Quo in the Holy Places*, p. 31.

Appendix to Chapter Seven

CONSULAR AGENCIES ESTABLISHED IN THE HOLY LAND IN THE OTTOMAN PERIOD

Starting in the mid-nineteenth century, the principal European Powers and the United States of America established consulates in Jerusalem and consular agencies in other towns in the Holy Land. Their main purpose was to protect and assist their nationals who were residents in the Holy Land, as well as the local religious institutions, and the pilgrims visiting the Holy Places. Under the prevailing "Capitulations agreement", the consuls had jurisdictional powers with regard to their nationals and the "protegés" of their country. These were entitled to submit their lawsuits to special law courts maintained by their consuls.

The first consulate to be established was that of Great Britain in Jerusalem. It opened in 1839, when the country was still under the rule of Ibrahim Pasha. Next came Prussia, which inaugurated a consulate in 1842. The Kingdom of Sardinia established the first Catholic consulate in Jerusalem in 1843. Its function was to counter the growing influence of the Protestant missions, which were backed by the consuls of Great Britain and Prussia. However, the Sardinian consulate was short-lived. It closed in 1849, the year which saw the defeat of this small kingdom at the hands of Austria. Not until 1872 did an Italian consulate open in Jerusalem, following the establishment of national unity in Italy.

A French consulate was established, or rather re-established in 1843, a few months after the Sardinian consulate. France had possessed a consulate as early as the seventeenth century, under the Capitulations' agreement which granted France privileged status regarding the Holy Places of Christianity. Consequently, the French consuls claimed the right of precedence over their Catholic colleagues when attending religious ceremonies or processions, and justified the exercise of such prerogatives as wearing a special uniform, sword and decorations, and hoisting the national flag.

The Austrian monarchy opened its consulate in Jerusalem in 1847. A special post office was set up in a building inside Jaffa Gate. (Today, the renovated premises house the Franciscans' Christian Information Center.)

The United States opened a consulate in 1844. The consulate's activities were interrupted by an unexpected occurrence. The first American consul, Warden Cresson, decided to convert to Judaism, a move which contrasted sharply with the proselytizing attitudes of his colleagues. The American consulate recommenced its functions in 1857.

The year 1853 saw the opening of the Spanish consulate. Links between Spain's Catholic rulers and the Holy Land had been forged as far back as the fourteenth century, when James of Aragon succeeded in obtaining important concessions from the Sultan of Egypt, ruler of the Holy Land.

Of special political significance was the establishment of a Russian consulate in 1858, following the Crimean War. It was located in the Russian compound.

From the second half of the eighteenth century onward, Tzarist Russia had assumed the role of patron of Orthodox Christianity, thus rivalling France, which supported Catholic claims regarding the possession of the Holy Places. Until the middle of the nineteenth century, Russia's intervention had been in support of the Greek Orthodox Patriarchate. Thereafter, however, Russia initiated an independent policy directed at furthering its own religious and political aims.

Greece, which had gained political independence in 1830, and enlarged its territory in the years that followed, opened a consulate in Jerusalem in the second half of the nineteenth century. Its function was to perpetuate the specifically Hellenic character of the Greek Orthodox Patriarchate.

Romania, one of the Orthodox States which gained independence from Turkey, also established a consulate in Jerusalem.

Ethiopia, too, which had enjoyed ties with the Holy Land throughout the Christian era, opened a consulate in the Holy City.

Chapter Eight

THE BRITISH MANDATORY PERIOD
(1917–1947)

INTRODUCTION

The First World War meant a serious setback for the Christian Churches in the Holy Land. Ecclesiastical properties were taken over by the Turkish Government as barracks or military hospitals, and any that belonged to Allied States were only perfunctorily looked after. The clergy and other religious personnel also suffered. Many were jailed or banished, not a few succumbed to the hardship inflicted. Seminary students of Turkish nationality were conscripted into unendurable military privations in an army not celebrated for its comforts. Exile did not spare even the Latin and the Greek Orthodox Patriarchs. And that was not all. The population was desperately hungry and sick, and the plight of non-Moslems was bound to be sorrier than most. It was scarcely surprising, in such circumstances, that the British entry into the Holy Land should also bring relief and satisfaction to the majority of its Christians.

Marching north from Egypt, the British Expeditionary Force took Gaza and Beersheba in the autumn of 1917 and, on December 11, General Allenby walked on foot into the Holy City of Jerusalem, to end a Moslem domination which had lasted since 1244. His first proclamation told the inhabitants that every sacred building, monument, holy spot, shrine, traditional site, endowment, pious bequest or customary place of worship, in whatever form, partaining to Christianity, Judaism and Islam, would be protected and maintained, according to the existing customs and beliefs of the faith to which it was sacred.

A military administration was set up, whose primary task was to undo the human wastages of war and famine. Next, political issues had to be resolved with justice and equity. Here was Christian Britain, come to govern a country where, in the main, Moslems dwelt, but in which it had taken upon itself a solemn and

143

internationally acknowledged obligation to further the establishment of a national home for the Jewish people.

And it had, also, the extremely delicate task of securing the religious rights of Christendom as a whole, with equity to the historical and often conflicting rights of the Churches.

In July 1920, the military regime was replaced by a civil administration under a High Commissioner, and on September 29, 1922, the Palestine Mandate was approved by the League of Nations. Under Article 8, privileges and immunities granted by the Capitulations by Ottoman usage were shelved for the lifetime of the Mandate.

Article 9 guaranteed respect for the personal status of peoples and communities and their respective religious interests, and continuity of control and management of Moslem charitable foundations, *"waqfs"*, in accordance with Islamic law and the wishes of the founders. Article 13 bound the Mandatory to sustain existing rights and to ensure free access to the Holy Places, to religious buildings and sites, and stipulated freedom of worship.

The Palestine Order-in-Council of 1922 and its amendments prescribed rules for the jurisdiction of religious tribunals in matters of personal status and pious endowments, in conformity with these general principles. This meant exclusive jurisdiction for the ecclesiastical courts of the recognized Christian communities in matters of marriage and divorce, alimony, and confirmation of wills, in other matters of personal status if all parties consented to their jurisdiction, and in any case concerning the constitution or internal administration of a *waqf* established before a religious court conformably to the canon law of the community in question.

The Palestine (Holy Places) Order-in-Council of 1924 left every dispute as to the Holy Places, religious buildings or sites in Palestine, or as to communal rights and claims, to the decision of the High Commissioner. Another statute that concerned the activities of the Churches is the Antiquities Ordinance of 1929, which was applied to the Holy Sepulchre because of the building's precarious state of preservation. The intervention of the Mandatory authorities was necessary, as the Churches directly responsible could not easily come to an agreement and begin repairs on their own within the prescriptions of the *status quo*.

The overall improvement of the conditions after the British occupation led to a steady rise in the Christian population. At the census of 1922, it came to about seventy-one thousand. At the census of 1931, it was about ninety thousand, apart from twenty thousand in Trans-Jordan, and it belonged to the following denominations: Greek Orthodox, Roman Catholic, Greek Catholic Melkite, Maronite, Chaldean, Armenian Gregorian, Armenian Catholic, Syrian Orthodox, Syrian Catholic, Coptic, Ethiopian, Anglican, Lutheran, and sundry Protestant Churches and sects. Under a schedule to the Order-in-Council issued in 1939, the first nine Churches,[1] enjoying the status of recognized religious communities, each had its religious courts.

The Greek Orthodox, Roman Catholic and Armenian Gregorian communities were headed severally by a Patriarch resident in Jerusalem; the Greek Catholic had an Archbishop resident in Haifa; the other Uniate Catholic communities were represented in Jerusalem by a Patriarchal Vicar. The Syrian Orthodox (or Jacobites), the Ethiopians and Anglicans had their Bishops and the Copts an Archbishop.

The duty of the Mandatory was far from simple: it frequently had to steer a middle course between the vying claims of nationalities and faith, disputes between Jews and Arabs, and chronic controversy in the Christian element.

At this distance of time, we may venture a detached judgement of the policy of the Mandatory towards the Christian communities: it was, we feel, inspired by a substantial degree of impartiality and prompted by respect for Church aspirations. It is a rare testimony of this objective approach that neither the Church of England nor the Church of Scotland, overwhelmingly though they mattered to Britain, was accorded—indeed it was doubtful if they ever sought—special privileges for Protantism in the Holy Land or communal recognition for themselves.

---

1) Eastern (Orthodox) Community; Latin (Catholic) Community; Gregorian (Armenian) Community; Armenian (Catholic) Community; Syrian (Catholic) Community; Chaldean (Uniate) Community; Greek (Catholic) Melkite Community; Maronite Community; Syrian (Orthodox) Community.

THE ANGLICAN CHURCH AND THE
PROTESTANT CHURCHES

This did not prevent the Protestant Churches from doing exceptionally well in the thirty years of the Mandate, both in numbers and in establishments.

The Anglican Church

The Anglican Church found a wonderful opportunity in civil servants, British garrison and constabulary. New churches, charitable and cultural institutions were founded and, incidentally, Arab membership was enlarged by proselytes from Greek Orthodox and the Eastern Churches. The Roman Catholics were not unmoved by this and the rivalry of the English scholastic establishment was all the more vexatious to them, seeing that there was a reasonable presumption that graduates from English schools stood a better chance of getting clerical jobs in the Administration.

Though, then, it prospered during the thirty years of the British Administration, the period immediately following the ravages of the First World War was a difficult one for the Anglican Church. Bishop Rennie MacInnes, who could enter the Holy Land only in 1918, found the work at a standstill, with the native Arabic clergy, such as had not been deported to the interior as pro-British, carrying on as best they could without outside help. As starvation and disease devasted the whole country, the first task of the Bishop was to provide relief.

The war had also deprived the Church Missionary Society of much of its financial resources and of the skilled teachers needed to maintain a widespread system of village-education for Arabs. Meanwhile, the inauguration of a modern system of education by British Mandatory authorities made the village school work of the Society less essential, and it was decided to concentrate its energies on medical work: the beneficiaries were the hospitals of Nablus, Jaffa, Gaza and Hebron.

Bishop Graham Brown (1932–1943) succeeded Bishop

146

MacInnes. He spent a great deal of his endeavors on improving the schools under his jurisdiction.

During the last years of the Mandate, the following Anglican schools existed: the Jerusalem Girls' College (since 1943 in a new building in the Rehavia quarter) and the British community school in Jerusalem (maintained jointly by the Church Mission to the Jews, the Church Missionary Society, and the Jerusalem and the East Mission); Christ Church School in Jerusalem and the English High School for Girls in Jaffa (maintained by the Church Mission to the Jews);[2] Bishop Gobat School in Jerusalem and schools in Jaffa, Lydda, Gaza, Shfaram, Nazareth, Nablus and Zababdeh, maintained by the Church Missionary Society and intended mainly for Anglican Arabs; schools in Nazareth and Haifa (maintained by the Palestine Native Church Council and the Jerusalem and the East Mission); St. George's School in Jerusalem, St. Luke's School in Haifa and the English High School for Girls, also in Haifa (maintained by the Jerusalem and the East Mission.)

In 1931, the visit to the Holy Land by the Archbishop of Canterbury, Cosmo Gordon Lang, aroused concern in Roman Catholic quarters that its purpose was to bring about an infringment in the *status quo* in the Holy Places. Before the outbreak of the Second World War, Miss A.M. Carey presented to the Anglican Bishop a large building above Ein Kerem, which was to be used to promote interreligious understanding. It was the Bishop's intention to invite an Anglican sisterhood to serve there, but the idea came to nought.

The Church of Scotland

Buildings belonging to the Church of Scotland, which were damaged in the war, were rapidly repaired. Educational and

2) The English High School for Girls in Jaffa was located in the building later known as Immanuel House. Built by Baron Ustinov in 1884, it served as a hotel (Park Hotel) and was a graceful feature of the German Templers' colony. Wilhelm II of Germany stayed there during his pilgrimage in 1898. The building was bought in 1927 by the Church Mission to the Jews. After 1978, it was renovated and used by the Israel Trust of the Anglican Church as a hostel and study center.

147

medical work was soon resumed, this time under the much more favorable conditions offered under the British Mandate.

Schools in Jaffa and Safed were reopened, though not those in Tiberias. In 1936, the educational work in Safed was also given up.

A special pride of the Church of Scotland was St. Andrew's Church in Jerusalem, dedicated in November 1930, in memory of men of Scots regiments who died to free the Holy Land. The Scots like to trace their connection with Jerusalem back to 1329, when King Robert the Bruce, on his death-bed, asked that his heart be buried in Jerusalem to redeem his vow to visit the Holy Land. His request could not be carried out, but in partial fulfilment of it, a plaque was placed in the floor of St. Andrew's Church, recording King Robert's pious wish.

The Lutheran Church

The German institutions quickly revived the work which the war interrupted. Schneller's orphanage, reopened in 1921, did splendid service in caring for a great increment of war orphans. A branch was later opened in Nazareth. In 1923, the Jerusalem hospital of the Kaiserswerth Diakonissen was given back to its owners; it had been used as a military hospital and, as often happens after military occupation, a lot of repairs had to be carried out to restore it to use. The Talitha Kumi girls' school and the German Evangelical school were reopened soon after. The building of the Augusta Victoria Stiftung on the Mount of Olives, occupied until 1928 by the British Mandatory Administration, was then returned to its German owners.[3] Already at that time there was a project to transform it into a hospital, but the idea was only realized after the Second World War.

Meanwhile, the many former pupils of the German Lutheran institutions favored the formation of an Arab congregation, which needed a setting other than that of the Evangelical Association

---

3) During the First World War it had housed the Turkish and German military headquarters.

founded in 1853 and intended for Germans. Consequently, in 1929, a Palestine Evangelical congregation was established.

In the 'thirties, the activity of the German Lutherans grew steadily outside Jerusalem as well, in Jaffa, Haifa, Waldheim and al-Bassa, a village near the Lebanese border.

Most of the members of the German community were arrested when the Second World War broke out, placed in special camps, and eventually deported to Australia. The majority of the personnel of Lutheran educational and charitable institutions had to go and the country-wide work of the community was disrupted. German property was vested in a Custodian of Enemy Property. Ecclesiastical buildings were taken over by the Anglican Church, the German hospital became a Government one, the Augusta Victoria Stiftung served as a British military hospital, the Syrian Orphanage housed British families evacuated from Egypt. The schools in Bethlehem and Beit Jala were closed and in Jerusalem, St. John's Hospice and the Church of the Redeemer likewise ceased activities.

At the end of the hostilities, the general atmosphere in the Holy Land was far from favorable for any renewal of activity by Germans: memory of Nazi persecutions and the horrors of the concentration camps was too fresh, too grim. In the circumstances, direct action by the German Church was not to be thought of. The initiative of looking into the matters pertaining to the German Lutheran Church in the Holy Land was entrusted to the Lutherans of the States and, at the end of 1946, the National Lutheran Council there sent out Dr. Erwin Mull, who opened negotiations with the British Mandatory Administration to regain at least some of the confiscated property. But the Mandatory Administration was itself drawing to its close, and all that Dr. Mull could do was to revive some of the interests of the Arab Lutheran community, which had suffered less than the German community during the Second World War. Later on, the outbreak of Jewish-Arab hostilities and, subsequently, the partition of Palestine, opened up possibilities for a fairly rapid revival of German Lutheran work in that part of the Holy Land which was included within the Kingdom of Jordan.

The Templers had prospered between the World Wars, and their number had risen to two thousand, no longer, however, men and women sworn to the religious ideals of their precursors, but

149

willing tools of Goebbels' propaganda. Most of the young people went back to Germany before fighting began, the remnant, as we saw, were deported to Australia and their property was vested in the Custodian. In 1962, the Government of Israel agreed to pay a sum of 31.5 million Israeli pounds in indemnification for German ecclesiastical and private assets which had reverted from the British Custodian to Israel's ownership with the proclamation of the State.

Other Protestant Missionary Societies

In the interval between the two World Wars, other Protestant missionary societies from the USA, Great Britain and Scandinavia had established places of worship, schools and Bible shops in the Holy Land and proselytized as they could.

The Southern Baptist Convention started its work in 1923, when two missionary couples were sent to the Holy Land. Dr. J. Wash Watt and his wife stayed five years, laying the foundation to the Baptist presence in the country. Active were also the *Adventists* (who, during the British Mandate, founded Jerusalem's Adventist House), *the Brethren*, and the *Society of Friends*.

The Church of God (Seventh-Day Adventists in Salem, West Virginia) sent Elder A.N. Dugger to Jerusalem in 1931. He stayed there for two years and operated a small press.

The Finnish Missionary Society started its work in 1924, carrying out various programs. At the end of the British Mandatory, it opened a boarding school in Jerusalem.

The Church of the Nazarene, the largest of the Holiness Churches, started its work in 1918 in Jerusalem, mostly among the Armenians.

Several *Pentecostal groups* were also active, notably the Rev. William L. Hull who, in 1935, established the Zion Christian Mission.

The work of the *Church of God* in the Holy Land dates from the visit of Rev. J. H. Ingram to the Middle East. At the Church's Assembly in 1946, Rev. D. B. Hatfield was assigned to the Holy Land. He landed in Haifa at the very end of the British Mandate and in due course established his headquarters in Cyprus, directing the Church's work in Israel, Jordan and Egypt from there. The *Jerusalem YMCA* came into being in 1878. Its constitution, adopted in that year, was written in Arabic. Like many other associations linked with countries at war with the Ottoman Empire, it was closed from 1914 to 1917, and then could start again, returning to the Holy Land with Allenby's force. Dr. A. C. Harte arrived and began the work which resulted in the present building and program of the YMCA. On July 23, 1928, the cornerstone was laid by Lord Plumer, High Commissioner of Palestine. For most of the funds necessary to provide this magnificent edifice the Association is indebted to the munificence of J.N. Jarvie of Mount Clair, New Jersey. Its dedication by Lord Allenby followed in 1933. From this unique center, the YMCA continues to do most valuable social and cultural work.

THE ORTHODOX CHURCHES

The Greek Orthodox Church

When the British forces entered Jerusalem, the highest-ranking Greek Orthodox priest was an Archimandrite, for the Turks had removed Patriarch Damianos and several members of the Synod to Damascus. In the spring of 1918, Damianos was still in exile, and the British Military Governor of Jerusalem, anxious to have Easter celebrated in dignity, invited Porphyrios II, Archbishop of Mount Sinai, to come to Jerusalem as officiant. Eventually, in 1919, Damianos returned. Relations between him and the Mandatory authorities were excellent. No Brotherhood was more loyally pro-British than the Orthodox. The birthday of the British king and the anniversary of the liberation of Jerusalem were marked by special prayers. Loyalty to the established government, following the precepts of the Gospel, is characteristic of the Greek Patriarchate, while the British Administration adhered to the Ottoman *status quo*, which allowed the Orthodox Church certain preferences. Between the Patriarchate and the Anglican

151

Church likewise, there had always been goodwill from the days of Patriarch Nicodemos, who, in 1885, lavished "hospitality" on the representatives of the Church of England, allowing the Anglicans to hold their services in the chapel of the upper floor of the Orthodox Monastery of Abraham,[4] a courtesy still extended, though the use of the chapel must be solicited in writing each time anew. Another such courtesy is the permission to the Anglicans to worship in the southern courtyard of the Greek Monastery of the Nativity in Bethlehem, at nine o'clock on Christmas Eve.[5] Furthermore, and under the same conditions, members of the Order of St. John (Anglican branch) may worship on June 24 in the lower Church of St. John in the Muristan.

The British Administration, finding the Patriarchate in an unhappy plight, on the verge of bankruptcy[6] and distracted by unending friction between Patriarch Damianos and the Brotherhood of the Holy Sepulchre, appointed the Bertram-Luke Commission in 1921 to investigate its affairs and suggest a workable solution of its troubles. The Commission favored the Patriarch on the constitutional issue and recommended that a commission of financial control be set up. This was done, in spite of the vehement opposition of Patriarch and Brotherhood alike, and the finances of the Patriarchate were handsomely retrieved. Its near-insolvency had been due principally to the cutting off of almost all its sources by repercussions of the First World War. It was income from pilgrims, from gifts of well-wishers in Russia and the Balkans, from the rents of overseas properties; the Russian revolution of 1917 led to the confiscation of many of these properties and also brought all intercourse between Russia and the Holy Land to an abrupt halt.

In 1925, a second enquiry was undertaken by Bertram and

4) According to a Christian tradition, the chapel is the site of Isaac's sacrifice.

5) In case of rain, they may worship in the chapel of St. George.

6) The debts amounted to some 600,000 pounds sterling, with steadily growing interest. In 1922, in order to meet its increasing obligations, the Greek Patriarchate sold a large tract of land in Jerusalem to a Jewish Society. This was to become the site of the elegant Rehavia neighborhood. The sale provoked an outcry from Arab circles. In this context, it should be mentioned that the successive transactions by the Greek Orthodox Patriarchate were for the most part long-term leases and not the sale of landed property. After the establishment of the State of Israel, important long-term leases were contracted, enabling the Patriarchate to regain a secure financial footing.

Young into the controversies between the Patriarchate and the Arab laity, but the Patriarch never accepted the findings. The protests of the laity were prompted by the lack of interest in their needs on the part of the Brotherhood of the Holy Sepulchre, which directed most of its energies to the guardianship of the Holy Places of the Church. The official Orthodox attitude, held even today, was expressed by Patriarch Damianos in his reply to the British Governor of Jerusalem when that official argued the Arab position. It reflects the Patriarchate's immemorial attitude. Damianos said this: "The guardianship of the Holy Places was the real and original purpose of the Orthodox Church in the Holy Land, which (its members) had maintained, often with their lives, through many centuries of infidel domination. Their endowments were the result of foreign and not Arab munificence, and Christian ministrations, in the accepted sense, though admittedly important and desirable, were a supererogation beyond their primary scope."

Because of this unwillingness of the Patriarch to consider the needs of the Arab-speaking Orthodox, and because of insufficient concern for their affairs, there was, during the whole Mandatory period, a steady drift into the Catholic and the Protestant Churches.

According to the census of 1931, the community was still the most numerous, comprising forty thousand members, with twenty thousand more in Trans-Jordan. But it was a decisive downward trend, which eventually led to an alteration of the existing proportions in favor of Catholicism and Protestantism.

On the death of Patriarch Damianos in 1931, there was a long interregnum, because of the opposition of the Arab Orthodox. Ultimately, the Synod proceeded to the election without the Arabs taking part and chose Monsignor Timotheus Temelis, who, like his predecessor, was originally from the island of Samos, but the protestations of the indigenous element were the cause of the royal assent of the British monarch being delayed until September 1939.

At the beginning of Timotheus' incumbency, the British Administration tried to settle the differences between the Brotherhood and the Arab Orthodox community. To this end, an ordinance was enacted in November 1941, which determined the competences of the Patriarch, the Synod and the mixed Council, and the local

153

Councils, fixing the procedure to be followed for the election of the Patriarch and dealing with the functions of the religious courts. It was, however, bitterly resisted by the Brotherhood and could never be enforced.

The Russian Orthodox Church

The Russian churches, monasteries and hospices which, until the First World War, had been centers of a busy, bustling religious life, were in jeopardy, and throughout the Mandate they eked out a meagre existence, their personnel slowly dwindling away, no recruits procurable. The Mandatory thought it well to appoint an administrator of Russian property in the Holy Land, which had formerly belonged to a number of institutions in Tzarist Russia, notably the Russian Ecclesiastical Mission and the Orthodox Society.

The successive administrators,who were under the supervision of the District Commissioner of Jerusalem, took charge of the property. They employed its revenues to maintain the local Russian churches and for the relief and support of Russian Orthodox monasteries and other religious institutions in Palestine, and their personnel residing in the Holy Land. By an Ordinance of 1926, amended in 1936 and 1938 (Administration of Russian Properties), the dependants of residents in Palestine who were connected with the Russian religious institutions were added to the beneficiaries of their revenues.

It is relevant that, because of the legal status of landed property in the Ottoman Empire, Church property had often to be registered under fictitious names.

In February 1948, the Mandatory Administration attempted to enact an ordinance recognizing the board of administrators of Russian ecclesiastical property as a corporate body, but the Mandate came to an end, and the ordinance was never gazetted nor, therefore, became effective in Israel.[7]

---

7) Russian Ecclesiastical Mission (Administration of Properties) Order, 1948 (Legislation Enacted and Notices Issued, which have not been Gazetted, p. 27— Government of Palestine, London & Jerusalem, 1948.)
Orthodox Palestine Society (Administration of Properties) Order, 1948

At the end of the British Mandate (May 1948), the Mission in Jerusalem was headed by Archimandrite Anthony, who was affiliated to the Russian Church Outside Russia. He had his seat in the monastery located within the Russian Compound which, when the British left, came under the authority of the Israeli commander of the northern sector of Jerusalem. The Archimandrite refused to recognize the authority of the military commander on the ground that the city's status was still in dispute. Moreover, he objected to the prerogatives granted to the Israeli-appointed supervisor of Russian ecclesiastical property, who replaced the British District Commissioner of Jerusalem.

Meanwhile, Soviet Russia had recognized the reborn State of Israel and established diplomatic relations with it. Perceiving an opportunity to further its aims of displacing the Jerusalem representatives of the Church Outside Russia, the Soviet authorities sent a Mission from Moscow, early in 1949. Archimandrite Leonide and a number of monks and nuns took up residence in the Gorny Convent in Ein Karem. Archimandrite Anthony, who from the start had refused to cooperate with the representatives of the new State, left for the monastery in Jordanian-occupied East Jerusalem, thus facilitating the installation of the Moscow-based Mission.

The Romanian Orthodox Church

There were strong links between the Romanian Orthodox Church and the Holy Land, even before Romania became an independent State. The Greek Patriarchate had benefitted from large religious endowments in the principalities of Walachia and Moldavia, ever since these two regions were tributaries of the Porte. It was only in 1938 that a Romanian monastery and chapel were built in Jerusalem. The coat of arms of the ruling king of Romania, from the House of Hohenzollern-Sigmaringen, is still visible in the wooden panels of the monastery's portal.

(Legislation Enacted and Notices Issued, which have not been Gazetted, p. 30, Government of Palestine, London & Jerusalem, 1948.)

THE ROMAN CATHOLIC CHURCH

The Roman Catholic Church soon recovered from the set-back of the First World War. The swift revival, made possible by the far better conditions that the Christian Churches enjoyed under the Mandate, was undoubtedly also due to a great extent to the energy of Patriarch Louis Barlassina (1920–1947). His endeavors were directed, first of all, to repairing the theological seminary in Beit Jala, which had suffered from military occupation during the War. In 1921, it was reopened and entrusted a year later to the Benedictine Fathers, who were replaced in 1931 by the Fathers of Betharram.

Many other buildings belonging to ecclesiastical institutions, especially those connected with countries at war with Turkey, likewise suffered from military occupation.

The missions previously founded began to take up their work again. Ten new ones were established; in Cis-Jordan, the missions of Tulkarm, Jenin and Beit She'an should be mentioned. New religious congregations entered upon their work in the Holy Land, among them the Hijas del Calvario,[8] the Sisters of St. Anne, the Sisters of Dorothy, the Jesuit Fathers, the Polish Sisters of St. Elisabeth, the Tertiary Franciscan Sisters from Austria, the Consolators from Czechoslovakia and the Sisters of Nigrizia. But, above all, the Patriarchate of Barlassina was a period of exceptional building activity. Some of the most beautiful churches date back to it. Among them are the Transfiguration on Mount Tabor and the Church of the Agony in Gethsemane, both designed by the architect Antonio Barluzzi, and inaugurated in 1924 by Cardinal Oreste Giorgi, a special Pontifical Delegate. The Church of the Visitation in Ein Karem and the Church of the Beatitudes near Capernaum, also designed by Barluzzi, were inaugurated in 1935 and 1940, respectively. In 1927, the Jesuits opened a Jerusalem branch of the Biblical Pontifical Institute. A hospice was built in Haifa by the Discalced Carmelite Fathers and, in the same city, a hospital was opened by the Society for Assisting Italian Missionaries Abroad. In Nazareth, the Salesians founded the beautiful church and the vocational school of Jesus Adolescent. Other

8) They opened a Spanish college in 1922.

buildings of this epoch are the Church of Our Lady of the Holy Arch of the Alliance in Abu Ghosh, the chapel of the Convent of the Sisters of St. Charles Borromeus in Jerusalem, the Convent of the Franciscan Missionary Sisters of Mary and the Convent of St. Paul, both of them near Damascus Gate in Jerusalem. The Rosary Sisters, too, built their mother-house and a large chapel in the Holy City.

Among the buildings sponsored by the Patriarchate was the Church of Our Lady Queen of Palestine in Deir Rafat. The land was bought in 1866, and the church and the monastery were put up in 1925. Sponsored by the Patriarchate were also the parish church in Ramallah and convents and schools in the missions of Nablus, Beit She'an and Rameh. In 1945, a large church was constructed in Beit Sahour, on the site of an earlier one built in 1877, during the Patriarchate of Monsignor Valerga. In addition, the Patriarchate bought a large farm in Tejasir, near Nablus.

But the Franciscans still outstripped all in this activity, as witness such impressive edifices as the churches conceived by Barluzzi. Also noteworthy were the Terra Sancta Colleges in Jerusalem and Nazareth, the Monastery of the Annunciation in Nazareth, the monastery near the Coenaculum on Mount Zion, the Church of St. Anthony and a boys' school in Jaffa, a chapel, a monastery and a boys' school in Jericho (1924), as well as the Church of St. Peter in Tiberias, near the monastery and the hospice dating from 1843.

Although many religious Orders and conventual Congregations had established themselves in the Holy Land in the last decades of Ottoman rule and at the time of the British Mandate, the Franciscans had a special eminence as the custodians of the most prestigious shrines in the possession of the Latin Church. Until the period of the Mandate, the traditional rights of the principal Catholic nations were acknowledged in the assignment of the main offices within the Franciscan Custody to Italian, French and Spanish monks. The privileges of the Spanish monks were sanctioned by Pope Benedict XIV, with the Brief "In Supremo", in January 1746.[9]

9) According to the practice in force in the Custody until recent times, the Custos was always an Italian, his vicar was French and the procurator in charge of finances was from Spain. In the most important monasteries (of the Holy Sepul-

Among the enterprises of Patriarch Barlassina, the establishment of the printing press of the Patriarchate merits record: since 1933, it has issued the official bulletin of the Patriarchate, "Le Moniteur Diocésain."

In his interventions on behalf of Catholic interests, Patriarch Barlassina sometimes clashed with the Mandatory authorities. As the Vatican was unwilling to recall him, an acceptable solution was found by appointing a British secretary, Father Keane, to serve alongside Mgr. Barlassina. A further step was the appointment, in 1925, of Franciscan Father Robinson as first Apostolic Visitor to Palestine. It was his task to relieve the Patriarch of some of his responsibilities regarding the delicate contacts with the British Government.[10]

The temporary arrangement was followed, in March 1929, by the nomination of an Apostolic Delegate who lived in Cairo, but kept also a residence in Jerusalem.[11] Before 1929, Jerusalem and Palestine had come under the Apostolic Delegation in Syria and Lebanon, which had its seat in Beirut. On February 11, 1948, Pope Pius XII created an Apostolic Delegation in Jerusalem, one independent of Egypt and which included Israel, Jordan and Cyprus. On September 14, 1940, during the term of office of Mgr. Barlassina, the British Mandatory authorities confirmed the exemptions from Customs duties which the religious institutions had enjoyed in the past.

At the 1931 census, there were nineteen thousand Latins in the Holy Land west of the Jordan and, at the onset of the Second World War, probably twenty-five thousand, but the war naturally interfered a good deal with the freedom of the Latin Church in the Holy Land, not least as concerned Italian and German institutions under enemy patronate. "Aliens" were taken from monastery or convent and placed under Police supervision. Monsignor Bar-

---

chre, Nativity and Annunciation), Italian, French and Spanish superiors served in rotation after an initial triennial period. Other monasteries were traditionally entrusted to an Italian or a Spanish superior. In recent times, most of these regulations have been abolished.

10) See: M. G. Enardu: *Palestine in Anglo-Vatican Relations, 1936-1939*, p. 7, CLUSF Cooperativa Universitaria, Firenze.

11) The first Apostolic Delegate, Mgr. Valerio Valeri, Titular Archbishop of Ephesus, had jurisdiction over an area which included Egypt, Eritrea and Ethiopia. Later, Egypt became an Inter-Nunciature distinct from Palestine.

lassina induced the British authorities to agree that the religious personnel be not interned in civilian camps, but concentrated in religious institutions, mainly in the Monastery of Deir Rafat and the Convent of St. Charles in the German "colony" of Jerusalem. Latin buildings were commandeered for military uses. Wartime restrictions, in general, temporarily held up progress in the manifold work of the Church.

UNIATE CHURCHES

The Uniate Churches also took advantage of the "Pax Mandatoria" to multiply and diversify their interests, but always, although attached to Rome and recognizing the Pope's supremacy, clinging to their own liturgy and customs more or less.

The Greek Catholics (Melkites)

The most important local denomination were the *Greek Catholics (Melkites)*, mainly in Haifa and Nazareth and in villages in Galilee. At the census of 1931, they came to some twelve thousand, but during the years that followed, they won over many converts from the Greek Orthodox community.

During the British Mandatory period, the Episcopal See of Acre (comprising Haifa, Nazareth and Galilee) was held successively by Mgr. Gregory Hajjar, Mgr. Joseph Maallouf and, from 1943, by Mgr. George Hakim. The last proved himself a very gifted and energetic leader. He was instrumental in the construction of the new churches of Rama and Ikrit and, in 1944, founded the magazine *Ar-Rabita*, which is until today the periodical of the Greek Catholic eparchy.

The Maronites

In 1931, the *Maronite Church* counted but a few thousand members in Galilean villages along the border with Lebanon, which is the stronghold of the Maronite persuasion. During the

159

rest of the Mandatory period, the parishes in Haifa and Jaffa rose considerably in numbers, with a constant influx of newcomers from Lebanon. This form of immigration, like so much other Arab entry into Palestine during the Mandate, was uncontrolled and unrestricted across long stretches of land frontiers, where no official check or criterion was attempted.

The Syrian Catholics

The activities of the *Syrian Catholics* expanded, like those of other Christian communities. A number of Syrian Orthodox joined the Syrian Catholic community, particularly in Bethlehem. So, Father Rabbani bought a plot there, and, in 1924, a small school was established on it by Mgr. Hanna Karroum. Later, a church was built close by at the initiative of the parish priest Ephrem Jarjour[12] and consecrated on May 31, 1930, by the Syrian Catholic Patriarch, Cardinal Tappouni. The work on the seminary in Jerusalem, interrupted during the First World War, had been resumed in 1919. Ten years later, in a re-organization of Syrian Catholic institutions, the seminarists of the higher grades were transferred to the seminary in Sharfe, Lebanon; the pupils of the lower seminary grades joined the seminary on the Mount of Olives, where all junior students were thus concentrated.

A schedule added to the Order-in-Council of 1939 made the Syrian Catholic Church one of the nine Christian communities recognized by the Mandatory.

The Armenian Catholics

The Armenian Catholics were represented in Jerusalem by a Patriarchal Vicar. Their church, called "Our Lady of the Spasm," was built over earlier churches which, according to tradition, marked the site of the Third and Fourth Stations of the Via Do

---

12) Fifty years after the consecration of the church, a solemn liturgy was celebrated there by the former parish priest, Ephrem Jarjour, who had meanwhile been appointed a Bishop.

lorosa. Mgr. Joachim Toumayan, who undertook the construction of the church, died in 1929 and was buried within its walls.

The Chaldeans

In 1933, the *Chaldean community* was given scheduled recognition. In 1944, Father Butros Shaye, in due course promoted to Monsignor, was appointed Patriarchal Vicar. He succeeded in building a chapel and the Vicar's residence, in 1955. The adherents of the community in the Holy Land number only a handful.

MONOPHYSITE CHURCHES

The Armenian Orthodox Patriarchate

On the British occupation of Jerusalem, the lamentable state of affairs within the Armenian Patriarchate, and the vacancy of the Jerusalem See, prompted the Military Governor, in March 1919, to appoint an administrative commission to supervise the financial interests of the Patriarchate and safeguard the precious objects and jewels of the Church; Bishop Yegishe Chilingiarian was made president.[13] On September 5, 1921, after a vacancy lasting eleven years, Mgr. Yegishe (Elisha) Tourian, former Patriarch of Constantinople, was elected Patriarch of Jerusalem, under the procedures of the constitution of 1888, except that the confirmation was given by the British crown, not by the Sultan. In 1929, the jurisdiction of the Patriarch, which till then had embraced the dioceses of Beyrouth, Damascus and Latakia, was circumscribed to Palestine and Trans-Jordan. In 1929, during Patriarch Tourian's tenure, Tarkmanchatz School was established with kindergarten and elementary classes. A secondary school was added in 1952. In 1984, the school had an enrolment of 200 pupils.

13) After the First World War, there was an influx into Palestine of displaced Armenians. This was a very valuable accretion to the local community, for the newcomers were deeply imbued with Armenian culture and tradition.

In June 1931, Patriarch Thorkom Koushagian was enthroned. During his term of office, the constitution of the Fraternity of St. James was modified to vest authority for the election of the Patriarch in the General Assembly of the Brotherhood of Jerusalem exclusively. Upon the death of Patriarch Koushagian on February 10, 1939, Archbishop Mesrop Nishanian became Patriarch on April 9 of that year. The next incumbent was Patriarch Guregh II Israelian, elected on October 20, 1944.

The Ethiopian Church

In 1933, the Monastery of Deir Al-Ahbash was built beside the River Jordan by Empress Ethegeh, consort of Emperor Haile Selassie. The monastery and the adjacent church were dedicated to the "Holy Trinity."

In 1921, an Ethiopian noblewoman who became a nun rented a plot in Jericho and had a chapel built on the site.

Chapter Nine

THE STATE OF ISRAEL
(1948 – June 1967)

INTRODUCTION

Many Christians, indeed, were among the Arabs who were frightened or misled by their leaders into fleeing what was to become the territory of the State of Israel, before and during its invasion by the neighboring Arab States. It was an invasion launched in defiance of the Resolution adopted by the General Assembly of the United Nations on November 29, 1947, to set up Jewish an Arab States within the confines of Mandated Palestine, in economic union.

But the percentage of Christian Arabs who left—and that is understandable—was much less than of Arab Moslems, and so after the war of 1948, the ratio which was one to eight during the Mandate, grew to a ratio of one to five. It was especially Christian Arabs from Haifa, Jaffa and Jerusalem, from Acre, Ramla and Lydda, who chose to go away, but the Christian element in Nazareth was doubled by the arrival of brethren from areas of unease, and most of them settled there for good.

The birthrate of Christian Arabs was, however, high and, with consequent local pressures on the economy, the villagers tended to look for work in the industrial centers. Even, therefore, though the number of Christian centers in the principal towns diminished pronouncedly as a result of the invasion of Israel by the Arab States, sizable congregations soon reappeared. The Reunion of Families scheme, whereunder the Government of Israel permitted broken Arab households to be restored by the admission of kinsfolk who had fled to neighboring Arab territory, has been a further means of communal recovery.

With reasonable normalcy restored in mid-1949, requisitioned buildings of several Churches were handed back to previous ownership, and the State of Israel indemnified Churches for structural damages or loss which an unprovoked incursion by

163

Arab States, and the assertion by the Third Jewish Commonwealth of its right of self-preservation, had brought about. It took a few years to recondition and reconstruct; in no-man's-land, between the Old City of Jerusalem and the New, some wreckage was visible until recently, to recall the havoc of war.[1]

THE LEGAL STATUS OF THE CHRISTIAN COMMUNITIES IN THE STATE OF ISRAEL

From the first day of its rebirth, the statesmen of Israel realized the necessity of making plain how the State would comport itself towards religious and ethnic minorities. And so, in the Proclamation of Israel's Independence, which, until a Constitution is written, is the charter of the fundamental principles of the State, the following words appear:

"THE STATE OF ISRAEL...will be based on the principles of liberty, justice and peace as conceived by the Prophets of Israel; will uphold the full social and political equality of all its citizens, without distinction of religion, race or sex; will guarantee freedom of religion, conscience, education and culture; will safeguard the Holy Places of all religions; and will loyally uphold the principles of the United Nations Charter."

This set of affirmations found practical echo in law and procedures. All in all, the State has taken up a most circumspect stand as regards the rights and prerogatives of the Churches. In remarkable measure, it has adhered to the *status quo* and in particular to the *millet* of Ottoman and Mandatory days. Only in the rarest cases has pre-existing legislation been modified to meet exigent new needs and circumstances. For example, the very first ordinance of the State provided that matters which, in the past, were within the competence of the Mandatory Administration should be transferred to the jurisdiction of the new Government. This, in our context, means that the authority of the British High

---

1) Since the War of June 1967, following the re-unification of the Holy City, war damages caused to buildings formerly situated in the front-line were all repaired.

Commissioner in respect of the Holy Places was vested in the Minister of Religious Affairs: that Minister and his Ministry, his establishment of civil servants, were accordingly concerned from the outset with the religious requirements and problems of Israel's several denominations. To look after the religious interests of the Churches and their congregants, there was established a special Division in the Ministry; their internal affairs, spiritual and secular, are not within its compass, and it has been, and is today, scrupulous to avoid any interference in them. Its chief task is to aid, protect and counsel the Churches, to safeguard their historical rights and to work for harmony and mutual understanding within and between all Christian creeds in the State. The mere existence and operation of a Ministry of Religious Affairs underlines the importance which the State attaches to the spiritual aspect of life in the Land that is called Holy; indeed, the Hebrew title is "Ministry of Religions", a pointer that the State of Israel freely recognizes a plurality of faiths and is organized ministerially to do for each faith all that a State should.

Within the pre-June 1967 boundaries of Israel, Judaism was professed by eighty-nine percent of the population, yet it may not claim to be the State religion. The letter and the spirit of the Proclamation of Independence, and the laws that stem from it, vouchsafe equality of rights to all recognized denominations and identical protection by, and in, the State. It would be strange if a distinct Jewish atmosphere were not discernible in everyday manifestations, but that is in no sense prejudicial to the legal status of the Churches or of their members. If any Christian in Israel should form the impression that he is a victim of discrimination, he may appeal to the High Court of Justice, a tribunal of incontestable impartiality. Ordinarily, however, the Ministry of Religious Affairs settles matters of that kind by administrative process. This was true during the whole period between 1948 and 1967 and it is no less true today. Nothing can be more mistaken than to believe that the Republic of Israel is a theocracy. That the bulk of the population is Jewish, makes it inevitable that the country's ways and modes should be impressively influenced by Jewish tradition and thinking, but every law must run the gauntlet of a parliament where procedures are governed, often demonstratively, by democratic principles.

165

It is the case, certainly, that the area of jurisprudence which embraces matters of personal status is regulated by religious law, but here again, each community comes under its own canon.

Comparing all this with the patterns of the West, we may submit that Church and State are kept apart in Israel, save that issues of personal status, as formerly, are adjudicated according to the *millet* system.

The Churches also continued to enjoy concessions in payment of import duty and of taxes on landed property: in this connection, French and Italian institutions were and are more favorably placed, by virtue of agreements signed by Israel with France and Italy, agreements that evoke much older pacts.

CHRISTIANS IN ISRAEL

That the great majority of Christians in Israel are Arabs was and is bound to color Christian affairs. In the nature of things, "political" problems of the Arab inhabitants as such can hardly fail to be linked at times with Church problems, if not deliberately confused with them. For much of any consequent irksomeness, both to the State and the community, the hostility of Israel's Arab neighbors must be blamed but, all the same, the Christian Arabs of Israel possess rights and privileges which, considering the conditions that prevail, any disinterested observer will regard as ample and fair. The political rights are guaranteed, *inter alia*, by parliamentary representation: of the hundred and twenty members of the sixth Knesset, three were Christian Arabs, although the community within the old borders made up only 2.2 percent of the population. All Christian Arabs of local birth are, automatically, citizens of the State. Foreigners may acquire citizenship by naturalization after three or five years' residence. Apart from those who are native-born, many members of the priesthood have become naturalized in that way, outstanding the Roman Catholic Bishop. Parenthetically, the truth of the Father Daniel (Rufeisen) case is that the Supreme Court felt that this convert from Judaism could not rightly claim citizenship of Israel "by return" as a Jew, for he was no longer one; and he duly accepted naturalization.

A striking example of how fully Christian Arabs entered the

166

economy and society of Israel is their membership in the Histadrut, as it is called, the country-wide Labor Federation which guards the rights of workers and provides all manner of help and amenity for the sick, the disabled and unemployed, as well as a variety of cultural and educational interests; the former Greek Catholic Archbishop belonged to the Federation, and all his clerics still belong to it.

Young Christian Arabs are organized in their own scout movement, within an Israeli Federation, with the various troops connected with the several Churches, Roman Catholic, Greek Catholic, Greek Orthodox, and so forth, and there are a number of Arab associations which pursue cultural and benevolent activity on specially Christian lines, including parish circles and clubs, welfare organizations, Catholic Action and the Legion of Mary.

By an ordinance of June 3, 1948, Christians in Israel were authorized to keep Sunday and all Church holidays as days of rest but, as the majority of people in Israel rest on the Sabbath, some Christians may be in a certain amount of practical difficulty about Sunday observance. The Churches are flexible in their approach to this question: to avoid financial loss, Christian employees of Jewish enterprises that keep open on Sunday may attend Catholic Masses and Protestant services especially conducted for them on Saturday or on Sunday evening. Similar arrangements with regards to Mass, for example, are granted in Catholic countries to those who wish to go on excursion on Sundays. Assuredly, there was within Israel's pre-June 1967 borders every facility for the traditional celebration of feasts, of solemn procession and festive assembly, for example, St. Elias, St. George and the Lady of the Carmel.

Christian schools have existed in the Holy Land since the last century, and within the pre-June 1967 borders there were and still are fifty-four of them with some eleven thousand pupils. There has been a marked trend on their part to adopt the governmental program in full, and thus be recognized by the Ministry of Education and Culture. The enrolment mentioned was over and above primary and secondary Government schools for Arab and Druze boys and girls, which not a few Christian children attended, in particular from villages that lack "confessional" schools. In every Government school where there are Christian pupils, their religious upbringing was and is still cared for by catechists appointed by the Church concerned and paid for by the Government. Hebrew is taught as a language in all Arab and Druze Government schools and, generally, in private Christian schools also. Indeed, Hebrew was soon enough spoken, or at any rate understood, by many Christian Arab grown-ups, and it is not surprising that Christian clerics should be conversant with it, both for its scholarly applications and pragmatically as the official language of a sovereign State. It was already normal in pre-June 1967 Israel, for priest, pastor or nun taking up residence to be first enrolled in an"ulpan", attending the concentrated course in Hebrew which is given there to Jewish newcomers. Protestant hymns have been rendered in Hebrew, there are modern Hebrew versions of the Roman Catholic Mass and of the Greek Catholic Byzantine liturgy. Already in pre-June 1967 Israel, Christian clergy preached and lectured fluently in the language. Hebrew can also be a *lingua franca* of communication between priests of different provenances and denominations: at official receptions, a French Catholic priest was seen talking Hebrew to a Russian Orthodox Archimandrite, a Lutheran German deaconess employed the accents of the Bible in conversation with an Arab Catholic nun.

Kol Israel, the State radio corporation, broadcasted, already in pre-June 1967 Israel, Christian religious services from the churches on the occasion of the most important feasts and festivals, and on Sunday afternoon it had a program of ecclesiastical music and sermons.

Christian scholars and students were already, in pre-June 1967 Israel, very interested in the curriculum of the Hebrew University of Jerusalem. They eagerly attended lectures on the Bible and on such topics as archaeology, comparative Semitics and Jewish history. Lectures on the New Testament by Jews who, out of penetrating familiarity with the Hebrew sources, are equipped to present, illuminatingly, the historical and spiritual background of early Christianity, attracted many Christian listeners. Friendly and fruitful collaboration between Christian and Jewish *savants* distinguish every realm of science and research, and there is no cultural bond or partnership but affords proof of honest endeavor to attain better understanding in general and dispel ancient prejudices.

All the Presidents of the State have shown a deep interest in and concern for the welfare of Israel's Christians. The presidential reception for all notables of the Christian Churches on New Year's Eve, with the President's message of seasonal greetings and good wishes, has become a traditional State ceremony.

The Holy Places of Christianity, so bound up with the history of the Holy Land, have been a matter of the closest concern to the State of Israel since its establishment, as witness the pledge to safeguard them which is part of the Proclamation of Independence. Especial and unremitting heed is paid to the honoring of that pledge. There was also no likelihood of contesting claims by Christian denominations to user or to ownership, for most of their Holy Places within the pre-June 1967 jurisdiction of Israel were marked by twin houses of prayer, of the Latins and the Greeks respectively. In this regard, circumstances in the Hashemite Kingdom had differed somewhat: the sites, mostly in the Old City of Jerusalem and Bethlehem, are regulated by the *status quo*, and can be sources of friction so that, for example, the restoration of the Basilica of the Holy Sepulchre, carried out by the Latins, Greeks and Armenians, entailed years of difficult negotiations.

The Christian Holy Places in Israel, the Old City of Jerusalem specifically included, are not only safeguarded. The Government of Israel tries, as far as it can, to assist their custodians in keeping them in proper repair and, in particular, in maintaining the seemliness of the precincts and in securing free and convenient accessibility. Reference is invited to the Protection of Holy Places Law, enacted by the Knesset, Israel's Parliament, in June 1967: its provisions, mindful, considerate and custodial, are set out in Chapter XI.

Sensitiveness on the former Israel-Jordan armistice line presented certain problems, which the Government of Israel did its utmost to mitigate. Clergy from Jordan were given every facility to cross into Israel and in the reverse direction throughout the year on their religious duties; the movement of thousands of Israeli Christians into Jordan at Christmastide, to make their devotions

at the Churches of the Holy Sepulchre and the Nativity, was authorized and facilitated. Pilgrims and tourists found it comparatively simple to pass from Israel into Jordan or *vice versa*; Jordan's un-cooperativeness meant that passage could be only in one
direction.

CHRISTIAN COMMUNITIES IN ISRAEL

The Christian population in Israel, in 1967, numbered about
fifty-five thousand, mostly Arab-speaking, in some twenty-four
denominations. Eighty-five percent were concentrated in the
north, sixty-one percent lived in towns and the rest in twenty-five
villages, in Galilee mainly. If Christian Arabs are, generally,
better educated than Moslem Arabs, it is because the Christians
are largely urbanized and had ampler opportunity to go to the
schools of foreign missions.

The *millet* was and is still the framework of communal organization, although the original basis of the system is infirm today
as a result of intermarriage, changing social ideas and a more
ardent nationalism. But it is far from moribund, and may rightly
be the starting point of any detailed description and classifica-
tion.

The Catholic Churches

The *Catholic Churches* were, until the Six-Day War, the most
important: they embraced the largest number of adherents—
thirty-five thousand, possessed most Holy Places and kept up
many charities and schools. In total, there were from nine to ten
thousand Roman Catholics or Latins, twenty-two thousand Greek
Catholics, two thousand eight hundred Maronites, and followers of
the other Uniate Churches.

The Latins. The *Latins* in Israel, as in Jordan and Cyprus,
are the ecclesiastical wards of the Latin Patriarch of Jerusalem;
their number within the Patriarchate was said to be about fifty
thousand; in Israel before June 1967, there were about seven thou-

sand Arab and, subject to fluctuation, some two to three thousand non-Arab Latins.

Many Arab Latins left Israel and settled in Jordan as a consequence of a demographic displacement for which the Arab States, by their invasion of the new State, were responsible, and the life of the remnant had to be reorganized ánd readjusted to a new set of conditions and circumstances. The purposes of several religious institutions were changed: some school and hospital buildings became hostels for pilgrims; what was no longer essential for worship was advantageously rented to Jewish schools and charities.

The process was swift, matching the dynamism of a forward-looking society. With cheap Arab labor no longer forthcoming, a large farm of the Patriarchate mechanized itself in emulation of neighboring Jewish settlements. Hospitals, not required to treat ailing indigents now that the several Sick Funds had taken over the task, entered in agreement with the Funds to admit their members. National expansion at every turn added enormously to the value of real estate, and all property-owning establishments could make substantial gains.

In May 1948, the Patriarchate was being administered, *ad interim*, by the Apostolic Delegate, Mgr. Gustavo Testa, subsequently a Cardinal; the Patriarch Barlassina had died in the previous year.

Monsignor Testa, residing in the Old City, found communication difficult with his clergy in Israel. Mgr. Antonio Vergani, Patriarchal Vicar in the north, was the only high-ranking Latin priest to stay on, and not seldom, in that situation, had to handle affairs on his own firm responsibility and in his tactful discretion: his wisdom and energy, his grasp of the new order of things, contributed immensely to a return to normal in his flock and, in the years that followed, he was to act a major part in establishing friendship and understanding between the Catholic Church and the new State.

In 1949, Alberto Gori, Custos of the Holy Land, as we recorded earlier, became Patriarch of Jerusalem, but contact with him was still awkward, and Father Terence Kuehn, an American Franciscan, was made Patriarchal Vicar in the south of Israel. As soon, however, as stability allowed, his Vicariate was abolished and Mgr. Vergani was appointed Vicar-General for all Israel, representing the Patriarch vis-à-vis the Government. On his death in 1960, Mgr. Piergiorgio Chiappero, a Franciscan, succeeded him, with the rank of Bishop, an elevation not without significance in the context of Catholic regard for the Jewish State.

Bishop Chiappero died suddenly in 1963; his successor was Mgr. John Kaldany, Doctor in Canon and International Law, who had been adjutant of the two previous incumbents for many years. Mgr. Kaldany, a local Christian, was elevated to episcopal dignity by Pope Paul VI during the papal pilgrimage to the Holy Land early in 1964, a proper recognition of his worth.

The Vicariate-General within the former demarcation of Israel had twelve parishes: Nazareth, Acre, Cana, Tiberias, Jerusalem, Jaffa, Ramla—all with Franciscans to minister to them; Haifa with a Carmelite Father as ministrant; and Yafiye, Rameh, Reneh and Shfaram, ministered to by secular priests of the Latin Patriarchate. Nazareth was the largest of these parishes by far, with about three thousand five hundred parishioners, and there, too, sat the Latin religious court, applying the Canon Law of the Roman Catholic Church and a special ordinance concerning matters of personal status, promulgated by the Patriarch in 1954.

The religious cadre of the Latin community in Israel, in June 1967, comprised a hundred and fifty-one monks, seven secular priests and six hundred and thirty-five nuns. The monks belonged to the following thirteen Orders: Assumptionists, Benedictines, Brothers of the Christian Schools, Brothers of St. John of God, Carmelites, Dominicans, Fathers of Betharram, Fathers of Zion, Franciscans, Jesuits, Lazarists, Little Brothers of Jesus and Salesians.

The conventual Congregations were: the Carmelite Sisters, Carmel St. Joseph, Carmel St. Thérèse, Franciscan Sisters of the Immaculate Heart of Mary, Franciscan Missionary Sisters of Mary, Salesian Sisters, Sisters of St. Anne, Sisters of St. Charles Borromeus, Sistes of Charity St. Vincent of Paul, Sisters of St. Claire, Sisters of St. Dorothy, Sisters of St. Elisabeth, Sisters of St. Joseph of the Apparition, Sisters of Nazareth, Sisters of Nigrizia, Sisters of the Rosary and Sisters of Our Lady of Sion.

The Latin community, again within the pre-war lines, administered thirty-five schools and kindergartens, five hospitals, four clinics and thirteen hospices for pilgrims; the Franciscan Order alone was responsible for eighteen monasteries and a number of schools and hospices, apart from its charge of most of the Holy Places which are in Latin care; the Benedictines and the Carmelites were and still are guardians of the others.

No other Christian community had in pre-June 1967 Israel as many places of worship—some seventy churches and chapels, including, among recent constructions, the great new Basilica of the Annunciation in Nazareth and a convent and chapel of the Franciscan Sisters of Mary of Nazareth, the Parish Church of St. Joseph and the Carmelite Monastery in Haifa, churches in Rama, Shfaram, and Reneh, a Benedictine chapel and monastery in Tabgha and a chapel and convent of the Sisters of the Rosary in Jish. Extensive restoration or enlargement, besides, had been carried out in Nazareth at the French Hospital and the Hospital of the Holy Family, the Casa Nova Hospice, the Monastery of the Salesian Fathers, and the school of the Franciscan Sisters of the Immaculate Heart of Mary; in Haifa, at the school of the Carmelite Sisters of St. Thérèse and the Italian Hospital; in Jaffa, at the school of the Sisters of St. Joseph; in Jerusalem, at the Franciscan Convent adjoining the Coenaculum. Plans were under way to build a center and a chapel in Beersheba, to satisfy the spiritual needs of pilgrims to the Negev.

The Franciscans contemplated building a new church where the Chapel of the Primacy of St. Peter stands, as well as a new chapel in Migdal (Magdala) on the shore of Lake Tiberias, in honor of Mary Magdalene.

Following the establishment of the State of Israel, it was felt necessary in Catholic quarters to provide pastoral care for non-Arab Catholics. Consequently "Oeuvre Saint James the Apostle" was founded and approved on February 11, 1955, by Patriarch Gori. The main tasks of this institution are the creation of centers for Hebrew-speaking communities (such centers were established in Jerusalem, Haifa and Tel Aviv-Jaffa,) and activities designed to foster reconciliation between Christians and Jews.

Constant and constructive amity with the local Latin hierarchy was uncomplemented by formal relations between the Government of Israel and the Vatican. This was not to say that valuable and representative contacts were lacking. The Ambassador

173

of Israel in Rome, and Israel delegations were invited to attend ceremonies of the Holy See, messages were exchanged on solemn occasions between the Pontiff and the President of the State, and there was the momentous pilgrimage of Pope Paul VI to the Holy Land; its strictly religious character still left room for a certain hopefulness that, out of the impressions and exchanges which it surely inspired, there may flow an eventual solvent of the theological conservatism of the Catholic Church, and of its "political" constraints, where Israel and Jewry are concerned.

Moreover, new and hopeful horizons of understanding and goodwill between Judaism and Christianity have been opened by the terms and sentiment of the text of the document regarding the relationship of the Catholic Church to non-Christian religions; although the text finally approved failed to meet all expectations in full, it may be considered significant progress. Here again, according to official statements from the Vatican, only a theological meaning attaches to the Jewish document but, in the sphere of Church activity, worldly aims are often a by-product of spiritual. It is in no sense underrating the efforts of other Church leaders in producing the document to suggest that two names go down in history in this regard: those of Pope John XXIII and Cardinal Augustin Bea.

The Greek Catholics. The *Greek Catholics* were the most numerous Catholic community within Israel up to June 1967, with twenty-two thousand souls. Archbishop George Hakim led the eparchy of Acre from 1943 to 1967, the year in which he was elected Greek Catholic Melkite Patriarch. On November 18, 1964, the See of Acre was made archepiscopal. Until then, the eparchy had been episcopal only, but its religious heads claimed that historical reasons gave them the right to the title of Archbishop, and Archbishop Hakim obtained recognition of the title from the Vatican. Archbishop Hakim showed himself to be a gifted religious leader and an outstanding public figure.

The eparchy embraced twenty-six parishes, with twenty-one local and four foreign priests to minister to them, ten with a complete curriculum of theological study behind them, the others less qualified and mostly married. Nineteen nuns of the Sisters of the

174

Annunciation, the Salvatorian Sisters and the Little Sisters of Jesus were in charge of Greek Catholic institutions. There were thirty-one places of worship. To the vigor and energy of Archbishop Hakim must be credited many of the churches and important buildings constructed since the State was established: the churches of Isfiya, Illabun and Mugrar, and St. Joseph the Worker of Nazareth, the episcopal residence in Haifa and, all in Nazareth, a convent of the Sisters of the Annunciation, a seminary and secondary school of St. Joseph, and the Mother Mary home and school for girls. Father Gauthier had been largely instrumental in the construction of a residential quarter, a project in which Archbishop Hakim was most active, and the Government and the Labor Federation rendered substantial help.

There were, besides, a boys' orphanage and clinic in Haifa, an old-age home in Acre, elementary schools in Shfaram and Nazareth; the community's other elementary schools had, by agreement, been taken over by the Ministry of Education and Culture. A hospital was under construction in Shfaram.

The Greek Catholic religious court was and still is in Nazareth; it applies the canon law of the Eastern Churches.

Summing up the activity of Archbishop Hakim during his tenure as head of the Greek Catholic community in Israel, it can be said that he was always very cooperative with the Israeli authorities for the sake of his community's interests. But after his elevation to the Patriarchal See, with residence in Beirut and Damascus, he did not miss any opportunity to express strongest criticism regarding Israel.

The Maronites. The Maronites, two thousand eight hundred strong in Israel in June 1967, had parishes in Haifa, Nazareth, Acre, Jish and Jaffa and they were cared for spiritually by four priests under the jurisdiction of the Archbishop of Tyre (Lebanon), Monsignor Joseph Khouri; Monsignor Jacques Raad, parish priest of Jaffa, was the Archbishop's Vicar in Israel. In the sixties, two newly-ordained local priests, after studying in St. Sulpice Seminary in Paris, joined the establishment. Plans were being made to put up a new parish church in Jish. The Maronite religious court, in Nazareth or Haifa, according to circumstances, also applies the Eastern canon.

The Orthodox Churches

The Greek Orthodox Church. In April 1951, the Greek Orthodox Patriarch, Timotheos Temelis, arrived in the Israeli sector of
the then-divided city of Jerusalem on his first visit to Israel. He
was in very ill health and until his death in 1955 many of his duties were performed by the Synod. After an interregnum of one
year, Mgr. Benedictos Papadopoulos, Titular Archbishop of
Tiberias succeeded Patriarch Timotheos as 95th Greek Orthodox
Patriarch of Jerusalem.[2] Until June 1967, Benedictos I, head of the
autocephalous Patriarchate of Jerusalem, which embraces Israel
and Jordan, was the spiritual leader of the sixteen thousand Greek
Orthodox in Israel. He was represented in Nazareth by
Metropolitan Isidoros Myrsiades, whose authority was limited to
spiritual matters. Administrative or financial affairs had to be
decided by the Patriarch and the Holy Synod within the Brotherhood of the Holy Sepulchre.

Within Israel's pre-June 1967 borders, the Patriarchate owned
fourteen historical churches and monasteries: Jerusalem-Holy
Cross, Mt. Zion and St. Simon; Lod-St. George; Ramla-St.
George; Jaffa-St. Michael; Acre-St. George; Haifa-St. Elias;
Nazareth-St. Gabriel; Mt. Tabor-Transfiguration; and churches
in Cana, Tiberias, Capernaum and Caesarea. They were tended
by the Metropolitan and eleven Greek monks, members of the
Brotherhood of the Holy Sepulchre.

There are a score of secondary churches, mostly in villages,
and there are thirteen native priests, non-celibate, to look after
them; new churches were lately built in Turan and Shfaram.
There are religious courts in Jaffa, Acre and Nazareth, in which
Byzantine law is applied.

The Patriarchate's large holdings earned enough revenues to
cover its expenses, not to mention the many pious endowments belonging to the local Orthodox communities, administered by the
local committees of the Arab congregations concerned, in
Nazareth, Haifa, Ramla, Lod, Acre, Jaffa and Rama.

The community of Nazareth conducts an elementary school of

---

2) On the complications surrounding the confirmation of Benedictos' election,
see Chapter Ten.

eight classes; that of Haifa has a secondary school in a newly constructed building; there are Sunday schools in Jaffa and in Ramla.

Within the area of the Greek Orthodox Patriarchate there are also ecclesiastical Missions of the Russian and the Rumanian Orthodox Patriarchates.

The Russion Orthodox Mission. The Russian Orthodox Mission, representing the Patriarchate of Moscow with its headquarters in Jerusalem is headed by an Archimandrite,[3] with an Igumen or monastic Superior as deputy, a deacon and an administrator as staff, and a number of serving nuns. The Patriarchate of Moscow, renewing its rapport with the Holy Land in 1949, took over and has carefully repaired and renovated the convents and churches in Israel: among then the Cathedral of the Holy Trinity in Jerusalem, and the "Gorny" Convent and Church in Ein Karem, St. Peter in Jaffa with the Tomb of Tabitha, and St. Elias on Mount Carmel; a church dedicated to Mary Magdalene has recently been built at the Sea of Galilee.

The tenure of the head of the Mission is only two years, as a rule, whereafter, recalled to Russia, he is customarily made a Bishop; thus Metropolitan Nicodeme, a former head, was put in charge of the Foreign Mission's Department of the Patriarchate.

Pilgrimages from Russia, which reached their peak before World War I, stopped entirely following the political upheaval which occurred in 1917. The only pilgrims visiting the Holy Land are a handful of highranking clerics and their retinue of deacons, who come to celebrate the Feast of the Holy Trinity to which the Russian Cathedral in Jerusalem is dedicated.

In October 1964, the Soviet Union signed an agreement with the Government of Israel for the sale to it of Russian property, not Russian Church property but only real estate that had been acquired in the last century. Properties in Jerusalem still belonging to the Russian Church after this transaction are the Cathedral of

---

3) From the establishment of the Mission in Jerusalem in 1949 to the present (1987), seventeen Archimandrites successively headed the Mission. They are: 1) Leonid, 2) Vladimir, 3) Policarp, 4) Michael, 5) Pimen, 6) Nicodeme, 7) Augustine, 8) Warfolomey, 9) Yuvenaly, 10) Germogen, 11) Anthony, 12) Yeronim, 13) Clement, 14) Seraphim, 15) Nicolay, 16) Panteleimon, and 17) Pavel.

the Holy Trinity, the large building nearby which houses the Mission, the Sergei building and a plot near the southern entrance to the compound.

The Romanian Orthodox Mission. The Romanian Orthodox *Mission* was re-established in Jerusalem in 1964, after a long interruption; its head, later appointed Archimandrite, was the only priest in charge of the Romanian religious property. The monastery and the chapel in Jerusalem, which had suffered from the war of 1948, have been repaired and even embellished artistically.

The Monophysite Churches

Until June 1967, their local membership was less than one thousand two hundred, but their age-old traditions and distinct and colorful customs lent them a more than numerical importance.

The Armenian Orthodox Church. The Armenian Orthodox *Church* had within pre-June 1967 borders six hundred members in eight towns, Jaffa and Haifa principally, and a single village. They come under the Patriarch of Jerusalem, Yegishe Derderian, residing in the Old City and, until June 1967, were represented in Israel by Archimandrite Houssig Bagdasian, who was the only cleric of his denomination in the State. The Archimandrite celebrated services in the community's four churches, in Jaffa, Ramla, Jerusalem and Haifa, in rotation; there are Sunday schools in Jaffa and Haifa where Armenian is also taught.

The religious court sat in Jaffa or Jerusalem as necessary but, in the circumstances, was rarely convened. The Patriarchate's property in Israel is extensive and yields a large income.

The Coptic Church. The Coptic *Church* was also an important landlord in Israel before 1967, but counted only a few hundred members, for the most part in Jaffa and Nazareth, with a church and a monastery, and a priest, in each place. The church in Nazareth, built in 1950, was the first new church in the new State and was consecrated by the then-Coptic Archbishop, a citizen of Egypt, then an enemy country; his successor, Archbishop Basilios, resident in the Old City, is also an Egyptian.

The Ethiopian Orthodox Church. *The Ethiopian Orthodox Church* had only a handful of adherents in West Jerusalem, where there is the one Ethiopian church, dedicated to the Virgin Mary, and adjoining it, a monastery; of the twelve monks in it, two were students at the Hebrew University. Bishop Youssef was head of the Church in the Holy Land. Little though it was, the Ethiopian community kept up an intense and devoutly traditional religious life. Pilgrimages from Ethiopia were more frequent in recent times and the Patriarch of the Church himself and Ethiopian royalty have been among the distinguished visitors.

The Syrian Orthodox Church. *The Syrian Orthodox (Jacobite) Church* had up to June 1967 about fifty Israeli followers.

Anglican and Protestant Churches

The denominations represented up to June 1967 were the Anglican Church, the Church of Scotland, the Lutheran Church, the Southern Baptist Convention, the Church of the Nazarene, the Church of Christ, the Church of God of the Seventh Day, the Pentecostal Movement, the Seventh-Day Adventists, the Brethren, the Mennonites and Jehovah's Witnesses.

There were also some Protestant Churches of an inter-denominational character, for example, the Church and Missionary Alliance.

But none enjoyed in pre-June 1967 Israel the status of a recognized community, according to the Ottoman and Mandatory precedents. The legal status of these denominations was, generally, that accorded by registration under the Ottoman Law of Societies, and thirty-one registrations already existed, with religious personnel numbering two hundred and fifty.

The Anglican Church. *The Anglican Church,* though still the largest denomination, was no longer as significant as it was un-

179

der the Mandate. Its spiritual head, from 1957 to 1968, was the Archbishop in Jerusalem, Angus Campbell MacInnes, one-time Bishop in Jerusalem, and then with a diocese stretching from Morocco to the Persian Gulf. His establishment in Israel had consisted of five English and four Arab clergymen, in respective spiritual charge of the Church's European and Arab members. Three of the Arab ministers were consecrated on October 16, 1966. The Arab branch, or Arab-Episcopal Church, as it is called, with some nine hundred followers in Israel, was remarkably autonomous in administration and finance, and recognized the Archbishop's authority only in spiritual matters; its congregations were and still are to be found in Nazareth, Shfaram, Rene, Kfar Yassif, Acre, Haifa, Jaffa, Ramla and Jerusalem, and in most of these places there is a church, besides the elementary schools in Haifa and Nazareth with four hundred pupils each.[4] St. Margaret's Girls' Orphanage was founded in Nazareth in 1883, in association with the Jerusalem and the Near East Mission. Later its functions changed and it now serves as a home and school for retarded children, subsidized by the Government.

The European branch, concentrated in Jerusalem, Jaffa, Haifa and Lod was much smaller, although it owned a great deal of property: it has a school in Jerusalem, located in the buildings of the formed CMJ hospital. Its enrolment in 1983 was 357 students, representing forty different nationalities. On Mount Carmel, the "Stella Carmel" cultural center and hospice is still run by the European branch of the Anglican Church. A number of teachers and nurses served and still serve these Anglican institutions.

The Church of Scotland. The Church of Scotland, too, was less influential than it was during the British Mandate and the congregations were sparse, but its cultural activity and good works were still manifold and praiseworthy in a church and hostel in Jerusalem, a church, school, cultural center and clinic in Jaffa, a church and hospice in Tiberias and a hospital in Nazareth. A school to train Arab nurses was founded near the hospital in Nazareth, with a chapel in the enlarged precincts.

---

4) The enrolment included pupils of other denominations as well.

Until June 1967, the Church of Scotland had a cadre of about fifty doctors and pastors, teachers and nurses.

The Lutheran Church. The work of the *Lutheran Church* was disrupted by the outbreak of the Second World War, the German branch liquidated and its property vested in a British Custodian. In 1951, the State of Israel entered into an agreement with the Lutheran World Federation to buy all the Lutheran property, except for two churches.

Scandinavian Lutheran Missions, by contrast, functioned expansively in pre-June 1967 Israel. A Norwegian Mission worked and still works in Haifa and Jaffa, the Scandinavian Seamen's Church cared for Scandinavian sailors in Haifa and Ashdod ports, and continues to do so. Jerusalem has a Swedish theological seminary for overseas Lutheran clergy,[5] and an elementary school of the Finnish Lutheran Church, which has recently put up a new building.

Since 1957, the *German Lutherans* have been anxious to reestablish contact, notably the Marienschwestern of Darmstadt, an Order of deaconesses founded by Mother Basilea Schlink, in contrition for Nazi evildoing, to redeem the wrong that Hitler wreaked upon Jewry. The deaconesses have opened a hostel called Abraham's House in the Talpiot quarter of Jerusalem, and another house on the Mount of Olives called "Beit Gaudia Dei," for victims of that barbarity. A "Beth El" with the same purpose is conducted in Nahariya by another small sect of German Protestants.

Also within the category of activities carried out with the intention of atoning for the Holocaust of the Jewish people is the work being done by the German "Aktion Suehnezeichen" (Operation Atonement.) In the sixties, the head of this group in Germany was Dr. Franz von Hammerstein, who later became Secretary of the

---

5) It is still located in Tabor House, a building erected in 1883 by the German architect, Conrad Schick, who also built Talitha Kumi School. Tabor House was originally designed as a private residence for Schick. In 1960, it was bought by the Methodist Church of America, as a seminary for missionaries to be trained for work in Islamic countries. In 1951, the building was rented by the Swedish Church, and in 1967, it was purchased and later handed over to the Church Mission.

World Council of Churches' "Agency for Consultation of the Church and the Jewish People."

Since October 1961, groups of German youngsters have been spending a year in Israel, working without pay in social welfare projects, for example constructing a home for blind people and helping crippled children.

The Southern Baptist Convention. The *Southern Baptist Convention* had, up to June 1967, a membership of about one hundred and seventy in Israel, with six Baptist and two Mennonite ministers. Few though they are, the Baptists, generously subsidized by co-religionists in the USA, were probably the busiest Protestant Church in Israel, principally in Nazareth, with a church and an elementary and secondary school of about five hundred and seventy pupils. From Nazareth, activity among the Arabs had been widespread, churches have been built in Cana, Rama, Turan and Acre; the George Truet Orphanage, formerly in Nazareth, occupies modern buildings in Petah Tikva, serving as a cultural center, with a farm annexed.

Nor were the Baptists idle in the Jewish sector; there is a church in Jerusalem and there are centers in Tel Aviv and Haifa. Grasping the importance of a knowledge of Hebrew in this regard, they ran a publishing house, "Dugit," in Tel Aviv, and issued a Hebrew monthly.

The Church of the Nazarene. The *Church of the Nazarene* had a mission in Jerusalem; it built in the sixties a church in Nazareth and established a center with a chapel in Haifa.

The Pentecostal Movement. The *Pentecostal Movement* is represented by several American, British and Scandinavian missionary organizations; local congregations are very small. One of these organizations, the Church of God of Prophecy, put up a memorial on the Horns of Hittin, a hill midway between Nazareth and Tiberias. A World Pentecostal Conference in Israel which the Movement organized in 1962 drew three thousand delegates.

Of note among the Pentecostal groups is the *Assemblies of God.* At the time of the British Mandate its members were active among the Arabs, transferring their attention, after 1948, to the

Jews. In 1962, the official representative of the Assemblies left, and their building in Jerusalem's Agron Street was taken over by the Messianic Assembly. In the seventies, the building was sold and the activities of the Messianic Assembly came to a halt.

The Seventh-Day Adventists. The Seventh-Day Adventists have a mission in Jerusalem, and several Adventist families worked as farmers in villages throughout the country, attracted by the facilities afforded them to keep the Sabbath.

The Church of Christ. The Church of Christ maintained a center in West Jerusalem and opened a secondary school in the village of Eilabun in Galilee, with an enrolment from the surrounding villages.

The Society of Friends. In 1950, the *American Friends Service Committee* (AFSC) started a program of relief in Galilee mainly in the village of Tur'an. It also opened a community center in Acre.

The Y.M.C.A. In numbers and works, the denominations listed hardly call for any description or commentary. But a prominent institution of broad cultural character, of no denominational affiliation, is the *Young Men's Christian Association.* Its headquarters, in Jerusalem, continues to engage in many cultural and sporting interests; a sister-building was dedicated in Nazareth in April 1965 and, on the Tiberias lake-shore, there is a small hospice, named after Dr. Harte, with a recently consecrated chapel for Protestant pilgrims to the Holy Places nearby.

The American Institute of Holy Land Studies. The *American Institute of Holy Land Studies* was founded by Dr. Douglas Young in 1959 as an inter-denominational finishing seminary for Protestant clergy, and also means to bring American and Israeli scholars of the Bible closer together.

The United Christian Council in Israel. Most of the Protestant denominations are federated in the *United Christian Council in Israel* (UCCI), a voluntary, independent organization, established in 1956 by Christian groups for mutual advice, cooperation and fellowship. It publishes a quarterly, UCCI News, and holds an annual convention, usually in Tiberias. In 1984, the Council had a membership of nineteen Churches and Missions.

Chapter Ten

THE WEST BANK UNDER
JORDAN ADMINISTRATION
(1948–1967)

INTRODUCTION

The causes of the Arab-Israel War of 1948, which resulted in great distress to the inhabitants of the Holy Land and in heavy damage to property, have been outlined in an earlier chapter. Consideration of the problem of the Arab refugees often overlooks that a nearly equal mass of Jewish refugees fled their centuries-old domiciles in Arab States under duress of Moslem hostility, following that war. Moreover, to form a true appraisal of the situation, one has to take into account that the number of Arab refugees—as given by Arab politicians—has been enormously inflated. But whatever one may think about responsibility for the outbreak of the war, and weighty as all other circumstances may be, the plight of the Palestinian refugees cannot be disregarded by any person of humanitarian instincts.

Christians made up less than ten percent of the exodus. They found their way, certainly at first, to Lebanon, to Jordan-occupied areas of Palestine and to Trans-Jordan, where substantial Christian congregations already existed, seeking shelter in the homes of kinsfolk and Christian charitable institutions. Assistance was extended to the refugees, Christian and Moslem alike, not only by the local charities, but also, and with by far larger resources, by international organizations. Besides UNRWA, the relief funds of several Churches offered help, notably the Palestine Relief Committee and the Belgian Catholic Mission. In April 1949, the Vatican founded the Pontifical Mission for Palestine, with generous means provided by the Catholic Relief Service[1] and the National Catholic Welfare Conference; Mgr. Thomas MacMahon, secre-

---

1) The Catholic Relief Service was founded in 1943 by the U.S.A. episcopate. In Israel, it has its center in Ratisbonne Monastery in Jerusalem.

185

tary of the Catholic Near East Welfare Association (C.N.E.W.A.) was appointed its first president. He organized local committees of the Pontifical Mission in Jerusalem and in the principal cities of the Near East.[2] The Lutheran World Federation, the Mennonite Central Committee and the Near-East Council of Churches were no less active.

The influx of Christian refugees had the virtue of multiplying the membership of what had been exiguous congregations. Larger communities called for new churches, bigger schools, more clinics. Urgent appeals to potential benefactors could justifiably be launched and the eventual response was open–handed.

The war of 1948 had left East Jerusalem, Samaria and most of Judea under Jordanian occupation.

On April 24, 1950, the Jordanians changed their *de facto* occupation of the so-called West Bank into definite annexation, and the new unity became the Hashemite Kingdom of Jordan.

On July 20, 1951, King Abdallah, an experienced ruler, was murdered by a hireling of the notorious, pro-Nazi ex-Mufti of Jerusalem, while he was leaving the Mosque of el-Aqsa, where he had attended the Friday morning prayers.

Jordan's kings considered themselves the lawful successors to the former rulers of the Holy Land in all matters pertaining to the Holy Places and the regulations of the *status quo* and, on January 15, 1951, Abdallah had appointed a Moslem to be inspector and administrator of the Haram es-Sherif, the Dome of the Rock, who also acted as chief custodian of the Christian Holy Places. Though scrupulous in their observance of the rules of the *status quo*, the Jordanian authorities sought to enhance the Moslem character of the Holy Land by erecting towering mosques in the vicinity of the Christian shrines.

On January 8, 1951, a new constitution was enacted in Jordan. By it, Islam was declared the State religion and the king had to be of Moslem faith. Otherwise, the Christian minority, which constituted seven percent of the population, was given, at least on paper, the same rights as the Moslem majority.

But, in spite of the professed principle of equality of all citi-

2) Since 1966, Mgr. John G. Nolan has been the President of the Pontifical Mission in Palestine.

zens, without distinction of creed, race or language, the Jordanian authorities followed a line of conduct favoring the nationalistic Arab aims, identifying themselves with Islam in the main. This found expression in more than one law, and the matter was of deep concern to Church leaders.

On February 16, 1953, for example, the Jordanian Government published a Law on charitable societies, of which several sections were thought to threaten the very existence of the many religious institutions engaged in charitable work. Christian protests led to the promulgation of a new Law on March 17, 1956, more liberal towards societies already established.

A Law of April 16, 1953 was designed to restrict ownership of real estate by religious societies, whether Jordanian or foreign: to acquire or own real estate contiguous to a Holy Place they had to get Cabinet approval and foreign societies had to register and accept Government control over their immovables; of any part of them which was considered by the Government to be owned in excess, the sale could be ordered.

A Law of April 16, 1955, on education, prescribed that:

"no indigenous school may be opened without acquiring first a permit from the Ministry of Education. Both indigenous and foreign schools must teach the Arab language, history and geography, according to the official curriculum. The lessons and examinations in these subjects must be given in Arabic. All schools must declare their financial sources to the Ministry. In no school may pupils be taught a religion which is not according to their faith. In case of transgression, the licence of the school can be revoked. There is prohibition of establishing new schools or enlarging existing ones. Schoolbooks must be approved by the Ministry. Moslem holidays must be considered as official ones, and as such have to be respected. Moslem curriculum in Christian private schools must include the teaching of the Moslem religion to Moslem pupils."

Vehement objection from Christian quarters was successful in mitigating the severity with which some of these provisions were enforced. But it is plain that the authorities were prejudiced against what was Christian and foreign, even if they dared not implement their policy in full, and even if it was always possible for the Churches to contrive the palliation of overly harsh measures.

On the positive side, one should mention a Jordanian Law of 1952, which granted Christian religious courts the same jurisdictional powers as those enjoyed by the Moslem religious courts, an equality that did not exist under British Mandatory Administration.

THE CATHOLIC CHURCHES

The Roman Catholic Church

After the death of Patriarch Barlassina, at one of the most critical moments in the affairs of the diocese, Monsignor Vincent Gelat was appointed Apostolic Administrator. In May 1948, Archbishop Gustav Testa arrived as Regent of the Patriarchate and Apostolic Delegate. Monsignor Testa, later Cardinal and Secretary of the Oriental Congregation, was not a newcomer to the Holy Land, having previously held the office of Apostolic Delegate. His regency lasted eighteen months, until Monsignor Alberto Gori, formerly a Franciscan Custos of the Holy Land, was elevated to the Patriarchal See.

The upheaval of 1948 impelled a movement of emigration, especially to the two Americas, and internal migratory currents were set in motion, too. The re-distribution of the Latins changed the physiognomy of the diocese radically, and this gave rise to an urgent need for new chapels, schools and other institutions, and many had to be built during the years 1948–1967.

The Latin Patriarchate was foremost in this constructive work. It opened the college of el-Ahliyah in Ramallah, schools in Beit Jala and Aboud, and one in Gaza, then under Egyptian administration. It built new churches in Beit Sahour (1950), in Ein Arik (1951), in Aboud (1953) and in Gaza (1953), and presbyteries in Beit Sahour and Jenin. The seminary in Beit Jala was enlarged at the same time.

The Franciscans, faithful to their tradition of marking with artistic shrines the sites holy to Christianity, entrusted Architect

Barluzzi with the design and building of the Church of St. Lazarus in Bethany, and the Chapels "Angelorum ad Pastores" in Beit Sahour and "Dominus Flevit" on the Mount of Olives. They restored the Grotto of Gethsemane and the Chapel of the Baptism near the Jordan, which had been badly damaged by an earthquake in 1933.

The other religious Orders and Congregations were not bad seconds. The Passionist Fathers built St. Martha's Church in Bethany (1965), and the Trappists a church for their monastery in Latrun. Activity in the educational field was no less remarkable. The Christian Brothers in Jerusalem and the Salesians in Bethlehem had their schools enlarged and renovated. New schools were opened in Jerusalem and elsewhere. The Franciscan Fathers built their Terra Sancta Boys' School in 1958, the Sisters of St. Charles their new Schmidt's Girls' School near St. Paul's Hospice, likewise in Jerusalem, in 1962. Educational institutions were started in the Holy City by the Daughters of Calvary and the Theresian Institute; in Nablus, the Sisters of St. Joseph opened a primary and secondary school; schools were opened by the Rosary Sisters in Beit Jala, by the Franciscan Sisters in Bethlehem, and in Jericho by the Franciscan Fathers for boys and by the Franciscan Sisters for girls.

The Rosary Sisters, with their mother-house in Israel since 1948, built a new convent and novitiate in Beit Hanina, near Jerusalem; the Sisters of St. Joseph, for a similar reason, a new hospital in East Jerusalem; the Sisters of Charity of St. Vincent a boys' orphanage in Bethany; and the Daughters of Our Lady of Grief a home for the aged in Jerusalem.

The additional personnel required by all this expansion was provided by new Orders which established branches in the Holy Land during this period, among them the Mercedarians, the Tertiary Franciscan Sisters of Maribor, the Theresians and the Sisters of Our Lady of Calvary.

The Franciscan Order was very active in archaeological excavations, anxious to discover surer evidence of the location of the events recorded in the Scriptures; it has, for instance, dug on Mount Nebo, at "Dominus Flevit" on the Mount of Olives, at the Herodion and in Beit Sahour.

The Greek Catholic Church

The Greek Catholics built several churches and schools during the Jordanian interval, the new churches often replacing the simpler edifices of the previous century. In Beit Sahour, the Church of Our Lady of Shepherds, was consecrated by Patriarch Maximos IV on May 1, 1955, and a vocational school for girls, directed by the Salvatorian Sisters, and a junior seminary were opened there: the transfer of the lower classes of the Seminary of St. Anne to Rayak in Lebanon in 1946 made this junior seminary essential to provide clergy for the growing community.

In the same neighborhood, the Compagnons du Père Paul Gauthier, formerly active in Nazareth, did welfare work among the needy. In Ramallah, which was the largest Greek Catholic congregation in all of Judea, a new church and a modern primary and secondary school for boys and girls had been built in 1951. Beit Sahour likewise had a new mixed primary and secondary school. At various times, churches and presbyteries have been built in Bethlehem, Nablus and Taibe.

The Sixth Station of the Via Dolorosa had been thoroughly restored in 1957, and the Little Sisters of Jesus set up their headquarters and novitiate in the building.

Besides the Salvatorian Sisters in Ramallah and Beit Sahour, the Benedictine Sisters of the Congregation of Our Lady of the Apostles worked energetically in Bethlehem, and the Auxiliares Féminines Internationelles in Ramallah. In 1964, the Maison d'Abraham was founded in Jerusalem, according to the wish of Pope Paul VI, who came on pilgrimage to the Holy Land. Located in a former Syrian Catholic seminary, it was inaugurated on April 1965 by the Greek Catholic Patriarch Maximos IV. Maison d'Abraham serves pilgrims of poor means.

In the light of the expansion of the Greek Catholic communities and institutions in Judea and Samaria, the Synod, assembled in Jerusalem in July 1960, elevated the Patriarchal Vicar of Jerusalem, Monsignor Gabriel Abu Saada, to the rank of Archbishop. On his death in 1965, Monsignor Hilarion Capucci succeeded him.

THE GREEK ORTHODOX CHURCH

Patriarch Timotheos was ailing during the last years of his Patriarchate, and several of his duties were performed by his representative, Monsignor Athenagoras, Titular Archbishop of Sebaste, and by the Synod.

In 1953, the Patriarchate established a boarding school next to the Seminary of St. Dimitri, with about sixty students, two-thirds of them Greeks and the rest Arabs.

Patriarch Timotheos died on December 31, 1955. Two months before his death, he had appointed six new Archbishops, all of them until then Archimandrites, members of the Synod. Archbishop Athenagoras was appointed Locum Tenens of the Patriarchate.

The formalities for the election of a new Patriarch had to be carried out according to the statute of 1875, approved by the Turkish Government, for the ordinance issued by the British Mandatory Administration in 1941 had not been recognized by the Brotherhood of the Holy Sepulchre. The Arab Orthodox, whom the statute of 1875 denied all part in the elections, did their utmost to delay the proceedings. In this they had the support of the Jordanian Government, which naturally sympathized with the Arab aspirations. A meeting of the notables of the Arab Orthodox community in March 1956 put forward their minimal demands. They claimed, *inter alia*, an effective share in the election of the Patriarch and a say in the management of the revenues of the Patriarchate. A special committee of Arab Orthodox members was charged with the task of pressing the Government to accept the demands. There was a succession and alternation of appeals to the Government, and to the High Court by the Patriarchate and by the representatives of the Arab Orthodox community. The Government solved the impasse by issuing a new statute and at the same time allowing the election of a Patriarch under the statute of 1875. The Patriarch was elected on January 29, 1957, and the new statute was approved by the Jordanian Parliament on June 1, 1958. The election of Patriarch Benedictos I was sanctioned by royal decree. The approval of the Government of Israel was not asked for, whereas, in the case of the election of the Armenian Orthodox Patriarch in 1960, the approval of the Governments of both Israel and Jordan was sought and given.

191

The new statute promulgated by the Jordanian Government endeavored to reach a compromise between the Arab Orthodox community and the Brotherhood, but did not satisfy the ambitions of the community, nor could it be acquiesced in by the Brotherhood, which complied only with the provisions not in conflict with the Byzantine Canon Law. In 1950, for the first time, an Arab Archbishop was elected to the Brotherhood in Jerusalem under the new statute; his mother, it should be noted, was of Greek extraction.

Several new churches were built in East Jerusalem, such as St. Basilius and St. George's Monastery and Chapel, and the new Church of St. Stephen was started in the Kidron Valley, near Gethsemane. A new church was built in Beit Sahour, and a number of churches and chapels were restored by the efforts as well as at the expense of the priests in charge, who spared no personal sacrifice in beautifying the structures entrusted to them.

New schools were built in Ramallah, Gifne, Aboud and Taibe. In all, the Patriarchate maintained in the territory under its jurisdiction some forty educational institutions, most of them primary schools, but some secondary as well.

In recent decades, not a few autocephalous Patriarchs visited the Holy Land, with the aim of stressing the links between the Orthodox Churches. Foremost was the Ecumenical Patriarch Kir Athenagoras, who came in 1959 and again in 1964, when he met Pope Paul VI in Jerusalem. There were also Alexei of Moscow (1945 and 1961), German of Yugoslavia (1959) and Cyril of Bulgaria (1963). Patriarch Benedictos visited Constantinople and Greece in 1959, the United States of America, Canada, Great Britain and Yugoslavia in 1962, and the USSR, the Balkan countries and Cyprus in 1968. Leading prelates of the Holy Synod attended Orthodox international conferences in Rhodes, Belgrade and Geneva and were present at the Lambeth Conference in 1968.

ANGLICAN AND PROTESTANT CHURCHES

The Anglican Church

After the fighting of 1948, the Anglican Church in Jordan-administered territory had to be reorganized, with the number of its faithful dwindling as the Mandate ended and the country split into two political entities.

The last British High Commissioner, upon his departure from Palestine, had left at the portal of St. George's Cathedral the Royal Arms formerly kept at Government House. It was a significant gesture, as though to say that from then on the Church of England stood for Great Britain's presence in the Holy Land. The cathedral and the headquarters of the Anglican Church adjoining were now in the Jordan-held part of Jerusalem. The Bishop, W.H. Stewart, retired in 1957, and Archbishop (as he became) Campbell MacInnes took over in August of the same year. St. George's compound was enlarged in 1962 by the addition of a theological college and conference center.

Under the new dispensation, the Arab branch of the Church was able to seek more independence. In 1947, it had obtained the status of a recognized community in Trans-Jordan; corresponding recognition was now extended in Cis-Jordan.

The Church Missionary Society handed over to the Arab Evangelical Community its hospital in Nablus and its schools in Nablus and in Zebabdeh, and all its property in the West Bank. In Ramallah, Bir Zeit, Nablus and adjacent villages, property that comprised churches and buildings in their vicinity was also handed over to it and became *waqf*. In Bethlehem, a former school-building of the Society was rented to the Jordanian authorities as a Government school.

On the retirement of Bishop Stewart, the Bishopric was raised to an Archbishopric, which included a new Bishopric of Jordan, Lebanon and Syria, taking in all Anglican congregations in the three countries. Bishop Najib Cubain, first incumbent of the new Bishopric of Jordan, Lebanon and Syria, was consecrated on January 6, 1958. East Jerusalem came under a special arrangement, whereby both the Archbishop and the Bishop of Jordan were its Diocesan Bishops.

St. George's College was set up in order to prepare ordinands from Middle East countries and from overseas for the priesthood. The college was enlarged in 1969 to meet the growing needs of the worldwide Church.

Before the events of June 1967, there were larger Anglican

193

congregations in East Jerusalem and in Ramallah, smaller ones in Bethlehem, Bir Zeit, Nablus, Rafidiyah, Zebabdeh and Aboud. Anglican churches were to be found in all these places, with the exception of Bethlehem. Schools were maintained in Jerusalem and in Ramallah (two), in Nablus and in Rafidiyah. In Nablus, there was a hospital and in Hebron an orphanage. The Anglican community had a court of first instance and a court of appeal, applying the law of personal status adopted by its council in 1956 and confirmed by the Jordanian Parliament.

In connection with the establishment of the Bishopric of Jordan, Lebanon and Syria, a new Statute of the Arab Evangelical Episcopal community was published in 1958. The cultural and economic level of the members of this community is perhaps the highest among that of the local Christians. This is possibly because the Evangelical Episcopalians are mainly town-dwellers and belong to the middle class. Furthermore, they undoubtedly benefitted from their closer connection with the British establishment during the Mandate.[3]

The Lutheran Church

After the partition of the Holy Land in 1948, Lutheran Church property in East Jerusalem was composed mainly of the Muristan compound with the Church of the Redeemer, a school and a hospice[4] and of the Augusta Victoria Stiftung on the Mount of Olives. Outside Jerusalem, there were church buildings and educational institutions in Beit Jala, Bethlehem and Beit Sahour. In Jordan, the Lutheran Church was soon able to take up its work again with means supplied by the Lutheran World Federation, with the indemnities paid in respect of its properties in Israel, and by no means least, with funds collected in West Germany after its economic revival. Most of the German institutions which had previously operated in the western part of Jerusalem were re-estab-

---

3) Evidence of the superior level of the members of the Arab Evangelical Episcopal community can be seen in the fact that two members of that community were elected to the first Knesset, in spite of the fact that the Church body to which they belonged was numerically one of the smallest.

4) Construction of the hospice in the Muristan quarter started in 1910.

lished in the Jordan-occupied sector of the Holy Land. The Diakonissen of Kaiserswerth resumed in 1950 their educational work for girls in a house belonging to the Jerusalem Foundation in Beit Jala, until it could be transferred in 1960 to a splendid new Talitha Kumi building on a hill south-west of the town. The Leper Hospital, too, was reopened in temporary premises in East Jerusalem until a new, modern hospital was made available on the Mount of the Star, near Ramallah.[5] The Augusta Victoria Stiftung, occupied until 1948 by the British Army, was transformed into a huge hospital, first administered by the Red Cross and afterwards by the Lutheran World Federation, together with the United Nations Organization. A school for nurses, sponsored by the Lutheran World Federation, was established in the framework of the Augusta Victoria Hospital. The German Evangelical Institute for Archaeology in the Holy Land restarted its work. By contrast, the educational activities of Schneller were not restored in the Holy Land as such but, instead, in Trans-Jordan and Lebanon; so, too, with the Carmel Mission which once had its center in Haifa but now migrated to Lebanon.

The Lutheran Church buildings and schools serving an exclusively Arab population were kept by their respective congregations in East Jerusalem, Bethlehem, Beit Sahour and Beit Jala. As we shall see, the activity there actually increased, owing to the influx of refugees.

The years following the partition of Palestine saw the gradual rise of an Arab Evangelical community in the Jordanian-occupied part of the Holy Land. It consisted mainly of three Arab congregations: in Jerusalem, in Bethlehem and Beit Sahour, and in Beit Jala. In 1957, a fourth congregation was established in Ramallah which, in 1963, was provided with a new church—the Church of Hope, a pastor's residence and a handsome community center. Special attention was given to the development of the existing schools. The primary schools in Bethlehem and Beit Sahour were enlarged and modernized. The Martin Luther School in the Old City's Muristan quarter was built in 1964. It replaced the former school, established in 1873, which had begun its classes in

---

5) With the dramatic fall in the number of lepers in recent times, the hospital on the Mount of the Star has been converted into a rehabilitation center for youth.

rooms adjoining the cloister in the Muristan building. To meet the need which was felt to provide secondary education, a school of that level was opened in Bethlehem with a boarding annex in Beit Jala.

On May 17, 1959, the Evangelical Lutheran Church in Jordan (ELCJ) was granted official recognition;[6] its membership then numbered about one thousand five hundred. A synod of four clergymen and fourteen laymen was entrusted with the administration of its interests.

Although the Lutheran community was composed of Arabs in the main, there is still a small German Lutheran congregation in Jerusalem. Jerusalem is also the See of the Propst, his headquarters being in the Muristan compound. Services are held in the nearby Church of the Redeemer, with a continuously rising attendance of German pilgrims. In the compound there is also a youth hostel.

The Lutheran community does not have religious courts of its own. In matters of personal status, members of the Lutheran community can avail themselves of the offices of the courts of the Evangelical Episcopal community.

The German Evangelical Institute for Archaeological Research in the Holy Land is one of the institutions supported by the Evangelical Churches in Germany.

It was founded in 1901, to explore the Holy Land and its history, especially its biblical past. The first seat of the Institute was a building in Prophets' Street, Jerusalem, and until the First World War its director was Prof. Gustaf Dalman. After interruption by the Second World War, it resumed its work in 1953. In 1966, the new director, Prof. Martin Noth, transferred the Institute to a handsome building in Jerusalem's Sheik Jarrah quarter.

Other Protestant Denominations

Besides the long-established Anglican and Lutheran Churches, which had attained the status of recognized communi-

---

6) A French translation of the Statute of the Evangelical Lutheran Church in Jordan (ELCJ) appears in the periodical, *Proche Orient Chrétien*, 1960, p. 369.

ties under Jordanian rule, a number of smaller denominations, Evangelical and Fundamentalist mostly, with their headquarters in the United States, pursued missionary activities in the Jordan-administered part of Palestine, establishing there places of worship, schools and charitable institutions.

The missionary activity pursued by Fundamentalist denominations and by the Jehovah's Witnesses was opposed by the long-established larger Churches, the members of which were the main object of their proselytizing activity. The Jordanian Government, eager to appear to subscribe to principles of religious liberty, obstructed missionary activity by administrative means only.

The Southern Baptists have a small congregation with a center and a bookstore in East Jerusalem, and a center in Ramallah. In 1954, the Southern Baptist Convention took over the hospital founded in Gaza in 1908 by the Anglican Church Missionary Society, and services were held in the chapel belonging to the hospital complex. Another Baptist organization, the *First Baptist Bible Church,* has chapels in East Jerusalem and Ramallah. *The Church of the Nazarene* has two small congregations in East Jerusalem—one, on Nablus Road, is Arab and the other is Armenian, located near the Armenian quarter. *The Seventh-Day Adventists* run a center in East Jerusalem and so does the *Church of Christ*. Among the *Pentecostal* groups active in East Jerusalem are the *Churches of God*, with their headquarters in Tennessee.

The Mennonite Central Committee with headquarters in Akron, Pennsylvania, started its work on the West Bank in 1950. It has distinguished itself in educational projects: a self-help needle-work center in Jerusalem, a boys' school in Beit Jala, a sewing-center in the village of Surif near Hebron, and a free kitchen in Jericho.

The Society of Friends continued its school work in Ramallah, which began in Ottoman times.

Among the Protestant missions is the *Independent Presbyterian Mission*, connected with the (Fundamentalist) Council of American Churches of Reverend MacIntyre; it maintains a church, a hospital and an educational center in Bethlehem. Among the interdenominational institutions, the *YMCA* is foremost. It built a new hostel called "Aelia Capitolina" in East Jerusalem, when the splendid building erected in the 'thirties in the western sector ceased to be accessible to East Jerusalemites upon the splitting of the city. It also opened a center in Beit Sahour near Shepherds' Field, and a vocational school in Jericho.

Prominent among the institutions connected with Great Britain is the *Ophthalmic Hospital of the Order of St. John.* A new building was put up in East Jerusalem after the city was divided.

An object of special veneration to many Protestants is the *Garden Tomb,* regarded by them as the site of Golgotha and of the Tomb of Christ. It was General Gordon of Khartoum who, in 1882, during a visit to the Holy Land, formed the view that a hill some 250 meters north of the Damascus Gate was the site of the Crucifixion and identified a tomb hewn in the rock not far away as that of Christ. He induced an influential body of people in England to raise funds wherewith to purchase the site, and in 1894 the *Garden Tomb (Jerusalem) Association* was established in London. The Association still pays for the upkeep of the Garden, in which there now are a warden's residence and restrooms for visitors.

It will not cause any surprise that Christians who regard the Church of the Holy Sepulchre as the authentic site of the Crucifixion and the Tomb of Christ, and they are the majority, should strongly resist any seeming encroachment upon the tradition to which they are vowed.

THE MONOPHYSITE CHURCHES

The Armenian Church

After the death of Patriarch Guregh II Israelian (October 19, 1949), Monsignor Yegishe (Elisha) Derderian became Locum Tenens. From that moment, the Armenian Patriarchate of Jerusalem entered upon a period of disquiet which was to last eleven years. Opposing trends within the Brotherhood and the community struggled for leadership in the See. It is not easy to ascertain the underlying cause of the dissensions, whether conflicting political orientations, personal ambitions or the highly independent and fighting spirit ingrained in the Armenian people. When, at last, in 1956, Monsignor Derderian was likely to be elected Patriarch, this was prevented by Monsignor Tiran Nersoyan, an Archbishop resident in the United States; he came to Jerusalem and persuaded the Jordanian authorities to expel Derderian who, on the eve of his departure for Armenia, appointed Archbishop Harig Aslanian to be Vicar. On October 9, 1956, the Jordanian Government deported Archbishop Nersoyan, not without strong protests from his followers within the Jerusalem community and he, in turn, appointed Archbishop Souren Kemhadjian as his Vicar. Nersoyan, however, succeeded in overcoming the resistance of the Jordanian authorities, returned to Jerusalem, was recognized as Locum Tenens and subsequently elected in March 1957 to the Patriarchal See by the General Assembly of the Armenian Fraternity of Jerusalem. But Archbishop Derderian, returning now to Amman, contrived to hold up confirmation of the election by the Government. In January 1958, Archbishop Nersoyan was again served with an official order of expulsion but it was held in suspense, lest its carrying out inflame the religious feelings of the Christian citizens of the Holy City. In August of the same year, however, Nersoyan was forcibly required to return to the States. After an absence of three years, Archbishop Derderian could return again, was elected by the Fraternity and confirmed as Patriarch by the King of Jordan; he sought and was granted confirmation also by the Government of Israel, in 1960.

On October 13, 1963, a major event took place in the religious life of the Armenian community, when His Beatitude Vasken I, the Catholicos of All Armenians, with the See in Etchmijadzin (Armenia), visited Jerusalem. A solemn liturgy was held by him in St. James Cathedral, in the presence of Patriarch Derderian and of the Catholicos of Cilicia, Khoren I.

The Syrian Orthodox Church

The Syrian Orthodox community has enjoyed official recognition since the Mandatory period. Most of its faithful live in East Jerusalem and Bethlehem. It is headed by an Archbishop, who is assisted by a number of monks. Prominent among the Archbishops who have occupied the See is Anastasios Joshua Samuel, who was instrumental in the original purchase of several of the Dead

Sea Scrolls and their conveyance to America. Archbishop Boulos Geleph, who was in office until a few years ago, went over to the Syrian Catholics owing to a misunderstanding with his own Church. His successor was Archbishop Dioscoros Lukas Shaya. The Archbishop of Jerusalem is dependent on the Syrian Orthodox Patriarch of Antioch and All the East, Mar Ignatios Zaka, who resides in Damascus.

The Ethiopian Church

On February 12, 1961, the Ethiopians obtained from the Jordanian Government the right to be reinstalled in the Chapels of St. Michael and of the Four Living Creatures, but the privilege was revoked within a few weeks. Deir el-Sultan is claimed by them, whilst the Copts base themselves on the *status quo*. The Ethiopians live in miserable hovels in the courtyard of Deir el-Sultan on the roof of the Chapel of St. Helena, which is part of the Church of the Holy Sepulchre. The Copts consider the Ethiopians as their "guests" and maintain strict control over the ceremonies and other activities of the latter. The Ethiopians worshipped in the small Chapel of the Savior, west of the dome of the Chapel of St. Helena: the constricted size allowed only one priest to officiate at a time.

The Emperor of Ethiopia and the imperial family always took a direct interest in the institutions of the Ethiopian Church in the Holy Land and this attachment was strengthened by the fact that the Emperor resided in Jerusalem when, after the conquest of his country by the Italians in 1935, he was forced to go into exile.

As well as the Monastery of Takla Haymanot in the Old City, built in 1891, the Ethiopians have another monastery near the handsome Cathedral Debre Genet. On the western bank of the Jordan River, they have a third, a new building completed a few years ago, dedicated to the Holy Trinity, paid for by the late Empress Menen.

Chapter Eleven

THE HOLY LAND IN THE AFTERMATH OF THE JUNE 1967 WAR

INTRODUCTION

With the ceasefire of June 1967, the artificial barriers that had severed the Holy Land and the City of Jerusalem for nineteen years finally came down.

The reunification of the Holy City was an event which transcended every consideration of a political or strategic nature, and aroused deep emotion throughout the world.

Apart, however, from reactions of sentiment and sanctity, other factors had to be taken into account concerning the inhabitants of the country, and the citizens in Jerusalem in particular. For them, the reunification brought about a radical change which made itself felt strongly in everyday life, in new contacts between races and religions, and in new horizons opening for the most diverse activities in the spiritual and material realms.

Reviewing the situation in the wake of the June 1967 War from the point of view of Christian interests, the salient facts were as follows:

— the most important Holy Places of Christianity were now situated in sovereign territory of the State of Israel,

— the Heads of the Christian Churches of the Holy Land, who had their seat in East Jerusalem, now found themselves in Israel,

— the Christian population of the Holy Land, no longer divided, had nearly doubled in size by comparison with its numbers in the State of Israel prior to the Six-Day War.

That war, which was forced upon Israel by its Arab neighbors, inevitably took its toll of human life and property, but unprejudiced observers, and notably the Heads of the local Churches, acknowledged that Israel acted with the most reverent and solicitous concern for the safety and accessibility of the Holy Places.

After the reunification of Jerusalem, the Prime Minister of Israel at once called in the two Chief Rabbis, the representatives of the Moslem clergy, and the Heads of the Christian communities,

201

among them the Apostolic Delegate and the Roman Catholic, the Greek Orthodox and the Armenian Patriarchs. At that historic meeting, he affirmed that the Government of Israel held it to be an essential principle of its policy to safeguard all the Holy Places, emphasizing that the internal administration of their sites and the measures to be taken for their management would be left entirely to the spiritual Heads concerned.

That very day, June 27, 1967, the Knesset (Parliament) passed a law which came into instant effect, the Protection of Holy Places Law, prescribing that whoever, in any way, desecrates or violates a Holy Place is liable to seven years' imprisonment, and whoever is found guilty of preventing free access to such a place is liable to five years' imprisonment.

To prevent improper behavior or the wearing of immodest attire at sacred sites, the Ministry of Religious Affairs, in agreement with the Heads of the Churches, issued instructions setting out the standard of deportment to be observed.

DEVELOPMENTS IN EAST JERUSALEM AFTER THE REUNIFICATION

On June 28, 1967, the Minister of Interior delivered to the Mayor of Jerusalem an administrative order enlarging Jerusalem's limits to include the Old City and several extramural quarters of the eastern part. One of the main consequences was to extend Israel law to the city in its entirety.

From the moment the cease-fire came into force, the Israeli authorities exerted themselves to restore life in East Jerusalem to normal. Attention was first directed to supplying the population with provisions and reinstating essential services which had been disrupted in the fighting. The central and local authorities then systematically proceeded to furnish East Jerusalem with all the amenities enjoyed by the western part of the city in such spheres as education, social welfare and sanitation.

The existing relief services of the Churches also promptly extended their assistance to those in distress as a result of the political upheaval. Jerusalem *Caritas*, a Catholic organization created in order to centralize charitable activities in the Jerusalem area, started its work as early as June 12, 1967.

In Jerusalem, contacts between Jews of the western, and Moslems and Christians of the eastern part were from the start more frequent and of a closer nature than in the administered areas. This was due not only to the physical proximity of domicile, but also to the extension of Israeli law to East Jerusalem, a circumstance that fostered uniformity in everyday life.

There was evidently a gap between Arabs whose close contact with Israeli Jews began only in June 1967 and Arabs who had been Israelis for two or three decades. The long spell of coexistance between Jews and Arabs, especially the Christians among them, had led to a remarkable assimilation of the Arabs to the Israeli environment that showed itself in the most varied ways: technical progress, living conditions, mode of dress, social services, spread of culture and so forth.

The process of integration, although slower and less pronounced, soon became evident among the Arabs of East Jerusalem. Shortly after the reunification of the city, no fewer than five thousand among them were working in Jewish enterprises and a large number joined the Israel Labor Federation and could share in the membership benefits and security afforded by organized labor.

After the reunification of the city, Israel put its medical facilities at the disposal of the Arabs of East Jerusalem and the administered areas. The Hadassah-Hebrew University Hospital, the most modern among such institutions in the Middle East, was eagerly called upon, as were other hospitals in Jerusalem and the clinics of the Labor Federation's Sick Fund.

Well aware of the importance of Christian religious life for Jerusalem's ambience, the guardians of the law sought to ensure, from the time of reunification, that the city's special character be safeguarded, guaranteeing, not least, the orderly conduct of ceremonies and processions.

After the reunification of the Holy City, Church dignitaries were unanimous in the opinion that never in the past had their Christmas and Easter celebrations been held with such decorum and dignity.

The City Fathers, well aware of the exceptional responsibility vested in them, also showed concern for the practical problems of the ecclesiastical institutions which the municipality could help solve. Special meetings were held periodically in the first years of the city's reunification, enabling leading ministers and superiors of monasteries and convents to bring up their problems, and these were not infrequently settled to mutual satisfaction without administrative delays.

Respect on the part of the Israeli authorities for the sacred character of Jerusalem did not circumscribe itself to the safeguarding of the holy shrines and the main religious institutions. The municipality issued a by-law for the reunited city requiring Christian shopkeepers to close their places of business on Sundays, and Moslem shopkeepers on Fridays. (Jewish shops in West Jerusalem have always closed on Saturday, the Jewish Sabbath.)

The Government's concern for the Churches also expressed itself in a decision to pay compensation for the damage they sustained during the fighting. A special commission was set up to examine and assess the damage they sustained during the fighting. In the spring and summer of 1968, contractual compensation agreements were signed with some fifteen major Churches and ecclesiastical organizations and payment of compensation was made totalling six million Israeli pounds (then equivalent to $1,715,000). The damage was caused only in part by the action of the Israel Defence Forces, and the compensation was certainly appreciated by the Churches, which were not unaware of the many urgent and considerable financial obligations which the young State had to meet.

After the reunification, the Old City of Jerusalem within the imposing sixteenth-century walls found itself in a state of utter delapidation, a condition which demanded immediate action for general renovation and infrastructure renewal.

The East Jerusalem Development Corporation, a joint State-Municipal body, was entrusted with the extensive project of renovation, the implementation of which, by the close of 1987, had already cost several millions of dollars. Among the buildings repaired figure those which, according to Christian tradition, are connected with the 7th and 8th Stations of the Via Dolorosa. Their foundations had to be reinforced and the buildings, which were near collapse, were preserved. The wall of the Armenian monastery, likewise in danger, was also saved. A monastery belonging to the Maronites, which was in delapidated condition, was entirely rebuilt at the expense of the Corporation.

In the Christian Quarter of the Old City, the main streets, formerly muddy and totally neglected, were properly paved. On the Via Dolorosa, the same work was carried out, giving special emphasis to the emplacement of the Stations by means of a semi-circle of distinctive paving at each one. Excavation along the Via Dolorosa revealed a six-meter stretch, near the Third Station, dating from the first centuries of the Christian era. This was only one of the many archaeological finds that came to light in the Old City. Paramount among the archaeological discoveries was the "Nea", the famous sixth-century church built by Emperor Justinian.

An entirely new infrastructure was installed with separate drainage and sewage systems, as well as a new water network. No less important in the process of renewal was the installation of underground electricity and telephone cables and cables linked to a central television antenna, to replace the multitude of antennae marring the skyline of the Old City.

Whilst all these remarkable works were carried out by the Development Corporation, many buildings were erected and old ones restored at the initiative of the various Churches. The latter profited from large customs duty exemptions granted by the Government.

DEVELOPMENTS IN THE ADMINISTERED TERRITORIES

Though Christian life in the Holy Land is the main subject of the present book, an account of the conditions prevailing in the administered territories seems to be appropriate.

In the immediate aftermath of the Israeli take-over, the inhabitants of Judea, Samaria and the Gaza district showed a certain willingness to cooperate with the military administration. With the physical barriers down, they could at least look directly into the reality of Israel's life, not being misled by distorted images created by hostile propaganda. Consequently, many prejudices and preconceived ideas could be rectified.

The initial calm was soon modified by anti-Israel pressure from beyond the borders and by the Arab inhabitants' newly-acquired self-confidence in the wake of the 1973 War. The military administration's policy was to minimize interference in the lives of the local inhabitants. Perhaps the most striking aspect of this policy was the fact that Jordanian law remained in force in Judea and Samaria, and Egyptian law in the Gaza district. Free movement was permitted to all within the territories and across the "Green Line", previously separating the territories from Israel proper. In addition, under Israel's "Open Bridges" policy, residents in the Arab countries were allowed to visit their relatives in the territories and in Israel. These visits totalled 150,000 in 1982 alone. Consequently, a continuous relationship, familial, social, cultural and economic, could be maintained with Jordan and other Arab countries.

Involvement on the part of the Israeli administration was above all directed at furthering such areas of civil life as education, health, agriculture, social welfare and municipal facilities and services. Intervention by military authorities had to be confined to measures necessary to ensure the preservation of law and order, and the prevention of any action which could adversely affect Israel's security. The measures by the military administration were, however, restrained by the right to petition the Israeli High Court of Justice on any question regarding alleged misuse of power by the administrative authorities. This right was granted to every member of the local population.

The administration strove above all to ensure economic prosperity and social stability in the occupied territories. Interaction with Israel's economy since 1967, continued access to Arab markets via the open bridges across the Jordan River, and the retention of Jordanian currency as legal tender have stimulated economic development in Judea-Samaria and the Gaza district, and have brought the inhabitants a steady rise in their standard of living. Since the beginning of Israeli administration, the per capita GNP has climbed an average of 8.8 percent per year, in real terms.

The main thrust of the administration's policy was to guarantee the inhabitants of the territories full employment, a concern which was not shown under the regimes which ruled in the territories before 1967, with the consequence that the population suffered from high rates of unemployment.

In line with this policy, the administration set up extensive vocational training programs.

Moreover, tens of thousands of Arab workers sought employment in enterprises within the "Green Line." Their number, including those from East Jerusalem, reached 100,000 in 1987. In this way, Arabs from territories formerly ruled by Jordan or Egypt were given the opportunity to become acquainted with a more advanced technology and fairer labor relations. Many of them soon became conversant in Hebrew, a factor helping the progress of integration.

Special care was given to the advancement of agriculture, farming being the occupation of many among the inhabitants of the territories. In this area, the Israeli administration could do much for the benefit of the local farmers, given Israel's experience in agricultural technology.

Before 1967, very little industry existed in Judea-Samaria and in the Gaza district. Since then, hundreds of medium and small plants have been put into operation. More recently, factories have been opened as well.

Social services were also reorganized by the administration. In this context, one should mention the activities of several international and Church-sponsored organizations which support a wide variety of health, education and welfare initiatives in the territories. These organizations include the Lutheran World Federation, the Catholic Relief Services, the American Friends' Committee, the Mennonite Central Committee, and the Near East Council of Churches.

Special care was given by the Israeli administration to the advancement of education on every level. The most striking progress, however, was made in the field of higher learning. Whilst under Jordanian rule no university could be founded because of opposition from the Government, four university-level academic institutes have been established in Judea-Samaria since 1967, in addition to five colleges which provide higher education.

Prominent among the universities are the Vatican-sponsored University of Bethlehem, and Bir Zeit University, supported by

Protestant organizations. Unfortunately, the students of the universities in the territories are engaged in internal struggles, due to their allegiance to different Arab parties and trends, and in political activities hostile to the State of Israel. In this context, we should remember that university students everywhere and at all periods have been in the forefront of national and revolutionary movements. This was undoubtedly the main reason why the Jordanian Government opposed the establishment of institutions of higher learning in Judea and Samaria.

The historic peace agreement between Egypt and Israel, signed on November 17, 1978, was not welcomed in Arab quarters. On the contrary, it stirred discontent and was interpreted as treason against the Arab cause. At the Camp David Conference of March 1979, where negotiations were held between the late President Sadat and Prime Minister Begin, with the active participation of President Carter, a plan was outlined aimed at settling the status of the Palestinian Arabs. The plan provided for the establishment of full autonomy for the Arab Palestinian inhabitants of Judea, Samaria and the Gaza district.

In its autonomy proposals, Israel agreed to grant the Arab inhabitants of the areas self-governing authority in the following domains: administration of justice, agriculture, finance, civil service, education and culture, health, housing and public works, transportation, communications and posts, labor and social welfare, municipal affairs, local law enforcement, religious affairs, industry, commerce and tourism.

Israel did not intend to give the local population control of foreign affairs and security. The parties to the negotiations agreed on a transitional period of five years, after which negotiations were to take place to determine the final status of Judea, Samaria and the Gaza district.

In order to advance the autonomy plan, the Israeli Government abolished the military administration, replacing it, in November 1981, with a civil administration. This administrative change, heralding the implementation of the autonomy plan, met with the strong opposition of the Arab inhabitants of the administered areas.

The consequent absence of any mutually-acceptable solution

to the problem of the administered areas and the status of their inhabitants has engendered civil unrest which, at the end of December 1987, erupted in widespread disturbances. It is believed by many that the existing situation in Judea, Samaria and the Gaza district calls for a political settlement based on compromise.

THE CHRISTIAN ESTABLISHMENT UP TO 1987

Prior to June 1967, the Israeli authorities had become accustomed to deal with a plurality of Christian communities and Churches. Since June 1967, the problems have become more complex, for additional ecclesiastical bodies are now represented in East Jerusalem and in Judea and Samaria. This multiplicity is a reflection of the understandable desire of every Christian denomination to have its own spiritual center or mission in the Holy Land and, if at all possible, near the most venerated shrines. The number of religious personnel residing in the Holy Land is, consequently, high in proportion to that of the local faithful. It is estimated that about two thousand five hundred priests, monks, nuns, pastors and missionaries are serving in the Holy Land in one or other capacity. True, they care not only for the spiritual needs of the one hundred and thirty-five thousand local Christians, but also for pilgrims and visitors, and not a few follow the purely contemplative life.

Detailed information on the various denominations, religious institutions and personnel is presented in the chapters on Christian life in the State of Israel and in Jordan between 1948 and 1967, but certain supplementary data on the latest developments may be of interest.

The Roman Catholic Church

The Roman Catholic Church had a following of 28,000 in Israel and in the administered territories at the end of 1987. The religious personnel is very large, numbering about 450 clerics, of

209

whom most belong to twenty monastic Orders,[1] the others being secular priests of the Latin Patriarchate. There are, in addition, 1,130 nuns belonging to forty-five conventual Congregations.[2] Heading the hierarchy for twenty-one years was the Latin Patriarch Alberto Gori. Elevated to the Patriarchal See, he held the position until his death in November 1970. During his lifetime, he was appointed a coadjutor with right of succession in the person of Bishop James Joseph Beltritti. Thus, after the demise of Patriarch Gori, there was no electoral bickering, nor the usual interregnum. Monsignor Beltritti was automatically enthroned as seventh Latin Patriarch of Jerusalem since the reinstallation of the See in 1847.

The Latin Patriarch's Vicar-General in Israel is Bishop Hanna Kaldany. Patriarch Beltritti has served as Chairman of

---

1) List of monastic Orders:
Assumptionists, Benedictines, Brothers of the Christian Schools, Brothers of St. John of God, Discalced Carmelites, Dominicans, Fathers of Betharram, Fathers of Zion, Franciscans, Jesuits, Lazarists, Little Brothers of Jesus, Little Family of the Annunciation (Dossetti), Passionists, Salesians, Servants of Charity (charitable institution of Don Gonella), Trappists and White Fathers.

In 1980, a male branch of the Focolari Movement became active in Jerusalem. Since 1982, several Fathers of the Holy Sacrament have responded to an invitation by Dr. Gedda to serve at an institution for twin research which he founded on the slopes of the Mount of Olives.

2) Conventual Congregations: Benedictine Sisters of Emmanuel, Benedictine Sisters of Our Lady of Calvary, Benedictine Sisters of St. Francis of Rome, Carmelite Sisters (cloistered), Carmelite Sisters of St. Joseph, Carmelite Sisters of St. Thérèse, Community of the Lion of Judas and the Immolated Lamb, Daughters of the Calvary, Dominican Sisters of the Presentation of Tours, Dominican Fraternity of Bethesda, Franciscan Sisters of the Heart of Jesus, Franciscan Sisters of the Immaculate Heart of Mary, Franciscan Sisters of the Eucharist, Franciscan Elisabethan Sisters of Padua, Franciscans of Mary, Handmaids of the Holy Heart of Jesus, Pious Mothers of Nigrizia, Little Family of the Annunciation, Religious Daughters of Mary Auxiliatrix (Salesians), Sisters of St. Anne, Sisters of Charity of St. Vincent of Paul, Sisters of St. Charles Borromeus, Sisters of St. Claire, Sisters of Dorothy, Sisters of the Cross, Sisters of the Holy Cross of Jerusalem, Sisters of St. Elisabeth, Sisters of St. John the Baptist, Sisters of the Immaculate Conception of Ivrea, Sisters of St. Joseph of the Apparition, Sisters of St. Paul of Chartres, Sisters of Nazareth, Sisters of Our Lady of the Apostles, Sisters of Our Lady of the Hortus Conclusus, Sisters of Our Lady of Mercy, Sisters of Our Lady of Zion, Sisters of Our Lady of Sorrow, Sisters of Maria Bambina, International Female Auxiliaries, Caritas Socialis, Oevre de Marie (Focolari) Sisters of the Rosary, Theresian Institute, Tertiary Sisters of St. Francis Voclabruck, Community of Work of Bregenz, Silent Workers of the Cross.

the Conference of Bishops of the Arab Regions (C.E.L.R.A.), and as Grand Prior of the Order of the Holy Sepulchre.[3] The Patriarch, on reaching the age of 75, asked to be relieved of his office, as is customary in the Catholic Church. His request, at that time, was denied. At the end of 1987, however, Pope John Paul II decided to appoint a new incumbent in the person of Mgr. Michel Asa'ad Sabbah, a native of Nazareth. The appointment was a further step in the process of the indigenization of the local hierarchy, a trend which has also been prominent in the Anglican and Lutheran Churches in the Holy Land. Mgr. Sabbah, a graduate of the Sorbonne and Rector of Bethlehem University, was consecrated Bishop in St. Peter's Cathedral in Rome on January 6, 1988, the Feast of the Epiphany.

Within the entire territory of the Holy Land there are 170 Roman Catholic churches and chapels, of which a third are considered Holy Places, and 186 religious establishments: biblical and archaeological institutions and seminaries, 75 secondary and primary schools, kindergartens and orphanages, eight hospitals, twenty clinics and several homes for the aged. Roughly half of the total are situated in Israel, within the pre-June 1967 borders; the other half are in East Jerusalem and in the administered territories.

This is an impressive array of places of worship and educational and charitable institutions—convincing testimony of the deep interest of the Catholic world in the Holy Land. Besides their charitable work under direct Church auspices, nuns were sometimes asked by the Jordanian authorities to serve as nurses in Government hospitals, when experienced lay staff were lacking; this was so with the Salvatorian Sisters, who for several years did duty at the hospital in Ramallah; the Sisters of Dorothy are still active in the mental hospital of Bethlehem and the Sisters of our Lady of Mercy in the Hussein Ibn Talal Hospital in Beit Jala.

Building activity has been unabated during the past few years. Recent construction includes the new Convent of the Sisters of St. Claire in Nazareth near the Church of the Tremor and, in the same town, that of the Franciscan Sisters of Mary. A residence for

---

3) The donations and other contributions by the knights of the Order are an important source of income for the Patriarchate, enabling it to put up new churches and to maintain its numerous educational and charitable institutions.

the Latin Patriarchal Vicar in Nazareth which replaces the former delapidated quarters is nearing completion.[4]

In January 1982, the foundation-stone of a memorial-church, sponsored by the Franciscan Custody of the Holy Land, was laid in Capernaum, at the traditional site of the house of St. Peter. The ceremony was attended by the General Minister of the Franciscan Order and by H.E. Mgr. Forlani, President of the Pontifical Committee of Sacred Art. The memorial was planned by Architect Ildo Avetta. In this context, it should be mentioned that the site where the memorial will stand was bought by the Franciscans in 1894, the excavations were started in 1905 and continued over the subsequent seventy years.

In Ramallah, a new building to serve as a family center was inaugurated in March 1977. In July 1986, a new residence for the Rosary Sisters was put up. In the villages of Zababde, Bir Zeit, Yafiya, Burquin and Taibe new churches have been built at the initiative of the Latin Patriarchate. In Taibe, a clinic has been opened with funds provided by Caritas. On April 17, 1986, the Latin Patriarchate opened a retreat center there for priests, religious and laity, named after Charles de Foucauld. In the town of Gaza, the Latin Patriarchate has erected a school with the financial help of the Knights of the Holy Sepulchre. New schools have also been built in Beit Sahour and Rafidiya. At the initiative of the Franciscan Fathers, the ancient "Casa Nova" hospice in Nazareth was renovated and converted into a modern, comfortable hostel. The Franciscans have likewise provided a new home for the aged to replace the former obsolete premises. Also in Nazareth, a building housing the local branch of Catholic Action has undergone considerable renovation. A spacious new school-building has gone up in the village of Yafiya, on the outskirts of Nazareth, and there are new school premises in the Galilean villages of Reneh, Zippori and Jish, and in the town of Akko (Acre).

At Tabgha, the traditional site of the Multiplication of the Loaves and Fishes, a new church was built at the initiative of the German Association for the Holy Land, and solemnly inaugu-

---

4) In this connection, one might note the rather Spartan life-style of the Latin Patriarch, his Vicar and his clergy, which offers a striking contrast to that of the heads of the Eastern Churches. The latter, it seems, are aware that their flock expect a degree of ostentation.

rated on May 23, 1982, in the presence of Cardinal Hoeffner of Cologne and ten Bishops.

Growth and development within the Christian communities is especially apparent in Jerusalem. The Benedictine Fathers of the Dormition Abbey on Mount Zion were instrumental in creating a seminary, "Beit Joseph", where clerics from German-speaking countries are trained in subjects connected with the Holy Land. The Basilica of the Dormition, which had suffered some damage during the Arab-Israeli conflict in 1948, was thoroughly restored and in August 1982 a magnificent new organ was installed there. In 1985, a new wing was added to the Abbey to accommodate the increasing number of monks.

The Latin Concathedral is undergoing thorough restoration.

The crypt in the Crusader Church of St. Anne in Jerusalem has been duly restored and embellished. The Franciscans have transformed the old hospice in the Jerusalem suburb of Ein Karem into a comfortable modern dormitory for foreign and Arab students enrolled at the Hebrew University. The Franciscans have also opened a "Pilgrim Information Center" near Jerusalem's Jaffa Gate in a building which once served as the Austrian post office. The friars have also built several rooms on the terrace overlooking the Church of the Holy Sepulchre, for the use of the monks who permanently guard the shrine.

The Institute of Medical Genetics and Twin Studies, sponsored by Professor Gedda, has been built on the slopes of the Mount of Olives. Beit Hanina, a suburb of Jerusalem, now has a church named for St. James the Less, with an adjoining cultural center. Construction of the church had been held up by the Jordanian authorities before 1967, in line with their policy of curbing the proliferation of Christian institutions in the Jerusalem area. A plot near the church and center is the site of a new housing estate with eighty apartments for Arab families. The project is financed by contributions of the Franciscan Mission Associates of the Franciscan Province of the Immaculate Conception in the United States.

In Kiryat Ye'arim, the Sisters of St. Joseph have put up a new house for religious retreats.

Bethlehem has also benefitted from Catholic building initiatives. Besides the Franciscans' renovation of the "Casa Nova" hospice, an institute for deaf mutes, called Ephpheta (see Mark 7:32), was sponsored by the late Pope Paul VI; a pediatric hospital has been established with the financial help of the German and Swiss Caritas; a secondary school, owned by the Christian Brothers, has been enlarged by the addition of a new wing to house Bethlehem University.

One of the most prestigious institutions built in recent years is the Ecumenical Institute for Theological Research at Tantur, halfway between Jerusalem and Bethlehem.

In Beit Jala, a fourth floor was added to the School of the Latin Patriarchate.

Special mention should be made of the restoration of Church property situated near the former Israeli-Jordanian border and damaged during the hostilities of 1948 and 1967. After the reunification of the city, the damage was soon put right with much of the repair work financed by indemnities awarded by the State of Israel. A notable example of war damage was that suffered by the monumental Notre Dame de France building. The hospice, located on the front line of the then divided city, had been the target of Jordanian artillery, and the whole wing facing the city wall was seriously damaged. The owners, the Assumptionist Fathers, could not find a suitable function for the impaired, eighty-five-year-old building and resolved to sell it. The hospice was purchased from the Assumptionist Order by a subsidiary of the Jewish National Fund on behalf of the Hebrew University. The Holy See contested the transaction which had been performed without its approbation, contrary to the provisions of Canon Law. Aware of the importance attributed by the Vatican to the ownership of Notre Dame, the Government of Israel allowed the resale of the building to the Holy See.

Extensive repairs were carried out in the huge edifice to convert it into a modern guesthouse for religious personnel and pilgrims, and for cultural activities. The restoration and redesign of the building was planned by Architect Frank Montana, who was also responsible for the Ecumenical Institute at Tantur and the building extensions for Bethlehem University. On December 13, 1978, the Notre Dame of Jerusalem Center was decreed a Pontifical Institute with the status "Praelatura Nullius." Recently, several new buildings were put up on a plot adjacent to Notre Dame to house meetings, religious conventions, lectures and similar activities. On the occasion of the first centennial of Notre Dame (June 1985), the ceremonial blessing of the cornerstone for a new cultural center took place at Notre Dame. In 1986, a long-standing dispute between the Vatican-owned Notre Dame Center and the Municipality of Jerusalem concerning taxes was resolved amicably.

The Uniate Churches

Among the *Uniate Churches* represented in the Holy Land, the *Greek Catholic* is the most important. It has about thirty-nine thousand adherents in the Eparchy of Acre-Ptolemais, which includes Haifa, Nazareth, and Galilee, and two thousand five hundred in the ecclesiastical district which is part of the Greek Catholic Patriarchate and comprehends Jerusalem, Judea and Samaria.

From 1968 to 1974, the faithful of the Eparchy of Acre came under the spiritual authority of Archbishop Joseph Raya. The latter, previously a parish priest in the United States, had succeeded Archbishop George Hakim on his preferment to the Patriarchal See of Antioch. Archbishop Raya, a learned and ecumenically-minded prelate, resigned in 1974 over a disagreement with the leader of his Church regarding the administration of Church property.[5] His successor was Monsignor Maximos Salloum, who had served as Vicar under the two preceeding Archbishops and, therefore, was well acquainted with all the problems of the Archdiocese of Acre.

The Archdiocese has twenty-nine parishes and twenty-five priests. There is an evident shortage of ministering clergy, since several are in charge of seminaries and religious courts, or perform administrative tasks.

The following religious orders and conventual congregations are associated with the Eparchy of Acre: the Sisters of the Annunciation, the Sisters of Charity of Jesus and Mary (in Isfyia), the

5) In December 1987, Archbishop Raya ended his exile in Canada and was appointed Archbishop of Marjayoun and Southern Lebanon.

215

Franciscans of Mary (in Maghar and Ramah), the monks of the Lavra Netufa Community, the Little Sisters of Jesus (in Haifa), the Salvatorian Sisters (in Nazareth), and the Sisters of St. Joseph (in Ibellin, Mi'ilia and Fassouta).

During the past decade, the Greek Catholic community has taken a leading role in the construction of religious buildings. A new church was inaugurated in 1976 in the village of Hurfeish, and churches in seven towns and villages were extensively restored. Community centers went up in the villages of Fassouta, Mi'illia, Maghar, Ibellin and Yefiye, testifying to an eagerness on the part of the Greek Catholics to foster cultural and social life. In 1972, Fraternity House, a home for the aged with seventeen beds, was opened in Isfiya. In 1980, the construction began on a new building which will have fifty beds. In Nazareth, a three-storey center near St. Joseph's Seminary is designed to promote religious, liturgical and spiritual life, as well as social and cultural activities. A locale for community activities, named Brotherhood Center, was inaugurated in Haifa in 1979. The city also has a new Greek Catholic funerary chapel.

In the village of Mi'ilia a new kindergarten was founded, and in Ibellin the secondary school of St. Elias was established with the help of German contributors. Enrolment at the seven schools of the Greek Catholic Eparchy totals 2,900.

A lavra of Greek Catholic monks was founded in Netofa, near Deir Hanna, in 1963. It seeks to follow the tradition of the anchorite colonies in the first centuries of the Christian era. In 1979, a group of Greek Catholic Melkite monks connected with the Community of the Theophany in France, established itself in the Monastery of St. John in the Desert, near Ein Kerem.

A smaller Greek Catholic community lives in Jerusalem, Judea and Samaria. Its spiritual leader serves as Patriarchal Vicar of the Patriarch of Antioch. Within the boundaries of the Vicariate there are seven parishes: Jerusalem, Beit Sahour, Bethlehem, Jaffa, Nablus-Rafidiya, Ramallah and Taibe. From 1965 to 1974, the incumbent was Archbishop Hilarion Capucci. The following Religious Orders and Conventual Congregations are associated with the Greek Catholic Patriarchal Vicariate of Jerusalem: the International Female Auxiliaries (in Jerusalem and in Ramallah), the Sisters of Emmanuel (in Bethlehem), the

Carmelites des Campagnes (in Jerusalem), the Auxiliaries of the Apostolate (in Jerusalem), the Paulist Fathers (in Ramallah), the Little Sisters of Jesus (in Bethany, Bethlehem, Ramallah and at the Sixth Station in Jerusalem), the Salvatorian Sisters (in Beit Sahour and Emmaus-Qubeibeh), the Salvatorian Basileans (in Beit Sahour, Tantur, Emmaus-Qubeibeh and in Jerusalem). Archbishop Capucci saw to the renovation of the Greek Catholic Cathedral of the Annunciation, built in 1948, and the Archbishop's residence near the Cathedral was enlarged. A new wing and further floors were added to the building, transforming it into a modern hospice for pilgrims. The project was supported by contributions from German Catholic circles. One notable benefactor to Greek Catholic institutions in the Holy Land was the late Mgr. Nettekoven, who gave his name to the Peter Nettekoven School in Beit Sahour, which was built with German Catholic sponsorship.

Archbishop Capucci, a native of Syria, was known as an ardent Arab nationalist. But his high ecclesiastical rank required that he be given complete freedom of movement, including permission to travel by car to neighboring countries, hostile to Israel. On one such trip, in June 1974, the Archbishop's car was searched on his return from Beirut. A cache of arms and explosives was discovered, leaving little doubt that the Archbishop was acting as courier, bringing weapons and lethal materials into Israel for use by terrorists. The offence was so serious that there was no alternative but to bring Mgr. Capucci to trial. The district court of Jerusalem found him guilty, and sentenced him to twelve years in prison. During his incarceration, the Archbishop was given the benefit of special conditions and received frequent visits from Vatican representatives and members of his clergy.

In November 1977, he was released, having served only a quarter of his sentence. The decision to reduce the term of imprisonment was taken by the President of the State of Israel, following a personal request from Pope Paul VI, and his undertaking that Mgr. Capucci would not be allowed to serve in the Near East and that he would refrain from any political activity detrimental to the State of Israel. In spite of those guarantees, Archbishop Capucci soon began to engage in hostile activity against Israel, moving freely in Arab countries.

It would seem that the Vatican is powerless to bar its clergy from undesirable activities when there are broader political interests at stake.

After the removal of Mgr. Capucci, Archimandrite Lutfi Laham, a learned Basilian Salvatorian monk, was appointed Patriarchal Administrator of the vacant See, and in 1978 was confirmed as Patriarchal Vicar. As the former incumbents of the Vicariate had been Titular Archbishops, the Greek Catholic Synod decided to elevate the worthy Archimandrite Laham to episcopal rank. Political pressure from Arab nationalist quarters succeeded, however, in delaying the consecration. Finally, a compromise was reached, according to which Mgr. Capucci would serve as Titular Archbishop of Caesarea and representative of the Melkite Patriarch in charge of the Greek Catholic Melkite community in Western Europe, while Mgr. Laham, as incumbent of the Titular See of Tarsus, would administer the local affairs of the community. The obstacles having been thus overcome, the consecration ceremony was held on November 27, 1981, and the episcopal title of Tarsus was bestowed on Mgr. Laham, Patriarchal Vicar of the Greek Catholic Church in Jerusalem.

Financial assistance from German Catholics enabled Archbishop Laham to put up six residential buildings, comprising thirty-six apartments, for local Christians in the North Jerusalem suburb of Beit Hanina, where the Prelate also built a community center containing a parish hall, pastoral facilities, a garden and a clinic. Within the Beit Hanina complex is the Church of Hypopante ("Encounter", in Greek), which was consecrated by the Archbishop in February 1987.

At the initiative of Mgr. Laham, an Eastern Churches Center was inaugurated at the Greek Catholic Melkite Patriarchate, with the aim of fostering acquaintance with the Eastern Churches, their life and institutions, and their spiritual and liturgical traditions.

The Maronite Community has some six thousand followers, the majority of them living in Israel within the pre-June 1967 borders, and forty-seven families divided between Jerusalem, Bethlehem, Beit Jala and Abu Dis. Mgr. Augustin Harfouche, a Baladite monk, has served as Patriarchal Vicar since 1974 and is in charge of the spiritual needs of the Maronites in Israel, the administered territories and Jordan. The parishes in Israel are served by five parish priests. Recently, Father Kamal Farah, a specialist in Canon Law, was named to the Maronite ecclesiastical court of first instance. The monastery in the Old City of Jerusalem, which was in delapidated condition, was entirely rebuilt at the expense of the Government of Israel and the Municipality of Jerusalem.

In the village of Isfiya on Mount Carmel, a new Maronite church dedicated to St. Charbel and a community center are nearing completion. In March 1982, the cornerstone of a new church and community center was laid in the village of Jish in Galilee. The Maronite Sisters of St. Thérèse of the Infant Jesus are associated with the Maronite Church in the Holy Land. In 1986, a Maronite center, Beit St. Charbel, was completed in Bethlehem. The spiritual and socio-cultural services of the center will be supervised by the monks from St. Esprit University in Lebanon.

In August 1983, Mgr. Harfouche initiated the construction of fifty apartments in Jaffa, on land belonging to the Lebanese Maronite Order, to provide suitable housing for Christian families in that city.

The Armenian Catholic Church, with but a few hundred faithful, mostly concentrated in Jerusalem, was led by Mgr. John Gamsaragan from 1966 until his retirement in 1979, when he was succeeded by Mgr. Joseph Chadarévian. On Mgr. Chadarévian's demise in 1985, Church leadership was invested in Mgr. Joseph Rubian.

The Syrian Catholic Church also with only a few hundred members concentrated in East Jerusalem and Bethlehem, has been headed, since the death of the Patriarchal Vicar Mgr. Yacoub Naoum in 1977, by Mgr. Butros Abdul-Ahad, formerly Syrian Catholic parish priest in Bethlehem. After the Six-Day War, the Church was granted full compensation by the Government of Israel for its property near the Damascus Gate, which had to be evacuated on the outbreak of hostilities in 1948. The compensation enabled the late Mgr. Naoum to purchase a building in East Jerusalem, in the neighborhood of the Ecole Biblique. A chapel was consecrated in the building in December 1975. The premises also serve as the residence of the Syrian Catholic Patriarchal Vicar. On July 3, 1986, the Feast of St. Thomas, a new church, dedicated to the Saint, was consecrated in Jerusalem by Bishop Ephrem Jarjour.

In Bethlehem, the Syrian Catholic Church maintains a small school, where teaching is entrusted to the Congregation of the Dominicans of St. Catherine of Siena.

The *Chaldeans*, a very small community, have been headed, since the death of Mgr. Butros Shaya in August 1978, by Mgr. Henri Constantine Gouillon.

A tiny *Coptic Catholic Congregation*, which seceded from the Coptic Orthodox Community, is entrusted to the spiritual care of the Franciscan Father Joseph Leonbruni. It worships in a chapel belonging to the Franciscans and situated at the Seventh Station of the Via Dolorosa.

The Orthodox Churches

The Greek Orthodox Church had, after the June 1967 War, some thirty-eight thousand faithful within Israel and the administered territories. In 1987, it numbered some forty-five thousand. This ancient autocephalous Church was headed from 1957 until 1980 by Patriarch Benedictos I, assisted in his spiritual and administrative functions by a Holy Synod. According to the constitution of the Patriarchate the Synod may number eighteen members, but in the period following the 1967 War, there were only fourteen.

Administrative posts in the Synod were held at that time by Mgr. Germanos, Titular Archbishop of Sebaste, who was the representative of the Patriarch, and by Mgr. Vassilios, Titular Archbishop of Jordan, who was the chief secretary of the Patriarchate.[6]

In June 1967, the Brotherhood of the Holy Sepulchre, in charge of the Church's religious activities in the Holy Land and in the Kingdom of Jordan, had a total of one-hundred and five members. In addition, there were thirty-seven parish priests. Forty students

---

6) Archbishop Germanos was elevated to the rank of Metropolitan of Petra, and Archbishop Vassilios to the rank of Metropolitan of Caesarea. In 1981, Metropolitan Vassilios was appointed General Representative of the Patriarch.

were enrolled in the seminary conducted by the Patriarchate.[7] The latter also maintains six schools, primary and secondary, in the Holy Land, and sixteen in Jordan.

Of special concern for the Patriarchate since its establishment more than fifteen centuries ago has been the guardianship of the Holy Places and the performance in them of the traditional religious rites. The Greek Orthodox Church has a pre-eminent status in the most important shrines of Christianity, as well as owning many ancient and deeply venerated monasteries all over the Holy Land. At least a third of its ninety churches and monasteries are considered Holy Places.

The tenure of Patriarch Benedictos I, as mentioned above, lasted twenty-three years. The situation of a Church leader with authority in two countries hostile to one another required special political ability. Patriarch Benedictos overcame the difficulties and succeeded in maintaining excellent relations with the authorities of both countries. During the incumbency of this wise Church leader, the financial situation of the Patriarchate, which in the past was on the verge of bankruptcy, improved remarkably. This was the result of the compensation paid by the Government of Israel, and of successfully conducted transactions. The Patriarchate stuck to its principle of retaining ownership of the Church's landed property, but agreed to lease urban property for appropriate payment. The Patriarchate was consequently in a position to undertake a significant program of restoration in its historical churches and monasteries, which were in great need of repair.

Notable among these ancient buildings were the Monastery of the Holy Cross, the Church of Modestos and Procopios, and the Monastery on Mount Zion, all of them in Jerusalem. To the Monastery on Mount Zion was transferred the Greek Orthodox Seminary, which till then had its seat at the central monastery of the Patriarchate. Repairs were also carried out in the Monastery of Mar Elias, on the road from Jerusalem to Bethlehem, in the Church and Monastery of St. George in Ramleh and in Lydda, in the church in Tiberias and in the church at Capernaum.

---

7) According to the *Imerologion* (Calendar) 1987 of the Patriarchate, the Brotherhood had in that year one hundred members; the novices were twenty-five. The number of the Arab Orthodox parish priests in 1987 remained approximately the same as in 1967.

Most prominent in scope and significance was the work executed in the Basilica of the Holy Sepulchre. In this most venerated sanctuary, extensive repairs were carried out in the central Greek Orthodox Catholicon, and a splendid marble iconostasis was installed. Before the construction of the iconostasis and the renovation of the chancel, important archaeological excavations were carried out under the supervision of architect Athanasios Iconopoulos. The excavations uncovered remains of the Martyrion, the fourth-century basilica of Constantine's day.

In addition to the extensive restoration work in many ancient churches and monasteries, the Orthodox Patriarchate embarked upon the construction of new churches, among them the Church of St. Stephen in the Kidron Valley in Jerusalem, the new church at Shepherds' Field near Bethlehem, a church in Bethfage on the slopes of the Mount of Olives, a church above the tomb of Lazarus in Bethany near Jerusalem, and a parish church in the village of Zebabde.

In addition to buildings of a religious character, cultural and welfare institutions were provided for the Orthodox community, such as an outpatient clinic in the main building of the Patriarchate in Jerusalem, and a cultural center in Ramla. The latter profited from a substantial contribution from the Ministry of Religious Affairs.

After the demise of Patriarch Benedictos I in December 1980 and a four week mourning period, a "Topoteretes" (Locum Tenens) was appointed and the electoral procedure started. The elections were held for the first time according to the Statute given to the Greek Orthodox Patriarchate in 1958 by the Government of Jordan. According to that Statute, the members of the electoral body as well as the candidates for the Patriarchal See must be Jordanian citizens. Most members of the Brotherhood of the Holy Sepulchre have double citizenship, Greek and Jordanian. The Statute also gives Arab parish priests a certain share in the election of the Patriarch, even though they are not members of the Brotherhood.

According to the Statute, there are three stages in the election of the Greek Orthodox Patriarch. Participating in the first round are members of the Synod, Bishops who are not members of the Synod, and twelve Arab married priests, delegated by the main Orthodox parishes.[8] Each delegate chooses his candidate, who must possess the necessary qualifications (age, ecclesiastical degree, Jordanian citizenship). The list of candidates, according to the law, must be submitted to the Jordanian Government and approved by it.[9] The next step is the selection of three candidates from the list of those chosen and approved. At this stage the electoral body is composed of the members of the Synod, the Archimandrites and the Protosynkeloi (chief overseers in the churches) resident in Jerusalem, and twelve Arab priests. Finally, the Patriarch is chosen from three candidates by the members of the Synod only.

The elections were held in a rather agitated atmosphere with political interference not alien to the process. Diodoros, Titular Archbishop of Hieropolis and religious leader of the Orthodox faithful of Jordan, was elected and solemnly enthroned in March 1981. Diodoros I is 96th in the sequence of Greek Orthodox Patriarchs of Jerusalem. The newly-elected Patriarch was presented with a formal writ of recognition (*bérat*) by the Minister of Religious Affairs of the State of Israel in the name of the Israel Government.[10]

One of the first steps taken by the new incumbent was a series of appointments: Mgr. Constantine was made a Metropolitan with the historical title of Scythopolis, and four members of the Brotherhood were consecrated as Archbishops: Daniel, Arcadios, Ambrosios and Irenaios were named Titular Archbishops of Tabor, Ascalon, Neapolis and Hierapolis, respectively. In 1981, the Patriarch appointed Archimandrite Yoannes Titular Bishop of Porphyripolis and, in 1984, Archimandrite Hesyhios Titular

8) Arab parish priests who held only Israeli citizenship were admitted to the electoral body, in spite of the fact that this contravened the Statute of 1958.

9) At the election of Patriarch Diodoros, the list of candidates was also duly submitted for the approbation of the Government of Israel. This formality was not followed during the procedure which brought to the election of Patriarch Benedictos, when Jerusalem was still under Jordanian rule.

10) According to an important decision handed down in June 1982 by the Israel Supreme Court, the status of a legal person was accorded to the Greek Orthodox Patriarchate. The Supreme Court decided that the *Bérats* (writs of appointment of the Greek Patriarchs) given by the Ottoman Sultans and later likewise issued by Governments successively ruling in the Holy Land, were valid documents, conferring the status of legal person on the Patriarchate. This precluded ambiguities which could give lawyers legal means of obstructing actions brought to court by the Patriarchate.

Bishop of Abila and Archimandrite Gregorios Titular Bishop of Jamnia. In 1985, Archishop Hymenaios was appointed Metropolitan of Vostra.

Patriarch Diodoros planned a number of improvements in the administrative system of the Patriarchate. Repairs and extensions are projected for the ancient building that houses the Patriarchate. In 1984, a new museum was inaugurated in a Crusader structure within the Monastery of St. Nicholas. In addition to archaeological exhibits, the museum has on display old manuscripts, ritual articles, vestments, antique embroideries and historical documents.

Contacts between spiritual leaders of the various autocephalous Churches had always been maintained, but in recent times they have markedly increased. After the reunification of Jerusalem, several heads of Orthodox Churches came as pilgrims to the Holy Land: Patriarch German of Serbia in 1971, Patriarch Pimen of Moscow in 1972, Patriarch Maxim of Bulgaria in 1973, Patriarch Justinian of Romania in 1975, Patriarch Elias of Georgia in 1980, Archbishop Chrysostomos, Ethnarch of Cyprus, in 1984 and, in 1985, Metropolitan Serafim, spiritual leader of the Orthodox Church in Greece.

In turn, a delegation of the Patriarchate of Jerusalem attended the enthronement of the Patriarch of Moscow in 1971, and representatives of the Jerusalem Patriarchate again visited Moscow in 1974. Leading members of the Patriarchate also attended ceremonies celebrated by other autocephalous Sister-Churches and participated in consultations and meetings held in the framework of Orthodox and ecumenical relations. Thus, representatives of the Patriarchate were present at the fourth General Assembly of the World Council of Churches in Uppsala in 1968, and again at the WCC meeting in Nairobi in 1975. Leading members of the Brotherhood attended discussions held between the Orthodox and the non-Chalcedonian Churches in Addis Ababa in 1971, with the Anglicans in Helsinki (1971), in Oxford (1973), in Cambridge (1977), and in Athens (1978). Representatives of the Patriarchate were likewise present at the Pan-Orthodox conferences held in Rhodes, and at the consultations held by the Lutherans in Sigtuna (Sweden) in 1978 and in Espoo (Finland) in 1981. In Patmos and

Rhodes, representatives of the Patriarchate met in 1980 with Catholic theologians for doctrinal consultations.

The Ecumenical Patriarch of Constantinople, Demetrios, arrived in Israel in May 1987. In his party were Archbishop Iakovos, Primate of the Greek Orthodox Church in North and South America and five Metropolitans. This was the first visit to the Holy Land of an incumbent Ecumenical Patriarch since that of Patriarch Athenagoras in 1964, on the occasion of his historic meeting with Pope Paul VI.

The head of the Georgian Orthodox Church, Catholicos Elias II, visited Israel in October 1987, his second pilgrimage to the Holy Land. The Georgians, in the seventeenth century, burdened by heavy debts, had to give up the Monastery of the Holy Cross, but they still hope to be reinstated in it. Parthenios III, Patriarch of Alexandria, came on pilgrimage to Israel in January 1988.

In line with his policy of strengthening ties with the autocephalous Orthodox Sister-Churches, Patriarch Diodoros I visited the religious Sees of Moscow, Georgia, Constantinople, Greece, Romania, Bulgaria, Serbia, Cyprus and Sinai. During his visit to Russia, the Patriarch was awarded the title of Doctor Honoris Causa by the Theological Academy of Leningrad. In autumn 1982, he paid a six-week pastoral visit to Greek Orthodox congregations in the USA.

The ancient, Greek Orthodox *Monastery of St. Catherine in the Sinai Peninsula,* which owes its foundation to Emperor Justinian, has enjoyed the status of an autonomous ecclesiastical entity since 1575, in recognition of its special importance. However, the Archbishop of Sinai is still consecrated by the Patriarch of Jerusalem. During Israel administration of Sinai from 1967 to 1980, there were three successive Archbishops: Porphyrios, who died in 1969 at the age of ninety; his successor, Gregorios Maniatopoulos, who passed away in 1973, and the present incumbent, Damianos Samartzis, who was duly ordained Archbishop of Sinai, Pharan and Raithouin.

Two independent *Russian Ecclesiastical Missions* are now to be found in Israel and the administered areas. One is connected with the Patriarchate of Moscow, the other with the Russian Orthodox Church outside Russia, which has its administrative center in

New York. Both are in charge of churches, monasteries and convents at sites that have important religious associations. Their landed property, acquired a century ago, has no little commercial value. The number of clerics in each is very small; in each, however, scores of nuns serve. Each Mission claims to be the sole legal representative of the Russian Pravoslav Church. The State of Israel, therefore, finds itself in the delicate position of having to strike a balance in its relations with two Russian Churches which openly question each other's legitimacy. The situation worsened in the early seventies when the Church, which has its headquarters in New York, started an action in the Israeli court against the Moscow-based Church. The case is still *sub judice*. Besides the purely juridical arguments, political considerations have their weight in a matter pertinent to the interests of two world powers. It is to be noted that Patriarch Pimen of Moscow came on pilgrimage to the Holy Land in 1972, as did Metropolitan Philaret, head of the New York-based Russian Church, in the early seventies. In mid-1986, the Soviet Union made the overture to Jerusalem for a consular mission to be allowed to check up on Soviet Russian Church property in Israel. Permission was granted and a Russian consular mission spent several months in Israel to study the state of Russian property in Israel within the pre-June 1967 borders.

In July 1987, a delegation of Russian Orthodox priests, led by Metropolitan Philaret, head of the Moscow Patriarchate's foreign affairs secretariat, came on pilgrimage to the Holy Land to commemorate the 140th anniversary of the establishment of the Russian Orthodox Mission in Jerusalem.

The anniversary was also commemorated by a hundred-member pilgrimage headed by Bishop Hilarion of New York, representing the Russian Orthodox Church in Exile.

In January 1988, a symposium marking the milennium of the baptism of the Russian people was held in Jerusalem at the headquarters of the Russian Orthodox Mission connected with Moscow. Most of the speeches were delivered by members of a Church delegation from the USSR, led by Bishop Theophan of the Russian Orthodox Church division for external affairs.

The Romanian Orthodox Church has a monastery in Jerusalem, the chapel of which was recently restored and embellished, and another monastery near the traditional site of Jesus' baptism beside the River Jordan. The monasteries are administered by an Archimandrite assisted by several nuns.

An important event in the life of the Romanian Orthodox Mission in Jerusalem was the pilgrimage, in 1975, of the head of the Church, Patriarch Justinian, who was accompanied on his visit to the Holy Land by a retinue of Church dignitaries: Metropolitans, Archbishops and lesser clerics.

The Anglican and the Protestant Churches

The Anglican Church has about two thousand five hundred members in Israel and in the administered territories. Most of them are Arabic-speaking and until January 1976 were organized within the Arab Episcopal Church, the Arab branch of the Anglican Church. There are nine congregations, with four ministers within the bounds of pre-June 1967 Israel, and four in the administered areas, also with four ministers. Until his retirement, Bishop Najib Cuba'in was head of all Arabic-speaking congregations. The spiritual care of the non-Arabs is entrusted to nine English ministers.[11]

The Anglican Archbishop in Jerusalem, Dr. Angus Campbell MacInnes, resigned at the end of 1968 from an office he had occupied since 1957, having also previously served for many years in Jerusalem in other capacities. He had been in charge of an Archdiocese stretching over the whole Middle East and North Africa. Before his resignation, Archbishop MacInnes applied formally to the Government of Israel for official recognition of the local Anglican community. The Anglican Church in Palestine, in which the Arab element predominated, was not given the status of a recognized community during the thirty years of the British Mandate. It may seem strange that Great Britain should withhold from members of what is the "Established Church" a standing which would have provided them with fuller legal guarantees. The reason, first of all, might have been an instinctive reluctance of An-

11) For further details of places of worship and educational institutions, see Chapters Nine and Ten, as the data given for the period preceding June 1967 remain basically unchanged.

glicans to adapt themselves to the obsolete *millet* system of communities, so evocative of religious minorities in Moslem lands. There might, too, have been in those "colonial" days a certain diffidence in English-Anglican quarters about conceding an independent position to the rising Arab element within the Anglican Church. That element, though staunch in its allegiance to the Church of England in purely spiritual matters, strove for autonomy in other spheres. Parenthetically, the lack of special Anglican religious courts did not cause undue hardship under the British Mandate, as the civil courts were competent to deal with most of the legal problems arising in the community.

In 1969, the Most Reverend George Appleton, formerly Archbishop of West Australia, was appointed as successor to Archbishop MacInnes. Archbishop Appleton, whose tenure lasted five years, distinguished himself in his ecumenical approach and his endeavors to create an atmosphere of understanding among the various confessions and nationalities in the Holy Land.

On April 12, 1970, during the incumbency of Archbishop Appleton, the Government of Israel granted official recognition to the Evangelical Episcopal Church. It was the first Christian community to be recognized by the State of Israel. Nine other communities had previously been recognized by the Mandatory authorities.

A more liberal attitude on the part of the Anglican Church regarding autonomy for local Churches enabled the Government of Israel to find a formula acceptable to both the European and the Arab branches of the Church. Formal recognition also removed the anomalous situation in which the Arab Episcopal Church was a recognized community in the administered territories, but not in Israel proper. As noted in Chapter 10, with the end of the British Mandate the Jordanian authorities had granted the Arab Episcopal Church the coveted status.

Official recognition of the Arab Episcopal Church was, as will be seen, only a first step towards the complete autonomy of the local Church. After Archbishop Appleton's retirement in 1973, Bishop Robert Stopford, former Bishop of London, was appointed Vicar-General of the Archbishop of Canterbury in Jerusalem. His task was to supervise the appointment of a local Bishop to the See of Jerusalem. The policy was, as Bishop Stopford termed it, the decolonization of the Church. After long consultation, Canon Faik

Haddad of the Arab Episcopal Church was appointed and installed on January 6, 1976. He had been consecrated a Bishop on August 29, 1974. As Bishop in Jerusalem, his sphere of jurisdiction took in Israel, Jordan, Lebanon and Syria.

The appointment of Bishop Faik Haddad was part of a far-reaching change that brought about the suppression of the former Archdiocese. The ecclesiastical province, comprising a smaller area, is administered by a synod of four Bishops, of which Bishop Haddad was one. The presidency of the synod is rotatable among the four Bishops.

July 1982 saw the episcopal consecration in Jerualem of Archdeacon Samir Kafeity. The new Bishop served as coadjutorwith Bishop Haddad. On January 6, 1984, the Right Rev. Samir Kafeity was enthroned as twelfth Anglican Bishop in Jerusalem.

The Arab Evangelical Episcopal Church maintains in the Holy Land an extended network of schools. They are located in the following towns and villages: West Jerusalem, with an enrolment of 350; East Jerualem, 800; Ramallah (two schools), Haifa, Nazareth, Kufr Yassif, Nablus, Rafidiya and Hebron. At St. George's College there are plans to add a third floor to the expanding study center. St. Luke's Hospital in Nablus has been completely renovated; it has an affiliated nursing school nearby. Al-Ahi Hospital in Gaza has been adopted by the Anglican diocese, while the nurses' training school is still the responsibility of the Southern Baptist Convention. In 1986, Bishop Kafeity ordained five deacons, four of them from villages in Galilee.

The Arab Evangelical Episcopal Church is supported by several Sister-Churches. With the help of the Church of the Nazarene, a house in Lod belonging to the C.M.S., which had been closed for fifteen years, was renovated, and three rooms on the ground floor are used as a kindergarten for Arab children. A new hall was built near Immanuel Church in Ramla with the help of the Finnish Missionary Society. The church was founded in 1913 by Miss Morphew, a C.M.S. worker. Permission to use the church building in Acre was given by the Evangelical Episcopals to the Baptists, who have taken responsibility for maintenance.

The Protestant Churches in Israel and in the administered areas are about a score in number, but their fellowship does not come to more than two thousand five hundred, about half of them Lutherans.

After the Six-Day War, missionaries in West and East Jerusalem, connected with the same organizations abroad but who had begun their work only after the partition of 1948, had for the first time the opportunity to meet.

In 1968, an application for official recognition of a Protestant community in Israel was submitted by a group of Protestant Churches, including the Lutheran Church, the Baptist Convention in Israel, the Church of the Nazarene, the Bible-Evangelistic Mission (British Pentecostal Fellowship), the Christian and Missionary Alliance, and the Mennonite Church. Of these only the Lutheran Church enjoyed official status in Jordan.

This was a notable precedent in the Holy Land of a group of missionary bodies, all of them Evangelical, but differing in theological approach and organization, seeking the status of a "religious community." Some of the bodies were numerically unimportant, with only a score or two of followers and, in the past, in the Ottoman conception, communal status was awarded only to numerically stronger groups, which were, in general, ethnically homogeneous and also possessed a common religious heritage and shared the same customs and traditions. Consequently, an application by the above-mentioned Churches and Missions was rejected on the grounds that they did not have the requisite qualifications.

In this context, it should be pointed out that, under the former régimes, the Protestant Churches—unlike the old-established Orthodox, Catholic and Monophysite Churches—were not organized as *millets* (religious communities). Their legal status was that of Ottoman Societies (according to a Turkish law of the year 1910). The main benefit deriving from the community status is the right to conduct religious courts which deal with matters of personal status.[12] When the Ottoman law of 1910 concerning Societies was abolished in 1980, and in its place came the law of *Amutot*, the status of the former Protestant Churches and Missions organized as

---

12) Under the term of a special law passed by the Knesset, persons who do not belong to a recognized community can apply to a civil court in case of divorce. Moreover, Protestants can avail themselves of the religious courts of the Evangelical Episcopal Church.

Ottoman Societies appeared endangered. However, the legal adviser of the Ministry of Interior informed the religious bodies concerned that the United Christian Council in Israel and its member bodies, which were formerly Ottoman Societies, could be registered as *Amutot*. They were, moreover, assured that it was in no way imperative that the structure and functioning of their religious organizations should be regulated by the rules of the *Amutot*, and that the organization could conduct its internal affairs independently according to its own confessional precepts and principles.

The Lutheran Church. The main Lutheran body in the Holy Land is the Evangelical Lutheran Church "in Jordan," which was granted official recognition by the Jordan Government in 1959. Its headquarters are in the Muristan Quarter in Jerusalem's Old City.

In the late seventies, the Arab branch of the Lutheran Church showed a marked trend towards separation from the German Lutheran Mother Church. This culminated in the consecration of Pastor Daoud S. Haddad as the first Arab Lutheran Bishop, in a solemn ceremony held on October 31, 1979 (the Feast of the Reformation), at the Church of the Redeemer in Jerusalem.

His installation signified the establishment of an independent Arab branch of the Lutheran Church. The selection of a local Bishop has also been favored by other Christian denominations, notably the Evangelical Episcopal Church.

The new Arab Bishop heads a community of about one thousand faithful in Israel and the administered territories, and several hundred more in Jordan. A German Provost continues to administer to the spiritual needs of the German congregation, which has some seventy members and serves the many pilgrims visiting the Holy Land.

The German Mother Church still supports the needs of the local Lutheran institutions. Recently, it financed the extensive renovation of the Church of the Redeemer and the installation of a new organ in the church.

The English-speaking Lutheran congregation in Jerusalem is served by an American pastor; a pastor from Denmark is in charge of the Danish congregation. The Jesus Brotherhood and the

Jesus Sisterhood, which function in the framework of the Lutheran Church, are active in various capacities in Jerusalem. The two fraternities were founded in the sixties in Wiesbaden, and have their headquarters in Gnadental, near Frankfurt. One group of Brothers and Sisters has settled near Latrun on land leased from the Trappist monks. The community has restored ruined Crusader buildings to serve as their chapel and living quarters.

The Evangelical Lutheran Church runs a number of schools with a total enrolment of 1300 boys and girls of whom only a minority are Lutherans.

Five schools are maintained by the Church, in Jerusalem, Bethlehem, Beit Sahour, Beit Jala and Ramallah. The Talitha Kumi School, near Beit Jala, is run by the Lutheran Deaconesses of Kaiserswerth. In 1983, a new classroom wing and a gymnasium were added to the school. In 1980, a third floor was added to the Lutheran school in Ramallah and an extension was built enabling the opening of a full secondary school. In September 1987, a new Evangelical Lutheran home was inaugurated in Beit Jala, which will provide modern lodgings for fifty-four boys enrolled in the local Lutheran school.

The Lutheran World Federation, with headquarters in Geneva, maintains a representative in Jerusalem. The federation assumed charge of the Augusta Victoria Stiftung on Mount Scopus in Jerusalem, and transformed it into a major hospital. On the crest of the Mount, the Federation has erected a complex comprising an administrative center, an assembly hall and lodgings for students. The Federation also maintains a Vocational Training Center in Beit Hanina, near Jerusalem.

Scandinavian Lutheran Missions active in the Holy Land were likewise eager to provide their institutions with modern facilities.

The Norwegian Lutheran Mission built Elias Lutheran Church and Community Center in the former German Colony in Haifa. In the spring of 1976, it opened the Ebenezer Home for the Aged nearby. In 1984, the Board of Missions of the Church of Norway decided to transfer to the congregational councils the authority and administrative responsibility for its congregations in Haifa and Tel Aviv-Jaffa. The decision parallels similar steps towards indigenization taken in recent years by other denominations.

Under the auspices of the Norwegian Mission to Israel, in cooperation with the Finnish Missionary Society, the *Caspari Center* of Biblical and Jewish Studies was dedicated in Jerusalem on November 14, 1982. It is named after Carl Paul Caspari, a scholar of the late 19th century. Caspari was a Jew who converted to Christianity. The Center's aim is to conduct theological studies on biblical and Jewish topics, with emphasis on the Church and the Jewish People.

In March 1986, the Caspari Center moved from French Hill in Jerusalem to new office quarters at the Finnish School.

The Scandinavian Carmel Institute is directed by the Norwegian Pastor, Per Faye Hansen. In Haifa, he transferred the Institute's hostel for Scandinavian seamen to newer and larger premises. With the opening of the seaport at Ashdod, he set up a hostel in that town, too, so that no Scandinavian seaman coming ashore in the Holy Land would be without pastoral attention. Pastor Faye Hansen also saw the need to provide a pied-à-terre in Jerusalem for the growing numbers of Scandinavian seamen wishing to visit the Holy City. An impressive three-storey building in the former German Colony became *Beit Norvegia*, a hostel for the seafaring pilgrims. A staunch believer in the fulfilment of biblical prophecy, Pastor Faye Hansen professes an identification with the destiny of the people of Israel in its historical homeland.

The Finnish Missionary Society, a branch of the Lutheran Church in Finland, closed its boarding school in Jerusalem in 1976, thirty years after it began its activities. In the same premises, the Mission now runs two kindergartens and the *Shalhevet-Yah* (Flame of God) Center, where lectures are held. The center also serves the many Finnish pilgrims who visit the country and volunteers from Finland working on *kibbutzim*. Representatives of the F.M.S. run the Ebenezer Home for the Aged in Haifa. Several are also active in the Evangelical Community in Ramla and Lydda and in St. Luke's Hospital in Nablus. In Beit Jala, missionaries work in cooperation with the Lutheran congregation.

The Danish Israel Missionary Society, founded in 1855 as a missionary society within the Danish Lutheran Church, started its work in Israel in 1953 when Rev. Anker Gjerding served as teacher at Tabitha School in Jaffa and, for some time, as pastor. The present minister, Rev. Erik Nikolaysen, devotes his care to the many Danish volunteers on *kibbutzim*. Services are held in Tiberias, using the chapels of other churches. The Mission in Denmark raises funds and prepares study material about Israel, Judaism and Jewish-Christian relations.

The Swedish Lutheran Church, which formerly owned property in Jerusalem near the boundary that bisected the city, today sponsers a school in Bethlehem. The most prominent Lutheran institution in Israel is the Swedish Theological Institute in Jerusalem.

Other Protestant Denominations and Church-Bodies. The Southern Baptist Convention is foremost among the Protestant denominations in the Holy Land.

The Southern Baptists began their work during the British Mandate in Palestine. Their activities developed rapidly thanks to an efficient staff of pastors and communal workers. However, while work proceeded steadily in the Christian Arab milieu, proselytizing activity among the Jews met with strong opposition. Aware of the strength of national and religious feelings among the Jews in the reborn State of Israel, the Baptists are wisely taking such sensibilities into account in the conduct of their activities.[13]

Although Baptists took care not to provoke antagonism on account of proselytizing activities, their chapel in the center of Jerusalem was the object of an arsonist attack in October 1982. The criminal act, the perpetrator of which has not yet been identified, was strongly condemned by representatives of the Government and of the Jerusalem municipality. Many Jewish residents of the city showed solidarity with the Baptists by making monetary contributions towards the rebuilding of the chapel.

---

13) Opposition to Christian proselytism is common to all sectors of the Jewish population. It is most vociferous, however, among the Orthodox Jews. On the initiative of a representative of the religious party, *Agudat Israel*, the Knesset passed an amendment to the Penal Law, outlawing the use of bribery for religious conversion. To the best of the author's knowledge, there has been no case of indictment under the new legislation.

The Baptists maintain centers, or have representatives, in many towns and villages throughout the country. The Baptist School in Nazareth, which in 1961 moved from rented premises to a new building, added to it a new auditorium and, in 1982, science laboratories. Enrolment at the school totalled 587 pupils in 1983. In 1964, a center associated with the Seminary Extension Department opened in Haifa. It has expanded and its courses have been followed by a large percentage of the present leadership in the Arabic-speaking Churches.

A recent project was the community center in the Arab village of Yafiye, near Nazareth, which can accommodate the expanding local congregation, and a local kindergarten.

The Baptists are also active in East Jerusalem and in the administered territories, in various educational, charitable and medical services. In East Jerusalem, the Southern Baptist Convention maintains a chapel and a bookstore.

In 1971, the Convention opened a center for Arab and foreign students who are enrolled at the Hebrew University of Jerusalem. There is also a Baptist presence in Ramallah.

In Gaza, the hospital which once belonged to the Anglican Church was run until 1982 by a Baptist team from the United States, assisted by local Arabs. A school of public health still operates in the framework of the hospital. Religious services are held in the hospital chapel. In 1971, the Baptists opened a cultural center in Gaza.

On September 1, 1985, "A Covenant of Relationship" was signed between representatives of the Baptist Convention in Israel and the Association of Baptist Churches in Israel. The Covenant affects education, church development, building budgets, personnel and associated matters.

The Council of the Association of Baptist Churches in Israel has received recognition by the Israel Government as an *Amuta* or "Friendly Society." In the past, such status was enjoyed only by the Baptist Convention in Israel.

A growing number of *Protestant denominations*, eager to gain a foothold in the Holy Land or to expand their existing presence, are sending out representatives and inaugurating new centers.

The American Friends Service Committee operates a Legal Aid and Community Center in East Jerusalem, thirteen kindergartens in the Gaza strip, and an Institute for Information and Consultation on Mental Retardation in Beersheba.

The Church of Jesus Christ of Latter-Day Saints (Mormons), based in Salt Lake City, Utah, has sent young couples to Jerusalem in recent years to work as volunteer missionaries for a period of one or two years. Their meetings are held in a hotel. In October 1979, two thousand members of the Church arrived from the United States, under the leadership of the Church's president, to participate in the dedication of the Orson Hyde Memorial Garden on the slopes of the Mount of Olives. In 1984, the Mormon Church-affiliated Brigham Young University announced plans to build a permanent center for Near Eastern Studies on Mount Scopus. When work for the new study center started, strong opposition was voiced by Jewish Orthodox quarters, lest the center would become involved in missionary activity. The Mormon institution responsible for the center declared itself ready to provide a written commitment not to engage in proselytization.

In 1982, the West German Evangelical Institute for Archaeological Research in the Holy Land moved from rented premises in the Sheikh Jarrah neighborhood of Jerusalem to the Evangelical Church's Canaan House on the Mount of Olives. The Institute is directed by Dr. Ute Wagner-Lux.

The activities of the German Templers came to an abrupt end during the Second World War. All that remained of the former Templer colonies were the cemeteries. In 1971, following an agreement between the Governments of Israel and West Germany, the remains of the former Templer colonists of Waldheim, and Bethlehem of Galilee were reburied in the Protestant cemetery of Haifa, while the former colonists of Wilhelma were interred in the Templer cemetery in Jerusalem. After burial, a short religious ceremony was held, attended by representatives of the German Embassy and of Israel's Ministry of Religious Affairs.

Standing in contradiction to the above organizations is Aktion Suehnezeichen ("Action Atonement") (see Chapter Nine). Volunteers from West Germany work in welfare projects in Israel after a preparatory course at the "Pax House" in Jerusalem and intensive Hebrew tuition on a kibbutz. Some volunteers in "Action Atonement" are working in the Swedish Village for retarded children in Jerusalem, others with disadvantaged youth and the blind, and with the elderly, many of whom are Holocaust survivors.

The German pietistic *Beit-El Movement* is another group that has recently taken root in the Land of Israel. It was started in the middle of this century in South Germany by Emma Berger. The movement has much in common with the initial aims of the Templers. Both religious sects had their origin in Wuertemberg and took a Fundamentalist approach to the Scriptures. Like the Templers, Beit-El followers believe in the Second Coming of the Messiah, and were convinced that they could hasten his coming by settling in the Holy Land.

In 1963, Sister Emma Berger and a few followers purchased a former guesthouse and landed property in the town of Zichron Ya'akov. There followed other property purchases, both in the town and in neighboring localities. Soon others arrived from West Germany to live and work in Emma Berger's center. Its steady expansion in the heart of a Jewish town met with strong opposition from the local population, among whose older members the recollection of Nazi atrocities was still vivid. The local council of Zichron Ya'akov sought to expropriate the landed property of Emma Berger. However, Israel's High Court of Justice, to which Sister Berger appealed, ruled that the expropriation order was illegal.

Since 1974, Emma Berger's community has been organized on the lines of a *kibbutz* and registered as the Beit-El Society in Israel. Besides the small kernel of permanent members, there are visiting groups which come to work and participate in the spiritual enterprise for a limited period. The movement is manifestly friendly to Israel, but in light of the still recent memories of the Holocaust, most observers are of the view that local opposition has to be taken into account and the movement should not be allowed to expand beyond certain limits.

Sister Berger died in 1984 at the age of 64; the future of Beit-El without its charismatic leader remains to be seen.

One Protestant organization which recently established a branch in the Holy Land is the *Sisterhood of Grandchamp*, a contemplative society of women which was founded in Switzerland in the fifties. In November 1981, it established a branch near the Monastery of St. John in the Desert, just outside Jerusalem. The small house occupied by three Sisters of Grandchamp is named after Elisabeth, the mother of St. John. The Sisters lead a mainly contemplative life and devote part of their study time to deepening their knowledge of Judaism.

A group which recently established contact with Israel is the *Beit Shalom Movement*, founded and directed by Dr. Wim Malgo. Rooted in the Bible, Beit Shalom has a large following in Switzerland, the Netherlands and West Germany. It expresses its solidarity with Israel through projects in the fields of medicine, education, social rehabilitation and enrivonmental improvement. The movement runs a guest-house on Mount Carmel in Haifa, and similar institutions are planned for the future elsewhere.

In September 1980, a group of evangelical Christians who believe in the fulfilment of biblical prophecy relating to the People of Israel, established the *International Christian Embassy* in Jerusalem. The initiative was taken in reaction to the abandonment of the city by thirteen foreign embassies. The spokesman for the embassy is the Rev. Willem van der Hoeven, a former warden of the Garden Tomb. The new embassy assists pilgrims visiting the country and functions as a public relations bureau in cooperation with like-minded Christians in other countries. Each year the Embassy organizes an international Christian celebration during the Feast of Tabernacles. This is attended by evangelical Christians who come from all over the world to affirm their solidarity with Israel.

Christian Action for Israel is an organization which likewise gives moral and financial support to Israel. Its representative in Jerusalem is the Protestant minister Claude Miller Duvernoy.

Another Protestant initiative, the *American Institute of Holy Land Studies*, was founded in 1959 by the late Dr. Douglas Young. It was with deep faith in Divine Providence that he signed, prior to June 1967, the longterm lease of a severely damaged building on Mount Zion in Jerualem, a site of great importance by reason of its historical and religious associations, but dangerously near the border of the divided city. He repaired it at large cost to house his American Institute of Holy Land Studies. This act of faith was handsomely rewarded after the reunification of Jerusalem for the Institute now commands an ideal setting in the very heart of the Holy City.

At the start of the academic year 1978–79, Dr. Young retired from his position as director of the Institute. His successor was Dr. George Giacumakis, a specialist in Mediterranean studies. Dr. Young then went on to launch a program called "Bridges for Peace," with the aim of improving relations between Christians and Jews and bringing Christians to an awareness of the Jewish roots of their faith. This devoted friend of Israel passed away early in 1980. In 1985, Dr. Morris Inch succeeded Dr. Giacumakis as director of the Institute.

The Mennonites in Israel, within the pre-June 1967 boundaries, continued to serve through various congregations: with the E.M.M.S. Hospital in Nazareth, with the Bethesda Congregation in Haifa and with the Immanuel House Congregation in Jaffa,where Mennonite Pastor Roy Kreider served as director of the Study Center.

The Mennonite Central Committee has an office on Nablus Road in East Jerusalem. Its activities in the administered territories include agricultural and community development. The Committee runs a self-help needlework program in East Jerusalem, the Hope Secondary School in Beit Jala, and kindergarten training seminaries.

The Christian and Missionary Alliance organizes Bible studies in Beit Hanina, a suburb of Jerusalem, and in Ramallah.

The Bethlehem Bible College started its activities in September 1979. It is an independent, indigenous Bible College with a board of directors belonging to several Christian denominations. Its chief purpose is to train Christian religious teachers in the administered territories.

The Monophysite Churches

The Armenian Orthodox Church. Foremost among the *Monophysite Churches* is the *Armenian Orthodox.* Its spiritual and administrative center is in the walled Armenian Quarter within the Old City of Jerusalem. This is verily a citadel, and of old provided the Armenians of Jerusalem with a place of refuge from the threats of hostile neighbors. But above all, the Armenian Quarter is a citadel of faith, learning and beauty. St. James' Cathedral and the nearby patriarchal residence, the Church of St. Theodoros and the Convent of the Archangels (the traditional House of Annas) are among the finest examples of Armenian art.

During the past decade, the Armenian Patriarchate has embarked on a series of ambitious projects, foremost among them being the restoration of the Armenian wing of the Basilica of the Holy Sepulchre and the Chapel of St. Helena within the Basilica. Behind the apse of the Chapel important archaeological excavations were carried out which threw light on the history of the shrine. The Chapel of St. James, facing the parvis of the Basilica, also underwent thorough renovation. On Mount Zion, a monumental church dedicated to the Savior, is nearing completion.Most important among the new buildings is the Theological Seminary.[14] Sponsored by Alex and Maria Manookian from Detroit, it was inaugurated in June 1975 in the presence of Vasken I, Catholicos of the Armenian Orthodox Church. The theological seminary, with a present roll of forty, gives training for holy orders. It supplies not only the priests needed by the Patriarchate of Jerusalem, but also religious personnel sent to do pastoral duty in congregations of the far-flung Armenian Diaspora.

Besides the seminary, the Patriarchate conducts the Tarkmanchatz (Holy Translators) Secondary School, an elementary school and a kindergarten with a total enrolment of 300 pupils. A new wing was recently added to the building to house the secondary school.

The valuable role played by the Patriarchate's theological seminary was highlighted by a meeting held in August 1980 in Jerusalem of some sixty Armenian prelates, all of them graduates of the Jerusalem seminary, who now serve in various countries of the Armenian Diaspora.

To the Armenian complex belongs the Gulbenkian Library, as well as a library of manuscripts and a printing press from which the Armenian Diaspora gets its religious and secular books. A museum of Armenian religious objects was opened in the Arme

---

14) The theological seminary was founded in 1843 and was housed in an old building in the Armenian Quarter until 1975, when it was transferred to the new premises.

nian Quarter in Jeruaslem, named for Helen and Edward Mardigian.

The Brotherhood of St. James numbers 56 members, about half of whom serve as Bishops or parish priests in congregations in different parts of the world. The religious personnel in the Holy Land, including seminarists and nuns, exceeds eighty.

During the past few years, Patriarch Derderian has attended various meetings abroad and participated in religious ceremonies in Etchmiadzin. In 1976, Archimandrite Guregh Kapikian, custodian of Armenian Holy Places and headmaster of Tarkmanchatz School, was elevated to episcopal rank.

In March 1981, Archbishop Karekian Kazandjian, formerly serving in Australia, joined St. James Brotherhood and was elected Grand Sacristan. He became the center of a controversy, when in November 1982, the Ministry of the Interior informed him that his visa would not be renewed and that he would have to leave the country. Archbishop Kazandjian remained in Jerusalem and in view of the delicate situation prevailing in the city regarding Church matters, the ruling of the Ministry was not enforced.

Another controversy arose during the second half of 1982, this time among leading members of the Patriarchate. Dissension in the upper hierarchy is not without precedent. In the 1950's, tempers flared high during the procedure for the election of Patriarch Derderian. At that time, the headquarters of the Patriarchate in East Jerusalem was under Jordanian rule, and the Government was compelled to intervene, expelling the candidates for the Patriarchal See.

The dispute of 1982 was between Patriarch Derderian and Archbishop Shahe Ajamian, who until then had served as Grand Sacristan of the Patriarchate. The Archbishop, having been suspended from all his functions in the Patriarchate, requested the intervention of Catholicos Vasken I, the supreme leader of the Armenian Church, whose seat is in Etchmiadzin (Armenia). In the absence of any explicit response, the Archbishop continued to reside within the precincts of the Armenian Quarter in Jerusalem, without performing any functions. The relative lull ended in May 1984, when Archbishop Ajamian's home was attacked by arsonists and severely damaged. At the same time, violence broke out in East Jerusalem between Armenians supporting

241

the Patriarch Derderian and those supporting Archbishop Ajamian.

In November 1986, Archbishop Ajamian was arrested on suspicion of bribery, but released on bail.

Another dispute, this time between the Armenian Patriarch and some members of his community, resulted in a Jerusalem Court ruling (1985), which gave the Patriarch and, by extension, other heads of Churches, almost unlimited power within the precincts of Church property.

The Syrian Orthodox Church. In September 1980, Syrian Orthodox Archbishop Lukas Dioskoros Shaya took part in the enthronement of Mar Ignatios Zaka, Syrian Orthodox Patriarch of Antioch and all the East. Archbishop Shaya then relinquished the See of Jerusalem and, in October 1980, Father Yacoub was appointed Patriarchal Vicar in Jerusalem. On his departure for the U.S.A., Bishop Dyonasaios Behnam Yacoub Jajjawi was appointed head of this ancient Church. He is assisted in his religious functions by three priests and three deacons.

With the aid of the municipality of Jerusalem and the Ministry of Religious Affairs a kindergarten for the children of the community was established in Jerusalem. The municipality of Jerusalem and the Government have also taken the initiative in assisting the small Syrian Orthodox community in the Holy City to prepare the premises for a new school which will promote the study among their youth of the ancient Syriac language and traditions.

The Coptic Orthodox Church. It is led by Archbishop Dr. Anba Basilios, who is assisted by twenty priests and twelve deacons. The Church maintains educational and social welfare establishments in Jerusalem: St. Anthony's College, with all primary and secondary classes and an enrolment of 250 pupils; St. Dimiana's Secondary Girls' School, with an enrolment of 200; a mixed primary school with elementary classes, and a kindergarten with 300 boys and girls. The Coptic Patriarchate also maintains an orphanage for boys.

A list of Coptic Holy Places and churches is given in Chapter Seven. A Coptic monastery was built in Jericho in the fifties. In a

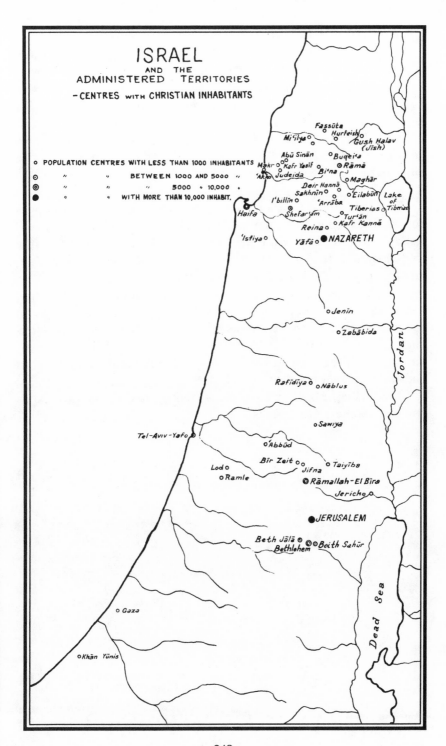

ISRAEL
AND THE
ADMINISTERED TERRITORIES
-CENTRES with CHRISTIAN INHABITANTS

o   POPULATION CENTRES WITH LESS THAN 1000 INHABITANTS
⊙   "   "   BETWEEN 1000 AND 5000   "
◎   "   "   5000 ⊹ 10,000 ⊹
●   "   "   WITH MORE THAN 10,000 INHABIT.

Fassūta
Mi'ilya o   Hurfeish o
Gush Halav
(Jish)
Abū Sinān   o Buqei'a
Makr o o Kafr Yasif   o ⊙ Rāmā
'Akko Judeida   Bi'na o
Deir Hannā   o Maghār
Sakhnīn o   o 'Eilabūn Lake
I'billīn o   'Arrāba   of
Haifa   o Shefar'ām   Tiberias o Tiberias
Reina o   o Tur'ān
'Isfiya o   o Kafr Kannā
Yāfā o ● NAZARETH

o Jenin

o Zabābida

Rafidīya o o Nāblus

o Sawiya

Tel-Aviv-Yafo ⊙   o 'Abbūd
Bīr Zeit o o   o Taiyība
Lod o   Jifna
o Ramle   ◎ Rāmallah - El Bīra
Jericho o

● JERUSALEM

Beth Jālā ◎ ◎◎ Beith Sahūr
Bethlehem

o Gaza

o Khān Yūnis

Jordan

Dead Sea

243

village near Ramallah, the Coptic Church has put up several houses for Church members. There is another project for the construction of a church, a monastery and new premises for St. Anthony's College on a plot of two and a half acres owned by the Coptic Church in Beit Hanina, a suburb of Jerusalem. On February 28, 1986, the Government finally approved the construction of the College.

The Ethiopian Church. Until 1972, the *Ethiopian Church* was headed by Bishop Joseph Fantaya, who was succeeded by Archbishop Matthew. In 1973, Patriarch Theophilos came from Ethiopia on pilgrimage to Jerusalem. In 1980, his successor, Takle Haymanot, came to the Holy City to celebrate Easter.

In 1974, a new Ethiopian monastery was consecrated at Bethany, near Jerusalem, on a plot which will also serve as a cemetery. The adjacent chapel is dedicated to St. Takle Haymanot, who lived in the thirteenth century.[15] The Ethiopian community is represented in the Holy Land by 52 monks and nuns, in addition to some families and students.

Archbishop Matthew was succeeded by Archbishop Barnabas and Archbishop Athanasios.

15) The present Patriarch chose the name of the Saint upon his election to the Patriarchal See.

Chapter Twelve

CHRISTIAN ZIONISM

Christian Zionism is found principally in Protestant Churches and sects that are particularly attached to the Hebrew Bible, or Old Testament. The strength of this connection reveals itself in Church ceremonies and in family circles, where reading from the Old Testament is a widespread tradition. Inevitably, biblical prophecies and revelations have had a powerful impact on Protestant religious movements and their attitude towards the destiny of the Jewish People.

Only a brief account will be given here of Protestant theological beliefs and messianic expectations concerning the return of the Jewish People to their homeland, since this is tangential to the main aim of the book.

The belief that the Jews should go back to the Land of their forefathers in accordance with biblical prophecies, can be traced to the time of the Reformation, notably among pietistic Protestants and certain groups of English Puritans. It was based on the pre-millenarian concept which, on the basis of a literal interpretation of the apocalyptic prophecies, believed that the Second Coming of Jesus was at hand and that he would rule from Jerusalem for a thousand years. The followers of the millenarian concept envisaged the return of the Jews to their ancestral homeland and, at the same time, their conversion to Christianity. Those two conditions were pre-requisites for the Second Coming (the Advent).

From England these beliefs spread to other countries, notably in the 18th century to the United States.

These earlier theological concepts engendered further developments in the 19th century, including the foundation of several Churches and sects, among them the Plymouth Brethren, the Christadelphians, the Mormons and a number of Fundamentalist Movements. All these Churches believed in the permanent value of the prophecies of the Holy Scripture with regard to the Jewish People.

One of the Churches which originated in the United States in the first half of the 19th century with a commitment to the pre-millenarian view was the Adventist movement. Yet William Miller, its founder, disassociated himself from the belief that the restoration of the Jews to Palestine was a precondition for the millennium. It was only in the second half of that century that Zionist Adventist sects definitively emerged. They were the Church of God (Abrahamic Faith), the Church of God of the Seventh Day (Denver, Colorado), and its rival offshoot, the Church of God (Salem, West Virginia).

A unique Adventist group was founded in 1870 by Charles Taze Russell. The attitude of this sect towards the Jewish return to Zion was initially positive, but later turned hostile towards the State of Israel. The name of the group, after successive changes, was finalized in 1931 as Jehovah's Witnesses. Russell visited Palestine twice and addressed Zionist gatherings abroad. His successor in the leadership of the movement came to adopt a negative stand on Jews and Zionism, an attitude which characterizes the sect to this day.

In the Pentecostal movement which emerged at the end of the 19th century, an important place is given to eschatology. Within its doctrine of the Last Days, there is considerable reference to the Jewish People, Zionism and the State of Israel.

The Churches connected with this movement include the Assemblies of God and several Churches of God.

The Dispensationalist movement also came into being at the end of the 19th century. In its eschatology, which espouses the most extreme pre-millenarian view, the Jewish People and its future occupy a central place in the millennium. The outstanding leader of the movement was William Blackstone, who visited Palestine and promoted the Zionist ideal.

The present survey is principally concerned with those groups or individuals who realized their theological beliefs by settling in the Holy Land or, at least, staying there for a certain period.

In this context, it should be stressed that, until the first decades of the 19th century, Christian settlement in Palestine was virtually impossible under the Ottoman régime. New prospects opened for Christian Zionism during the rule of Mehmed Ali in Palestine (1831–1839). With law and order reasonably stable during his term, Christian clergymen and scholars who were interested in biblical and archaeological research were able to come more freely, and their writings and oral descriptions stimulated interest in the Holy Land. When the Turks reconquered Palestine after 1839, they could not reverse the liberal trend inaugurated by Mehmed Ali, and the climate favorable to Christian visitors was maintained. As far as the local Jews were concerned, the intention of these early pioneers was essentially missionary, but the return of the Jewish People after their long exile was also considered.

One of the early visitors who had a special interest in the destiny of the Jewish People was Orson Hyde of the Church of Jesus Christ of Latter-Day Saints (Mormons). A member of the Quorum of the Twelve Apostles, he was delegated by the head of the Church, Joseph Smith, to travel to the Holy Land. On October 24, 1841, Orson Hyde stood on the Mount of Olives and offered a dedicatory prayer for the Jewish People and their constitution as a distinct nation and government. His pronouncement was recently commemorated when, in October 1979, two thousand members of the Church arrived under the leadership of the Church's president to participate in the dedication of the Orson Hyde Memorial Garden on the slope of the Mount of Olives.

In the 19th century, there were several attempts by millenarian sects to settle in the Holy Land, in order to await the Second Advent.

Of special note was the agricultural settlement created in 1851 by Clorinda S. Minor of Philadelphia, U.S.A., at Mount Hope near Jaffa, and the settlement founded nearby in 1866 by G. Adams and a group of Americans of the Church of the Messiah. Both experiments failed miserably.

Among the individual proponents of the Jewish return to Zion was Laurence Oliphant (1829–1885). Born in Cape Town, South Africa, to a Scottish family, this writer, politician and traveller was moved by religious and mystical impulses to take a lively interest in the Holy Land and Jewish settlement there. Political and economic considerations also played a part in his interventions on behalf of the Jewish People. Equipped with recommendations from prominent British statesmen, Oliphant started negotiations with the Turkish Government to secure concessions for the early Jewish colonists in Palestine. His interventions in Con-

stantinople, which at the time stirred great hopes in the Jewish settlers, did not succeed. But Oliphant persisted in his efforts to help
the early Jewish colonists. In 1882, Oliphant settled in Palestine
with his wife and built his house in Haifa, devoting his time to
mystical and messianic meditations.

In the second half of the 19th century, several Protestant
Christians were moved by religious beliefs to assist the return of
the Jewish People to the Promised Land. They included politi-
cians, theologians and clergymen, such as Lord Anthony Asley
Cooper, Earl of Shaftesbury, the Canadian Henry Wentwork
Monk, and Herzl's friend, the Reverend William H. Hechler.

The Balfour Declaration, a turning-point in the fulfilment of
Zionist aspirations, was undoubtedly motivated by political considerations. Yet moral and religious reasons might also have lent
their weight. Of Lord A.J. Balfour, sponsor of the declaration, it is
said that he was a rationalist, but his Scottish ancestry with its Old
Testament tradition might have influenced his political decisions.

Political developments in the wake of the Balfour Declaration
and, more than any other event, the establishment of the State of
Israel, reinforced the views held by Christian Zionists regarding
the fulfilment of the biblical prophecy.

In 1931, a small offshoot of the Adventist movement, the
Church of the Seventh Day (Salem, West Virginia), sent Elder
A.N. Dugger to Jerusalem. He stayed in the city for eighteen
months and, using the printing press given to him by his Church,
published Gospel tracts. Elder Dugger returned to the Holy Land
in 1954, after disassociating himself from the Church to which he
had belonged and founding his own split group. In Jerusalem, he
began publication of the monthly magazine, *The Mount Zion Re-
porter*. His sect included several Adventist families who settled as
farmers in various rural parts of Israel.

Pentecostal missions which started their activity in Palestine
at the beginning of the twentieth century remained in the country
after the establishment of the State, and directed their missionary
activity at the Jewish population, arousing criticism and opposition. These Pentecostal missions hailed from Great Britian and
from Scandinavian countries. Notable among the Pentecostal denominations is the Zion Christian Mission founded by the Rev.

William L. Hull of Canada in 1935. From the beginning of his stay in Mandatory Palestine, the Rev. Hull was an enthusiastic exponent of Christian Zionism. His pro-Zionist opinions were voiced in the magazine, *Pentecost in Israel*, which after 1948 became *Christian Voice in Israel*. In 1954, William Hull published *The Fall and Rise of Israel*, a book which he dedicated to David Ben-Gurion. In his book, the Rev. Hull interprets historical events from the First Commonwealth to our time from a radically millenarian viewpoint.

One branch of the American Pentecostalists which had links with Israel are the Churches of God. These were formed at the end of the nineteenth century during the revival movement, and can be traced back to A.J. Tomlinson. He founded the Church of God with its center in Cleveland, Tennessee; after his death, the Church split into a number of sects. One of these was the Church of Prophecy, also based in Cleveland, and led by A.J. Tomlinson's son, Milton, who took no definitive stand regarding the State of Israel. Accompanied by a forty-member delegation (called the Bible Landmark Expedition), Milton Tomlinson visited Israel in 1962 and erected a monument in memory of the Twelve Apostles on the peak of Mount Hittin in Galilee. Some years later, he proposed another memorial project in the neighborhood of Caesarea.

Milton's brother, Homer Tomlinson, was positively disposed towards Zionism and founded a group named the Church of God (World Headquarters, with its center in New York). In 1946, he visited Palestine and raised his banner on the Mount of Olives, on Mount Zion, and on the Horns of Hittin. He predicted that the State of Israel would be established in Palestine. As head of his Church, Homer Tomlinson often wrote on Zionism in the Church bulletin on the basis of his eschatological views.

A milestone in the development of the Pentecostal movement was the Sixth World Conference of the Pentecostal Churches held in Jerusalem in June 1961, with the participation of over 2500 delegates from thirty countries. Notwithstanding the exceptional attendance and the choice of Jerusalem as venue, the delegates refrained from formulating a positive interpretation of Pentecostal ideology with respect to Zionism and Israel.

After the establishment of the State of Israel, it becomes necessary to distinguish between pro-Zionist Christian Protestants and those, undoubtedly the majority, who conform with Jesus' saying, "Render unto Caesar what is Caesar's."

Prominent among the Protestant clergymen committed to biblical prophecy regarding the Jewish People is the Norwegian Pastor Per Faye-Hansen, who founded the Carmel movement and established several hostels for seamen visiting Israel. Another staunch supporter of the Zionist ideal is the French Pastor Claude Duvernoy, author of the book *Le Prince et le Prophète*. In it he describes the life of the Rev. W. Hechler who helped Dr. Herzl in his political endeavors. The book gives the author an opportunity to express his own political credo of Christian Zionism. The Rev. Duvernoy, who settled in Israel, continues to support the policies of the State of Israel through tracts and letters to newspapers.

Outstanding among Christian Zionists was the late Rev. Dr. G. Douglas Young who founded the American Institute of Holy Land Studies on Mount Zion. This biblical scholar, who was associated with the Evangelical movement in America and deeply committed to biblical prophecies concerning the Jewish People, was entirely devoted to Israel's cause.

The Fundamentalist position on the re-establishment of Israel in accordance with scripture, a view held by a number of Protestant Churches, found expression in the establishment of the International Christian Embassy in Jerusalem. It was conceived by a group of Fundamentalist Christians as a response to the departure of thirteen foreign embassies from Jerusalem and as an expression of their deep religious persuasion.

Christian Zionism has no similar links with the Catholic Church. Unlike the Protestant emphasis on the Old Testament, in Catholic doctrine the importance of the Old Testament lies mainly in its witness of the meaningful events recounted in the New Testament. In the opinion of the celebrated medieval theologian, Thomas Aquinas, the Old Testament's value is "Ad testimonium et non ad usum." The declarations issued by a number of Roman Pontiffs confirm the negative attitude of the Catholic Church regarding the return of the Jewish People to their ancestral homeland. To be noted in this context is the meeting between Pope Pius X and Dr. Theodore Herzl, as well as the Consistorial allocutions "Causa Nobis" by Pope Benedict XV, and "Vehementer gratum" by Pope Pius XI.

Yet, after the establishment of the State of Israel and the significant declaration of Vatican Council II, there may have been some attenuation of the Catholic Church's former negative attitude towards Zionism. The fact is that the disposition of the Holy See does not prevent individual Catholic clergymen from adopting, in certain instances, staunch pro-Israeli views.

PART TWO

People, Holy Places, Institutions, Interreligious Relations

Chapter Thirteen

CURRENT PROBLEMS STEMMING FROM THE STATUS QUO IN THE HOLY PLACES

After the Six-Day War, with the extension of its jurisdiction to East Jerusalem, Judea and Samaria, the Government of Israel was directly confronted with the problems arising out of the *status quo*. It is there that are located the Christian shrines of paramount religious significance that are the objects of conflicting claims by the several Christian denominations. True, the rights and privileges of the communities had been defined in the *firman* of 1852. But to master the subtle intricacies of the *status quo*, study of the *firman* is not enough: one must acquire a thorough knowledge of the *de facto* situation prevailing in the shrines from a perusal of the many precedents set and the decisions promulgated by the Governments which successively ruled in the Holy Land.

Very helpful in this connection is *An Account of the Practice Concerning the Status Quo in the Holy Places*, published in 1929 by L.C.A. (afterwards Sir Lionel) Cust, a former District Officer of Jerusalem. This account had no official authority under the British Mandatory Administration, and was not binding, but it was extensively used in adjusting conflicts that kept arising as to the application of the *status quo*.

From the strictly legal point-of-view, the rules of the *status quo* apply to five Christian shrines only:

1) The Church of the Holy Sepulchre with all its dependencies;
2) Deir el-Sultan, near the Holy Sepulchre;
3) The Sanctuary of the Ascension on the Mount of Olives;
4) The Tomb of the Virgin Mary in the Valley of Jehoshaphat; and
5) The Church and the Grotto of the Nativity in Bethlehem.

There are other Holy Places, subject to conflicting claims, for which adherence to the existing *de facto* situation is demanded, but they do not "technically" come under the rules of the *status quo*. A notable example is the maintenance of the Room of the Last Supper.

The matters affected by the *status quo* concern, in the main, the three denominations which enjoy a pre-eminent position in the Holy Places, namely, the Greek Orthodox, the Latins, and the Armenians. Three other Monophysite denominations—the Copts, the Syrians and the Ethiopians—are grouped with the Armenians, as their clients, in Turkish their "Yamaklak."

In the past, other denominations, such as the Nestorians, the Georgians and the Maronites also possessed rights in the Holy Places, but forfeited them because poverty made it impossible for them to make over the crippling bribes demanded by the local and central Moslem governors.

The rights and the privileges of the denominations officiating in the Holy Places must be meticulously observed in rigid conformance with what has been done in the past. This applies to the manner of public worship and its timing, to the decoration of altars and shrines, the use of lamps and candelabra, of tapestry and pictures. So, too, the categories of the officiants. Thus, the Franciscans alone of the Roman Catholic Orders may attend, and the Latin Patriarch has, of course, the right to pontificate. The clergy of the Uniate Catholic Churches, however, are excluded from all office in the Holy Places, and equally so those of the autocephalous Orthodox Churches other than the Orthodox Patriarchate of Jerusalem; the Russian Orthodox Church has been uniformly unsuccessful in its endeavors to attain a standing in the Holy Places. Russian clergy are allowed to take part in services. During his pilgrimage in 1975, the Romanian Orthodox Patriarch attempted to join in the liturgy conducted by the Greek Orthodox Patriarch in the Basilica of the Holy Sepulchre. There followed a protest from the Latin Patriarch, denouncing the behavior of the Romanian Patriarch as a violation of the *status quo.*

In the administration of the *status quo*, the following are the basic principles: the authority to repair a roof, a floor or a wall implies the repairer's right to exclusive possession of it; the right to hang or displace a lamp or a picture is recognition of exclusive possession of the wall or pillar in question; and the right of other communities to cense a chapel means that the ownership of the chapel is not exclusive.

To define the kinds of rights bearing upon the Holy Places or their component parts, Cust divides them into five classes:

1) The parts which are accepted to be the common property of three denominations in equal shares;
2) The parts claimed by one denomination as its exclusive jurisdiction, but in which the other denominations claim joint proprietorship;
3) The parts of which the ownership is disputed between two denominations;
4) The parts of which one denomination has the exclusive use, but qualified by the right of the others to cense and visit it during the offices; and,
5) The parts which are comprised within the ensemble of the Holy Places.

When parts in dispute are concerned, no innovation or repair may be made by any party. If the matter is urgent, the work must be carried out by the Government or by the municipality. Sometimes, the dispute is settled by an arrangement whereby work is permitted in the disputed part, subject to the denomination that conceded the permission being compensated by indulgence to carry out an equivalent work in another disputed place.

In other cases, formal notice of every intended work must be given by the denomination in occupation, but fundamental innovations fall under special procedures.

The Church of the Holy Sepulchre

This is the foremost among the Holy Places governed by the *status quo*. As in other sites, only the three Patriarchates—the Greek Orthodox, the Latin and the Armenian Orthodox—have possessory rights in the church, with the exception of the small chapel behind the edicule, which is in the possession of the Copts. The Copts do not hold daily services, but have the right to cense at the shrine. Similarly, the Syrian Orthodox have no formal residence, and may officiate only on holidays. They are, however, permitted to use three rooms belonging to the Armenians during

CHURCH OF THE HOLY SEPULCHRE

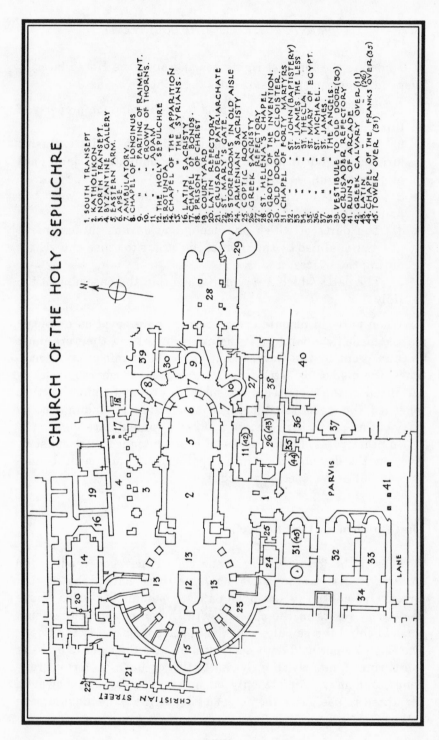

N.

1. SOUTH TRANSEPT
2. KATHOLIKON
3. NORTH TRANSEPT.
4. BYZANTINE GALLERY
5. EASTERN ARM.
6. APSE.
7. AMBULATORY.
8. CHAPEL OF LONGINUS.
9. " " PARTING OF RAIMENT.
10. " " CROWN OF THORNS.
11. THE HOLY SEPULCHRE
12. ROTUNDA
14. CHAPEL OF THE APPARITION
15. " " THE SYRIANS.
16. LATIN SACRISTY
17. CHAPEL OF BONDS.
18. PRISON OF CHRIST
19. COURTYARD
20. LATIN REFECTORY
21. CRUSADER PATRIARCHATE
23. ST. MARY'S GATE.
24. STOREROOMS IN OLD AISLE
24. ARMENIAN SACRISTY
25. COPTIC ROOM
26. GREEK SACRISTY
27. " REFECTORY
28. ST. HELENA'S CHAPEL.
29. GROTTO OF THE INVENTION.
30. OLD DOOR TO CLOISTER.
31. CHAPEL OF FORTY MARTYRS
32. " ST. JOHN (BAPTISTERY)
33. " ST. JAMES, THE LESS
34. " ST. THECLA
35. " ST. MARY OF EGYPT.
36. " ST. MICHAEL.
37. " ST. JAMES.
38. " THE ANGELS.
39. VESTIBULE TO OLD DOOR.(30)
40. CRUSADER REFECTORY
41. RUINS OF ARCADE
42. GREEK CALVARY OVER.(11)
43. LATIN " " (11)
44. CHAPEL OF THE FRANKS OVER.(35)
45. TOWER OVER (31)

CHRISTIAN STREET

PARVIS

LANE

258

Holy Week and Easter. The Ethiopians are confined to the roof of St. Helena's Chapel.

In the component parts of the church, the situation is this:

1) The entrance doorway and the facade, the Stone of Unction, the parvis and the rotunda, the great dome and the edicule are common property of the three main denominations, the cost of any work of repair being shared by them in equal parts.

2) The dome of the Katholikon is claimed by the Greek Orthodox, St. Helena's Chapel by the Armenians, and the Chapel of the Invention of the Cross by the Latins. Each claim is challenged by the other two communities, and in each case it is considered that the place in question is part of the general fabric of the church.

3) The ownership of the Seven Arches of the Virgin was in dispute between the Latins and the Greek Orthodox. In December 1963, however, an agreement was reached between the two denominations. The ownership of the Chapel of St. Nicodemos is in dispute between the Armenians and the Syrians, and that of Deir el-Sultan between the Copts and the Ethiopians. In no case will either part agree that any work of repair be carried out by another community, or that the costs be divided.

4) The Chapel of the Apparition, the Calvary chapels and the commemorative shrines are in the exclusive possession of one or other denomination, but non-possessors enjoy certain rights of office there. Projected innovations or works of repair must be notified to the other denominations.

5) The Katholikon, the galleries and the chapels in the courtyard (other than the Orthodox chapels on the west) are under exclusive jurisdiction of one or other of the denominations, but subject to the main principles of the *status quo*, being within the ensemble of the Church of the Holy Sepulchre.

A Summary Description of the Main Part of the Church of the Holy Sepulchre. The church is entered from the parvis by a single portal, closed by a wooden door with two leaves; a second portal nearby had been walled up. The procedure of opening is complicated. The key of the door is in the custody of the Moslem janitors, who occupy a divan just within: from most ancient times, the Judeh family has held the actual key, and the Insaibe family has been in charge of the opening of the door, a system introduced by the Moslem rulers to prevent quarrels between the Christian denominations. The janitors get a fixed payment from the interested denominations. The entrance-fee formerly exacted from the pilgrims was abolished in 1831 by Ibrahim Pasha. A special right of requiring the door to be opened is enjoyed by the three Patriarchs. The priests dwelling in the church cannot leave it after nightfall.

Just within the entrance is the *Stone of Unction*, commemorating the spot where Jesus was anointed before burial. The Stone is common property and above it are suspended lamps belonging to a number of denominations. Between the Stone and the rotunda is the *Station of the Holy Women*, in charge of the Armenians and in its vicinity is the Priory of the Armenians. Nearby is the *rotunda*, eighteen pillars supporting the iron dome and the galleries that enclose the *edicule* over the tomb.[1] Behind the edicule is a small chapel belonging to the Copts. The eighteen pillars belong to different denominations. All around the rotunda and opening into it, are small rooms occupied by the clergy; the most important of them is the edicule itself, enclosing the Chapel of the *Angel* and the tomb. The edicule is common property of the three denominations. A number of lamps, belonging to the several denominations and always left burning, hang above the tomb. In the west end of the rotunda is the Chapel of *St. Nicodemus*, in dispute between Syrian and Armenian Orthodox, and repairs can only be carried out by the Government. Syrian Orthodox officiate in the chapel on Sundays and on holidays. The portion of the rotunda between the edicule and the Orthodox Katholikon is known as the *Latin Choir*, and in it the Latins hold regular services. The Katholikon, with a stone in it that marks the center of the world, is Orthodox property, but, being within the ensemble of the church, any important or structural innovation should properly be notified to the other denominations. Furthermore, certain commemorative shrines are included in the church, recalling the episodes of the Passion. Among them—north of the rotunda—is the Chapel of the *Apparition of the Virgin*, where the *Column of the Flagellation* is pre-

1) The edicule was built in 1810, after the fire which swept the church, by the imperial architect, Kalfa Komnenos, originally from Mytilene on the Island of Lesbos.

served. It belongs to the Latins and the Franciscan convent adjoins it. The part at the north of the Katholikon is known as the *Seven Arches of the Virgin*, whose ownership was in dispute between the Greek Orthodox and the Latins. In December 1963, however, an agreement was reached between the two denominations. To the east of the arches is the *Prison of Christ*, in Greek possession. Opening out from the eastern ambulatory are the Chapels of *St. Longinus* (Greek Orthodox), of the *Parting of the Raiment* (Armenian), and of the *Derision or Mock Coronation* (Greek Orthodox). Between the two last-mentioned chapels a stairway leads to the Chapel of St. Helena (Armenian) and to the Chapel of the *Invention of the Cross*. The Latins claim exclusive possession of the second chapel, but certain rights in it are claimed by the Greek Orthodox; the Armenians and the Syrian Orthodox hold services there on the Feast of the Invention of the Cross.

Most important are the *Calvary* chapels, which are reached by two steep staircases, at the right of the main entrance of the church. The Greek Orthodox have the possession of the northern part of the Calvary, known as the Chapel of *Plantation or Exaltation of the Cross*, and the Latins that of the southern part, namely, the *Place of the Crucifixion*. The altar between the two, the "Stabat", belongs to the Latins. A grill looks out on the Latin Chapel of the *Agony*. Below the Calvary is the Greek Orthodox Chapel of *Adam*.

The Upper Parts of the Holy Sepulchre. Various galleries are in possession respectively of the Armenians, the Latins and the Greek Orthodox.

Around the parvis stand the following six chapels: St. James, St. John, the Chapel of the Fourteen Martyrs, and the Monastery of St. Abraham, all four of them Greek Orthodox; the Chapel of St. John (Armenian) and the Chapel of St. Michael (held by the Ethiopians, but claimed by the Copts). The belfry, built between 1160 and 1180, is in possession of the Greek Orthodox. In 1545, an earthquake destroyed its upper part.

The Monastery of Deir El-Sultan

The Monastery of *Deir el-Sultan* is adjacent to the Church of

261

the Holy Sepulchre on the east side. It consists of a courtyard with a central dome (the dome of the Chapel of St. Helena) and a cluster of ramshackle dwellings occupied by Ethiopian monks, under a Coptic guardian. Attached to the monastery are the Chapels of the *Four Living Creatures* and of *St. Michael*, which open on to the parvis of the Holy Sepulchre. Both Copts and Ethiopians claim possession of Deir el-Sultan but, until April 1970, the Copts held the two chapels in physical fact and maintain that the Ethiopians are only their guests. The Ethiopians have the use of a small chapel which opens on the courtyard; they may hold services at Easter and on the Feast of the Cross in the courtyard on the roof of St. Helena's Chapel, but the Copts will not permit them to carry out any work of repairs or innovation, which explains the miserable aspect of the shacks in which the monks have to live.

The Ethiopian Church has never ceased to claim its right in Deir el-Sultan. According to its version, the Copts occupied its property in 1838 when a plague raged in Jerusalem and all the Ethiopian monks succumbed. It likewise claims that, at that time Jerusalem was ruled by Ali Pasha, and the Copts, being Egyptians, had the support of Ibrahim Pasha's Government in occupying the monastery.

It was, however, only in 1889 that the Ethiopians, who until then officiated in the Chapel of the Four Living Creatures, were denied the privilege, in retaliation for their opposing the wish of the Copts to pull down a wall near Deir el-Sultan.

During the Jordanian rule, the Ethiopians managed to secure their partial reinstatement in Deir el-Sultan, but within forty days the favorable decision was reversed by Amman under Egyptian pressure.

After the reunification of Jerusalem, the Ethiopian Church addressed itself to the Government of Israel, asking to have its rights to the chapels restored. However, although the matter was investigated, no decisive action was taken by the Israeli authorities. With no settlement forthcoming from the Government, the Ethiopians took matters into their own hands. On the eve of Easter (on April 25, 1970), while the Copts were praying in the Church of the Holy Sepulchre, Ethiopian monks changed the locks on the doors at each end of the passageway linking the Chapel of the Four Creatures and the Chapel of St. Michael. They then occupied the shrines. Having tried to repossess the chapels with scant assistance from the police, the Copts then applied to the High Court of Justice. In its decision the High Court expressed misgivings regarding the behavior of the police which, although on the spot, did not obstruct the trespass committed by the Ethiopians. However, the judges decided the execution of the order absolute to be postponed, to enable the Government, if it thought it right, to exercise the powers available to it and deal with the substantive dispute.

The High Court was prevented from deciding the question of the ownership of the two chapels by the terms of Article 2 of the Palestine (Holy Places) Order-in-Council, 1924, which provides that "no cause or matter in connection with the Holy Places or religious buildings or sites in Palestine shall be heard or determined by any court in Palestine." (See also Chapter Eight.)

Following the instructions of the High Court, the Government referred the matter to a ministerial committee, whose efforts were intended to move the sides to an agreed solution. During the past eighteen years, no solution was found in a matter in which, besides the ruling of the *status quo*, momentous political considerations are involved, concerning Israel's relations with Ethiopia and with Egypt. As there was no progress in the matter, the Coptic Church addressed two subsequent petitions to the High Court, seeking the restoration of the chapels.

As in previous decisions taken in this matter, the Court ruled that it could not issue any order pertaining to the possession of the chapels, as this was the prerogative of the Government.

In November 1981, there was a new development with the appointment of a new ministerial committee headed by the Minister of Religious Affairs.

Summing up the terms of the dispute, there is reliable historical evidence that, in the past, the Ethiopians were in possession of the two chapels. On the other hand, there is no doubt about the fact that the Copts were holding the chapels at the time when the well-known *firman* (February 1852) entered into force, a circumstance which enabled the Copts to invoke the observance of the *status quo*.

In the author's opinion, only the advancement of ecumenism promises a viable solution on which the twin Monophysite denominations would share the two chapels and conduct alternative services there.

The Sanctuary of the Ascension

The Sanctuary of the Ascension in el-Tor village on the top of the Mount of Olives has been for many centuries in Moslem hands, being part of a mosque. It consists of a circular yard enclosed by a wall: in the center of the yard is a round, domed building above a rock, on which the imprint of the foot of Jesus is shown.

Services are held by the denominations at the site on their respective Ascension days: the Latins hold theirs inside the chapel, the Eastern Church under tents, pitched for the occasion. A meticulous schedule of ceremonies is drawn up by the communities, especially in years when the feasts of the Eastern and Western Churches coincide. The Armenians, besides holding their Ascension Day ceremonies with the Eastern Churches, have the shrine at their disposal on the sixth Saturday and Sunday of Lent.

The Tomb of the Virgin

The Tomb of the Virgin is in the Valley of Jehoshaphat, near the Garden of Gethsemane. The church built over the tomb is a medieval building, constructed, in great part, underground. It is under the joint control of the Greek Orthodox and the Armenians; the Copts and Syrians have the right to hold services on the Armenian altars.

The Latins, having been dispossessed from the church in 1757, were permitted to hold services in it under the *firman* of 1852, but never made use of the concession, so as not to derogate from their claim to the right of exclusive possession of the shrine. However, the Franciscan Fathers make three official visits to the shrine during the year to hold a short prayer service. Of the altars within the church, the one dedicated to St. Joachim and St. Anne is Greek Orthodox, the one to St. Joseph is Armenian and the one to St. Nicholas is again Greek Orthodox. In the right-hand apse is the Tomb of the Virgin and the chapel behind it is Greek Orthodox. The altar in honor of St. Bartholomew is Armenian and the Syrians are permitted to officiate at it once a week. The altar in honor of St. Stephen is Orthodox, and that of the Presentation is Armenian, the Copts having the right to officiate at it twice a week.

The Church of the Nativity in Bethlehem

The Church of the Nativity in Bethlehem is strictly governed by the *status quo* . Since 1757, it has been mainly in the possession of the Greek Orthodox. In 1881, the Latins, evicted from most parts of the main building, constructed the Church of St. Catherine nearby, and most of their services are held there. In the north transept is the Armenian church, where certain rights are also granted to the Copts and Syrians.

Repairs and innovations are regulated by the *status quo*, which applies to the *Parvis*, the *entrance doorway*, the *Nartex*, the *Nave*, the *Katholikon*, the *Grotto* and the *Manger*.[2]

The key of the door is kept by the Greek Orthodox; the Armenians have one, too; the Latins had one formerly, but it was taken from them, and the opening of the door for them has now to follow a set procedure when special services are to be held, especially at Christmas.

In the nave, all the items, lanterns and lamps belong to the Greek Orthodox, among whose rights is that of holding a number of processions in the nave. The Latins have the right of passage from the entrance of their convent door, between the first and second pillars of the northern rows. The Armenians have the right of passage through the nave, but it must be exercised in complaince with certain rules.

The Katholikon and the Church of St. Nicholas are used exclusively by the Greek Orthodox.

The Armenian church in the northern part of the transept, being across the line of passage of the Latins to the grotto, special rules had to be formulated to preclude interference and incidents. During the Christmas festivals of the Greek Orthodox, the Copts hold services on the main altar of the Armenian church, and the Syrians on a side altar. As the Armenians have their distinct date for Christmas (January 19), the altars are available for the feasts of the Copts and Syrians as they fall due.

The grotto of the Nativity, under the Katholikon, consists of two parts: the altar of the Nativity, belonging to the Greek Ortho-

---

2) In November 1982, at the request of the denominations in possession of the shrine, the civilian administration of Judea carried out repairs to the roof of the Church of the Nativity, which was in poor condition.

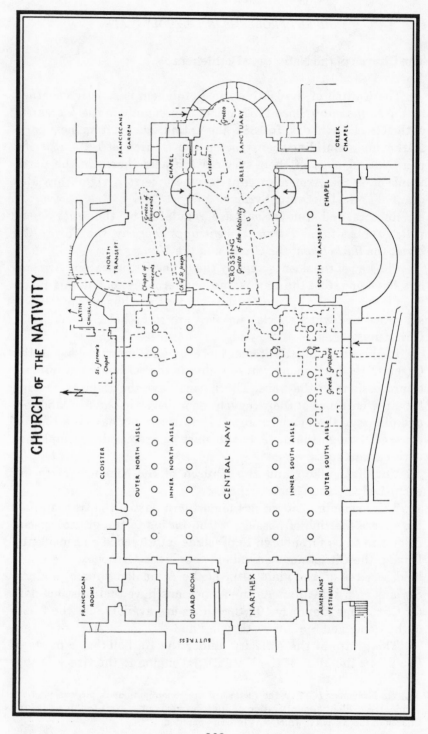

CHURCH OF THE NATIVITY

dox and the Armenians, at which the Copts and Syrian Orthodox may officiate, and the altar of the Manger, in sole Latin use.[3]

The order of services is highly complicated, and arrangements for it must be made in unison by representatives of the three main denominations. Lamps and furniture are the property of all three and no alterations are allowed either in their number of in their position. The grotto is divided into two sections—the lower with the star, the upper with the altar.

A grotto in which tradition has it that St. Jerome lived is connected by a wooden door with the grotto of the Nativity. Nearby are the tombs of the saint himself and his disciples, two women of Rome's aristocracy, Paula and her daughter Eustochium.

***

The prescriptions of the *status quo* in the Holy Places have rendered restoration most difficult, even where it was very much and urgently needed. This was so with the Church of the Holy Sepulchre, in which fire, earthquake and the ravages of time had brought about a dangerous state that excited real concern for the stability of the venerable edifice.

As the dénominations that had a say in it were unwilling to come to an agreement, the Mandatory Administration was compelled to take the matter into its own hands and safety measures were adopted after the tremors of 1927 and in the forties. The iron scaffolding put up to buttress the facade and the interior until recent days disfigured the major sanctuary of Christianity. In 1951, Greeks, Latins and Armenians started preliminary negotiations and, as the outcome, several projects were planned. An agreement was reached on May 27, 1959, between Patriarch Benedictos, the Franciscan Custos of the Holy Land Polidori, and the Armenian Vicar-General, Bishop Souren Mekhadjian.[4]

Actual work only began in 1962 and followed the plans of the chief architects—Trouvelot (Latin), Orlandos (Greek Orthodox)

---

3) According to a pious tradition, the wooden manger, which was discovered in the grotto, is now deposited in the Basilica of Santa Maria Maggiore in Rome and displayed there every Christmas.

4) On December 5, 1963, a similar agreement concerning the situation in the Basilica of the Nativity was reached between the Greek Patriarch and the Franciscan Custos of the Holy Land.

and Altonian (Armenian)—being directed locally by a technical office of which architects Coüasnon, Colas and Diran were in charge.

The main concern of those in charge of the extensive restoration of the Basilica was to perform the complicated work without interrupting the liturgical ceremonies and the processions that go on night and day.

During the past few years, major repairs were carried out on the southern facade facing the parvis as well as on the northern one, which was likewise delapidated. The pillars supporting the roof of the rotunda, which were also damaged, had to be changed stone by stone. Of particular note is the restoration of the Katholikon, the major church in the Basilica complex. Work there had to be combined with archaeological excavations, which uncovered the remains of the Martyrion, the fourth-century Constantinian Basilica. The iconostasis of the Katholikon was replaced by a new one in stone and marble, designed by a renowned Greek architect.

The Armenian gallery and priory were artistically renovated and embellished by the addition of stone bas-reliefs and mosaics, in keeping with the best Armenian artistic tradition. Likewise were restored all the chapels in Armenian possession and particularly the Chapel of St. Helena, where a magnificent floor mosaic was inset before the main altar.

The Franciscan friars saw to the repair of those chapels and parts of the sanctuary in their exclusive possession. They furthermore built several rooms on the terrace above the Basilica for the use of friars keeping watch over the shrine.

By far the most challenging project was the dismantling and replacement of the dome which crowns the columned rotunda. The work was carried out by a British construction company, Freeman-Kershaw, and costs were borne equally by the three communities having historical rights in the Basilica: the Greek Orthodox and Armenian Patriarchates, and the Franciscan Custody of the Holy Land. Government participation is precluded under the provisions of the *status quo*, since such participation would imply partial ownership of the shrine. However, Government assistance was forthcoming in the form of tax exemption for all three communities on building materials. Moreover, at the request of the three, the Municipality of Jerusalem installed new drainage pipes beneath the worn flagstones next to the Basilica, to put an end to the annual hazard of winter flooding.

The *status quo* contains no provisions for Protestant believers. The omission is explained by their particular approach to the holiness of the Land of the Bible. The devotion of the Protestants is less localized than that of other Christian believers. Their veneration is not directed at shrines marking sites mentioned in Gospel tradition, but rather comprehends the broader biblical landscape as such. In the Protestant view, Jerusalem, Bethlehem, Galilee and the River Jordan can produce in their entirety a unique and moving experience, permitting the visualization of biblical ideas and events in their actual setting.

Appendices to Chapter Thirteen

THE ROOM OF THE LAST SUPPER
(Coenaculum-Cenacle)

The Room of the Last Supper is a shrine which does not come under the rules of the *status quo*. It is nevertheless the object of conflicting claims by the three monotheistic faiths.

According to Christian tradition, it is the site where Jesus and the disciples partook of the Last Supper and where such hallowed events as the Pentecost took place. Furthermore, it is considered to be the site of the gathering of the first Christian believers and is known as the Mother Church. In Jewish and Moslem tradition, the site is connected with King David's burial place. As King David is venerated by Moslems as Nebi Daoud (the Prophet David), they converted the premises into a mosque and it became a *waqf* (religious endowment).

The Room of the Last Supper was bought in 1333 by Robert of Anjou, King of Naples, and his wife Sancha of Mallorca, from the Mamluk Sultan of Egypt and entrusted to the care of the Franciscan Fathers. In 1552, however, the Franciscans were ejected from the shrine by the Moslems, who converted it into the Mosque of Nebi Daoud. During the more liberal régime of Muhammed Ali, the Franciscans were permitted to visit the Room of the Last Supper twice during the year (on Good Friday and on Pentecost), but had to confine themselves to reading passages from the New Testament, and were not allowed to kneel.

During the first half of the twentieth century, great efforts were made by the Italian Government to recover the Room of the Last Supper. The Italian claim was based on the assertion that the King of Italy was the legitimate heir of Robert of Anjou, King of Naples.[1] A similar claim was put forward by the Spanish Government on behalf of the King of Spain on the grounds that he had inherited the rights of Sancha of Mallorca. Catholic claims supported by the Holy See were of no avail in the face of Moslem oppo-

---

1) See the article by S.I. Minerbi in the periodical *Cathedra* (Hebrew), October 1982, "Italian Efforts to Recover the Coenaculum."

sition. Under Israeli rule, the Room of the Last Supper is open to visitors of all creeds, but since the site remains a Moslem endowment, there are some restrictions regarding worship by other faiths. Israel's Ministry of Religious Affairs, acting as neutral agent in the dispute between the Franciscans and the Moslems, has recently carried out repairs in the shrine.

APPROACH ROADS TO CHRISTIAN SHRINES

Since the establishment of the State of Israel, an impressive network of roads has been built, making travel swift and easy and giving access to even the most remote village. This development benefitted the local inhabitants as well as tourists and pilgrims visiting the Holy Places of their faith. However, there are isolated sanctuaries where pious men chose to detach themselves from the world's tumult and live in prayer and ascetic solitude. In the past, these places could be reached only by mule tracks or steep paths. The Israeli Government, at its own initiative or in response to the request of Church leaders, saw to the construction of good roads, giving easy access to sanctuaries which had been virtually cut off.

The roads built in recent times include those leading to the Mount of the Beatitudes and to Capernaum, the road ascending Mount Tabor, and the road opened on Mount Zion to enable Pope Paul VI, during his pilgrimage in 1964, to travel by car to the Dormition Abbey and the Coenaculum. The road to the Church of the Visitation in Ein Karem was renewed and in Jerusalem's Old City the Via Dolorosa was repaved in the ancient style.

In the Judean Wilderness, the rugged track leading to the renowed Monastery of Mar Saba has been widened and paved, and now serves as an approach road.

In April 1985, a new road was opened in the dry river bed leading to the St. George of Chosiba Monastery in Wadi Kelt.

The approach road to the Quarantal Monastery, on the eastern face of the Mount of Temptation, overlooking Jericho, has been improved and paved. The work was carried out by the civil administration at the request of the Greek Orthodox Patriarch of Jerusalem. His Beatitude Diodoros I participated on June 15, 1987, in the dedication ceremony.

The road leading to the Latin Church's Shepherds' Field, east of Bethlehem, was substantially extended so as to provide an easier and safer approach for the many Christians who make devotional visits to the site.

Chapter Fourteen

CHRISTIAN EDUCATIONAL AND CULTURAL INSTITUTIONS IN THE HOLY LAND

Whilst deeply concerned with the right to worship unhindered in their hallowed shrines, the Churches are no less anxious to pursue freely their educational work among the youth of their flock. To this end, the Christian denominations in the Holy Land maintain one hundred primary and secondary schools with an enrolment of thirty thousand boys and girls, mostly Christians, but also Moslems.

About three-quarters of those schools are administered by Catholic Orders and Congregations. The greater part of them are under Italian or French patronage. Besides these there are a large number of educational institutions run by the Anglicans, by Protestant denominations, by the Greek Orthodox Patriarchate, and by several Monophysite Churches.

In Israel within its pre-June 1967 borders there is an established network of Government schools for the Arab sector of the population. This has not made the mission schools redundant, since parents often prefer to send their children to be educated in a traditional Christian spirit. That is especially true for girls, given the traditional upbringing of women in Arab patriarchal society.

Primary schools which adopt the curriculum of Israel's Ministry of Education and Culture profit from a Government subsidy. In secondary private schools which follow suit, school fees for children of indigent families are covered by a special fund.

A recent development in the cooperative relations of Church and State in Israel concerns the funding of Christian schools in the country. In the past, the Churches have sought to maintain the independence of the schools which they run. But a number of years ago, the Greek Catholic Archbishop of Acre, Haifa and Galilee asked the State to grant official recognition of his community's schools and to assume the burden of the teachers' salaries. The Ministry of Education and Culture accepted the Archbishop's request and, in fact, also agreed that although the teachers' salaries are now largely paid by the State, the teachers nonetheless remain the employees of the Church rather than of the Government. A similar request from the Baptists for their school in Nazareth has also been approved. A later request, from the Latin Patriarchate of Jerusalem, which originally opposed the action taken by the Greek Catholic Archbishop, involving thirty-two schools, is presently under consideration. Until now, the request has been granted for the schools run by the Franciscan Fathers in Acre and in Nazareth. A similar request has also been submitted by the Anglican Bishop in Jerusalem.

More and more Christian private schools in Israel, within the pre-June 1967 borders, are adapting their curricula to that of the Government system, so that their pupils may pass the Government matriculation and thereby qualify for admission to an Israeli university. Over two thousand Israeli Arabs, Christian and Moslem, are studying today at Israel's several universities.

In the territories which came under Israeli administration in 1967, the prevailing educational system in each area has been allowed to continue: Jordanian in Judea and Samaria, and Egyptian in the Gaza district. The role of the Christian schools is particularly beneficial in those areas where local educational institutions are below European and American standards.

Besides the numerous lay schools, there are theological seminaries to train young men for the priesthood. Seminaries of this sort are maintained by the Latin, Greek and Armenian Patriarchates. In 1983–84, the seminary of the Latin Patriarchate had an enrolment of 75 in the junior sector and 14 in the senior sector. The Armenian seminary also trains ministers for congregations in the Armenian diaspora. The Greek Catholic Church in the Holy Land also maintains a junior seminary. Furthermore, there are novitiates for monks and nuns run by monastic Orders and conventual Congregations.

Of special importance are the biblical and archaeological institutes sponsored by Catholics and Protestants alike.

As far as cultural activities are concerned, it is indicative that in Israel, and particularly in Jerusalem, a number of Christian institutions publish books and periodicals, often of a high scientific and scholarly level. At the biennial Jerusalem Book Fair, in which hundreds of local and foreign publishing houses participate, books and periodicals by local Churches (see special chapter) are on display.

In a previous chapter (1), mention was made of the increasing diffusion of Hebrew among Israeli Arabs. Especially keen to avail themselves of Israel's facilities to learn the language of the Bible are members of the clergy, both foreign and local.

In 1986, an agreement was signed between Prof. Moshé Bar Asher of the Hebrew University of Jerusalem and Prof. A. Roest Crollius of the Gregorian University of Rome, providing for exchanges of professors and students for bestowal of scholarships and organization of lectures and other research projects.

Over the past few years, more than a hundred students of the Pontifical Biblical Institute of Rome have attended special courses at the Hebrew University of Jerusalem. A similar program has been organized by the Committee for Church and Judaism of the Evangelical Church in West Germany. Since 1978, Evangelical students of theology can attend seminaries set up by the working circle "Studium in Israel," in collaboration with the Hebrew University of Jerusalem. Christian scholars from the United States and Europe in 1986 attended courses at the Shalom Hartman Institute for Advanced Judaic Studies in Jerusalem. On March 30, 1980, a collaborative agreement was signed between the Hebrew University in Jerusalem and the Pontifical University in Rome. The agreement calls for an exchange of scholars and students, scholarships for exchange students, collaborative research projects, scholarly conferences and mutual visits. Three Christian scholars, two Catholics and a Protestant, have joined the academic staff of Israeli universities. Father Marcel Dubois, a learned Dominican monk who has lectured at the Hebrew University of Jerusalem since 1968, was recently appointed head of the University's philosophy department.

Rewarding cooperation in the realm of biblical studies has been established between the savants of prestigious biblical and theological institutes under the aegis of Protestants and Catholics alike and scholars at Israeli universities.

Among the cultural events which insert themselves harmoniously in the framework of the land of the Bible are Jerusalem's Bible contests which attract Jewish, Protestant and Catholic contestants from all over the world.

Cultural values shared by the various faiths in the Holy Land are not confined to biblical studies, but encompass a broad spectrum of interests. Foremost among these is music, speaking a universal tongue to the ear and heart of man, unconfined by the boundaries of nation or religion. The unifying power of music was well illustrated by a performance of Verdi's Requiem in Manger Square in Bethlehem by an internationally renowned choir and orchestra, before a large cosmopolitan and interconfessional audience. There is also a great interest in concerts of religious music by Johann Sebastian Bach, regularly performed by an Israeli orchestra. During several years, these concerts took place in a church in Kiriat Ye'arim, near Jerusalem, the spot where the Ark of the Covenant rested. Also very well attended are organ concerts of religious music given in Jerusalem in the Lutheran Church of the Redeemer and, more recently, in the Catholic Church of the Dormition. Here, too, the audience is very large and interconfessional.

Mention should also be made of the International Harp Contest, periodically held in Jerusalem, with the participation of musicians from far and wide. The contest takes place in the very city where King David accompanied on the zither the rendering of his own sublime psalms.

In the context of Israel Radio's religious programs, there are regular broadcasts of Church ceremonies. In addition to the coverage of major feast-days, Sunday services are relayed every week. A new series is devoted to liturgical music of the Eastern Churches, performed by members of those Churches. The music is accompanied by appropriate explanations as to its liturgical significance.

After Israel gained control over East Jerusalem and Bethlehem, Israeli television started to transmit ceremonies marking the principal Christian holidays, both to local viewers and, by satellite, to the world at large.

Christian religious art has been handsomely represented in a striking exhibition of Armenian ritual objects and illuminated manuscripts, organized by the Armenian Patriarchate in

Jerusalem with the technical assistance of the staff of the Israel Museum in Jerusalem.

One cultural activity which calls for close collaboration between scholars of different nationalities and religions is archaeology.

Since the first half of the last century, excavations have been carried out all over the Holy Land under the auspices of universities and foreign Governments, with the aim of uncovering the historical and religious heritage of the Holy Land. In recent years, archaeological research has taken unprecedented strides. Hundreds of voluntary workers from Israel and abroad have given eager assistance to archaeologists engaged in digs throughout the country. Excavations initiated by Christian institutions are mostly at sites traditionally connected with the events of the Gospels. Of prime importance are the excavations conducted by the Franciscan Fathers, which have shed light on the early Christian period when the new-born Church had not yet become detached from Jewish customs and traditions.

Excavations near the Dead Sea are of paramount interest because of similarities between the followers of John the Baptist and members of the sect at Qumran. Christian scholars also follow with considerable interest the excavations carried out near the retaining wall of the Temple Mount, since the findings help to indicate the precise alignment of Jerusalem's ancient walls, and this has a bearing on the site of the Holy Sepulchre.

The discovery of scores of remains of Byzantine churches and monasteries has revealed the extent of the Christian establishment in the first centuries of the common era. Finally, the exploration of Crusader fortresses and other Crusader monuments offers no lesser appeal to scholars investigating this particular chapter of the Christian presence in the Holy Land.

Chapter Fifteen

CHURCH SPONSORED MEDICAL INSTITUTIONS IN THE HOLY LAND

Care of the infirm is considered a most worthy duty, especially if performed in the Holy Land. Pious Christians who follow this vocation see themselves as fulfilling Jesus' exhortation to his disciples "to cure the sick, rise the dead, cleanse the lepers" (Matt. 10:8). Not surprisingly, members of the religious Orders were foremost in this charitable work. From the beginning of the Christian era, they cared for pilgrims, protecting them from the prevalent hazards and privations.

Hospices affording shelter to pilgrims have existed in the Holy Land since the early Middle Ages. One example was the Benedictine hospice sponsored by Charlemagne; another, even more important in the light of subsequent developments, was the hospice founded in the eleventh century by the merchants of the Italian port-city of Amalfi. A century later, the hospice was taken over by the Knights of St. John and transformed into a hospital which could accommodate as many as two thousand infirm. The Knights, also known as "Hospitallers," transferred the hospital to Acre when Jerusalem was conquered by the Moslems.

During the Crusader Kingdom there was also a leprosary, dedicated to St. Lazarus and located outside Jerusalem's Damascus Gate. The leprosary, too, was transferred to Acre after the fall of Jerusalem.

When the Crusader Kingdom came to an end, Christian hospitals in the Holy Land ceased to function and the care of sick pilgrims was entrusted to the Franciscan friars. When a pestilence broke out during Napoleon's campaign in Palestine, the ailing soldiers were nursed by the Franciscan friars in Jaffa. After the siege of Acre, during the same campaign, wounded soldiers were tended by the Carmelite Fathers in their monastery on Mt. Carmel. There is record of only one Moslem hospital in olden Jerusalem: the *Muristan* (a Persian word meaning hospital.) The name now denotes a neighborhood in the Old City, the Muristan, where the Church of the Redeemer and other Lutheran institutions are located.

Not until the middle of the nineteenth century, when Ottoman rulers adopted more enlightened policies, were the Churches able to set up hospitals according to modern standards. They were very needed in backward Palestine. Catholic Orders and Congregations, Anglican and Protestant missionary societies as well as the Russian Orthodox Mission, were active in establishing medical institutions.

One Catholic Congregation which took a pioneering role in caring for the sick was that of the Sisters of St. Joseph of the Apparition. They came to the Holy Land at the invitation of the Latin Patriarch Valerga, and by 1851 they had established a small hospital inside Jerusalem's Jaffa Gate, named after the Crusader King Louis the Saint. In 1896, through the endeavors of Count A. de Piellat, the hospital was transferred to a new, stately building opposite New Gate. In 1950, when the hospital could not be used by the inhabitants of the then divided city, the Sisters built a new hospital, named after St. Joseph, in the eastern sector of Jerusalem. In 1881, thanks to the generosity of M. Guinet of Lyons, the Sisters of St. Joseph also built a large hospital in Jaffa. This is now used in part as a home for aged nuns. The charitable sisters also run clinics in Nablus and Ramallah.

In 1876, the Sovereign Order of Malta founded a small hospital at Tantur, site of the present-day Ecumenical Institute, and entrusted the infirm to the care of the Charitable Brothers of St. John of God. The Brothers opened their own hospital in Nazareth in 1884. The building was occupied by the military during the two World Wars and had to be thoroughly restored. The enlarged, renovated premises were reopened in 1959 and today it is a medical institution which meets the most modern standards.

In 1898, Nazareth also saw the establishment of a hospital, by the Charity Sisters of St. Vincent of Paul. This hospital has likewise been renovated and new wings added. In 1905, the German Sisters of St. Charles Borromeus opened a hospital in Haifa. However, it ceased to function as a medical institution and the premises are rented, providing an income for the German Sisters. Today the Sisters perform medical duties in a number of clinics. In Haifa, the "National Association for Assisting Italian Missionaries Abroad" runs a hospital which was recently enlarged and modernized. However, a hospital built by the Association in 1912 in Jerusalem was put in charge of the Custodian of Enemy Property by the British Mandatory Authorities during the Second World War. During the hostilities in 1948, when the building stood on the front-line of the then divided city, it suffered severe damage.

The property was sold to the Israeli Government, and today houses several departments of the Ministry of Education and Culture.

Newly-built hospitals include the Pediatric Hospital in Bethlehem which was founded by the German and Swiss "Caritas." Another building was put up nearby in 1984, to accommodate some of the hospital's departments. Mention should also be made of the Government hospitals in Beit Jala and Bethlehem, both of which are run by Catholic Sisters. These arrangements date from the time of the Jordanian administration. The French Hospital founded by the Sisters of St. Vincent of Paul in Bethlehem in 1889 was taken over early in 1985 by the Sovereign Order of Malta.

In the past, the Anglican Church established several hospitals with the aim of assisting the sick and winning adherents to the Church. The changes which occurred in the political and financial position of Great Britain, as well as mounting national feeling among the local population, have adversely affected the development of those Anglican institutions.

A hospital founded in Jerusalem by the "Society for Promoting Christianity among the Jews" and located in Jerusalem's Street of the Prophets, has now been converted into a school run by the Anglican Church. St. Luke's Hospital was started by the Mildmay Deaconesses in Haifa in 1892. Its personnel was transferred to a new hospital in Hebron in 1929, but this was later closed and rented to the Jordanian Government. St. Luke's Hospital in Nablus, founded in 1894, has been handed over to the Arab Evangelical Episcopal community. Another hospital which opened in Jaffa in 1844 under the direction of the Mildmay Deaconesses was also closed down. The Al Ahli Hospital in Gaza was taken over by the Southern Baptist Convention of the U.S.A. and run for several years by a dedicated team of American Baptists. In 1982, the Anglican Church took charge of the eighty-bed hospital.

In the past century, the Church of Scotland built a large hospital in Tiberias. With the appearance of new, modern hospitals in eastern Galilee, the Church of Scotland made the building a hostel for Protestant pilgrims. Another Scottish venture, a hospital built in Nazareth by the Edinburgh Medical Missionary Society, was renovated and a school for nurses added to it. In 1987, a new wing for the out-patient clinics was added to the hospital.

The Lutheran Deaconesses of Kaiserswerth founded a hospital in 1851 in Jerusalem, but its activity was interrupted at the outbreak of World War II. A leprosary called "Jesushilfe", also founded in Jerusalem by a Lutheran organization, was transferred to a new building on a hilltop near the small town of Beit Jala. The monumental Augusta Victoria Hospital founded in 1898 on Jerusalem's Mount Scopus is now administered by the Lutheran World Federation.

The Russian Orthodox Church used to run a hospital in the Russian Compound in Jerusalem. It was closed when the flow of Russian pilgrims dwindled, following the Soviet Revolution.

The Greek Orthodox Patriarchate also used to maintain a hospital in Jerusalem; today, it has only a clinic. In February 1973, the Armenian Orthodox Patriarchate also opened a clinic in a spacious center adjoining St. James Cathedral.

In addition to the hospitals and clinics, there are also several paramedical institutions in the Holy Land, such as hospices for retarded children, institutions for deaf-mutes, and homes for the aged, where medical assistance is also given.

The paramedical and reeducative institutions recently established include the London-based "Cheshire Home for the Physically Handicapped", founded in 1960. In 1975, this became the "Bethlehem Arab Society for the Physically Handicapped", offering patients board and lodging, physical therapy, medical care, elementary schooling and preliminary training. Since 1980, the German-sponsored "Christoffel Blindenmission" in Bethlehem has given vocational and technical training courses for young men.

It should be noted that the Church-administered hospitals have found a useful and advantageous place in the framework of Israeli medical institutions. By agreement with the Sick Fund of the Histadrut (the countrywide Labour Federation) and with the National Insurance Institute, they are reimbursed for the hospital expenses of patients, members of the Histadrut, in their care. Moreover, since October 1981, the three hospitals in Nazareth (the French Hospital of the Sisters of St. Vincent, the Italian Hospital of the Brothers of St. John of God, and the Hospital of the Edinburgh Association) have functioned as district hospitals.

Hostels for Pilgrims

In early times, pilgrims could find refuge and protection only in monasteries and in hostels kept in the vicinity of the main sanctuaries. Until the nineteenth century, indeed, the hospices or hostels maintained by the religious establishments were the cleanest and most comfortable lodgings available in a still backward country.

Napoleon Bonaparte, during his campaign in Palestine, slept in a Franciscan monastery, and Franz Josef I, Emperor of Austria, on his pilgrimage in 1869, lodged in the newly inaugurated Austrian Hospice in Jerusalem. In more recent times, with the increased number of pilgrims, the Christian hostels seek to remain competitive with the many luxury hotels in the Holy Land. Visitors seeking religious surroundings may prefer to stay in the hospices of the Catholic Orders and Congregations, or in Protestant hostels such as those run by the Y.M.C.A., the Anglican Church, or the Scottish Church.

Orthodox pilgrims who come in great numbers to the Holy Land, especially at Easter, can find lodging in the huge monasteries of the Greek Orthodox Patriarchate.

Since 1948, more hostels have been opened. In some cases former schools and hospitals have been converted to meet the needs of an ever-growing influx of pilgrims and visitors.

The various "Casa Nova" hostels run by the Franciscan Fathers have been thoroughly renovated. Notre Dame de France, after restoration, offers standards comparable to most modern hotels. The communal Christian villages of Nes Ammim and Yad Ha'Shemona also run guest-houses, as an additional source of income. A Norwegian Lutheran institution welcomes into its hostels the thousands of merchant seamen whose ships put in at

Israeli ports. Finally, one should mention such guest-houses as those established for Jews by the Marienschwestern of Darmstadt as an act of atonement for the Holocaust, and others founded as a gesture of solidarity by the Beit Shalom movement.

Christian Agricultural Villages

Life in the State of Israel is not confined to historical and biblical recollections nor to the veneration of Holy Places. Local Christians and those visiting from abroad are attracted by original patterns of social organization, which contribute to the ongoing process of national reconstruction.

It will be sufficient to refer to the *moshav* (cooperative village), the *kibbutz* (collective village) and the intermediate forms of agricultural communities, with more or less closed systems of cooperative output, which have important effects on the social and cultural life of the country.

The appeal of the cooperative and communal form of life has generated imitators in Christian quarters. In fact, the monastic way of life, although dissimilar in its spirituality, has a remarkable resemblance with the kibbutz in its social and economic aspects.

The most successful example of Christian settlement following the Israeli model is the cooperative village of "Nes Ammim". It was founded in Western Galilee by Dr. Johan Pilon and is settled mostly, but not exclusively, by pious Protestants hailing from Holland, Switzerland, West Germany and the U.S.A. The Hebrew words, "Nes Ammim", translated "Banner of the Nations", are taken from the Book of Isaiah (11:10). The settlers of this Christian village grow plants for industrial processing and flowers which are exported to Europe. They also have a carpentry shop which produces spiral staircases for the local market. The members of the village, who in 1987 numbered two hundred souls, and the visitors who flock to it, also devote themselves assiduously to spiritual matters. It is worth noting that they enjoy excellent relations with the neighboring Jewish and Arab settlements.

Another village founded by religious Protestants is "Yad Ha'Shemona", translated "The Memorial of the Eight." The settlement is located in the Judean Hills, west of Jerusalem, and its members are Bible-believing Finns. Their income derives from Scandinavian tourism and a small furniture factory.

Since 1974, Emma Berger's community in Zichron Ya'acov has also been organized on the lines of a kibbutz.

A similar enterprise is "Neve Shalom", meaning "House of Peace." It was founded by the Dominican Father Bruno Hussar near the Trappist Monastery of Latrun, on a site rich in Crusader history. Its program is intended to promote interconfessional accord not only in theory but also in practice, by demonstrating the vitality of a settlement where followers of the three monotheistic faiths live and work in harmony.

In addition to cooperative forms of agricultural activity, there are still Church-owned farms operated on traditional lines.

Chapter Sixteen

CHRISTIAN RELIGIOUS COURTS

The existence of Christian religious courts in Israel and in the administered territories, with jurisdiction in matters of personal status, is an inheritance of Ottoman rule. The system was adopted with a few changes by the British Mandatory Government, which replaced the Turkish after the First World War. Matters pertaining to the competence of these courts were recorded in an earlier chapter of this book.[1]

The following Christian communities maintain religious courts in the Holy Land: the Latins, Greek Catholics and Maronites, the Greek Orthodox, the Armenian Orthodox, the Syrian Orthodox and, more recently, the Evangelical Episcopal community.

The Latin Patriarchate maintains courts of first instance as well as courts of appeal in Nazareth and in Jerusalem.[2] The law applied by the Latin courts is the Codex Juris Canonici of the Roman Catholic Church. In addition, there is a special statute covering matters of personal status and comprising 308 articles. Issued by the Latin Patriarch of Jerusalem on October 31, 1954, it is written in Arabic and pertains to the following matters: betrothal, dowry and trousseau; parentage and legitimacy of children; adoption, authority of parents; alimony and maintenance; compensation in cases of nullity of marriage; guardianship, curatorship and interdiction; succession and wills; temporal property of the Church, *waqfs* (trusts); administration of property of absentees, donations and Holy Places.

The Greek Catholic Archdiocese of Acre, Nazareth and Galilee maintains a court of first instance and a court of appeal in Nazareth. In these tribunals, the Canon Law for the Uniate churches is applied. In addition, a statute for matters of personal

---

1) See Chapter Eight
2) Patriarchs and religious heads, whose jurisdiction extends to the Kingdom of Jordan, maintain religious courts there too, but the present survey does not cover the religious institutions east of the River Jordan.

status is in force. It was issued by the Archbishop of Acre in 1954 and is very similar to the statute of the Latins.

The Maronite Church has a court of first instance in Haifa. Concerning the court of appeal, there is cooperation with the Greek Catholics. The Maronites apply the Canon Law for the Uniate Churches and in addition a statute for matters of personal status, published in Beirut in 1929, comprehending 312 articles.

Other Uniate Churches with only a small following in the Holy Land cannot dispose of qualified religious judges and thus avail themselves of the offices of the Latin courts.

Such is the case of Greek Catholics who live in the area under the jurisdiction of the Patriarchal Vicariate of Jerusalem.

The Greek Orthodox Patriarchate maintains religious courts of first instance in Acre, Nazareth, Jaffa, Gaza and Jerusalem. The court of appeal, its seat in Jerusalem, has a Metropolitan, two Archbishops, and an Archimandrite with function of secretary. The Greek Orthodox tribunals apply the Byzantine ecclesiastical law, though this does not exist in the form of a Codex. In order to facilitate the work of the religious judges, a summary of the principal dispositions concerning matters of personal law was compiled by Miltiades Karpokides. This was translated into Arabic by George Sabsah during the period of the British Mandate for use in the Orthodox courts in Palestine.

The Coptic Orthodox Church does not maintain religious courts in the Holy Land, but instead uses the tribunals of the Greek Orthodox Church.

The Armenian Orthodox Church does not possess a Codex. A collection of various council canons and those by the Armenian Patriarchs was published in Armenian in 1964 by Vasken Hagopian. An earlier collection was compiled by Archbishop Meliktakian. A collection of laws in Armenian was published in Beirut in 1956 by Izmirlian for use in the religious courts in matters of personal status. There is an Arabic translation of this collection.

The Syrian Orthodox Archbishop maintains a court of first instance in Jerusalem. The court is composed of the Archbishop and three priests. It applies a collection of laws, dealing with matters of personal status, which was compiled in Jerusalem in 1929 by Father Juhanna Dolawani. The 300 articles and their contents resemble the statutes of the other communities. In the case of an appeal against the decision of the court of first instance, the case is heard by a court held in Damascus, near the Syrian Orthodox Patriarchate.

The Evangelical Episcopal (Anglican) Church maintains a court of first instance, with two ministers and a lawyer. The court of appeal has two Bishops, an Archdeacon and a lawyer. The law applied is a statute dealing with matters of personal status, which was compiled in 1954 by the Council of the Evangelical Episcopal Community in Jordan, Lebanon and Syria.

The Evangelical Episcopal Church allows Protestant denominations which have no religious courts of their own, to avail themselves of the Evangelical Episcopal tribunal. Lutherans occasionally make use of this option.

Chapter Seventeen

CHRISTIAN PERIODICALS
IN THE HOLY LAND

The Christian Churches in the Holy Land publish a number of periodicals dealing with religious, ecclesiastical and communal matters, past and present. They are a precious source of information on the manifold activities of the Churches, demonstrating freedom of expression and worship. Most are published in Jerusalem, where the majority of the communities have their headquarters, and where prestigious biblical and archaeological institutes are located.

The Catholic institutions are especially noteworthy for their diverse and reputed publications.

The monthly, *Jérusalem,* is the mouthpiece of the Latin Patriarchate. Founded in 1934, it is published in French by the Fathers of Betharram. It contains passages from the main papal encycles, pastoral letters and news concerning the diocese of Jerusalem.

La Terra Santa is an illustrated monthly put out by the Custody of the Holy Land. It appears in Italian, French and Spanish, with a quarterly edition in English and an Arabic version called *As-salam We al-Kheir* (Peace and Goodness). *La Terra Santa* is devoted mainly to issues concerning the Holy Places, but also contains articles and news of general Christian and historical interest.

La Revue Biblique was founded in 1892 by the learned Dominican Fathers of the French Biblical and Archaeological Institute in Jerusalem. Its carefully researched papers are intended for scholars in the fields of Bible and archaeology.

Proche-Orient Chrétien is a quarterly issued by the White Fathers of St. Anne's Monastery in Jerusalem. It was founded in 1951 with the aim of fostering interconfessional contacts among the various Christian Churches operating in the Near East. The first section of the periodical contains historical, liturgical and juridical articles relating to the Eastern Churches, while the second section is devoted to a chronicle of religious events in Egypt, Jordan, Israel, Lebanon, Syria and Turkey.

Lettre aux amis is a quarterly publication put out by the Dominican Fathers of Isaiah House. Focusing on the subject of dialogue with Judaism, it explores aspects of the State of Israel which invariably challenge Christians who live there.

Ar-Rabitah (The Link) is the official bulletin of the Greek Catholic Eparchy of Acre, Haifa and Galilee. Founded in 1944, it is published monthly in Arabic. The articles deal with religious and moral issues and with the problems confronting the Greek Catholic minority in Israel.

Message de Galilée is a French-language quarterly published by friends of the Greek Catholic Church in Galilee.

The Protestant Churches also produce bulletins concerned mainly with communal matters.

The quarterly *U.C.C.I. News*, published by the United Christian Council in Israel, was started in 1970. It carries articles on the activities of the Council's member Churches, giving details of new pastoral appointments, new schools and hospices, and missionary activity.

Gemeindebrief is a quarterly bulletin of the German Lutheran Church of Jerusalem. It has articles on religious and archaeological subjects and chronicles events in the everyday life of the Lutheran community.

The Southern Baptist Convention in Israel from 1961 to 1983 published the bulletin *Ha-Yahad* in English and in Hebrew. The bulletin gave the view-point of the Baptists in Israel, in opposition to the obsolete *millet* system. It also advocated a separation of religion and State, following the American pattern.

Miskan offers a theological forum for Jewish-Christian relations, Jewish Evangelism and Hebrew-Christians (Messianic Jews). The biannual journal is published by the United Christian Council in Israel, a federation of nineteen Protestant Churches and missionary societies.

Nea Sion-Ecclesiastical Periodikon Syngramma is a quarterly publication of the Greek Orthodox Patriarchate of Jerusalem. It deals with subjects relating to theology and the history, archaeology and topography of the Holy Land. It also reports on the ecclesiastical life of the Orthodox Churches, records ecclesiastical events, and devotes particular attention to the rights and interests of the Greek Orthodox Church in the Holy Places. *Nea Sion* is written in Greek and is directed mainly at clergymen in the Holy Land and in Greece. It is produced by the printing press of the Greek Orthodox Patriarchate of Jerusalem.

Inviera (Resurrection) is a periodical dealing with theology and Romanian culture. It is published by the representative of the Romanian Patriarchate in Jerusalem.

Sion is a monthly bulletin of the Armenian Patriarchate of Jerusalem. Published in Armenian, it contains essays on religion, literature and philology. *Sion* is printed by the press of the Armenian Patriarchate, the first printing press to be established in Jerusalem (1833).

Majalah El Nahda El Morcossian El Orthodox (Monthly of Morcossian Revival of the Orthodox Copts) is an illustrated review of religion and literature, published by the Coptic Archbishopric of Jerusalem.

Aram is a bulletin published by the local Syrian Orthodox Church

Christian News from Israel is, today, a semi-annual periodical published by the Ministry of Religious Affairs of Israel. It began publication in 1949 and was issued in several languages. It is widely praised for the objectivity and the exactitude of its far-ranging contents. Eminent Christian savants of every denomination contribute to its columns.

Christian Life in Israel is a bulletin published by the Israel Interfaith Association.

Immanuel is a semi-annual periodical issued by the Theological Research Fraternity in Israel in collaboration with other organizations.

Christian Comment is a monthly column appearing in *The Jerusalem Post*. Written by several Christian clerics and scholars under the pseudonym "Oekumenicos," it is devoted to ecumenical subjects. For a number of years, the main contributor was Dr. Wesley Brown, who left Jerusalem in 1984.

Chapter Eighteen

CHRISTIAN HOLIDAYS IN THE HOLY LAND

The Holy Land differs from other countries not only by reason of the plurality of its Christian denominations, but also because of the different dates on which those denominations keep their feasts and festivals. This is mainly due to the fact that the Julian calendar is still used in the Holy Land by the Oriental communities: thirteen days behind the Gregorian, it was abolished nearly everywhere else, but in the Holy Land, where, in all dates, a merit goes with tradition, it has abided. But there are other variants in the determination of the dates of the holy days, and they are, in general, of a theological character.

Thus Christmas is celebrated by both Catholics and Protestants on December 25, and by the Greek Orthodox, the Copts and the Syrian Orthodox on January 7, corresponding in the Julian calendar to December 25. The Armenian Orthodox, on the other hand, celebrate it on January 19, which corresponds to January 6 by the Julian calendar; they hold that Christmas and Epiphany happened on the same day, that Christ revealed himself to mankind on the very same day as that on which he was born.

That there are three divergent Christmas-tides has the advantage that several denominational services and ceremonies can take place in the Church of the Nativity with less mutual clash or interference.

New Year, too, has its different timings: January 1 for Catholics and Protestants, January 14 for Greek Orthodox, Armenians and Syrian Orthodox. The Copts and Ethiopians adhere to an entirely other anniversary—September 11.

Easter is celebrated by Catholics and Protestants according to the Gregorian calendar, and by the Orthodox and Monophysite Churches according to the Julian. It is, of course, a movable feast, and special reckonings are required to fix it annually, as it takes place on the first Sunday after the first full moon following the spring equinox; the difference of thirteen days between the Gregorian and the Julian calendars does not count, and the two Easters may coincide, or be separated by a week, or by five, or, very seldom, by four.

When they coincide, a very intricate time-table must be scrupulously followed to avoid overlap of ceremonies, for all of them are celebrated by the several denominations in the one Church of the Holy Sepulchre. This is the case even when the difference is one of a full week, as the Holy Week of the Orthodox synchronizes with the Easter of the Catholics.

As the dates of Easter of the Julian Calendar are not ordinarily recorded in calendars outside the Holy Land, we subjoin the dates of both Easters for the next thirteen years:

Year	Western	Eastern
1988	April 3	April 10
1989	March 26	April 10
1990	April 15	April 15
1991	March 31	April 7
1992	April 19	April 26
1993	April 11	April 18
1994	April 3	May 1
1995	April 16	April 23
1996	April 7	April 14
1997	March 30	April 27
1998	April 12	April 19
1999	April 4	April 11
2000	April 23	April 30

There are other movable feasts whose datings depend on that of Easter. Thus, Ascension is celebrated thirty-nine days after the first day of Easter, Pentecost on the fiftieth. Consequently, when Easter takes place on the same day for Western and Eastern Christians, Ascension Day also does and, for both, in the Chapel of the Ascension on the Mount of Olives, so that here, too, a timetable must be worked out by the communities. Pentecost is free from these complications.

Chapter Nineteen

THE QUESTION OF JERUSALEM
AND THE HOLY PLACES

A special holiness adheres to Jerusalem, the city so meaningful in its religious associations for the three monotheistic creeds. Those links of faiths have found, besides their scriptural references, a concrete embodiment in special sites conferring sanctity to them. Consequently, there develops a disposition to consider Jerusalem and the Holy Places as an inseparable entity and the problems inherent in them as calling for a single solution. This conclusion, based as it is on an incorrect assumption, cannot be sustained.

In any attempt to clarify the problems, one should bear in mind the precedents. At the end of the First World War, on the collapse of the Ottoman Empire, the League of Nations, with the assent of the Principal Powers, granted Great Britain the Mandate over Palestine, (12 June, 1922). According to Article 13 of the Mandate, all responsibility "in connection with the Holy Places, religious buildings or sites in Palestine, including that of preserving existing rights and of guaranteeing access to the Holy Places, religious buildings and sites, and free access of worship" was laid upon the Mandatory. The Mandatory, in turn, was responsible solely to the League in "all matters connected herewith." Article 14 required the appointment by the Mandatory of a special commission "to study, define, and determine the rights and claims in connection with the Holy Places and the rights and claims relating to the different religious communities in Palestine." The composition and the function of the commission had to be approved by the Council of the League. By article 15, the Mandatory was required "to see that complete freedom of conscience and free exercise of all forms of worship, subject only to the maintenance of public order and morals," were ensured to all.

Thus, the rights of the Mandatory were circumscribed and matters connected with the Holy Places were under the supervision of the League of Nations. A general supervision of the religious sites was acknowledged, but there was no question of territorial internationalization for the better guarantee of the religious aspects of Jerusalem and the Holy Places.

When Great Britain declared that it was no longer willing to administer the Mandate, the General Assembly of the United Nations, on November 29, 1947, adopted Resolution 189 II on the basis of suggestions presented by the United Nations Special Committee on Palestine. These suggestions called for the partition of Palestine into two States, one Jewish and one Arab, to be established within the boundaries laid down in the Resolution. Moreover, there was to be an economic union between the two States, and Jerusalem was to be internationalized. In other words, the partition, to be effective and viable, pre-supposed the continuation of an intimate link between the three separate entities created by it. But the situation envisaged did not materialize. The Jewish authorities accepted the Resolution, although it did not satisfy them completely, but the Arabs rejected it outright, and the armed forces of five neighboring Arab States invaded the newly declared Jewish State of Israel to prevent its implementation. Arab rejection of partition, Arab invasion of the Jewish State, destroyed the essential elements of the success of partition, and the whole plan was undone: there was no independent Arab State, no economic union, and the Israel Defence Forces, in sheer compulsion of survival, moved out of a strategy of resistance into a thrust that took them, in places, beyond the lines marked in the Resolution.

So it was that, during the whole period prior to June 1967, certain member-States of the United Nations set their faces against acceptance of the legitimacy of Israel's sovereignty over the New City of Jerusalem.[1] The physical internationalization of Jerusalem was uncompromisingly rejected throughout all these years by the parties directly concerned: Israel, which held the western half of the Holy City, and Jordan, which was in possession of the eastern part. From April 3, 1949, when the Armistice Agreement between Israel and Jordan was signed, the de facto division of Jerusalem, which was in effect a total negation of the concept of its internationalization, had been crystallized.

---

1) These member-States of the United Nations, albeit maintaining diplomatic relations with Israel, established their respective Embassies in Tel Aviv.

On April 15, 1949, Pope Pius XII issued the encyclical "Redemptoris Nostri," in which he expressed his concern for the safety of the Holy Places and recommended the adoption of a special regimen for Jerusalem and its surroundings, that is a juridical statute guaranteed by international law.[2]

The issue of the status of the Holy City was raised in United Nations circles again and again, not least by the representatives of the Arab States other than Jordan, which were persuaded that they could thus further their object of ousting Israel from its capital and eventually making for the State's complete collapse.

On December 9, 1949, the General Assembly had adopted a Resolution calling for the internationalization of the entire Jerusalem area and its environs, and on April 4, 1950, the Trusteeship Council adopted a draft statute, under which the city was to be constituted a *corpus separatum*. On June 14, 1950, the Council decided to submit its special report, containing this statute, to the General Assembly. The report was examined at the end of the same year by a committee of the Assembly. In the committee, Sweden and Belgium presented draft Resolutions of their own. Sweden proposed that Israel and Jordan each have jurisdiction over their respective parts of the city, but give guarantees to respect human rights, protect the Holy Places and ensure free access to them: a Commissioner on behalf of the United Nations was to be allowed to supervise the implementation of the guarantees. Belgium proposed a further study of the conditions of the settlement necessary to make certain of adequate protection of the Holy Places under the supervision of the United Nations. Neither proposal secured the required number of votes.

In 1952, the General Assembly, noting that its committee had failed to find a solution, affirmed that the Governments concerned had the primary responsibility of settling their outstanding differences in conformity with its Resolutions. On December 11, the Ad Hoc Political Committee resolved to invite the parties to

---

2) In the previous encyclical, *In Multiplicibus*, issued on November 24, 1948, when the fighting still raged, Pius XII had advocated an international regime protecting the Holy Places, enabling free access to them and guaranteeing freedom of worship to the various Christian communities and respect for their religious traditions as inherited from the past.

proceed accordingly, but in the Assembly, this move, again, lacked the modicum of support.

All along, Israel spoke against territorial internationalization as unrealistic and impracticable; in lieu, it suggested functional internationalization, involving an international answerability for freedom of access to the Holy Places and of worship at them.

Events in June 1967 put an abrupt end to the *de facto* situation. In July 1967, Israel re-unified Jerusalem. On July 17, 1967, the General Assembly passed a Resolution urging Israel to rescind all its measures of re-unification and to desist from taking any further action which might alter the city's status. No specific reference was made in the Resolution to internationalization, and it is proper to interpret it as touching only on the question of the re-unification. Israel's rejoinder was that it had not formally annexed East Jerusalem; it had confined itself to measures integrating that sector into the administrative and municipal complex of the capital and provided a legal basis for the protection of the Holy Places. The measures taken in no way ran counter to Israel's earlier suggestion of a functional internationalization of the Holy Places alone, guaranteeing their inviolability and absolute accessibility.

There was, however, a radical change in the juridical status of Jerusalem, as a result of the law issued on August 30, 1980 by the Knesset, which formally annexed Jerusalem and solemnly declared the united city the Eternal Capital of Israel. Thus, after thirteen years, the rather vague formulation of administrative measures in the eastern part of the city was replaced by a clearcut policy on Jerusalem.

There was no lack of response to the "Jerusalem Law," from foreign Governments as well as from ecclesiastical bodies, the latter's attitude evidently influenced by political considerations.

On the political level, thirteen foreign embassies moved from Jerusalem to Tel Aviv. On the ecclesiastical plane, the Central Committee of the World Council of Churches issued a statement in August 1980, expressing opposition to Israel's unilateral action in annexing Jerusalem under its exclusive sovereignty. The Central Committee urged the General Secretary of the Council to explore, in consultation with member Churches in the area and the

Vatican, possibilities of finding the best solution to the problem of Jerusalem. Consultations with Moslem and Jewish communities were also to be undertaken, in order to seek ways of consolidating justice and human coexistence in the City of Peace.

Regarding the position of the Holy See, it should be noted that from 1949 to 1967 it refrained from any explicit declaration on the issue of Jerusalem and the Holy Places. It was the War of 1967 which prompted Pope Paul VI to intervene and express his concern for the Holy City and the Christian sanctuaries. The Pontiff continued to underline his anxiety and his involvement in speeches to the Consistory. Pope Paul VI seemed, however, to have abandoned the plan for internationalization, in line with projects of the United Nations, and to incline instead to the idea of an internationally guaranteed statute for Jerusalem.

Pope John Paul II, in his address to the General Assembly of the United Nations on October 2, 1979, reiterated his predecessor's suggestion that a special internationally guaranteed statute should be given.

In this context, it is worth noting the opinion voiced by a leading member of the Greek Orthodox Church, who maintained that no head of another Christian denomination should be spokesman for all Christians in Jerusalem in an international forum. Regarding the particular interests of the Greek Orthodox Church, responsibility for the policy in Jerusalem rested exclusively with the Greek Orthodox Patriarchate in Jerusalem.

The Holy See's position on Jerusalem was even more clearly reflected in an editorial published by the Vatican paper, *Osservatore Romano*, on June 30–July 1, 1980. The editorial was written after the address by Pope John Paul II to President Carter on June 21, 1980. In it, the editor asserts that since the safeguarding of the sacred and universal character of Jerusalem is of primary importance, any nation exercising sovereignty over it, should pledge *vis-à-vis* the great world religions, to respect the special character of the city and to guarantee not only specific rights in connection with the Holy Places, but also the rights of the religious communities living in the hallowed city. This obligation should be secured through an appropriate juridical system, guaranteed by a higher international body.

During his visit to Otranto in southern Italy in October 1980,

Pope John Paul II said that he prayed for Jerusalem, wishing that the city, rather than being an object of dissension and disunity, might instead be a meeting-point, a center which Christians, Jews and Moslems alike looked upon as their common home, where they might feel like brethren, with no one claiming to be the other's superior.

The status of Jerusalem was also discussed during the meeting held on January 12, 1982, between Pope John Paul II and the then Minister of Foreign Affairs in Israel, Yizhak Shamir. According to the Vatican's press-communiqué, the Pontiff confirmed the well-known position of the Holy See, namely that the status of Jerusalem be determined according to a just and agreed solution. The Holy City should be a cross-roads for peaceful encounter between members of the three religions, Christianity, Judaism and Islam, whether residents or pilgrims, who venerate Jerusalem as the cradle of their faith.

On September 15, 1982, in his address to the crowds in St. Peter's Square after his meeting with PLO leader Yasser Arafat, Pope John Paul II restated the Church's position on Jerusalem, declaring that the rights of Christians, Jews and Moslems must be recognized in the Holy City. The Pontiff said there should be "recognized guarantees that the city is the sacred patrimony of all who carry out the activities that enoble man: adoration, meditation and brotherly works."

On April 20, 1984, the Pontiff delivered a comprehensive Apostolic Letter on Jerusalem to the bishops, priests and faithful of the Catholic Church. In it, he reiterated the Vatican's call for an internationally guaranteed statute for the city, as the sacred patrimony of all faithful and potential cross-roads of peace for the peoples of the Middle East.

On February 19, 1985, Israel's Prime Minister Shimon Peres was officially received at the Vatican. During the meeting between Pope John Paul II and the Prime Minister, the political situation in the Middle East, the status of Jerusalem and Christian-Jewish relations were discussed. The audience lasted almost an hour and was held in a friendly atmosphere.

During his flight from Nairobi to Morocco in August 1985, Pope John Paul II, speaking to reporters, called Jerusalem "the central point, the spiritual capital," of Christianity, Islam and Judaism.

Pope John Paul II's visit to the Synagogue in Rome on Sunday, April 13, 1986, could be considered a major landmark in Catholic-Jewish relations, but did not indicate a change in the Vatican's position towards the State of Israel.

The four-day visit to Israel of New York's Cardinal John O'Conner, in January 1987, was indeed a meaningful event, but it raised controversial issues. During his stay in Jerusalem, the Cardinal, in his addresses and his visit to the Western Wall and to the Memorial of the Holocaust, was eager to demonstrate his friendship for, and personal warm feelings towards the Jewish People. On the other hand, he disappointed the Israelis by his anxiety to avoid any move which might be understood as Church recognition of Israeli sovereignty over Jerusalem. Thus, a compromise arrangement had to be found when the Cardinal called upon President Herzog. His visit was at the President's home and not in the presidential office. The courtesy call upon Foreign Minister, Shimon Peres, likewise took place at the latter's private flat.

At a press conference held on his arrival in Rome, Cardinal O'Conner, wishing to clarify his stand during his visit to Jerusalem, stressed the following points: the Vatican's request of the necessity of a special statute affording international guarantees for Jerusalem; the creation of a homeland for the Palestinian people, together with a definition of Israel's permanent boundaries. The Cardinal furthermore stated the Vatican's concern for the security of the Christian minorities in the Middle East, who could be subjected to very severe persecutions in case of diplomatic recognition of the State of Israel.

On September 1, 1987, nine Jewish leaders met Pope John Paul II at his summer home at Castel Gandolfo in a bid to improve Jewish-Catholic relations which had been damaged by the Pontiff's audience with Austrian President Kurt Waldheim. The Jewish delegates, referring to the conversation held with the Pope, said that the Pontiff acknowledged "the centrality of Israel in the thinking of the Jews," but there had not been any sign that the Vatican could respond to Jewish requests that it establish diplomatic relations with Israel.

A successive encounter took place between the Pontiff and a large group of Jewish leaders in Miami (U.S.A.). In his address, John Paul II quoted from a statement he made in 1974 calling for security and tranquillity for the Jews of Israel, but made no response to Jewish appeals that the Vatican establish relations with Israel.

Chapter Twenty

STATISTICAL DATA ON THE CHRISTIAN POPULATION IN THE HOLY LAND

THE SITUATION IN ISRAEL AND IN THE ADMINISTERED TERRITORIES AFTER THE WAR OF JUNE 1967

According to the census of May 22, 1961, the Christian inhabitants of the State of Israel then numbered 50,543 souls. In 1967, when the census was taken in East Jerusalem and in the administered territories, the number of Christians in Israel, within the pre-June 1967 borders, might have been several thousands more as a result of natural increase. Besides, Christian partners in mixed marriages and their offspring often do not care to be registered as Christians, or come under the category of "religion unknown," and one may safely estimate Israel's Christian population, within the pre-June 1967 periphery, at 56,000.

The census taken in East Jerusalem on September 27, 1967, showed a Christian population of 10,975, and that of a few weeks earlier, in Samaria and Judea, one of 29,434; in the Gaza Strip, the figure was 2,490, and on the Golan Heights, forty-one. This gives us a total of 42,750 in the Israel-held territories. The possibility that some have been overlooked or their religion marked "unknown" would justify us in putting the number of Christians in the administered areas up to 43,500, making in 1964 an all-in-all Christian population within Israel's jurisdiction of 99,500.

While one may give credence to the exactitude of the global results of the censuses of 1961 and 1967, the distribution among the denominations in the official records was not set out in sufficient detail for precise study. First of all, the censuses referred only to the three major denominations and the lesser were considered as a whole, without sub-division. Furthermore, the connection with one of the three major denominations was often erroneously interpreted in the individual answers to the questions asked in the census-form, so that it may happen that Roman Catholics (Latins) were registered as Greek Catholics, as the Arab word for Greek Catholic is "Roum" Catholic; and Uniate Catholics (Maronites, Syrian Catholics, Armenian Catholics, Coptic Catholics and Chaldeans) were generally registered among the Greek Catholics, there being no special rubric for them. As a result, the number of the Greek Catholic community was inflated. The same imprecision affects the Coptic Orthodox or the Syrian Orthodox, who had no rubric of their own either, and may quite likely be among the Greek Orthodox, too.

When one comes to supplement imperfect official statistics of denominational distribution by the estimates of Church representatives themselves, one must be on one's guard against a propensity to exaggerate. There were several reasons for this. To begin with, the priests who kept the registers of the congregations not infrequently counted as present parishioners who had already left. Moreover, people who had changed their religious allegiance were often registered twice, once by the priest in charge of the congregation from which they had withdrawn, and again by him whose congregation they had joined. There were, as well, the cases of those faithful who worshipped temporarily in a church which was not of their own communion, for lack of one in the communicant's place of residence, and double registration might have ensued.

The following data were tentatively given for the year 1967 on the dual basis of the official statistics and the estimates of the Churches themselves.

Israel

Latins	11,000
Greek Catholics	22,500
Maronites	2,800
Other Uniates	—
Greek Orthodox	17,000
Armenian Orthodox	600
Anglicans	900
Protestants	800
Copts	300
Syrian Orthodox	50
Ethiopians	50
	56,000

East Jerusalem

Latins	3,800
Greek Catholics	300
Maronites	100
Other Uniates	400
Greek Orthodox	3,950
Armenian Orthodox	1,200
Anglicans	200
Protestants	300
Copts	500
Syrian Orthodox	200
Ethiopians	50
	11,000

Judea and Samaria

Latins	8,800
Greek Catholics	1,700
Maronites	100
Other Uniates	200
Greek Orthodox	15,300
Armenian Orthodox	300
Anglicans	1,200
Protestants	1,300
Copts	200
Syrian Orthodox	900
Ethiopians	—
	30,000

Gaza Strip

Latins	300
Greek Catholics	300
Maronites	50
Other Uniates	—
Greek Orthodox	1,200
Armenian Orthodox	50
Anglicans	—
Protestants	100
Copts	500
Syrian Orthodox	—
Ethiopians	=
	2,500

All Territories

Latins	23,900
Greek Catholics	24,800
Maronites	3,050
Other Uniates	600
Greek Orthodox	37,450
Armenian Orthodox	2,150
Anglicans	2,300
Protestants	2,500
Syrian Orthodox	1,150
Ethiopians	100
	99,500

In the State of Israel before the Six-Day War, the Christians were concentrated in the northern part of the country—in Nazareth, Haifa, Acre and in twenty-four villages in Galilee. Only a few thousand were to be found in Jaffa, Ramla and Lod.

The census of the Christian inhabitants of East Jerusalem in September 1967 gave, in round figures, a total of eleven thousand.

In Judea, Samaria and the Gaza Strip, the main concentrations of Christians, again in round figures were:

Bethlehem	6,400
Beit Jala	2,270
Beit Sahour	3,730
Ramallah and Bira	7,300
Aboud	500
Jifneh	540
Bir Zeit	1,350
Taibe	1,160
Zebabdeh	930
Jericho	540
Nablus	370
Rafidiyah	320
Gaza	1,650
Khan Yunis	320
	27,380

The Christian inhabitants of Nazareth, Bethlehem, Beit Sahour, Beit Jala and Ramallah accounted in 1967 for about 50 percent of the total population of those places.

One can see that the Christian population was still settled in the major towns and in a few villages, for the most part. Other interesting findings of the census done by the Israel Central Bureau of Statistics are these. Arab Christians in the Holy Land have, generally, more schooling than other Arabs, which is the consequence of the fact that the majority of Arab Christians live in cities and towns, but also of the facilities offered by educational institutions maintained by the Christian Missions. The circumstance that the Arab Christians are town-dwellers in the main and enjoy a higher educational standard tends to make them less prolific than their Moslem neighbors. Thirdly, more Christian than Moslem Arabs emigrate: this tendency was marked in the Middle East before the establishment of the State of Israel and the fighting of 1948 and 1967, and under the Turkish and British regimes; indeed, it can be observed in the Arab countries of the region where the fighting was not felt at all. Even in Lebanon, where the Christians accounted for half of the total population, this drift overseas existed before the present unrest. In the past hundred years, this trend has led to the establishment of large Arab Christian communities all over the world and particularly in the two Americas.

309

Since the above figures were recorded, the Christian population in the Holy Land has increased; according to Government and Church sources, it today numbers some 135,000 souls.

ESTIMATES OF THE CHRISTIAN POPULATION UP TO THE END OF 1987

According to the estimates of the Israeli Government statistician, the Christian inhabitants within the pre-June 1967 borders, including Jerusalem, numbered at the end of 1985, 102,000 souls.

In Jerusalem itself, there were in June 1983, 13,730 Christians, up 17.3 percent from 11,704 in 1972.[1]

In the Government statistics there are no precise figures for the membership of the various denominations within the total numbers. The estimates given by the heads of the Churches are not always reliable for the reasons mentioned above. Thus, the data for the Uniate Catholics which appear in the Yearbook of the Catholic Church (1984) and the figures published in the Calendar of the Orthodox Patriarchate, require some revision.

Within the pre-June 1967 borders and East Jerusalem a tentative estimate of the distribution of various denominations may be given as follows:

Latins	17,000
Greek Catholics	41,000
Maronites	6,300
Other Uniates	400
Greek Orthodox	31,000
Armenian Orthodox	2,000
Copts	1,000
Syrian Orthodox	500
Anglicans	1,500
Protestants	1,500
Ethiopians	300
	102,000

1) According to Roman Catholic sources, the Latin faithful in Jerusalem numbered 4,827. (See interview given in January 1986 by the Latin parish priest to the magazine *Terra Santa*.)

As regards the administered territories, it may be presumed that the population has remained roughly the same as in 1967, that is, around 33,000, because losses through emigration have been compensated by birth.

Chapter Twenty-One

ECUMENISM IN THE HOLY LAND

The ecumenical ideal has, during the past few decades, become one of the foremost aspirations of the Christian Churches. Having long since reached the conclusion that a divided Church is incompatible with a true Christian spirit, they are seeking new ways and new methods to bring together again what misunderstandings and prejudices have split in the past. These noble efforts are directed first to bring about a deeper unity and mutual understanding in the disunited family of the Churches, but are by no means circumscribed to this limited aim; the dialogue is also pursued with the other monotheistic religions, Judaism and Islam, and reference to the three creeds which have their origin in the Patriarch Abraham is not rare. And there is ever greater insistence on the common sources of Judaism and Christianity.

Of course, one might adduce not a few precedents and maintain that there is nothing specially new in all this talk about ecumenism and unity. Still, one must concede that there never was such an impetus, such an organized endeavor, such a display of goodwill.

In modern times, with the facilities afforded by the new means of transportation and communication, there is no serious obstacle to the arrangement of meetings among Church leaders and theologians of various denominations. Such meetings have become more and more frequent, and it is hardly possible to imagine a more suitable place for ecumenical encounters than the Holy Land. If this holds true for contacts between Judaism and Christianity, which had their birth in Palestine, it is even more so for a dialogue between the Christian denominations themselves, of which all consider the Holy Land their source and whose intercourse and discourse are furthered by physical presence in the Holy Land.

There are many indications of this improved relationship. During the Week of Prayer for Christian Unity, special ecumenical services are hosted by a number of different Churches in turn. An ecumenical Prayer Garden, created by Pastor Boegner and approved by Pope Paul VI, has been inaugurated on the slopes of the Mount of Olives.

The ecumenical spirit is, however, less apparent in the Greek Orthodox Patriarchate.[1] The latter's standpoint was stressed in a decree dated February, 1/14, 1969. Issued by the late Patriarch Benedictos I, it refers to the Holy Canons of the Orthodox Church, which debar priests and faithful from participating in the prayers of non-Orthodox believers. The decision of the Orthodox Patriarchate has to be understood in the local context. The intention was to discourage conversions to other Christian confessions and thus preserve the integrity of the Orthodox flock. During the Catholic-Orthodox dialogue held on the Island of Crete in summer 1984, Metropolitan Germanos read a protest of Diodoros, Patriarch of Jerusalem, concerning the proselytizing activity of the Catholics among the Orthodox in the area of the Patriarchate of Jerusalem.

Because of the proselytization allegedly carried out by the Catholics among the Orthodox, Metropolitan Germanos did not attend the Catholic-Orthodox dialogue held in 1986 in the town of Bari (Italy). A written declaration on behalf of Patriarch Diodoros of Jerusalem sent to the Orthodox co-president of the encounter explained the reason for the non-participation of the Greek-Orthodox Patriarchate of Jerusalem.

The visit of Pope Paul VI to the Holy Land in January 1964 should be looked upon not only as a pilgrimage, but also as a spiritual journey for ecumenical ends. This is underscored by his conversation in Jerusalem with the Ecumenical Patriarch Athenagoras and his talks with the Christian leaders in the Holy Land. This wide rapport undoubtedly contributed to the conception and realization of the plan to establish an Ecumenical Institute for Advanced Theological Studies proposed by two prominent Lutheran theologians and enthusiastically promoted by the Pontiff. The Institute stands on the outskirts of Jerusalem, on the road to Bethlehem, on land belonging to the Sovereign Order of Malta

---

1) The reticence of the Greek Orthodox Patriarchate of Jerusalem *vis-à-vis* interreligious dialogue is not shared by World Orthodoxy. This was evident in the encounter between Pope Paul VI and the Ecumenical Patriarch Athenagoras, which took place in January 1964 in Jerusalem, and in the exchange of ecclesiastical delegations between Rome and Constantinople.

and donated by the Order to the Pope.[2]
The Institute was intended to be fully ecumenical in spirit and structure. A group of theologians—Roman Catholic, Orthodox (Chalcedonian and non-Chalcedonian),[3] Protestant and Anglican—have formed themselves into its Academic Council.[4]

2) The land at Tantur, on a part of which the Institute now stands, had been given in 1110 by Baldwin I, King of Jerusalem, to the Knights of the Order of St. John. It had been lost by them after the Crusaders' defeat. Seven centuries later, it was re-purchased (1867) by Count Bernard Caboga, the Austro-Hungarian consul-general in Palestine, with money provided by Emperor Franz Joseph and the Knights of the Sovereign Order of Malta, Priorate of Bohemia. The Order established a hospice on the site and the nursing Brothers of St. John of God were called to administer it. Later, when the Brothers left Tantur, the buildings were entrusted to the Salesian Fathers.

3) Greek Orthodox, who initially participated in the academic activities of the Institute, later broke off relations with it, because the administration was in the hands of a Catholic religious Order, the Benedictine Fathers of Montserrat. This fact, according to their religious legislation, debarred the Orthodox from participation.

4) According to the proposed program of the Institute, "the object of research conducted in it must afford a wide scope and bear on points in which all Christians share an interest, bringing them together in a common theological task. It must help them to become aware of the universality of God's Word addressed to all men. The principal object, therefore, would be the significance of the "economy" of salvation for all humanity, touching on every dimension of the history of mankind. In this way, theologians of all the Churches will be able to give the world a single witness of their hope of salvation.

"Every problem discussed and studied should be truly relevant to the present-day Christian "problematic," to the so-called modern or secularized world, and to other religions at large. A mere inner Christian "problematic" would not suffice; any study coupled to this one perspective would necessarily be crippled. A theology deaf to the cry of the modern world would soon tend to become totally unheeding. A mere secular study without theology would be blind to any positive solution, for that can only come from a transcending of the purely natural data. The challenge to the Institute is not exclusively from within the Christian confessions, but also from each and every faith at large and from the secular world, which make up a good two-thirds of humanity today.

"It is necessary to begin by studying the Scriptures as a whole, the one source for all Christians. Thus, in the understanding of the Bible, it will be possible to rise above certain confessional limitations produced by historical influences. A work of this kind will bring to light the inexhaustible riches and the diversity of ways of Revelation, which is the action and Word of God. It will also be necessary to discover how Christian traditions have had the Word of God and responded to it; how, in the course of centuries, different theological, liturgical, spiritual and canonical traditions have developed. Hence, it is not a question of something which has historical interest and nothing besides, but a striving to find out how the revealing Word can be explained to contemporary men, and how the Christian, in his historical situation, must respond to it.

315

Since its inauguration in September 1972, the Ecumenical Institute has attracted many distinguished scholars and students from different countries belonging to various Christian persuasions. According to the ecumenical aims of the Institute, the position of rector alternates between Protestant and Catholic incumbents. The Institute is distinguished by intensive academic activity, comprising symposia, seminars, lecture courses and various research projects.

A major innovative contribution to the search for world harmony and understanding was taken on December 15, 1983, with the Tantur Interfaith Academy of Peace. Hosted by the Ecumenical Institute, the new Academy intends to bring together the world's leading theological peace-scholars for long term exchanges. During one fall term, for example, the Academy explored the foundations for peace in the sacred writings of Judaism and Christianity.

On a more modest scale, the spirit and purpose of the Ecumenical Institute are embodied in the *Theological Research Fraternity in Israel*. This is composed of a group of Christians, mostly clergy, belonging to different Christian denominations. They meet once a month, discussing subjects connected with ecumenical relations and a Christian approach to Judaism. Noteworthy among its initiatives is the publication of *Immanuel*,

---

"For Christian reunion, the unity within the multiplicity of Christian traditions must be recaptured, the universality of the Word of God be rediscovered.

"It seems that there are two ways of achieving this dual purpose: a return to the sources, and dialogue.

"*Return to the sources*: It is important to find our continuity with the past again. Jerusalem is a meeting-place of Eastern and Western traditions; moreover, the biblical origin shared by all Christians exercises an influence of reconciliation upon the thoughts and feelings of brethren parted. The search must go behind the philosophical and theological developments as well as beyond cultural and canonical applications. This at once raises a problem of central consequence: the critique of theological knowledge. We need to compile a history of theological method, tracing the course of the great turning-points which it has known. There are weighty problems here for scholars to work on.

"*Dialogue*: We must learn to extract anew the freshness and originality which touch on the essential elements in the history of salvation. The more we succeed in this, the more will we reveal how open is the "economy" of salvation to new cultures, as, for example, that of Africa, which in certain respects is so akin to the Bible setting."

a biannual magazine of religious thought and research in Israel.[5] Plans are underway for the group to acquire a permanent home and a specialized library.

Following the example of Jerusalem's Theological Research Fraternity, the *Ecumenical Theological Study Group* was formed in 1966 in Tel Aviv. Its aims are to deepen the Church's self-awareness in the Israeli setting, to further Christian relations with Jewry, Judaism and Israel, and to provide visiting Christian students from abroad with an instructional program on the religious, political and social situation in Israel.

Besides the Institute, the Fraternity and the Study Group, which are fully interdenominational and Christian, mixed groups of Christians and Jews have been formed, in which religious problems of common interest are debated. Such forums, directed to interfaith dialogue, are not infrequent in countries other than Israel; they have, however, a special meaning here, where the Jewish religion is that of the majority of the population and the position of Judaism can be articulated without reticence.

Prominent in the interconfessional dialogue is the *Rainbow* group, composed, as the name implies, of a diversified membership. There are fifteen Christian clergy belonging to several denominations, and a similar number of Jews, mainly theologians and professors of comparative religion, some of them of international repute. The group meets periodically to examine, compare and evaluate the religious traditions and tenets of its members.

Other discussion groups in Jerusalem which deal with religious problems in an ecumenical spirit are the *International Student Christian Forum*, sponsored by the Ecumenical Theological Research Fraternity in Israel, and the *Mamre Center*.

Foremost in the sphere of this inter-religious activity is the *Israel Interfaith Association*, founded in 1959, which tries to promote mutual understanding and the respect due to all creeds represented in Israel. Its program expresses the letter and the spirit of Israel's Proclamation of Independence and deserves to be quoted in essential part:

5) It is produced in cooperation with the Department of Comparative Religion at the Hebrew University of Jerusalem, the School of Jewish Studies at Tel Aviv University, the Interfaith Association, the Israel Office of the American Jewish Committee, and the Israel Office of the Anti-Defamation League of B'nei Brith.

"With the establishment of the State of Israel, the problem of relations between members of the Jewish faith and those of other faiths has taken on an exceptional degree of moral and social importance.

"Members of many diverse faiths are to be found among the citizens of Israel. Numerous Holy Places, numerous religious institutions, are scattered over the face of the country; millions of men and women in all parts of the world are tied to them by their very heartstrings; from them are drawn an intense inspiration and spirituality.

"Israel exercises sovereignty over citizens of many varying beliefs, and in a Land that is sanctified in the tradition of many peoples. A great responsibility thus rests not only upon the individual citizen but also upon the entire community of Israel.

"This is a circumstance which concerns, paramountly, the relationship that exists between members of the Jewish faith, who constitute a majority in Israel, and those who belong to other faiths. That relationship, in its turn, becomes a criterion of the human and spiritual content of Israel's sovereignty, and will inevitably affect the pattern of the relations of Israel with other nations.

"Among wide circles in Jewry, and among the Gentiles, there have grown up, in the course of centuries, feelings of suspicion and antagonism that obsess members of one creed against the other; ancient prejudices darken counsel and breed misunderstanding.

"While this misunderstanding prevails in certain quarters of the West, it is a simple lack of knowledge that persists in other vast areas of the world. The religious and spiritual impulsions which play so vital a role in the history of Israel are unknown to the peoples of Asia and Africa, which accordingly incline to regard whatever happens in our part of the world as a merely political process.

"The rise of Israel, its position as an independent State in a region steeped in religious sentiment, the existence of large Jewish communities throughout the world, antisemitism in its different forms—all this tends to invest with a special significance the attitudes which the community of Israel adopts regarding the question of interfaith relationship.

"We have, therefore, decided to set up a national committee in Israel, to study the problems of interfaith relationships and to act in this sphere:

"To foster a spirit of brotherhood and tolerance, without impairment to the integrity and identity of each religious group; to conduct educational work on a large scale; to influence institutions and individuals in that spirit through the medium of lectures, talks and conferences, and publication of written material; to keep a watchful eye on manifestations likely to offend Man's feelings in his chosen faith; to exchange correct and precise material; to remove misgivings and suspicions; to disseminate information, without minimizing existing difficulties, and to encourage mutual trust and to pave the way towards a communion of hearts."

In an effort to decentralize some of its activities and to encourage more active participation on the part of its members around the country, the Israel Interfaith Association established branches in Haifa, Upper Nazareth and Beersheba, in addition to the existing Tel Aviv branch.

Since its establishment in Israel, the Interfaith Association has abided by the letter and spirit of its program, and its activities in Israel and abroad have gathered momentum. The Association is constantly on the alert for infringements of human rights and religious liberty, issuing public statements and initiating action against manifestations of racism or racist expressions. Cordial working relations have been established with associations for Jewish-Christian dialogue in countries overseas. The Israel Associaton has also become a member of the International Council of Christians and Jews (ICCJ), a federation of seventeen national councils which has its headquarters in Heppenheim, Germany, in the Martin Buber House.

Representatives of the Israel Interfaith Association attend the joint consultations sponsored by the ICCJ, held annually in different countries. Of special significance was the ICCJ meeting in Jerusalem in 1976.

There is a growing inclination in Christian quarters to abandon the traditional methods of proselytizing, which are generally resented and rejected, and to have recourse to dialogue. This tendency was making itself felt in Israel even before the initiative of

Pope John XXIII; the ecumenical spirit aroused by Vatican Council II contributed much productive momentum to the trend.

The desire to establish a cordial relationship with Judaism on the basis of dialogue was first manifested in Israel by certain Protestant theologians. The vanguard in the heart of the Catholic Church in Israel soon followed suit. Examples of such activity, directed at fostering a better knowledge of Judaism among Catholics as a prelude to dialogue, are to be found in the work of Isaiah House of the Dominican Fathers in Jerusalem, and the Studium of the Sisters of Sion at Ratisbonne Monastery. The Studium was founded in 1976 with the aim of providing visiting Catholic and Protestant churchmen and educators with background material on the Jewish religion.

Among the Protestants, there is the village of Nes Ammim, "Banner of Nations," established in Galilee in 1962 by a Protestant group. The founding father and pioneering spirit behind the venture was Johan Pilon, a Bible-minded doctor from Holland. Since its creation in 1964, Nes Ammim developed as a cooperative village with a present population of about 200 permanent residents, many of them children of the settlers. The members of the village seek to promote ideological contacts with Jews and offer them the benefit of Protestant experience and knowledge in secular realms.

Outstanding for earnestness and depth are the spiritual and intellectual contacts between biblical and archaeological scholars in Church-sponsored institutes and their colleagues at Israeli universities. Among the Protestants, we may instance the American Institute of Holy Land Studies and the Swedish Theological Institute; among the Catholics, the Biblical Pontifical Institute of the Jesuits, the Studium Biblicum Franciscanum of the Flagellation Convent, the Biblical and Archaeological School of the Dominicans, Beit Joseph, an annex of the Benedictine Dormition Abbey, and the Christian Institute of Jewish Studies at the Ratisbonne Monastery of the Fathers of Sion.

After the re-unification of Jerusalem, the possibility of fruitful contacts was enhanced. The municipality of Jerusalem, under its dynamic mayor, Mr. Teddy Kollek, is very active in taking care of the needs of the Christian institutions and in promoting amity and mutual understanding among all the inhabitants of the Holy City—Jews, Christians and Moslems.

Interreligious relations in Israel have progressed significantly during the past three decades. Vatican Council II undoubtedly had an impact on the dialogue between the Catholic Church and Judaism. An important development in the sphere of Catholic-Jewish relations took place in October 1974 with the appointment of a special commission dealing with Judaism, which is linked with the Secretariat for Promoting Christian Unity. Another landmark was the "Guidelines and Suggestions for Implementing the Second Vatican Declaration *Nostra Aetate*" (December 1, 1974).

In January 1976, Pope Paul VI named eight consultants to the commission. One of these was Father Marcel Dubois, a French-born Dominican monk, prominent in interfaith dialogue, who has long been a citizen of Israel.

Early in the seventies, it was decided that Israelis should participate in interfaith consultations conducted by Jewish world organizations. Thus, the Jewish Council for Interreligious Consultations (JCICI) was formed. Meetings with representatives of the Catholic Church were held annually in various localities. By 1987, thirteen such encounters had taken place, notably the 1976 meeting in Jerusalem. The Jewish Council for Interreligious Consultations does not limit its contacts to the Catholic Church. There have also been meetings with the World Council of Churches, the umbrella organization which comprises the majority of the Protestant, Orthodox and Pre-Chalcedonian Churches. The JCICI has forged links with the Lutheran World Federation, several Lutheran national Churches, the Church of England and the Ecumenical Patriarchate of Constantinople.

In June 1985, the Vatican's Commission for Religious Relations with the Jews issued "Notes on the Correct Way to Present the Jews and Judaism in Preaching and Catechesis in the Roman Catholic Church." This document contains a number of positive features, such as its stress on the Jewish roots of Christianity and the Jewishness of Jesus, and its denial of the traditional negative Christian view of the Pharisees. However, in other respects, conservative views are expressed. Judaism is not seen as a legitimate path to salvation and Jews are said to have been chosen by God to prepare the coming of Christ. Reference is made to the Jews "preserving the memory of the land of their forefathers at the heart of the hope." However, "the existence of the State of Israel is not to be seen in a perspective which is in itself religious but in reference to the common principles of international law."

The allusion made in the "Notes" of June 1985 that Judaism should not be seen as a legitimate path to salvation, was unequivocally confirmed by a declaration of Cardinal Ratzinger, Prefect of the Congregation for the Doctrine of the Faith. The Cardinal's statement, which emphasizes that Jews' and Catholics' union with the faith of Abraham has to find its fulfilment in the reality of Jesus Christ, represents a setback in the ongoing Jewish-Christian dialogue. This reversion to conservative doctrine will no doubt be of deep concern to Catholic clergymen living in Israel who are anxious to advance the process of amity with Jews.

Yet the trend towards better interfaith understanding is evidenced by the growing frequency of congresses, symposia and seminars in Israel.

Summer seminars for African Christian clergy and Church leaders have been held in Jerusalem since 1975, in French and English alternatively. The idea was conceived in the wake of the Jerusalem Congress on "Black Africa and the Bible." A remarkable outgrowth of that initiative was the founding of a "Center for African Clergy" within the complex of St. Anne's Monastery.

Also noteworthy are the Israel-Spanish colloquia, organized by the Israel Interfaith Association and the Center for the Jewish-Christian Dialogue in Madrid. The ninth Symposium, held in Jerusalem from April 1 to 9, 1986, was attended by the Cardinal Archbishop of Madrid, Angel Suquia Goicoechea.

Jerusalem has also hosted seminars for Belgian and Dutch theologians, both Protestants and Catholics, since 1975.

The "Hope Interfaith Center," established in Jerusalem in 1973, seeks to bring together people who share the monotheistic tradition. Directed by Sister Marie Goldstein, R.S.H.M., it provides a forum for intellectual and spiritual discussions on matters of mutual interest.

On February 27, 1986, Christians, Jews and Moslems belonging to the Center were received in audience by Pope John Paul II, who in his address encouraged them in their efforts to seek mutual understanding and reconciliation.

Ecumenical events in Jerusalem which have attracted an international attendance of several thousands include the Conference of Biblical Prophecy, which took place in 1971, and the Conference of the Holy Spirit, in 1974 and 1975. Other recent gatherings in Jerusalem which carried an ecumenical imprint were the Conference for the Peace of Jerusalem, the Symposium "People, Land and State," the first and second Conference of Christians and Israelis, and the colloquia on "Law and Religious Liberty," and on "Majority and Minority Relations." Equally noteworthy was the symposium devoted to the theme, "Christians and Jews, Shared Responsibility for the Future," which was held under the joint sponsorship of the Israel Interfaith Association and the Central Committee of German Catholics.

In April 1985, an International Salvation Army Conference, with some 2000 members from around the world, was held in Jerusalem.

In April 1987, an international congress on "A Member of Another Religion in Religious Law," was sponsored by the Israel Matz Institute for Research in Jewish Law in cooperation with the universities of Jerusalem and Haifa. Discussion focused on the legal status of the "stranger" in Jewish, Catholic, Greek Orthodox, Islamic and Druze religious law during biblical, Byzantine, medieval and modern periods.

Chapter Twenty-Two

CONCLUSIONS

In retrospect of this survey, which traverses, in barest outline, nineteen centuries of a crowded and kaleidoscopic history, it is perhaps permissible to attempt a prediction of developments to come in the Christian Churches in the Holy Land.

Never once, in the antecedent lifetime of Christianity, were the links with the Holy Land broken. Long periods went by, indeed, in which the plight of local Christians was precarious, their number minute, their foothold insecure. But they held on stubbornly, and no adversity could drive them to desperation of abandonment. That was, and is, the strength of Christian concern for the Holy Places of the Christian faith, and as a whole, the Church has exercised that concern unremittingly in sacred and educational buildings, in pious work and in evangelical endeavor.

Today, Christianity the world-over seems still to be more solicitous of the welfare of co-religionists in Israel than of the outnumbered faithful that dwell in the Moslem lands of the Middle East. There is no difference in historical heritages that would appear to warrant it. It is possible that complex calculations of national policy, the uneasy balance of power between the Western and Eastern blocs, may underlie this apparent dichotomy of interest and intervention: there still lingers in this region, with States newly independent, a nervousness of "colonialism," Christians of European origin are methodically edged out, institutions to do with Christian Europe are wound up. Witness the systematic elimination of Greeks from Istanbul and Egypt, the *modus vivendi*, adjusting religious affairs and questions of Church property, between the Vatican and Tunis, the shrinking of the prosperous Christian community in Algeria, the expulsion of priests and missionaries from Sudan, the restraint and restrictions inflicted upon Christians in Egypt, one which culminated in the temporary dismissal of the Coptic Patriarch Shenouda III, the expropriation of Christian educational institutions in Syria, the nationalization of Christian schools in Iraq. Even Christians of native birth hardly enjoy an ideal existence wherever, by constitution, Islam is the State religion. We have already mentioned in Chapter Ten the attempts made in Jordan to curtail the free development of Christian educational and charitable institutions. Avoidance of overt discrimination cannot entirely save Christian elements from progressive atrophy by emigration to Western Europe and the Americas, whither prosperous Christian Arab "colonies" beckon so compellingly.

A further regression in Christian numbers and standing in most of the Mohammedan areas of the Mediterranean must, therefore, be expected. It is a process which has been going on for a hundred years, which slackened during the period of Mandatory administrations and protectorates, to start again in full swing when one Arab nation after another gained independence. Even Lebanon, with its relatively large Christian population, is not exempt from this trend. The civil war which began in 1975 and raged through the Land of the Cedars accentuated this course. Its Christian population, the most prosperous and educated sector in that variegated country, was the main victim of the chaotic situation which has prevailed there for the past twelve years. Opposing factions, divided along ethnic, religious or social lines, have been locked in an unremitting struggle. Meanwhile, Church property has been badly damaged and the clergy subjected to brutal attacks, such as that on the Greek Catholic Patriarch Maximos V Hakim, who was wounded by unidentified terrorists while travelling in his car.

Looking back, it would be quite wrong to surmise that Christendom would be so dispirited on that account as to succumb to defeatism or resignation in the Holy Land. Moreover, in Israel, there are decisive factors that safeguard Christian interests. If this was true previously to June 1967, it is no less so now that the most sacred shrines of Christendom are situated in Israel's sovereign territory, or in the administered areas. Though geographically in Asia, Israel is firmly linked with the civilization of the West. Willingly, and from a deep sense of cultural and conceptual affinity, it finds itself drawn naturally into friendship and exchange with the West. But the continuity of the Christians of Israel as a creatively viable and self-determining group, ethnic and religious, depends in largest part upon the Bible-influenced attitude of Judaism towards the stranger, on Jewish aversion to winning proselytes, and on the democratic principles that are at the base of Israeli legislation.

This attitude has undoubtedly gained encouragement from the recent ecumenical trends in Christianity, together with an enhanced Christian awareness of its Jewish heritage.

The progressive tendencies which are making themselves felt throughout the Christian world, and the ecumenical spirit gradually spreading, might also help to overcome all that is too static and crystallized in the Christian Churches in the Holy Land.

In this perspective, one can hope that, in the Holy Land, the cradle of the world's monotheistic faiths, a sound basis may be found within the ambience of the State of Israel for the advancement of the ideals and aspirations that they share.

Appendix A

LIST OF THE HOLY PLACES

Sanctuaries Owned by the Roman Catholics

Ortas:	Sanctuary of the Hortus Conclusus.	Sisters of Our Lady of the Hortus
Beit Sahour:	Field and Grotto of the Shepherds.	Franciscan Fathers
Bethlehem:	Sanctuary of the Nativity. Church of St. Catherine. House of St. Joseph. Milk Grotto.	Franciscan Fathers
Bethany:	Sanctuary of St. Lazarus.	Franciscan Fathers
Bethfage:	Sanctuary of the Palms.	Franciscan Fathers
Jericho:	Site of the Baptism of Christ.	Franciscan Fathers
Qubeibeh:	Site of the Apparition of Christ.	Franciscan Fathers
Amwas:	Sanctuary and House of Amwas.	Fathers of the Holy Heart of Betharram
Jerusalem:	Basilica of the Holy Sepulchre. Sanctuary of the Flagellation (two churches). Fifth Station of the Cross. Gethsemane: Basilica of the Agony.	

Gethsemane: Grotto of Gethsemane. Dominus Flevit.	Franciscan Fathers
Sanctuary of the Ecce Homo or of the Lithostratos.	Sisters of our Lady of Sion
Sanctuary of St. Anne and of the Nativity of the Virgin.	White Fathers
Sanctuary of St. Peter in Gallicantu.	Assumptionist Fathers
Sanctuary of the Pater Noster (Eleona).	Carmelite Sisters
Sanctuary of St. Stephen.	Dominican Fathers
The Church of the Dormition.	Benedictine Fathers
Monastery "Ad Coenaculum".	Franciscan Fathers
Ein Karem: Church of St. John the Baptist. Church of the Visitation. Monastery of St. John in the Desert.	Franciscan Fathers
Jaffa: Church of St. Peter.	Franciscan Fathers
Nazareth: Basilica of the Annunciation. Church of St.Joseph. Mensa Christi. Church of the Tremor.	Franciscan Fathers
Cana: Church of the First Miracle.	Franciscan Fathers

Mt. Tabor:	Basilica of the Transfiguration.	Franciscan Fathers
Tiberias:	Church of St. Peter.	Franciscan Fathers
Tabgha:	Church of the Multiplication of Loaves and Fishes.	Benedictine Fathers
	Church of the Primacy of St. Peter.	Franciscan Fathers
	Church of the Beatitudes.	Franciscan Fathers
Capernaum:	Ancient Synagogue.	Franciscan Fathers
Haifa: (Mt. Carmel)	Church of Stella Maris. Chapel of the Sacrifice (Muhraka).	Carmelite Fathers

Sanctuaries Owned by the Greek Catholics

Nazareth:	Synagogue.
Jerusalem:	Sixth Station of the Cross.

Sanctuaries Owned by the Armenian Catholics

Jerusalem:	Third Station of the Cross.
	Fourth Station of the Cross.

Sanctuaries Owned by the Greek Orthodox

Jerusalem:	Basilica of the Holy Sepulchre.
	Church of the Virgin Mary at Gethsemane.
	Compound of the Greek Orthodox Patriarchate.
	St. Constantine's and St. Helena's Monastery.
	Patriarch Abraham's Monastery.
	St. James' Cathedral.

Forty Martyrs' Church.
St. Haralampos' Monastery.
St. John the Baptist's Monastery.
St. Nicodemos' Monastery.
St. Onofrios' Monastery.
Christ's Prison Monastery.
St. Anne's Monastery.
"Viri Galilaei" on the Mount of Olives.
Virgin Mary's Nunnery (Megali Panaghia)
(with Tomb and Cell of Melania).
Monastery of the Cross.
Holy Sion Monastery.

Bethlehem: Church and Monastery of the Nativity.
St. Elijah's Monastery.

Beit Sahour: Church of the Forefathers.

Judean   St. Theodosios' Monastery.
Desert: St. Saba's Laura.

Bethany: Church of St. Lazarus and Martha.

Jericho: Church and Monastery of the Prophet Elisaios.
Monastery of the Mount of Temptation.
St. George's Monastery (Kozeba).

River Jordan: St. John the Baptist's Monastery.
St. Gerasimos' Monastery.

Lod: Church and Monastery of St. George.

Jaffa: Church and Monastery of St. Michael.

Nazareth: Church of St. Gabriel (Annunciation).

Mount Tabor: Church and Monastery of the Transfiguration.

Cana: Church of the First Miracle.

Tiberias: Church and Monastery.

Capernaum: Church.

Sanctuaries Owned by the Armenian Orthodox

Jerusalem: Church of the Holy Sepulchre.
Church of the Virgin Mary at Gethsemane.
St. James' Cathedral and Monastery.
Church and Monastery of the Archangels
(House of Annas).
Church and Monastery of St. Savior
(House of Caiaphas).

Bethlehem: Church of the Nativity.

Sanctuaries Owned by the Coptic Orthodox

Jerusalem: Church of the Holy Sepulchre (Chapel behind the
Edicule and various rights).
Church of St. Anthony.
St. Helena's Church and Church of the Virgin's
Apparition, near the Holy Sepulchre.
Monastery of Deir el-Sultan with Chapels of
St. Michael and the Four Living Bodiless
Creatures (disputed ownership).
Ninth Station of the Cross.
Church of the Virgin Mary in Gethsemane (right
to worship on certain dates, and on certain
altars).

Bethlehem: Church of the Nativity (right to worship on certain dates and on certain altars).

Jordan River: St. John the Baptist's Monastery.

Sanctuaries Owned by the Syrian Orthodox

Jerusalem: St. Mark's Monastery.
Church of the Holy Sepulchre: Chapel of Nicodemos (disputed ownership).
Church of the Virgin Mary in Gethsemane (right to worship on certain dates, and on certain altars).

Bethlehem: Church of the Nativity (right to celebrate on certain occasions).

Jordan River: Monastery on the bank of the River.

Sanctuaries Owned by the Russian Orthodox Church
(connected with the Patriarchate of Moscow)

Jaffa: Tomb of the Holy Tabitha in the Garden of St. Peter's Church.

The following churches and monasteries, located in surroundings considered holy:

> Gorny Convent in Ein Karem.
> Cathedral of the Holy Trinity in Jerusalem.
> St. Elias on Mount Carmel.
> St. Maria Magdalena on the shores of the Sea of Galilee.

Sanctuaries Owned by the Russian Orthodox Church
(connected with the Church Outside Russia)

All of the following churches are located in surroundings considered holy:

Jerusalem: Church of Maria Magdalena on the Mount of
Olives.
Church of the Ascension on the crest of the Mount
of Olives.
Church and Monastery Alexander Niewsky
(near the Church of the Holy Sepulchre).

Hebron: Monastery of Father Abraham.

Ein Farah: Monastery of St. Chariton.

Sanctuary Owned by the Romanian Orthodox Church

Monastery near the Jordan River.

Sanctuary Owned by the Anglicans and Protestants

Jerusalem: The Garden Tomb.

As mentioned in the list of the Holy Places, the major Christian Churches maintain chapels near the Jordan River, the traditional place of Jesus' baptism. After 1967, access to the site near the Israel-Jordan armistice line was restricted for security reasons.

The Israel Ministry of Religious Affairs recently inaugurated an alternative site on the River Jordan. Known as *Yardenit*, it is located south of the Lake of Galilee, beside one of the natural pools in the river's winding course. Here, Christian pilgrims can perform the baptismal rite and make use of the special modern facilities at the site.

With the improvement of security on the Israel-Jordan border, the Greek Orthodox Patriarch was granted permission to celebrate the ceremony of the Blessing of the Water on the Feast of Epiphany 1982, at the site long revered as the place where Jesus was baptized by John the Baptist. Since then, the ceremony has been performed by the Greek Orthodox every year.

On the first of November, 1985, the pilgrimage to the traditional site of the baptism of Jesus was also renewed by the Franciscans, led by the Custos of the Holy Land. The Franciscans, entrusted with the care of the Holy Places belonging to the Roman Catholic Church, had not made the pilgrimage since the Six-Day War in 1967.

Appendix B

CHRISTIAN CHURCH DIGNITARIES IN THE HOLY LAND (1987)

The Patriarchs and the Apostolic Delegate

The Greek Orthodox Patriarch of Jerusalem
His Beatitude Diodoros I

The Latin Patriarch of Jerusalem
His Beatitude Michel Asa'ad Sabbah

The Armenian Orthodox Patriarch of Jerusalem
His Beatitude Yeghishè Derderian

The Apostolic Delegate
His Excellency Monsignor Carlo Curis, Titular
Archbishop of Medeli

Archbishops §

His Excellency Abuna Athanasios	Ethiopian Archbishop in Jerusalem
His Grace Dr. Anba Basilios	Coptic Archbishop of Jerusalem and the Near East
His Excellency Dyonisiaios Behnam Yacoub Jajjawi	Patriarchal Vicar of the Syrian Orthodox Church in Jerusalem
His Excellency Monsignor Lutfi Laham, Titular Archbishop of Tarsus	Greek Catholic Patriarchal Vicar in Jerusalem

§ The order implies no rule of precedence.

His Excellency Maximos Salloum	Greek Catholic Archbishop of Acre, Nazareth and all Galilee

Bishops [§]

The Right Rev. Samir Kafeity	Evangelical Episcopal Bishop in Jerusalem, Jordan, Syria and Lebanon
His Excellency Dr. Hanna Kaldany, Titular Bishop of Gaba	Latin Patriarchal Vicar General in Israel
His Excellency Naim Nasser	Bishop in Jerusalem of the Evangelical Lutheran Church in Jordan

Other Church Leaders [§]

His Paternity Carlo Cecchitelli	The Franciscan Custos of the Holy Land
Rev. Provost Dr. Johannes Friedrich	Representative of the German Lutheran Church in Israel
Rev. Ray Hicks	Representative of the Southern Baptist Convention in Israel
Rev. Archimandrite Ireneos	Representative of the Romanian Orthodox Patriarchate in Jerusalem

[§]   The order implies no rule of precedence.

Rev. John Miller Scott M.A., D.D.,
T.S.A.

Minister of the Church of Scotland in Jerusalem

Rev. Archimandrite Pavel

Head of the Orthodox Mission of the Patriarchate of Moscow in Jerusalem

Rev. Dr. Ray G. Register

Chairman of the United Christian Council in Israel

Rev. Archimandrite Wladimir

Chief of the Russian Ecclesiastical Mission in Jerusalem of the Russian Orthodox Church Outside Russia

Patriarchal Vicars of the Uniate Churches [§]

Monsignor Pierre Abdel-Ahad

Patriarchal Vicar of the Syrian Catholic Church

Monsignor Henri Constantine Gouillon

Patriarchal Vicar of the Chaldean Church

Monsignor Augustin Harfouche

Maronite Episcopal Vicar in Israel and Patriarchal Vicar in Jerusalem

Monsignor Joseph Roubian

Patriarchal Vicar of the Armenian Catholic Church

§   The order implies no rule of precedence.

Appendix C

GREEK ORTHODOX BISHOPS AND, SINCE 451 C.E., PATRIARCHS OF JERUSALEM

* Yacovos (James),		Gordios	"
the brother of Jesus	died 62	Alexandros	213–251
Simeon	died 106–107	Mazabanis	251–260
Youstos I or Yudas	111	Imenaios	260–298
Zachaios	111–134	Zambdas	298–300
Tobias	"	Hermon	300–314
Binjamin I	"	*Makarios I	314–333
Yoannes I	"	*Maximos	333–348
Mathias I	"	*Kirillos	350–386
Philippos	"	Yoannes II	386–417
Senekas	"	Praulios	417–422
Youstos II	"	*Youvenalios	422–458
Levis	"	Anastasios	458–478
Ephraim	"	Martyrios	478–486
Yoseph I	"	Salloustios	486–494
Youdas	"	Ilias I	494–516
*Marcos	134–185	Yoannis III	516–524
Kassianos	"	Petros I	524–552
Pouplios	"	Makarios II	552,564–575
Maximos I	"	*Eustochios	552–564
Youlianos	"	Yoannis IV	575–594
Gaios I	"	Amos	594–601
Gaios II	"	Isakios	601–609
Simmachos	"	*Zacharias	609–632
Youlianos or Ualis	"	*Modestos	632–634
Kapion	"	*Sophronios I	634–638
Maximos II	"	*Anastasios II	706
Antonios	"	Yoannis V	706–635
Ualis	"	Theodoros	745–770
Dolichianos	"	Ilias II	770–797
Narkissos I	185–211	*Georgios	797–807
Dios	213	Thomas I	807–820
Germanion	"	Vassilios	820–838

Yoannis VI	838–842	Arsenios	1334
Sergios	842–844	Dorotheos	1376–1417
Solomon	855–860	Theophilos II	1417–1424
Theodosios	862–878	Theophanis I	1424–1431
Ilias III	878–907	Yoakim	1431–
Sergios II	908–911	Theophanis II	1450
Leontios I	912–929	Athanasios IV	1452
Athanasios I	929–927	Yakovos II	1460
Christodoulos	937	Avram	1468
Agathon	950–964	Grigorios III	1468–1493
Yoannis VII	964–966	Marcos III	1503
Christodoulos II	966–969	Dorotheos II	after 1505–1537
Thomas II	969–978	*Germanos	1537–1579
Yoseph II	980–983	Sophronios IV	1579–1608
Orestis	983–1005	Theophanis III	1608–1644
Theophilos I	1012–1020	*Paisios	1645–1660
Nikiphoros I	1020–1084	Nektarios	1660–1669
Ioanikios	"	*Dositheos	1669–1707
Sophronios II	"	*Chrysanthos	1707–1731
Evthymios	1084	Meletios	1731–1737
*Simeon II	1084–1106	Parthenios	1737–1766
Savvas	1106–1156	Ephraim II	1766–1771
Yoannis VIII	"	Sophronios I	1771–1775
Nicholaos	"	Avramios	1775–1787
Yoannis IX	1156–1166	Procopios I	1787–1788
Nikiphoros II	1166–1170	Anthimos	1788–1808
Leontios II	1170–1190	*Polycarpos	1808–1827
Dositheos I	1191	*Athanasios V	1827–1845
Marcos II	1191–	*Kyrillos II	1845–1872
Evthymios II	died before 1223	Prokopios	1872–1875
Athanasios II	1224–1236	*Hierotheos	1875–1882
*Sophronios III	1236–	*Nikodimos I	1883–1890
*Grigorios I	–1298	*Gerasimos I	1891–1897
Theddaios	–1298	*Damianos I	1897–1931
*Athanasios III		*Timotheos I	1935–1955
	before 1313–1334	*Benedictos I	1957–1980
Grigorios II	1332	*Diodoros I	1981–
*Lazaros	after 1334–1368		

Until the incumbency of Bishop Makarios, a contemporary of Emperor Constantine the Great, no exact dates can be given. There were troubled periods during which the patriarchal succession was interrupted. This occurred at the time of the Arab conquest (the incumbency of Sophronios), during the Crusades (the incumbency of Simeon) and during Mamluk rule. The Greek Orthodox Patriarchate attained stability under Germanos I (1537–1579) and his successors. Patriarchs mentioned in the book are indicated by an asterisk in the list above.

BIBLIOGRAPHY

GENERAL

Encyclopaedias

Encyclopaedia Britannica
Encyclopaedia Hebraica (Hebrew)
Enciclopedia Cattolica (Italian)
Encyclopaedia Judaica
Enziclopedia Leyediat Haaretz "Ariel", by Zeev Vilnay (Hebrew)
Die Religion in Geschichte und Gegenwart, Tuebingen, 1927 (German)

Periodicals

Christian News from Israel (1949-), published by the Ministry of Religious Affairs of the State of Israel, Jerusalem
Christian-Jewish Relations, a Documentary Survey, Institute of Jewish Affairs, London, Hartford Street 11
Das Heilige Land, Deutscher Verein vom Heiligen Land, Koeln (German)
Gemeindebrief, Evangelische Gemeinde Jerusalem (1974-) (German)
Jérusalem, Le Bulletin Diocésain du Patriarcat Latin (1932-) (French)
Proche Orient Chrétien, Sainte Anne, Jérusalem (1934-) (French)
Terra Santa, Rivista della Custodia Francescana, Gerusalemme (1950-) (Italian)
UCCI News, the United Christian Council in Israel (1974-)
The Jerusalem Post, a daily newspaper, Jerusalem (1932-)
Kardom, published by the Ministry of Tourism of the State of Israel (1978-) (Hebrew)

History

Atlas Carta Letoldot Israel, Carta, Jerusalem (Hebrew)

Bahat, Dan, *Carta's Historical Atlas of Jerusalem*, 1983

Musset, Henri, *Histoire du Christianisme, Specialement en Orient*, Impr. St. Paul Harissa, Liban 1949 (3 vol.) (French)

Nutting, Anthony, *The Arabs*, Mentor Books, Chicago, 1965

Odeh, Issa Anton, *Les Minorités Chrétiennes de Palestine à Travers les Siècles*, Franciscan Press, Jerusalem, 1976

Parkes, James, *A History of Palestine from 135 A.D. to Modern Times*, Victor Gollanz, Ltd., London, 1949

Parkes, James, *Whose Land? A History of the Peoples of Palestine*, Penguin Books Ltd., 1970

Stanley, Arthur P., Dean of Westminster, *Sinai and Palestine*, London, 1981

Storrs, Ronald, *Orientations*, Nicholson & Watson, London, 1945

Wardi, Chaim, *Christians in Israel –A Survey*, Jerusalem, 1950

Holy Places

Aline, Marie de Sion, *La Fortresse Antonia à Jérusalem et la Question du Prétoire*, Franciscan Printing Press, Jerusalem, 1955 (French)

Baldi, Donato, *Encheiridion Locorum Sanctorum*, Franciscan Press, Jerusalem, 1982 (Latin)

Baldi, Donato, *Guida di Terra Santa*, Centro Propoganda e Stampa, Milano, 1975 (Italian)

Béguerie, Auscher, Turnus, *Itinéraires Bibliques—Guide de Terre Sainte*, Edition Cerf, 1974, Maison Mame (French)

Collin B., *Rome, Jérusalem et les Lieux Saints*, Editions Franciscaines, Paris (French)

Collin B., *Le Probléme Juridique des Lieux Saints*, Presse Universitaire de France, Paris, 1969 (French)

Collin, B., *Recueil des Documents concernant Jérusalem et les Lieux Saints*, Franciscan Printing Press, Jérusalem, 1982 (French)

Coüasnon, Charles, *The Church of the Holy Sepulchre*, Oxford University Press, London, 1974

Cust, L.C.A., *An Account of the Practices Concerning the Status Quo in the Holy Places*, Government of Palestine, 1929
D'Amico, Bernardino, *Trattato delle Piante e delle Immagini dei Sacri Edifici di Terra Santa*, Firenze, 1620 (Italian)
De Santoli, Sabino, *Il Santo Sepolcro e il Calvario, (Cenni Storici)* Franciscan Press, Jerusalem, 1974 (Italian)
Kopp, C. *Die Heiligen Stätten der Evangelien*, Friedrich Pustet Verlag, Regensburg, 1969 (German)
Major Peace Treaties of Modern History, (1648-1967), Vol. II, New York, Chelsea House Publishers, 1967
Lauterpacht, E., *Jerusalem and the Holy Places*, Anglo-Israel Association, London, 1968
Pearson, L.T., *Where is the Calvary?* Brighton, Sussex, 1966
Rock, Alberto, *Lo Statu Quo dei Luoghi Santi*, Franciscan Press Jerusalem, 1977 (Italian)
Sayegh, S., *Le Status Quo des Lieux Saints, Nature Juridique et Portée Internationale*, Latran Corona Lateranensis, 21, Roma, 1971, (French)
Stiassny Joseph, *Nazareth* (French)
Volken, Lorenz, *Reisen und Wandern im Heiligen Lande*, Verein der Freunde der Benedictiner Abtei auf dem Sion, 1983, (German)
Zander, Walter, *Israel and the Holy Places of Christendom*, Weidenfeld and Nicolson, London, 1971

Pilgrimages

Leclerq, H., *Pélerinages aux Lieux Saints, Dictionnaire d'Archéologie Chrétienne* (Vol. XIV) (French)
Palestine Pilgrims' Text Society, London, (14 volumes)

RULERS OF PALESTINE

The Romans and Byzantines

Abel, F.M., *Histoire de la Palestine depuis la Conquète d'Alexandre jusqu'à l'invasion Arabe*, Tome II (French)

Avi-Yona, M., *In the Days of Rome and Byzantium*, Jerusalem, 1962 (Hebrew)

Bachi, R., *The Population of Israel*, The Hebrew University, Jerusalem,1974

Bagatti, B., *Alle Origini della Chiesa*, Libreria editrice Vaticana, 1981 (Italian)

Bagatti, B., *L'Eglise de la Circumcision*, Jérusalem, 1965 (French)

Bagatti, B., *L'Eglise de la Gentilité*, Jérusalem, 1968 (French)

Bagatti, B., *Antichi Villaggi Cristiani in Galilea*, Tipografia dei Padri Francescani di Gerusalemme, 1971 (Italian)

Bagatti, B., *Antichi Villaggi Cristiani in Samaria*, Tipografia dei PP. Francescani Gerusalemme, 1979 (Italian)

Bagatti, B., *Antichi Villaggi Christiani nella Giudea e nel Negev*, Franciscan Printing Press, Jerusalem 1983 (Italian)

Compagnoni, Pia, *Il Deserto di Giuda*, Franciscan Press, Jerusalem, 1975 (Italian)

Chouraqui, A., Danielou J., *Ebrei e Cristiani*, Borla Editore, Torino, 1967 (Italian)

Flusser, David, *Creeds and Beliefs of the Early Christian Church*, Jerusalem (Hebrew)

Mancini, Ignazio, and others, *Saint Jacques Le Mineur, Premier Evêque de Jérusalem*, Presse Franciscaine, Jerusalem, 1962 (French)

Mancini, Ignazio, *Le Scoperte Archeologiche dei Giudei Cristiani*, Assisi, 1978 (Italian)

Rubin, Rehav, B., *The Laura Monasteries in the Byzantine Period*, in *Cathedra*, 23, Ben Zvi Institute, Jerusalem (Hebrew)

The Crusades

Benvenisti, Meron, *The Crusaders in the Holy Land,* Keter Publishing House, 1970

De Santoli, Sabino, *Corpus Inscriptionum Crucesignatorum Terrae Sanctae*, Jerusalem, Franciscan Printing Press, 1974

Gabrieli, Francesco, *Arab Historians of the Crusades*, Routledge, Kegan, London, 1969

Hamilton, Bernard, *The Latin Church in the Crusader States*, Variorum Publications Ltd., London, 1980

Mayer, Hans Eberhard, *The Crusades*, Oxford University Press, 1972

Prawer, Yoshua, *The Latin Kingdom of Jerusalem*, Weidenfeld and Nicolson, London, 1972

Risley, Jonathan, *The Knights of St. John in Jerusalem and Cyprus*, Macmillan St. Martin Press, 1975

Runciman, S., *A History of the Crusades* (3 volumes, 1951, 1952, 1954), Cambridge University Press

Runciman, S., *The Sicilian Vespers*, A Penguin Book, 1961

Richter, B., *The Maps of Acre, A Historical Cartography*, published by the Municipality of Acre, 1973

The Mamluks

Ayalon, David, *The Organization and Structure of a Moslem Military Society in the Middle Ages*, Hebrew University, Jerusalem

Muir, Sir William, *The Mamluk or Slave Dynasty in Egypt*, Smith Elder, London, 1896

Quatriermere, M., *Histoire des Sultans Mamelouks de l'Egypt* (French)

Ottoman Rule

Bateh, George, *Les Chrétiens de Palestine sous la Domination Ottomane*, Pontificia Università Lateranense, Roma, 1963 (French)

Dib, Pierre, *L'Eglise Maronite sous les Ottomans*, Beirut, 1962, La Presse Catholique (French)

RELIGIOUS COMMUNITIES OF THE HOLY LAND

The Greek Orthodox Church

Agiotafitikon Himerologion tou Etous, Jerusalem, 1987 (Greek)

Baynes, H.N. and Moss, H. St. L.B., *Byzantium*, Oxford, Clarendon Press, 1961

Bertram and Lukes, *The Orthodox Patriarchate of Jerusalem*, Report of Commission, Oxford, 1921

Dowling, Archdeacon, *The Patriarchate of Jerusalem*, London 1909

Moscopoulos, N., *La Terre Sainte*, Athens, 1957 (French)

Moscopoulos, N., *La Question de la Palestine et le Patriarcat de Jérusalem*, Athens, 1948 (French)

Papadopoulos, Chrysostomos, *Historia Ecclesias Hierosolymon*, Athens 1971, (Greek)

Tsimsoni, Daphne, *Die Griechische Gemeinde in Jerusalem und West Bank*, in *Orient*, 1982, II (Zeitschrift des Deutschen Orient Institute) (German)

Ware, Timothy, *The Orthodox Church*, Penguin Books, Ltd., 1981

The Latin Church

Annuaire de l'Eglise Catholique en Terre Sainte, Jérusalem, 1984, Franciscan Printing Press

Annuario Pontificio, Città del Vaticano, Libreria editrice Vaticana, 1985 (Italian)

Bethlehem University Catalogue, Bethlehem

Bogolte, Michael, *Gesandtenaustausch der Karoliner mit den Abbasiden und dem Patriarchen von Jerusalem* (German)

Dovigneau, Pierre, *Une Vie pour Dieu et les âmes: Vincent Bracco, Patriarch de Jérusalem*, Imprimerie du Patriarcat Latin, 1981, (French)

Dovigneau, Pierre, *Une vie au Service de l'église: Joseph Valerga, Patriarch Latin de Jérusalem*, Imprimerie du Patriarcat Latin 1972 (French)

Enardu, Maria Grazia, *Palestine in Anglo-Vatican Relations, 1936-1939*, Università degli Studi, Firenze

Fedalto, G., *La Chiesa Latina in Oriente*, Casa editrice Mazziana, Verona, 1973 (Italian)

Friedman, Elias, *The Latin Hermits of Mount Carmel: A Study in Carmelite Origins*, Roma, Teresianum,1979

The Latin Patriarchate of Jerusalem and the Equestrian Order of the Holy Sepulchre, A Century of History (1847-1947) Jerusalem, 1966

Médebielle, Pierre, *The Diocese of the Latin Patriarchate of Jerusalem*. Typography Patriarchatus Latini, Jerusalem, 1963

Médebielle, Pierre, *L'Eglise Catholique aux Lieux Saints, encore à propos du Patriarcat Latin* (French)

Médebielle, Pierre, *Gaza*, Imprimerie du Patriarcat Latin, 1982

Mendes, Meir, *Ha-Vatican ve-Israel*, The Hebrew University of Jerusalem, 1983 (Hebrew)

Statuts et Documents concernant l'Ordre Equestre du Saint Sepulchre de Jérusalem entre 1868 et 1967 (French)

Tabella Pasquale per il Santo Sepolcro di Gerusalemme, Tipografia PP. Francescani, Gerusalemme, 1946 (Italian)

La Croisade Moderne, Ordre Souverain Militaire Hospitalier de Saint Jean de Jérusalem, dit de Rhodes, dit de Malte, Grafiche Palazzotti Roma I969

La Huella de España en Terra Santa, Rivista Geografica Española, Madrid (1951) (Spanish)

The Uniate Churches

La Sacra Congregazione per le Chiese Orientali nel Cinquantesimo della fondazione 1917-1967, Roma, 1969, Tipografia S. Nilo, Grottaferrata (Italian)

Dib, Pierre, *L'Eglise Maronite*, Tome III, Edition de la Sagesse, Beirut,1973

Dauber, Nicola, *Sainte Anne de Jérusalem*, Yabroud, 1959 (French)

Gora, Philippe, *Sainte Anne de Jérusalem*, Imprimerie de S. Paul, Liban, 1932 (French)

Hajjar. I., *Les Chrétiens Uniates du Proche Orient*, Paris 1961 (French)

Patriarcat Grec-Melchite, Catholicism ou Latinism? Harissa, Liban, 1961 (French)

La Sacra Congregazione delle Chiese Orientali, Oriente Cattolico, cenni storici e statistiche - Città del Vaticano 1974 (Italian)

The Russian Orthodox Church

Graham, Stephen, *With the Russian PIlgrims in Jerusalem*, Macmillian & Co., Ltd., London, 1913

Hopwood, T., *The Russian Presence in Syria and Palestine, 1843-1914*, Oxford University Press, 1969

Moscow Patriarchate, *The Russian Orthodox Church, Organization, Situation, Activity*, 1956

Theophays, G.S., *Russian Interests in Palestine, 1843-1914*, Thessaloniki, 1963

Ware, Timothy, *The Orthodox Church*, Penguin Books, Ltd., 1981

The Anglican Church, the Protestant Churches and their Missionary Activities

Baptists in the Holy Land, a pamphlet

Bible Lands, Magazine of the Jerusalem and Middle East Association, 1979

Church of Scotland-Tabitha (1863-1963), Printed by Corquodale, Ltd., Glasgow

C.M.J. in Action - The Church Ministry among the Jews, Olive Press, London

The Evangelical Lutheran Church in Jordan and its Schools, a pamphlet

Gidney, W.T., *The History of the London Society for Promoting Christianity among the Jews*, London, 1908

Handbook of the Anglican Bishopric in Jerusalem and the East, Ariel Press. Jerusalem, 1941

Hanselmann, *Deutsche Palästina Mission 1971, Verlag der Evangelischen* Lutherischen Mission, Erlangen (German)

Hertzberg, D. Hans Wilhelm, *Die Geschichte einer Gemeinde*, Kassel, 1965 (German)

Hendenquist, Goete, *The Church and the Jewish People*, Edinburgh House Press, London, 1954

Irgett, White and Hardcastell, *Jerusalem, the Garden Tomb*

Jocz, Jacob, *The Jewish People and Jesus Christ, A Study in the Controversy between Church and Synagogue*, London, 1954

Johannitenorden, Herausgegeben Johannitenorden, Bonn, 1974 (German)

Malachy, Yona, *American Fundamentalists and Israel*, The Hebrew University of Jerusalem, 1978

Pragai, Michael, *Faith and Fulfilment—Christians and the Return to the Holy Land*, London, Valentine Mitchel, 1985

Spafford, Vester B., *Jerusalem, My Home* (reprinted from the National Geographical Magazine, 1964)

Stevens, George H., *Go Tell My Brethren—A Short Popular History of the Church Mission to the Jews* (1809-1959)

Stolz, B., *La Propagande Protestante*, Réunion Ecclesiastique au Patriarcat Latin (French)

Tibawi, S.T., *British Interests in Palestine 1801-1901*, Oxford Press, 1961

Yearbook of American and Canadian Churches, 1979, published by Abingdon (Nashville)

Livingstone, W.T., *A Galilee Doctor (Life of Doctor D.W. Torrance of Tiberias)*, printed in Perth

The Armenian Orthodox Church

Assadour, Antreassian, *Jerusalem and the Armenians*, St. James Press, Jerusalem, 1968

Azaria, Victor, *The Armenian Quarter of Jerusalem*, 1984, University of California Press, Berkeley, Los Angeles, London

Hintlian, Kervork, *History of the Armenians in the Holy Land*, St. James Press, Jerusalem, 1976

Ormanian, Malachia, *L'église armenienne*, Imprimerie du Catholicossat de Celicie, Antelias, Liban, 1954 (French)

Brief Notes on the Armenian People and the Armenian Patriarchate of Jerusalem

The Ethiopian Church

Pedersen, Kirsten, *Ethiopian Institutions in Jerusalem*, Franciscan Press, Jerusalem

Philippos, Archbishop, *Know Jerusalem*, Bohannes Selam Haile Selassie I Printing Press, Ethiopia, 1962

Philippos, Archbishop, *The Rights of the Abyssinians in the Holy Places*, Documentary Authorities, 1959

Philippos, Archbishop, *The Rights of the Abyssinian Orthodox Church in the Holy Places*, Documentary Manuscripts, 1962

Correspondence Respecting Abyssinians and Jerusalem, 1850-1867, presented to the House of Commons, 1968

The Coptic Orthodox Church

Mainardus O.F.M., *The Copts in Jerusalem*, Cairo, American University, 1960

Risek, D., *El Akbat fi El Ard El Mukadassa*, Egypt, 1967 (Arabic)

Warkin, E., *A Lonely Minority* (The Modern Story of Egypt's Copts), 1963, New York

The Syrian Orthodox Church

Koriah, Yacoub, *The Syrian Orthodox Church in the Holy Land*, Jerusalem, 1976

St. Mark's Church and Monastery in Jerusalem, a pamphlet

International Treaties

Testa, Baron I., *Recueil de Traités de la Porte Ottomane avec les Puissances Etrangères depuis le premier Traité conclu en 1536 entre Suleyman I et Francois I jusqu'à nos jours*, Paris, 1864 (10 Vol.) (French)

Major Treaties of Modern History, Vol. II, 1684 - 1967, New York, Chelsea House Publishers, 1967

INDEX

Saul P. Colbi was born in Trieste, Italy, and graduated from the law faculty of the University of Rome. He practised law in his native city before settling in Mandatory Palestine in 1939. After the establishment of the State of Israel in 1948, he joined the Ministry of Religious Affairs and, as an expert in Canon Law, was entrusted with the Christian desk. He served in that capacity until his retirement in 1975.

Dr. Colbi is the author of several books and numerous articles on the Christian Churches in the Holy Land and on Christian-Jewish relations. He has been awarded the Order of Commander of St. Gregory the Great by the Holy See, and the Order of Commander of Merit of the Italian Republic by Italy's President.